The Philosophy and Common Sense Reader

Also Available at Bloomsbury

The Philosophy of Death Reader: Cross-Cultural Readings on Immortality and the Afterlife, edited by Markar Melkonian

Introduction to Existentialism: From Kierkegaard to The Seventh Seal, Robert L. Wicks

Epistemology: The Key Thinkers, Stephen Hetherington

Philosophy of Science: Key Concepts, Steven French

The Philosophy and Common Sense Reader

Writings on Critical Thinking

Edited and Annotated by
Markar Melkonian

BLOOMSBURY ACADEMIC
LONDON • NEW YORK • OXFORD • NEW DELHI • SYDNEY

BLOOMSBURY ACADEMIC
Bloomsbury Publishing Plc
50 Bedford Square, London, WC1B 3DP, UK
1385 Broadway, New York, NY 10018, USA

BLOOMSBURY, BLOOMSBURY ACADEMIC and the Diana logo are trademarks of
Bloomsbury Publishing Plc

First published in Great Britain 2020

For legal purposes the Acknowledgments on p. xiii constitute an extension
of this copyright page.

Cover image: The Netherlandish Proverbs (The Blue Cloak or The Topsy Turvy World, 1559)
by Pieter Bruegel the Elder (ca 1525–1569)
(© Fine Art Images / Heritage Images / Alamy Stock Photo)
To sample the numerous proverbs depicted, visit the annotated Google Art Project preview at:
https://commons.wikimedia.org/wiki/File:Pieter_Brueghel_the_Elder_-_The_Dutch_
Proverbs_-_Google_Art_Project.jpg

Bloomsbury Publishing Plc does not have any control over, or responsibility for, any
third-party websites referred to or in this book. All internet addresses given in this book
were correct at the time of going to press. The author and publisher regret any
inconvenience caused if addresses have changed or sites have ceased to exist,
but can accept no responsibility for any such changes.

A catalogue record for this book is available from the British Library.

A catalog record for this book is available from the Library of Congress.

ISBN: HB: 978-1-3500-7373-9
         PB: 978-1-3500-7374-6
       ePDF: 978-1-3500-7375-3
      eBook: 978-1-3500-7376-0

Typeset by Integra Software Services Pvt. Ltd.

To find out more about our authors and books visit www.bloomsbury.com
and sign up for our newsletters.

To Suzy,

for her critical common sense

Contents

Preface: What This Book Is (Not) About   x

Acknowledgments   xiii

General Introduction: Paradoxes of Plain Thinking   1

Part I: Common Sense and Skepticism

Introduction to Part I: Common Sense and Skepticism   **13**

1   The Human Mind and Common Sense (1785)
      Thomas Reid   **19**

2   A Defense of Common Sense (1925) *G. E. Moore*   **27**

3   From *On Certainty* (1951) *Ludwig Wittgenstein*   **47**

4   The Plain Truth about Common Sense (1995)
      Mark Kingwell   **55**

      For Discussion or Essays   **71**

      Further Readings for Part I   **72**

Part II: Common Sense and Science

Introduction to Part II: Common Sense and Science   **77**

5   The Scope and Language of Science (1954)
      W. V. O. Quine   **81**

6   Two Faces of Common Sense (1973) *Karl Popper*   **91**

7   Why Scientists Shouldn't Be Surprised by the Popularity
        of Intelligent Design (2006) *Scott O. Lilienfeld*   **113**

        For Discussion or Essays   **119**

        Further Readings for Part II   **121**

Part III: Common Sense and Religion

Introduction to Part III: Common Sense and Religion   **125**

8   A Cosmological Argument for the Existence of
        God (1705) *Samuel Clarke*   **127**

9   An Argument from Design (1802) *William Paley*   **133**

10   Good Sense without God (1772) *Baron d'Holbach*   **141**

11   Belief without Argument (1982) *Alvin Plantinga*   **155**

        For Discussion or Essays   **166**

        Further Readings for Part III   **167**

Part IV: Common Sense and Morality

Introduction to Part IV: Common Sense and Morality   **171**

12   The Evolution of the Moral Sense (1871) *Charles Darwin*   **173**

13   Common Sense and Human Nature (1966)
        Stanley Rosen   **191**

14   The Ethics of Common Sense (1970) *Mortimer J. Adler*   **205**

        For Discussion or Essays   **219**

        Further Readings for Part IV   **220**

Part V: Common Sense and Economics

Introduction to Part V: Common Sense and Economics   225

15   Ten Principles of Economics (2004) *N. Gregory Mankiw*   229

16   Income Inequality and Corporate Responsibility
         (2005, 2006) *Gary Becker and Richard A. Posner*   241

17   Economic Common Sense and the Depoliticization of
         the Economic (2008) *Jacinda Swanson*   251

         For Discussion or Essays   266

         Further Readings for Part V   268

Part VI: Common Sense and Politics

Introduction to Part VI: Common Sense and Politics   271

18   The Study of Philosophy (1932) *Antonio Gramsci*   275

19   The Intramural Warfare between Thought and
         Common Sense (1978) *Hannah Arendt*   293

20   Inherit the Whirlwind (2004) *Thomas Frank*   303

21   Common-Sense Neoliberalism (2013) *Stuart Hall and*
         Alan O'Shea   321

         For Discussion or Essays   331

         Further Readings for Part VI   333

Readings That Appear in This Book   335
Index   338

Preface: What This Book Is (Not) About

This book is about *the philosophical examination of common sense*. Some of the readings included in this book were themselves intended to be instances of common sense reasoning. The readings from Samuel Clarke, William Paley, Baron d'Holbach, and Gary Becker fall into this category. Most of the other readings are more or less *critical* philosophical examinations of common sense, as the authors have variously described it.

This is not a book on the philosophy *of* common sense. It will quickly become clear that common sense, whatever it may be, is not a kind of philosophy, nor is it a foundation for philosophy or a substitute for it. But this book also, most assuredly, does not try to inoculate readers against common sense in the conduct of their daily lives. Even the fanciest literary theorists defy the deliverances of common sense at their own peril. We do not denigrate either common sense or philosophy by pointing out their differences and trying to get to the bottom of the former.

In the pages that follow, we will consider such questions as:

- What might common sense be? Is it a mental capacity? Does it consist of just truisms and precepts? Does the term have any definite meaning at all?

- Has common sense been typical of competent people across the centuries and the continents, or is it a characteristically modern phenomenon?

- Is a common-sense understanding of common sense satisfactory? If not, why not, and in what respect?

- Is common sense opposed to philosophical skepticism? And if it is, so what?

- What is the relationship between common sense and the sciences? Is the former the "foundation" for the latter?

- Is there such a thing as common-sense religious belief?

- Is common sense the foundation of morality? Could it be?

- What are we to make of the frequent claim that common sense confirms the basic maxims of economics?

- Common sense is supposed to be practical and non-"ideological." What can we make of this claim?

- What can we make of the claim that common sense is "the political sense *par excellence*"?

- What is the relationship, if any, between common sense and democracy?

Our philosophical examination of common sense will take us into several consecrated fields of philosophy: in Part I, we'll find ourselves in the field of epistemology; in Part II we enter philosophy of science; in Part III, philosophy of religion; in Part IV, ethics and metaethics; in Part V, philosophy of economics; and in Part VI, political philosophy. As we will see, much can be said about the uses to which the term *common sense* has been put, and the social functions that common-sense talk has served. By critically examining common-sense talk within these fields, we might gain important insights into the rationales and self-conceptions of such institutions as modern science, religion, morality, economics, and political authority. A philosophical examination of common sense, then, may be most important not for what it tells us about common sense, but rather for what it tells us about certain important institutions and large fields of human endeavor. This last point might be more than enough to justify a book on philosophy and common sense even if, after the readings in Part I, some readers were to conclude that there is not much of philosophical interest to be said about common sense *per se.*

In addition to trying to get the bottom of a term that has appeared so frequently in modern discourse, there is another good reason for a philosophical examination of common sense. As it turns out, one can learn a great deal about some of the most influential modern philosophers by examining what they have to say about common sense. A quick perusal of the Table of Contents will reveal the names of several "top 40" twentieth-century philosophers, including G. E. Moore, Ludwig Wittgenstein, W. V. O. Quine, Karl Popper, and Hannah Arendt. But you will also notice the names of several nonphilosophers, including psychologist and science writer Scott Lilienfeld, economist Gary Becker, political scientist Jacinda Swanson, and historian and journalist Thomas Frank. The latter readings might provide support for one side or another in the debates in Parts V and VI—and some measure of relief for theory-weary readers, too.

In the course of our readings, it should become clear that common sense is fluid and highly contentious. Despite what our commonsensical assumptions about common sense may tell us, the beliefs of common sense are not guaranteed to be useful, true, or even coherent.[1] If science and philosophy do not confirm common sense, then that may (or may not) be regrettable, but this in itself is no failure of science or philosophy. The latter are under no obligation to conform to common sense. To paraphrase the American writer Flannery O'Connor, *common sense should not be consulted here; it is in the process of being formed.*[2]

---

[1]Of course, the same could be said of the sciences. But the sciences do not typically base their claims to validity on obviousness and common consent; moreover, the sciences put a much greater emphasis on *consistency*. More about this in Part II below.

[2]Flannery O'Connor, *Mystery and Manners: Occasional Prose* (New York: Farrar, Straus & Giroux, 1961), 140: "The high-school English teacher will be fulfilling his responsibility if he furnishes the student a guided opportunity, through the best writing of the past, to come, in time, to an understanding of the best writing of the present. [...] And if the student finds that this is not to his taste? Well, that is regrettable. Most regrettable. His taste should not be consulted; it is being formed."

Acknowledgments

I wish to thank Liza Thompson and Lucy Russell, my editors at Bloomsbury Academic, for their guidance and patience. Thanks to my colleague John Birmingham for helpful suggestions in an early stage of the writing. Long-overdue thanks to Maile Melkonian and Marcia Bedrosian, for their support over the years during my work on this and other books. Thanks also to Sureya, Tamar, and Narineh, for their forbearance—and for their good humor: the very idea that their father, of all people, would put together a book on common sense! And great appreciation, as always, to my students.

All efforts have been made to trace copyright holders. In the event of errors or omissions, please notify the publisher in writing of any corrections that need to be incorporated into future editions of this book.

General Introduction:
Paradoxes of Plain Thinking

Natural sense and imagination are not subject to absurdity.
    –Thomas Hobbes (1588–1679)

That which seems the height of absurdity in one generation often becomes the height of wisdom in the next.
    –John Stuart Mill (1806–1873)

The Sun orbits Earth. Two-plus-two always equals four. Objects fall when pushed off a table. Nothing comes from nothing. The whole is greater than the part. These have all been taken to be common sense beliefs. But what makes them so? And what is common sense, anyway?

Whatever common sense may be, it includes much else besides obvious and practically confirmed truisms. Consider the claims that heaven and earth are creations of God, that the soul and the body have different fates, and that men are created unequal. Although some thinkers have contested these claims over the centuries, far more people have accepted them as useful and obvious beyond doubt. Or consider the erstwhile common-sense claims that the Sun revolves around Earth, and that except for earthquakes our planet does not move. For educated adults today, these are no longer claims of common sense. Consider some further claims of contemporary astronomy:

- Earth spins on its axis at 1,600 kilometers per hour (about 900 miles per hour) at the equator, relative to a frame of reference at the center of the planet.

- Earth orbits our star, the Sun, at an average of 110,000 kilometers per hour relative to the Sun.

- The Sun and its planets spin with the Milky Way galaxy (the center of which is 30,000 light years from Earth) at the rate of 1 million miles per day.

- The Milky Way and its neighboring galaxies, the so-called Local Group, are moving at 600 kilometers per second (1.34 million miles per hour) in the direction of the constellation Hydra.

Of course, future astronomers might correct or falsify one or more of these claims. But even if this were to happen, the point has been settled: Earth is anything but unmoving. This is but one of many instances in which some of the best-established and most "intuitive" claims of the past have been cast out of common sense.

But are there claims that, *by their very nature*, could *not* be accepted as obvious by a large number of people? Well, surely 2 + 2 ≠ 5, and *there are no married bachelors*. But the truth of these claims follows from the meanings of the terms in which they are stated: a bachelor is *by definition* unmarried, and the symbol "≠" would lose its familiar use for us if it were *not* true that 2 + 2 ≠ 5. What about the claim that *there is no subject, no you, that has experiences*? This might appear absurd on the face of it, and upon even the slightest consideration, it might be taken to conflict with the surest and most direct knowledge. And yet the Scottish philosopher David Hume defended this view in his book *A Treatise of Human Nature* (1739–1740). Hume argued that selfhood, which other philosophers had accepted without argument, was really just a series of sense impressions and ideas, a loose "bundle" that is not bound together with anything extra—no container or bailing wire that could function as an enduring self, mind, or soul. Thus, according to Hume, nothing enduring "has" the impressions and ideas that you believe are occurring to you. However uncommonsensical Hume's bundle theory of the self might appear to be, it turns out that millions of people over the course of many centuries have accepted something very similar to this theory: although Hume probably was not aware of it, his bundle theory of the self had existed since ancient times, in the Buddhist doctrine of *anatman* or "no-mind."[1]

Another sort of claim that might be incompatible in principle with common sense are claims that appear to conflict with a basic principle of logic. For example, one might think that the ancient geometer Euclid's "common notion" that *the whole is greater than the part* follows from the definition of the terms "whole" and "part." And it does. This being the case, it would be a logical contradiction to deny the claim. But not even this seemingly trivial claim holds without qualification, since a subset of an infinite series is just as big as the original series: one half of infinity is just as big as infinity itself.

---

[1] See Derek Parfit, "Divided Minds and the Nature of Persons," in *Mindwaves*, ed. Colin Blakemore and Susan Greenfield (Oxford: Oxford University Press, 1987). Although this doctrine was central to Buddhist teaching, it is not clear that many lay Buddhists have subscribed to the doctrine or have been capable of sustaining it for long.

Of course, it is not difficult to find paradox when it comes to discussions of infinity. But not even the claim that *nothing comes from nothing* is beyond doubt.[2] In his best-selling book, *A Universe from Nothing*, physicist and popular science writer Lawrence Krauss is adamant about this:

> One thing is certain, however. The metaphysical "rule," which is held as an ironclad conviction by those with whom I have debated the issue of creation, namely that "*out of nothing nothing comes*," has no foundation in science.[3]

Quantum mechanics, our best current theory of the character and behavior of subatomic phenomena, allows for the fleeting appearance of energetic particles out of "empty space." But there is a question whether this "empty space" should really be described as *nothing*. The quantum vacuum, we learn, contains quantifiable, measurable energy. This is not surprising: physicists, presumably, would not need the term if it did not designate anything at all *determinate*. To the extent that such "empty space" is determinate in any respect—to the extent that it has any property or characteristic at all—perhaps it is misleading to describe it as nothing at all. Still, if some interpreters of quantum theory are right, then at least in one special sense of the word *nothing*, something can come from it after all.

Quantum theory and astronomy describe phenomena on unimaginably small and large scales, respectively, so perhaps it is not surprising that these fields so vividly defy common sense. We will return to the topic of common sense and the sciences in Part II. In any case, leaving aside perhaps formulations that genuinely violate a basic logical principle or that are false by definition, our quick survey has not turned up a claim that we could confidently set outside of any possible common sense.

In her book *Common Sense: A Political History*, professor of history Sophia Rosenfeld notes that the title of her book is paradoxical, since common sense is supposed to define "that which is the common property of all human beings regardless of the variance of time and space." Common sense is supposed to be a feature common to almost all adult humans, from ancient times to the present: it is supposed to be "the natural

---

[2] The philosopher Parmenides advanced this claim in the early fifth century BCE, but the Greeks were not the only ancients to hold this view. The *Katha Upanishad*, which was composed in India at around the same time as Parmenides, poses the rhetorical question: "How can anything come from nothing?" By contrast, consider Laozi (Lao Tzŭ), writing in the fourth century BCE: "The myriad creatures in the world are born from Something, and Something from Nothing." (*Tao Te Ching*, trans. D.C. Lau [New York: Penguin Books, 1963], Book II, Verse XL.)

[3] Lawrence Krauss, *A Universe from Nothing: Why Is There Something Rather than Nothing?* (New York: Atria, 2012), 174. It should be pointed out that Krauss never really answers the *Why?* question (or pseudo-question?) posed in the subtitle of his book. In his defense, though, this may be due to the consideration that like the formulation *What is the difference between an orange?* it is not really a question at all.

mother-tongue of thought," as the American philosopher and psychologist William James put it. If this common-sense understanding of common sense is accurate, then it doesn't appear to have much of a history at all, let alone a *political* history.

Rosenfeld herself does not subscribe to this common-sense understanding of common sense: to her, common sense is neither *common* nor is it a reservoir or source of direct and dependable knowledge. Thomas Reid, an eighteenth-century author whom we will meet in Part I, claimed that when it comes to common-sense beliefs, there is a "fixed list," "the same for all men."[4] This is a common view today, too. And yet as we have already seen and as Rosenfeld shows at length, common sense is variable in content, and the common sense of one party has not been obvious to opposing parties. If this is right, then it would appear to undermine (though perhaps not definitively vanquish) the claim that common sense is a feature of all reasonable humans, ancient and modern.

Here we encounter a question that will reappear in the readings that follow: is common sense something that arises from the shared experiences of mankind, or are there multiple common senses, specific to certain times and places? The answer to this question, of course, depends on how broadly one conceives of common sense: does it arise from the "shared experiences of mankind" by definition, or do we conceive of it more narrowly, as a property of "men with whom we can conduct business"? Is common sense transhistorical and transcultural, as a common-sense understanding of common sense would have it, or is it a distinctive feature of modern persons, notably adult males in market economies?

Surely our species has shared experiences, if for no other reason than that we do, after all, live on the same planet, share a common biophysical makeup, and have language. Beyond these truisms, though, a common-sense understanding of common sense becomes murky: common sense is supposed to deliver us from strife because it is plain and sure, and yet, as it turns out, both sides in one controversy after another have fought to redefine it and to claim it as their own. Common sense is "by definition, ahistorical terrain."[5] And yet, as Rosenfeld sees it, common sense has a history.

---

[4]John Coates, *The Claims of Common Sense: Moore, Wittgenstein, Keynes, and the Social Sciences* (Cambridge: Cambridge University Press, 1996), 20. Coates quotes from Thomas Reid's *Collected Papers* 5, paragraph 509.

[5]This and the following quotation are from Sophia Rosenfeld, *Common Sense: A Political History* (Cambridge, MA: Harvard University Press, 2011), 1. The familiar ahistorical view of common sense was expressed, for example, by British philosopher P. F. Strawson, who wrote that it is that "massive central core of human thinking which has no history—or none recorded in histories of thought" (P. F. Strawson, *Individuals: An Essay in Descriptive Metaphysics*, London: Routledge, 2006, 10). The influential early-twentieth-century British philosopher Bertrand Russell once described common sense as little more than "stone age metaphysics" (Stephen Boulter, *The Rediscovery of Common Sense Philosophy* (Basingstoke, UK: Palgrave Macmillan, 2007), xi).

We will encounter writers who would not endorse Rosenfeld's claim, starting with our first reading, by Thomas Reid, for whom common sense is a particular power or capacity of the mind, namely *"the power by which we compare [...] ideas and perceive their necessary agreements and disagreements."* In a reading in Part IV, American philosopher Stanley Rosen, while agreeing with several of Rosenfeld's cautionary observations, suggests that common sense predates philosophy. Indeed, Rosen describes the Greek epic poet Hesiod (active between 750 and 650 BC?) as "a great admirer of common sense."[6]

Much of the seeming difference of opinion here, too, has to do with how loosely we wish to define the term *common sense*, compared to narrower and more historically specific conceptions. Rosen, for example, connects common sense to the "common experience of mankind": "Common sense means at least the capacity to deal successfully with the commonly accessible world."[7] Thus, Rosen's usage, unsurprisingly, has a much broader application than Rosenfeld's more historically specific usage. This looser usage is part of how common sense—our current common sense—understands itself. In keeping with this usage, the American philosopher W. V. O. Quine, in our reading in Part II, identifies "archaic common sense" with an "archaic natural philosophy," which, he says, "we imbibe [...] with our mother's milk."

Having thus untangled this particular knot, the reader may now distinguish two distinct strings: a loose commonsensical conception of common sense, and a narrower, historically and culturally specific one. It is enough at this point, perhaps, to keep these two distinct usages in mind as we proceed.

There is another knot that we should untangle, too, before we can hope to make sense of the term *common sense*. Reviewing the literature, at least two closely connected but importantly distinct meanings of the term *common sense* emerge: it may be thought of either as (1) the "basic intellectual capacity of ordinary people," or as (2) the "elemental, shared assumptions" that inform and guide competent people in the conduct of their daily affairs.[8] In the former meaning, common sense is "the faculty of primary truths":[9] it is the innate power

---

[6]The claim appears in a passage not included in our selection from Rosen's essay.

[7]In a passage not included in our selection from Rosen's essay (Rosen, "Common Sense," *The Journal of General Education* 18, no. 2 (July 1966): 127).

[8]Rosenfeld, 222. In the essay "Ethics and Common Sense" (refer to the Further Readings section at the end of Part IV), Marcus G. Singer connects these two senses of "common sense," describing "Common Sense as a capacity and Common Sense as the product [...] of that capacity."

[9]Rosenfeld, 314, fn11.

of the mind which, against the menaces of skepticism and paradox, puts us into assured possession of such truths as *a thing is identical to itself, some objects are bigger than others*, and *the earth has existed for many years*. Common sense, according to this meaning, is the basic ability to *judge*, which is a mental capacity that all competent adults share, even if they cannot explain it. In this oracular sense of the term, common sense accords with the recommendation to *Use your common sense!* This appears to be the main sense in which Thomas Reid uses the term, in the reading in Part I.

According to the shared-assumptions meaning, by contrast, common sense is a cache of "the truisms about which all sensible people agree without argument or even discussion, including principles of amount, difference, prudence, cause and effect."[10] These truisms may or may not be drawn from a special faculty of the mind, and they may or may not be conscious. In the shared-assumptions usage, common sense is a contrast term for "nonsense"—that which is obviously absurd to any adult competent enough to take care of ordinary affairs. This appears to be the sense in which several of our authors use the term, including G. E. Moore, in the reading from Part I.[11]

In both of these cases, the items of common sense are either *products* of common sense as a mental faculty or inner sense,[12] or they are *instances* of common sense, in the form of explicit or unstated assumptions and beliefs. Items of common sense include truisms about what's what, as well as basic maxims, the most elementary know-how, routinely confirmed habits of thought, and intuitive beliefs. Rosenfeld describes how, since the late seventeenth century, these disparate maxims, practical dispositions, and noninferential knowledge were tossed together into the same heap and came to count as products or instances of a discrete something-or-other called common sense.

There is, of course, a straightforward explanation as to why these motley items— maxims, dispositions, and noninferential knowledge—have been heaped together like this: they are all *widely accepted* and *obvious* because *they work*. But even leaving aside the consideration that common sense arrived on the scene only recently in the career of our species, this commonsensical understanding of common sense

---

[10]Rosenfeld, 1.

[11]Refer also to the John Dewey paper, included in the Further Readings item for Part II.

[12]The Greek polymath Aristotle (384–322 BCE) described a certain capacity of the animating soul (the *psuche*), which he said, is distinct from basic sensory perception, sight, hearing, smell, and so on, and also distinct from rational thinking, but which cooperates with both of them, linking them. Two thousand years later, French philosopher Rene Descartes (1596–1650) took up this idea of common sense as a mental faculty that is analogous to the five "external senses" through which we see, hear, and so on, but is distinct from them. According to Descartes, common sense is one of three "inner senses" (along with imagination and memory), linking the body and its external sense organs with the immaterial human mind.

is unsatisfactory in more than one way. For one thing, the pronouncements of common sense often conflict: *caution is the better part of discretion*, but *he who hesitates is lost; out of sight, out of mind*, but *absence makes the heart fonder; birds of a feather flock together*, but *opposites attract; the proof of the pudding is in the eating*, but *eyes—and presumably taste buds, too—are deceiving; two heads are better than one*, but *you should paddle your own canoe*. The book of *Proverbs*, which we today mine for common-sense advice, tells us to "Answer not a fool according to his folly, lest thou also be like unto him"; however, in the very next verse we read, "Answer a fool according to his folly, lest he be wise in his own conceit."[13] So it appears that Rosenfeld is right: common sense, the supposed enemy of paradox, is itself paradoxical.

These two usages, common sense as a *shared ability* and common sense as *shared assumptions*, do not exhaust the range of definitions of *common sense* that have come down to us. The American philosopher C. S. Pierce (1839–1914), for example, described it as a certain sort of "belief-habits," and it is not clear that Pierce's formulation would fall neatly into either of the definitions mentioned.

But there is yet another view of common sense that we should consider, namely, common sense as an authority invoked primarily for purposes of persuasion. Italian thinker Antonio Gramsci prepared the ground for this view when he observed that even in the brain of one individual, the shared jumble of values, assumptions, expectations, and dispositions that each of us acquires in the course of life is "a chaotic aggregate of disparate conceptions, and one can find there anything that one likes."[14] The values, attitudes, beliefs, and instructions that make up common sense are fragmentary and often incoherent, and according to Gramsci they are also *spontaneous*: we typically absorb them from our environment without thinking about it much.[15] By thus stripping common sense of any special scientific or theoretical power, Gramsci suggests that it is chiefly a rhetorical tool, an instrument of persuasion more than accurate description. We will encounter Gramsci's views in Part VI below.

But there is a danger in speaking too dismissively of common sense. Outside of Humanities Departments and highbrow academic journals, as we have noted, grown-ups defy common sense at their own peril. Not only must we conduct our

---

[13]*Proverbs* (KJV), 26:4–5.

[14]Antonio Gramsci, *Selections from the Prison Notebooks* (refer to the Readings That Appear in This Book section at end of this book), 422.

[15]Gramsci, 198–9.

daily affairs in keeping with its deliverances, but as the American philosopher Richard W. Miller has observed, the empirical sciences would be impracticable without them: the chemist who rejects such truisms as "the apparent shape of a middle-sized object seen close-up in moderate sunlight usually is a product of its similar real shape"[16] could not confidently take a reading from a thermometer. Indeed, even magic cannot do without such truisms: as Miller points out, "Augurers had better think that they can reliably detect natural phenomena by looking in addition to augury, or else they will not be able to make out the spots on their birds' livers."[17]

Truisms, in the sense of beliefs that lots of people have repeatedly confirmed, have been around for a long time, but they have only recently counted as instances of this alleged something-or-other called common sense. Moreover, common sense has not been restricted to truisms, even ones that conflict. Claims that God created heaven and earth, for example, or that minds and bodies have different fates, or that "the rule of the many" would summon disaster—all of these have been items of common sense, but it is not clear that, on balance, they have proved more useful to more people than their negations.

Taking all of this into account, one might distinguish the truisms from the rest of common sense. Gramsci recommended doing so, and he called the aggregation of truisms *good sense* (*il buon senso*).[18] Good sense, the "healthy nucleus" of common sense, is made up of the practical and empirical (but not necessarily *scientific* or even *coherent*) elements of experience.[19] Accordingly, good sense would include such things as ordinary assumptions about quantity, size, power, or prudence, including such obvious and daily-confirmed items as *2 + 2 = 4, the Sun revolves around Earth* (or vice versa), and *nothing comes from nothing.* The best way to teach philosophy, Gramsci claimed, is to bring good sense to bear on the prevailing common sense.

But even if we limit our consideration to good sense, we are still confronted with a jumble of divergent and seemingly arbitrary elements. Let's see if we can make sense of this jumble.

* * *

---

[16]Richard W. Miller, *Fact and Method* (Princeton, NJ: Princeton University Press, 1987), 195.
[17]Miller, 494.
[18]This distinction must have impressed itself upon Gramsci by his early twenties. There was a great difference between the rural Sardinia where he grew up—a land of pervasive superstitions and folklore—and the industrialized, cosmopolitan city of Turin, where he migrated in early adulthood.
[19]Gramsci, 328.

The readings in Part I have to do with the relationship between common sense and skepticism. It is striking that, in the past three hundred years, some of the most vocal defenders of common sense have wielded "it" to banish skepticism, even as their opponents have invoked "it" to *promote* skepticism with respect to certain widely held assumptions and beliefs. In Part II, we will take up the related and much-contested question of the relationship between common sense and science. Part III is devoted to the equally controversial question of the relationship between common sense and religion. As more than one philosopher has noted, common sense has often been thought to have a strong connection with morality.[20] Part IV comprises several suggestive readings on this topic. No survey of common sense and philosophy would be complete without this. Finally, Parts V and VI focus on a topic that preceding readings have broached in passing, namely, the typically modern relationship of common sense to power. Part V takes up the "common sense foundations" of economics. One of the readings in Part V is about how mainstream economists, often citing the authority of common sense, represent economic institutions and practices as essentially distinct from politics and the state. This provides a good transition to the readings in Part VI, which examine common sense as an "unspectacular instrument" of political domination.

---

[20]Refer to the paper by Marcus G. Singer, listed in the Further Readings section for Part IV.

Part I

Common Sense and Skepticism

Introduction to Part I:
Common Sense and Skepticism

According to one common understanding of common sense, it is a dependable, direct sense of what's what, a sense that emerges from our experiences in the conduct of our day-to-day lives. Like the senses of sight and hearing, the direct, instinctive character of common sense and its basis in experience is what makes it dependable and what makes it a *sense*. What makes it *common* is that it is *shared*: it is the *body of ideas and beliefs* or the *mental capacity* that has been common to all adults who are competent enough to tend to their daily affairs. The French theologian François Fénelon (1651–1715) described a near synonym of common sense, namely, "good sense" (*le bon sens*), as the instinct that, when shocked, results in laughter.[1] Fénelon suggested that laughter, or a condescending smile, was the appropriate response to the extravagant claims of philosophers and skeptics of all stripes. Against the infallible and shared deliverances of common sense, skepticism cannot prevail. This, at least, was the conviction of the earliest modern champions of common sense.

The philosophy of common sense developed as a reaction against the skepticism of the Scottish enlightenment thinker, David Hume (1711–1776), and the subjective idealism of his contemporary, George Berkeley (1685–1753), the Anglo-Irish philosopher and Anglican Bishop of the city of Cloyne, in Ireland. Skepticism and subjective idealism both seemed to issue from the same source, namely an excessive stress on *ideas*, or *what is present to the mind*, at the expense of the *inborn capacities of the mind*. The skeptics' overemphasis on ideas provided what seemed to the common-sense philosophers to be a false start, leading inescapably from the fundamental premise that "all knowledge begins with ideas," to absurdities.

No one better personified the excesses of reason than Berkeley.[2] He argued for subjective idealism along the following lines: the only things that can be present to the mind are *ideas*—sensations, passions, memories, imaginations, and other "operations of the mind." Since, as Berkeley claimed, "ideas can only resemble ideas," every

---

[1]Rosenfeld, 114.

[2]See: George Berkeley, *A Treatise Concerning the Principles of Human Knowledge* (Dublin: Aaron Rhames, for Jeremy Pepyat, Bookseller, 1710).

thing that we confusedly take to be an object is really ideas "blended or combined together." You believe that an apple is something more than the *sensations* of a round red shape, a smooth spherical surface, a certain heft and aroma, and other ideas and perceptions; and yet, when you attend to these ideas and perceptions, you find that this "something more," this supposed material reality swinging entirely free of your mind, is impossible to imagine. Accordingly, Berkeley concluded that *to be* means nothing more than *to perceive* or *to be perceived*. Reality consists not of physical form and matter, but of *ideas* and the *minds* that "have" them. Since any reality independent of minds and ideas is incomprehensible—since we cannot even make sense of the term *material objects*—it is against common sense to accept any notion of mind-independent reality.

But if this were so, then it would seem that apples and all other objects would disappear the moment we stop perceiving them: the world would disappear "behind our backs." If that were the case, though, what would account for the regularity and consistency of our perceptions? What would account for the fact that, as I seem to turn the apple around in my hand, my perceptions of it change in very predictable ways? In response to this sort of question, Berkeley explained that the world—"all the choir of heaven and furniture of the earth"—is given its regularity and consistency by an infinite all-perceiving mind: the world exists as it does, even when we are not looking or listening, because it consists of ideas perceived by God. The only reason objects do not disappear behind our backs is because from moment to moment God keeps them in mind. We are, thus, entirely dependent on an all-knowing and all-sustaining God.

Berkeley's conclusion, perhaps, is not as surprising as the fact that he claimed it in the name of common sense.

As we will see in our first reading, Scottish philosopher Thomas Reid (1710–1796) could not have disagreed more sharply with Berkeley when it comes to mind-independent reality. Reid conceded Berkeley's point that reason could not establish the existence of mind-independent reality—at least not alone. This, however, served only to illustrate how helpless reason is in the face of skepticism. Indeed, as Reid noted, skepticism could be extended considerably further than Berkeley had acknowledged: Reid's fellow Scotsman and younger contemporary David Hume had shown in his then-recent book *A Treatise of Human Nature* (1738)[3] that reason could also doubt the existence of minds, as discrete entities! Just as Berkeley could find no idea corresponding to mind-independent reality, Hume reported that he could find

---

[3]David Hume, *A Treatise of Human Nature* (Oxford: Clarendon Press, 1888), 251–63.

no idea or perception corresponding to his self, except as a loose bundle of ideas and impressions. In the course of Hume's good-natured but devastating arguments, he went much further than Berkeley by casting into doubt the very notion of the continuity of personhood. What Hume left us with, then, is not minds and ideas, as Berkeley would have it, but mere passing ideas unattached to minds.[4]

If this is where philosophical skepticism leads us, Reid thought, then all the more reason to resist it. Far from conceding the point that reality independent of minds and ideas is incomprehensible, Reid held that we cannot avoid the nonphilosophical conviction that many of our impressions are caused by external objects. Indeed, for anyone but a complete skeptic, the idea of material objects must be taken as an unquestioned *first principle*. If the faculty of reason alone cannot establish the existence of either material objects or minds, then something else must underwrite our belief in these things. Fortunately, we have other inborn or *innate* capacities of the mind to fall back on, notably common sense. It is common sense—not reason alone—that certifies the existence of minds and material objects.

The next reading, "A Defence of Common Sense" (1925), is a classic of Anglo-American analytic philosophy. The author, G. E. Moore (1873–1958), convinced many British and American philosophers that it was not their business to question common certainties, but rather to *analyze* them, in a special meaning of that verb. In this essay, Moore presents his argument for "common-sense realism"—the view that things independent of thinkers exist. He argues that any reason a skeptic could give that we cannot know with certainty that mind-independent reality exists would be no more certain than the reasons we have to accept common sense claims about our knowledge of that reality.

Our third reading consists of remarks written in response to G. E. Moore's paper by the influential twentieth-century Austrian philosopher Ludwig Wittgenstein (1889–1951). From Wittgenstein's notes emerge, lightly sketched, a *holistic* view of knowledge and doubt, and a strikingly original response to the skeptical challenge. "If you are not certain of any fact," he writes, "you cannot be certain of the meaning of your words either"; thus, "the game of doubting itself presupposes certainty."[5] In a passage that is not included in our excerpt, Wittgenstein writes that, "... the questions

---

[4]Unlike Berkeley, though, Hume did not argue that this was all that existed; rather, he argued only that in the face of skeptical challenge, we could not rationally justify the existence of more than this. Hume was making a point about the limits of justification of matters of fact, and about the broad scope of skepticism.

[5]The quoted passages are from *On Certainty* (ed. G. E. M. Anscombe and G. H. von Wright [New York: Harper & Row, 1969]), 114 and 115 (Sections 17e and 18e).

that we raise and our doubts depend on the fact that some propositions are exempt from doubt, are as it were like hinges on which those turn." These propositions or statements, exemplified by Moore's utterance *This is a hand* (accompanied by the gesture of holding up his hand), are embedded in a much larger "nest of propositions." Any of these statements, taken singly, can of course be subject to skeptical doubt; nevertheless, such statements taken together constitute "an unmoving foundation" without which our actual language practices cannot take place. "Our knowledge forms an enormous system," Wittgenstein wrote, "and only within this system has a particular bit the value we give it."[6] It is only thanks to these hinge statements that certainty and doubting can take place. Banish all such statements and you banish doubt, along with linguistic practices themselves. Thus, "doubt itself rests only on what is beyond doubt."[7]

In the final reading in Part 1, Canadian philosopher Mark Kingwell tries his hand at making sense of common sense. Kingwell first distinguishes "plain common sense"—the untutored, unreflective common sense that most adults are supposed to have—from the more reflective "philosophical common sense." The latter sort of common sense is what the architect Frank Lloyd Wright was probably referring to when he quipped: "There is nothing more uncommon than common sense." Kingwell appears to take common sense, in both its plain and its philosophical versions, to be a mental capacity, rather than a set of beliefs and assumptions. He connects the "main features of plain common sense" with the claims that: (1) there is an objectively existing world external to me; (2) it has existed for a long time in the past and will continue to exist in the future; (3) I exist as both a subject and an object in this world; (4) I existed in the past and will exist in the future; and (5) there are numerous other thinking subjects like me, who exist in time and the external world. For Kingwell as for Moore, then, plain common sense is incompatible with skepticism about the existence of other minds, and it entails *metaphysical realism*, the view that the world is the way it is independently of how humans take it to be.

The guiding thought of plain common sense is: *a thing is what it is, and is not what it is not.* But this very insistence leads beyond plain common sense, because it sets the stage for the distinction between appearance and reality, guiding us to a *critical* sort of sound judgment. This is the critical common sense that says, "the oar in the water *appears* to be crooked, but it is not *really* crooked." As soon as we take seriously the

---

[6]Wittgenstein, *On Certainty*, 52e (Section 410).
[7]Wittgenstein, *On Certainty*, 68e (Section 519).

distinction between appearance and reality, we move from plain common sense to what Kingwell calls *philosophical common sense*. But once we do this, what becomes of the insistence that a thing is what it is? Common sense leads to criticism, but the beginning of criticism marks the limit for common sense in its plain variety. Thus, common sense appears to subvert its own authority. "Since common sense clashes with itself," Kingwell writes, "the requirement of consistency with common sense rules out common sense itself."[8]

If Kingwell provides a reliable survey of issues we've encountered in Part 1, it would seem that the term *common sense* typically flags something vague and nebulous at best—either a particular set of beliefs and assumptions or a certain mental capacity that produces these beliefs and assumptions. The beliefs are supposed to be widely shared and so reliable that they usually go without saying, but as it turns out, many of these beliefs are *not* widely shared across time and space, and some of them are not especially reliable, either. Indeed, some of these supposed beliefs, namely those that qualify as Kingwell's *common nonsense*, are not really even beliefs at all.

But whether or not a formulation is nonsense, to describe it as commonsensical is to rhetorically certify it. This fact, which is especially apparent when it comes to partisan claims and politics (as we will see in Parts V and VI), accounts at least in part for why common sense beliefs are so strikingly inconsistent. And the inconsistency, in turn, renders common sense incoherent. This is why, according to Kingwell, "we have no way of talking philosophically about it."

Actually, though, we *can* speak philosophically about it, as Kingwell himself demonstrates in this paper. We can speak philosophically about common sense, just as we can speak philosophically about, say, providence or human nature. But if Kingwell is right, then we cannot put common sense to *philosophical* work, and we should not try to use common sense as Reid and G. E. Moore wanted to use it—as an authority to certify knowledge claims and to banish skepticism as it arises from case to case. In the philosophical contest between common sense and skepticism, skepticism wins.

Although skepticism may carry the day when it comes to philosophy, it is no way to conduct our daily lives. We cannot *live in* skepticism: as Wittgenstein has reminded us, doubt itself rests on what is beyond doubt. Nevertheless, plain common sense constantly pushes us toward doubt. What then are we to do? Competent modern adults must in the course of their daily affairs defer to common sense; however, Kingwell suggests,

---

[8]Here Kingwell is quoting Timothy Sprigge, "Philosophy and Common Sense," *Revue Internationale de Philosophie* 40, no. 158(3) (1986): 203.

we should do so the way we would defer to a prudent but arrogant guide: let common sense be our guide in daily affairs, but do not believe its flattering self-descriptions. To speak seriously of common sense, we must *not* speak commonsensically about it. Kingwell concludes that the plain truth about common sense is that there is not much to say about it philosophically, except perhaps *ironically*.

But what of those of us who are "cursed with a peculiar kind of curiosity"—namely philosophical curiosity? It would seem that the best we can do is to *live with* skepticism. Kingwell suggests that Hume provides the model here: when philosophy starts to hurt our heads, we should beat a retreat to the backgammon board, a glass of sherry, and light conversation with friends.

Chapter 1

The Human Mind and Common Sense

Thomas Reid

Thomas Reid begins our first reading by distinguishing between two distinct meanings of the word *sense*: on the one hand, there is the non-philosophical meaning of *judgment* "in common language." This is the meaning that Reid will describe and defend. On the other hand, there is a meaning that the word took on in the writings of the "modern philosophers" whom Reid opposes, notably John Locke.[1] According to these philosophers, sense comprises sight, hearing, smell, taste, and touch—the powers "by which we receive certain ideas or impressions from objects"[2]—as well as the "internal senses," including consciousness, memory, reasoning, and other "operations of our own minds."

It might help to say a few more words about what the "modern philosophers" have to say about ideas. An idea, according to Locke, is anything present to the mind, any immediate object of thought, whether simple ("round") or complex ("apple"). Ideas broadly include visual images (colors, shapes, spatial relationships, motions, and so on), sounds, smells, tastes, and touches, as well as the "internal senses" that provide memories, emotions, feelings, the meanings of words, and concepts of logic and mathematics. The senses— both the five "external" senses that are familiar to us, as well as the "internal senses"—merely furnish the mind with "ideas," without providing anything in the way of knowledge or opinion. By this account, sense gives us the ideas of color, shape, sound, and other qualities of objects, as well as memories, feelings, and meanings, but it does not *judge*: it does not compare ideas and perceive their necessary relations. In the view of the "modern philosophers," then, judgment is a power distinct from sense, and judging comes *after* sensing.

---

[1]Reid mentions Locke and Francis Hutcheson as modern philosophers, but he also had Berkeley and Hume in mind.

[2]Locke, Berkeley, and Hume thought of impressions and "ideas" as mental *objects*. Reid, by contrast, thought of them as mental *activities*.

Reid, by contrast, argues that the word *sense* in the term *common sense* does not refer to just the internal and external senses, such as the senses of sight, hearing, smell, taste, or touch. For him common sense is a power of the mind by which we "judge concerning self-evident things" that exist independently of ourselves. When we perceive an apple, a man, or a horse, we immediately perceive them to exist, without inferring their existence from anything else (such as colors, shapes, sounds, motions, and so on). Common sense judgments, then, do not require an effort of reasoning: to understand a common sense judgment (as in the statement *the part is less than the whole*) is to believe it.[3]

For Reid, then, common sense is a certain power of judgment: it is the faculty of the mind that concerns sure knowledge. This usage corresponds to the expression *he is a man of sense*—that is, of good judgment. Common sense is "one branch (or degree) of reason—the capacity to judge concerning self-evident things." This, Reid says, is the extent of reason for the greater part of humanity: it is "the degree of judgment that is common to men with whom we can converse and transact business."

It is, moreover, a "gift of Heaven": most of us are born with this capacity of judgment, and for those who are not born with it, no amount of education can provide it. (After all, how could noninferential knowledge be taught?) For the greater part of mankind, no larger degree of reason is to be found than common sense. By contrast, the higher degree of reason, which involves reasoning from judgments of things self-evident to conclusions that are not self-evident, *can* be acquired by education and training.

From this it follows that, "It is absurd to conceive that there can be any opposition between reason and common sense." Thus, in the contest between the modern philosophers and "the opinions of the vulgar," Reid places himself squarely in the latter camp.

Reid was the leading figure in what has come to be called the Scottish School of Common Sense. He entered the ministry in 1737, and in 1752 he was appointed professor of philosophy at King's College in the town of Aberdeen, Scotland. There he cofounded the Aberdeen Philosophical Society, the so-called "Wise Club," whose members dedicated themselves to scholarly debate, carried on strictly within the realm of something they called *common sense*. The

---

[3]Reid appears sometimes to subscribe to a psychological conception of evidence, whereby what is evident produces belief in the human mind and forces assent (*Essays on the Intellectual Powers*, 2.20, 292, in the *The Works of Thomas Reid*, listed in the Readings That Appear in This Book section, at the end of this book).

members of the Club staunchly opposed the institution of slavery and they also opposed the twin evils of skepticism and "enthusiasm," or what we today call religious extremism. These are twin evils because they both tend to undermine civil authority by promoting dissention and sectarian violence, and they both directly or indirectly discredited the established church.[4] England had recently emerged from brutal civil war along religious lines, and the members of the Wise Club feared anything that posed a threat to civil peace.

Our selection consists of Chapter 2 from Reid's essay "Of Judgment," in his *Essays on the Intellectual Powers of Man*. The remarks in square brackets are those of A. D. Woozley, the editor of the 1941 edition of Reid's *Essays*.

Common Sense

The word *sense* seems to have a different meaning in common language from its meaning in the writings of philosophers, and those different meanings are apt to be muddled together, giving rise to embarrassment and error.

I shan't go back to ancient philosophy on this matter. Modern philosophers regard sense as a power that has nothing to do with judgment. They regard sense as the power by which we receive certain ideas or impressions from objects, and judgment as the power by which we compare those ideas and perceive their necessary agreements and disagreements.

The external senses give us the ideas of color, shape, sound, and other qualities—primary or secondary—of bodies. Locke called consciousness an "internal sense" because through it we have the ideas of thought, memory, reasoning, and other operations of our own minds. Hutcheson thought that we have simple and original ideas that can't be attributed either to the external senses or to consciousness, so he introduced other internal senses such as the sense of harmony, the sense of beauty, and the moral sense.[5] Ancient philosophers also spoke of "internal senses," of which memory was thought to be one.

---

[4]The skepticism that is the focus of the readings in Part I is primarily skepticism with regard to *knowledge* (epistemological skepticism), not skepticism with regard to *morality* (ethical skepticism). The latter sort of skepticism, to which we will return in Part IV, claims that *we cannot know whether there are any valid moral principles*. As Reid's colleagues were fond of pointing out, these two sorts of skepticism are related: skepticism with regard to knowledge in general opens the door to the denial of certainty when it comes to knowledge of moral laws.

[5]The Reverend Francis Hutcheson (1694–1746) is today ranked, with Reid and Hume, as a leading figure in the Scottish Enlightenment. Hutcheson believed that among the internal senses is a "moral sense," which he described as a "determination of the mind" by which we directly perceive virtue or vice.—Markar Melkonian (henceforth M. M.).

But all these "senses," whether external or internal, have been represented by philosophers as the providers to our minds of ideas, without including any kind of judgment. Hutcheson defines a sense as the mind's determination to receive ideas from the presence of an object independently of our will. And Priestley writes:

> Philosophers have used the word *sense* to name the faculties in consequence of which we are liable to feelings relative to ourselves only, and from which they haven't claimed to draw any conclusions concerning the nature of things; whereas truth is not relative but absolute and real.

Not so! In common language "sense" always implies judgment. A man of sense is a man of judgment. Good sense is good judgment. Nonsense is what is obviously contrary to right judgment. Common sense is the degree of judgment that is common to men with whom we can converse and transact business.

Philosophers call seeing and hearing "senses" because we have ideas by them; the vulgar call them "senses" because we judge by them. We judge colors by the eye, sounds by the ear, beauty and ugliness by taste, and right and wrong in conduct by our moral sense or conscience.

Philosophers who portray sense as having only one role, namely to provide us with ideas, slip without realizing it into the popular opinion that the senses are judging faculties. Thus Locke, writing about the thesis that the quality of color really exists and has a being outside me: "The best assurance I can have, the best my faculties are capable of, is the testimony of my eyes; they are the proper and sole judges of this thing" (*Essay* IV.xi.2). This popular meaning of the word *sense* is not peculiar to the English language. The corresponding words in Greek, Latin, and (I believe) all the European languages have the same meaning-spread. The Latin words *sentire, sententia, sensa, sensus*—from the last of which the English word *sense* is borrowed—stand for judgment or opinion, and are applied equally to objects of external sense, of taste, of morals, and of the understanding.

I can't claim to explain why a word that is not a technicality, and is familiar in common conversation, should have such a different meaning in philosophical writings. I merely remark that the philosophical meaning corresponds perfectly with the account that Locke and other modern philosophers give of judgment. For if the only role of the external and internal senses is to provide the mind with the ideas about which we judge and reason, it seems to be a natural consequence that the only role of judgment is to compare those ideas and to perceive their necessary relations.

These two opinions seem to be so connected that one may have been the cause of the other. Anyway, I think that if both are true, there is no room left for any knowledge or judgment either about the real existence of contingent things or about their contingent relations.

To return to the popular meaning of the word *sense*: it would be much harder to find good authors who never use the word with that meaning than to find ones who do. [Reid then quotes eight lines by the English poet Alexander Pope, in which "good sense" is described as "the gift of Heaven" and "a light which in yourself you must perceive."] This inner light or sense is given by heaven to different persons in different degrees. We must have a certain degree of it if we are to be subjects of law and government, capable of managing our own affairs, and responsible for our conduct toward others. This is called "common sense," because it is common to all men with whom we can transact business or hold accountable for their conduct.

The laws of all civilized nations distinguish those who have this gift of heaven from those who don't. The latter may have rights that ought not to be violated, but because they have no understanding of their own to direct their actions, the laws arrange for them to be guided by the understanding of others. Their lack of common sense is easily detected through its effects on their actions, through what they say, and even through their physical appearance. When there is a question as to whether or not a man has this natural gift of common sense, a judge or a jury can usually give a very confident answer after a short conversation with him.

The same degree of understanding that makes a man capable of acting with common prudence in the conduct of life makes him capable of discovering what is true and what is false in matters that are self-evident and that he is clear about in his mind.

All knowledge and all science must be built on principles that are self-evident, and every man who has common sense is a competent judge of such principles when he conceives them clearly. That is why disputes very often come down to appeals to common sense.

When the disputants agree on the first principles on which their arguments are based, there is room for reasoning, but when one of them denies something that seems to the other to be too obvious to need or to be capable of proof, reasoning seems to be at an end; an appeal is made to common sense, and each disputant is left to enjoy his own opinion.

There seems to be no cure for this, and no way to discuss such appeals to common sense, unless the decisions of common sense can be encoded in rules that all reasonable men accept. If this were possible it would be very desirable, and would give logic something it needs, and why shouldn't it be possible for reasonable men to agree on things that are self-evident?

All I want to do in this chapter is to explain the meaning of "common sense," so that it won't be treated (as some have treated it) as signifying something new or as a phrase without any meaning. I have tried to show that "sense," in its most common and therefore its most proper meaning, signifies judgment (though philosophers often use it with a different meaning). This makes it natural to think that "common sense" should mean common judgment, and so it does.

It may be hard to settle the precise limits separating common judgment from what is beyond it, on the one hand, and from what falls short of it, on the other. Men who agree about the meaning of the phrase *common sense* may disagree about where those limits lie, or may never have even thought of fixing them. There is nothing puzzling about this, any more than there is about the fact that all Englishmen mean the same thing by "the county of York," though not one in a hundred can point out its precise boundaries.

Indeed, it seems to me that "common sense" is as well understood and as free from ambiguity as "the county of York." We find the phrase in countless places in good writers; we hear it on countless occasions in conversation, and as far as I can tell it is always used with the same meaning. That is probably why it is so seldom defined or explained. [...]

Men rarely ask what common sense is, because everyone thinks that he has it. Yet I remember two very eminent authors who have asked this question, and we should hear their views on this topic that is so often mentioned and so rarely discussed.

It is well known that Lord Shaftesbury called one of his treatises *Sensus Communis:*[6] *An Essay on the Freedom of Wit and Humour, in a Letter to a Friend.* In this, he reminds his friend of a free-wheeling conversation they once had with some of their friends on the subjects of morality and religion. Amidst the different opinions launched and defended with great vivacity and ingenuity, every now and then someone would make an appeal to common sense. Everyone allowed the appeal; no one questioned the authority of the court, until someone whose intellect they had never questioned solemnly asked them to tell him what common sense is. He said:

> If by the word *sense* we were to understand opinion and judgment, and by the word *common* the whole or any considerable part of mankind, it would be hard to discover where there *is* any common sense; for views agreeing with the "sense" of one part of mankind would conflict with the "sense" of another part. And if "common sense" were to be determined by the *majority,* it would change as often as men changed.

---

[6]In Latin, literally "common sense."—M. M.

In religion, he said, common sense was as hard to determine as *catholic* or *orthodox*; one sect's absurdity was another's demonstration. He continued:

> In political matters, if plain British or Dutch "sense" were right, Turkish and French "sense" must certainly be wrong. Passive obedience—i.e. unquestioning obedience to a ruler with unlimited powers—seemed to us to be mere nonsense; but it turned out to be the "common sense" of a considerable proportion of our fellow-countrymen, a larger proportion in Europe, and perhaps a majority of all the world. As for morals, the difference is still wider; for even the philosophers can never agree on a single system. And even some of our most admired modern philosophers have openly told us that virtue and vice have no law or criterion except mere fashion and vogue.

That is the substance of the gentleman's speech. I think it explains the meaning of "common sense" perfectly, and contains the whole case—everything that has been said or can be said—against the authority of common sense and the permissibility of appeals to it.

There is no report of any immediate answer to this speech, which might incline us to think that the noble author agrees with the views of the intelligent gentleman whose speech he quotes. But that would be wrong, as is clear from the title *Sensus Communis* given to his work, from his frequent use of the phrase *common sense*, and from the whole tenor of the book. [Reid backs this up with a discussion of what Shaftesbury was up to in this work, and by quoting some passages, including this:]

> Some moral and philosophical truths are so evident in themselves that it would be easier to imagine that half mankind had run mad in precisely the same way than to admit as truth anything that was advanced against such natural knowledge, fundamental reason, and common sense.

[After adding one more quotation from Shaftesbury, again treating "common sense" as a criterion of truth, Reid presents passages from Fénelon, Cicero, Hume, and Priestley—all using the phrase "common sense" (or its French or Latin equivalent) to stand for a source of knowledge, and thus as implying that common sense involves *judgment*. Then:]

On the basis of this cloud of testimonies (and I could have given hundreds more), I think that whatever criticism is spread over those who have spoken of common sense as a source of knowledge, or who have appealed to it in matters that are self-evident, will fall lightly on any individual when there are so many to share in it! ...

From the account I have given of the meaning of the phrase *common sense*, it is easy to see how to use it properly and how to tell when it is being misused.

It is absurd to think that common sense could be in any way opposed to reason. It is indeed reason's firstborn, and just as they are commonly joined together in speech and in writing, they are inseparable in their nature.

We ascribe to reason two roles, or two degrees—to judge concerning self-evident things, and to draw conclusions that are not self-evident from premises that are. The former is the job of common sense—its only job. So the whole of common sense coincides with reason; indeed, "common sense" is only another name for one branch (or degree) of reason. "Why give it a name of its own, when you admit that it is only a degree of reason?" ... There is an obvious reason why this degree of reason should have its own special name. It's that in the vast majority of mankind no other degree of reason is to be found. It is this degree that entitles them to be called "reasonable creatures." It is this degree of reason—and only this—that makes a man capable of managing his own affairs and accountable for his conduct toward others. So there is the best reason why it should have its own special name.

These two degrees of reason differ in other respects, which would be sufficient to entitle them to distinct names.

The first is purely the gift of heaven, and where heaven hasn't given it, no education can make up for that. The second is learned by practice and rules when the first is not lacking. A man who has common sense may be taught to reason. But if someone doesn't have that gift, no teaching will enable him either to judge concerning first principles or to reason from them.

I have only one other point to make, namely that common sense has more work to do in refutation than in confirmation. A conclusion drawn by valid reasoning from true principles can't possibly contradict any decision of common sense, because truth will always be consistent with itself. And such a conclusion can't be confirmed by common sense, because it doesn't lie with common sense's jurisdiction.

But someone who sets out from false principles, or who makes a mistake in reasoning, may be led to a conclusion that contradicts the decisions of common sense. In this case the conclusion is within the jurisdiction of common sense, even though the reasoning on which it was based is not, and a man of common sense is entitled to reject the conclusion without being able to show the error of the reasoning that led to it.

[...]

Chapter 2

A Defense of Common Sense

G. E. Moore

As we have seen, Reid sometimes describes common sense as *a power of the mind*, or a mental faculty. In our next reading, G. E. Moore limits his view to common sense as *a set of truisms*. The first item that Moore mentions in his list of truisms (under heading (1)) is "There exists at present a living human body, which is my body." Notice that he did not write, "There exists at present a mind, which is my mind"—a claim that would have evoked René Descartes's famous first item of certainty, "I think, therefore I am." Moore, for his part, offers his item without preceding argument. Evidently, he is up to something very different from Descartes.

In Section I, Moore makes a case for the reality of many things that are neither my mind nor my present thoughts. These include: mind-independent objects (both animate and inanimate) in various spatial relations to each other; the past; other experiencing minds; and some of what I take to be my memories.

In a paragraph-long sentence under heading (2), Moore asserts a "single truism" that is key to his argument. He observes, commonsensically enough, that many humans believe, with regard to themselves and their respective bodies, a proposition[1] corresponding to each truism under heading (1). Moreover, he argues, these humans are *justified* in this belief. So since, as Moore has already assured us, each of the propositions under heading (1) is "wholly true," he concludes that his "single truism" counts as genuine knowledge.

---

[1]Moore makes a distinction between a *proposition* (something that can be true or false) and a *sentence* ("complete thoughts" people say in normal language). According to this view, *Le chat est sur le tapis* and *The cat is on the mat* are two different sentences, which might under certain circumstances express the same proposition. On the other hand, Moore writes, "a different proposition is meant at every different time at which an expression is used." Some philosophers reject this distinction, though (including W. V. O. Quine, whom we will meet in Part II), and for our purposes we will ignore it.

In the remainder of the first section (in Subsection B), Moore argues that idealist philosophers and skeptics are inconsistent if they hold that the truism under heading (2) is wholly true.

In Section II, Moore first distinguishes between two different sorts of facts: *physical* and *mental*, and identifies several possible sorts of mental facts, at least one of which, he says, certainly exists. He then makes the case that there is no good reason to suppose that every physical fact is *logically dependent* upon some mental fact, and that there is no good reason to suppose that every physical fact is *causally dependent* upon some mental fact.

Moore's immediate target here is a version of absolute idealism that he had at first accepted as a student of philosophy and that prevailed at the time of his writing, a version that owed much to the German philosopher Georg W. F. Hegel (1770–1831); however, his remarks apply just as well to an idealist philosopher whose views we have already encountered. If, as George Berkeley claimed, Nature is God's idea, then it would seem that things that we meet with in space are things that are not external to God's mind. According to this view, as we have seen, there is no reality independent of minds: only minds and ideas exist.

Among the consequences of Moore's discussion toward the end of Section II are his two conclusions in the brief Section III.

Clearly, Moore has not met the skeptical challenge with reference to the philosophical problem of Knowledge of the External World. But he did not set out to refute skepticism; rather, it appears that he is trying to convince us that a certain "common-sense view of the world" is the case.

George Edward Moore (1873–1958) was an English philosopher at the University of Cambridge who wrote influential papers on metaphysics, epistemology, and ethics. Along with Bertrand Russell, he is celebrated as a founder of analytic philosophy, a style of philosophy that still prevails among academics in Britain and the United States. Our selection consists of the first three-fifths of Moore's original paper.

In what follows I have merely tried to state, one by one, some of the most important points in which my philosophical position differs from positions which have been taken up by some other philosophers. It may be that the points which I have had room to mention are not really the most important, and possibly some of them may be points as to which no philosopher has ever really differed from me. But, to the best of my belief, each is a point as to which many have really differed, although (in most cases, at all events) each is also a point as to which many have agreed with me.

I

The first point is a point which embraces a great many other points. And it is one which I cannot state as clearly as I wish to state it, except at some length. The method I am going to use for stating it is this. I am going to begin by enunciating, under the heading (1), a whole long list of propositions, which may seem, at first sight, such obvious truisms as not to be worth stating: they are, in fact, a set of propositions, every one of which (in my own opinion) I know, with certainty, to be true. I shall, next, under the heading (2), state a single proposition which makes an assertion about a whole set of classes of propositions—each class being defined as the class consisting of all propositions which resemble one of the propositions in (1) in a certain respect; (2), therefore, is a proposition which could not be stated until the list of propositions in (1), or some similar list, had already been given; (2) is itself a proposition which may seem such an obvious truism as not to be worth stating, and it is also a proposition which (in my own opinion) I know, with certainty, to be true. But, nevertheless, it is, to the best of my belief, a proposition with regard to which many philosophers have, for different reasons, differed from me; even if they have not directly denied (2) itself, they have held views incompatible with it. My first point, then, may be said to be that (2), together with all its implications, some of which I shall expressly mention, is true.

(1) I begin, then, with my list of truisms, every one of which (in my own opinion) I know, with certainty, to be true. The propositions to be included in this list are the following:

There exists at present a living human body, which is *my* body. This body was born at a certain time in the past, and has existed continuously ever since, though not without undergoing changes; it was, for instance, much smaller when it was born, and for some time afterwards, than it is now. Ever since it was born, it has been either in contact with or not far from the surface of the earth, and, at every moment since it was born, there have also existed many other things, having shape and size in three dimensions (in the same familiar sense in which it has), from which it has been *at various distances* (in the familiar sense in which it is now at a distance both from that mantelpiece and from that bookcase, and at a greater distance from the bookcase than it is from the mantelpiece); also, there have (very often, at all events) existed some other things of this kind with which it was in contact (in the familiar sense in which it is now in contact with the pen I am holding in my right hand and with some of the clothes I am wearing). Among the things which have, in this sense, formed part of its environment (i.e., have been either in contact with it, or at *some* distance from it, however *great*) there have, at every moment since its birth, been large numbers of other living human bodies, each of which has, like it, (a) at some time been born, (b) continued to exist from some time after birth, (c) been, at every moment of its life after birth, either in contact with or not far from the surface of the earth, and many of these bodies have already died and ceased to exist. But the earth had existed also for many years before my body was born, and for many of these years, also, large numbers of human bodies had, at every moment, been alive upon it, and many of these bodies had died and ceased to exist before it was born. Finally (to come to a different class of propositions), I am a human being, and I have, at different times since my body was born, had many different experiences, of each of many different kinds: for example, I have often perceived both my own body and other things which formed part of its environment, including other human bodies; I have not only perceived things of this kind, but have also observed facts about them, such as, for instance, the fact which I am now observing, that that mantelpiece is at present nearer to my body than that bookcase; I have been aware of other facts, which I was not at the time observing, such as, for instance, the fact, of which I am now aware, that my body existed yesterday and was then also for some time nearer to that mantelpiece than to that bookcase; I have had expectations with regard to the future, and many beliefs of other kinds, both true and false; I have thought of imaginary things and persons and incidents, in the reality of which I did not believe; I have had dreams; and I have had feelings of many different kinds. And, just as my body has been the body of a human being, namely myself, who has, during his lifetime, had many experiences of each of these (and other) different kinds; so, in the case of very many of the other human bodies which have lived upon the earth, each has been the body of a different human being, who has, during the lifetime of that body, had many different experiences of each of these (and other) different kinds.

(2) I now come to the single truism which, as will be seen, could not be stated except by reference to the whole list of truisms, just given in (1). This truism also (in my own opinion) I *know*, with certainty to be true, and it is as follows:

In the case of *very many* (I do not say *all*) of the human beings belonging to the class (which includes myself) defined in the following way, i.e., as human beings who have had human bodies, that were born and lived for some time upon the earth, and who have, during the lifetime of those bodies, had many different experiences of each of the kinds mentioned in (1), it is true that each has frequently, during the life of his body, known, with regard to *himself* or *his* body, and with regard to some time earlier than any of the times at which I wrote down the propositions in (1), a proposition corresponding to each of the propositions in (1), in the sense that it asserts with regard to *himself* or *his* body and the earlier time in question (namely, in each case, the time at which he knew it), just what the corresponding proposition in (1) asserts with regard to *me* or *my* body and the time at which I wrote that proposition down.

In other words what (2) asserts is only (what seems an obvious enough truism) that each of *us* (meaning by "us," very many human beings of the class defined) has frequently *known*, with regard to *himself* or *his* body and the time at which he knew it, everything which, in writing down my list of propositions in (1), I was claiming to know about myself or *my* body and the time at which I wrote that proposition down, i.e., just as I knew (when I wrote it down) "There exists at present a living human body which is my body," so each of us has frequently known with regard to himself and some other time the different but corresponding proposition, which *he* could *then* have properly expressed by, "There exists *at present* a human body which is *my* body"; just as *I* know "Many human bodies other than mine have before now lived on the earth," so each of us has frequently known the different but corresponding proposition "Many human bodies other than *mine* have before *now* lived on the earth"; just as *I* know "Many human beings other than myself have before now perceived, and dreamed, and felt," so each of us has frequently known the different but corresponding proposition "Many human beings other than *myself* have before *now* perceived, and dreamed, and felt," and so on, in the case of *each* of the propositions enumerated in (1).

I hope there is no difficulty in understanding, so far, what this proposition (2) asserts. I have tried to make clear by examples what I mean by "propositions *corresponding* to each of the propositions in (1)." And what (2) asserts is merely that each of us has frequently known to be true a proposition *corresponding* (in that sense) to each of the propositions in (1)—a *different* corresponding proposition, of course, at each of the times at which he knew such a proposition to be true.

But there remain two points, which, in view of the way in which some philosophers have used the English language, ought, I think, to be expressly mentioned, if I am to make quite clear exactly how much I am asserting in asserting (2).

The first point is this. Some philosophers seem to have thought it legitimate to use the word "true" in such a sense that a proposition which is partially false may nevertheless also be true, and some of these, therefore, would perhaps say that propositions like those enumerated in (1) are, in their view, true, when all the time they believe that every such proposition is partially false. I wish, therefore, to make it quite plain that I am not using "true" in any such sense. I am using it in such a sense (and I think this is the ordinary usage) that if a proposition is partially false, it follows that it is not true, though, of course, it may be *partially* true. I am maintaining, in short, that all the propositions in (1), and also many propositions corresponding to each of these, are *wholly* true; I am asserting this in asserting (2). And hence any philosopher, who does in fact believe, with regard to any or all of these classes of propositions, that every proposition of the class in question is partially false, is, in fact, disagreeing with me and holding a view incompatible with (2), even though he may think himself justified in saying that he believes some propositions belonging to all of these classes to be "true."

And the second point is this. Some philosophers seem to have thought it legitimate to use such expressions as, e.g., "The earth has existed for many years past," as if they expressed something which they really believed, when in fact they believe that every proposition, which such an expression would *ordinarily* be understood to express, is, at least partially, false, and all they really believe is that there is some other set of propositions, related in a certain way to those which such expressions do actually express, which, unlike these, really are true. That is to say, they use the expression "The earth has existed for many years past" to express, not what it would ordinarily be understood to express, but the proposition that some proposition, related to this in a certain way, is true; when all the time they believe that the proposition, which this expression would ordinarily be understood to express, is, at least partially, false. I wish, therefore, to make it quite plain that I was not using the expressions I used in (1) in any such subtle sense. I meant by each of them precisely what every reader, in reading them, will have understood me to mean. And any philosopher, therefore, who holds that any of these expressions, if understood in this popular manner, expresses a proposition which embodies some popular error, is disagreeing with me and holding a view incompatible with (2), even though he may hold that there is some *other*, true, proposition which the expression in question might be legitimately used to express.

In what I have just said, I have assumed that there is some meaning which is *the* ordinary or popular meaning of such expressions as "The earth has existed for many years past." And this, I am afraid, is an assumption which some philosophers are capable of disputing. They seem to think that the question "Do you believe that the earth has existed for many years past?" is not a plain question, such as should be met either by a plain "Yes" or "No," or by a plain "I can't make up my mind," but is the sort of question which can be properly met by:

> It all depends on what you mean by "the earth" and "exists" and "years": if you mean so and so, and so and so, and so and so, then I do; but if you mean so and so, and so and so, and so and so, or so and so, and so and so, and so and so, or so and so, and so and so, and so and so, then I don't, or at least I think it is extremely doubtful.

It seems to me that such a view is as profoundly mistaken as any view can be. Such an expression as "The earth has existed for many years past" is the very type of an unambiguous expression, the meaning of which we all understand. Anyone who takes a contrary view must, I suppose, be confusing the question whether we understand its meaning (which we all certainly do) with the entirely different question whether we *know what it means*, in the sense that we are able to give *a correct analysis* of its meaning.[2] The question what is the correct analysis of *the* proposition meant *on any occasion* (for, of course, as I insisted in defining (2), a different proposition is meant at every different time at which the expression is used) by "The earth has existed for many years past" is, it seems to me, a profoundly difficult question, and one to which, as I shall presently urge, no one knows the answer. But to hold that we do not know what, in certain respects, is the analysis of what we understand by such an expression, is an entirely different thing from holding that we do not understand the expression. It is obvious that we cannot even raise the question how what we do understand by it is to be analyzed, unless we do understand it. So soon, therefore, as we know that a person who uses such an expression is using it in its ordinary sense, we understand his meaning. So that in explaining that I was using the expressions used in (1) in their ordinary sense (those of them which have an ordinary sense, which is not the case with quite all of them), I have done all that is required to make my meaning clear.

But now, assuming that the expressions which I have used to express (2) are understood, I think, as I have said, that many philosophers have really held views incompatible with (2). And the philosophers who have done so may, I think, be divided into two main groups. (A) What (2) asserts is, with regard to a whole set of *classes* of propositions, that we have, each of us, frequently *known* to be true propositions belonging to *each* of these classes. And one way of holding a view incompatible with this proposition is, of course, to hold, with regard to one or more of the classes in question, that no propositions of that class *are* true—that all of them are, at least partially, false; since if, in the case of any one of these classes, no propositions of that class *are* true, it is obvious that nobody can have *known* any propositions of that class to be true, and therefore that *we* cannot have known to be true propositions belonging to *each* of these classes. And my first group of philosophers consists of philosophers who have held views incompatible with (2) for this reason. They have held, with regard to one or more of the classes in question, simply that no propositions of that class *are* true. Some of them have held this with regard to *all* the classes in question, some only with regard to *some* of them. But, of course, whichever of these two views they have held, they have been holding a view inconsistent with (2). (B) Some philosophers, on the other hand, have not ventured to assert, with regard to any of the classes in (2),

---

[2]Moore believed that *analysis* is an essential tool or method for philosophy. For him, what is analyzed is a complex psychological fact. To give the analysis of "the earth has existed for many years past" would require describing what the expression has meant on each and every occasion in which it has been used. Moore's point here is that we can *understand* an expression without being able to *provide an analysis*, in this sense of the word, of what we understand by the expression. In any case, as he notes, we must first understand an expression before we will ever be able to provide an analysis of what we understand by it.—M. M.

that no propositions of that class are true, but what they have asserted is that, in the case of some of these classes, no human being has ever *known*, with certainty, that any propositions of the class in question are true. That is to say, they differ profoundly from philosophers of group A, in that they hold that propositions of *all* these classes *may* be true, but nevertheless they hold a view incompatible with (2) since they hold, with regard to some of these classes, that none of us has ever *known* a proposition of the class in question to be true.

A. I said that some philosophers, belonging to this group, have held that no propositions belonging to *any* of the classes in (2) are wholly true, while others have only held this with regard to *some* of the classes in (2). And I think the chief division of this kind has been the following. Some of the propositions in (1) (and, therefore, of course, all propositions belonging to the corresponding classes in (2)) are propositions which cannot be true, unless some *material things* have existed and have stood in *spatial relations* to one another: that is to say, they are propositions which, *in a certain sense*, imply *the reality of material things*, and *the reality of Space*. For example, the proposition that my body has existed for many years past, and has at every moment during that time been either in contact with or not far from the earth, is a proposition which implies both the *reality of material things* (provided you use "material things" in such a sense that to deny the reality of material things implies that no proposition which asserts that human bodies have existed, or that the earth has existed, is wholly true) and also the *reality of Space* (provided, again, that you use "Space" in such a sense that to deny the reality of Space implies that no proposition which asserts that anything has ever been in contact with or at a distance from another, in the familiar senses pointed out in (1), is wholly true). But others among the propositions in (1) (and, therefore, propositions belonging to the corresponding classes in (2)) do not (at least obviously) imply either the reality of material things or the reality of Space: for example, the propositions that I have often had dreams, and have had many different feelings at different times. It is true that propositions of this second class do imply one thing which is also implied by all propositions of the first, namely that (*in a certain sense*) *Time is real*, and imply also one thing not implied by propositions of the first class, namely that (*in a certain sense*) at least one *Self is real*. But I think there are some philosophers who, while denying that (in the senses in question) either material things or Space are real, have been willing to admit that Selves and Time are real, in the sense required. Other philosophers, on the other hand, have used the expression "Time is not real," to express some view that they held, and some, at least, of these have, I think, meant by this expression something which is incompatible with the truth of *any* of the propositions in (1)—they have meant, namely, that *every* proposition of the sort that is expressed by the use of "now" or "at present," e.g., "I am now both seeing and hearing" or "There exists at present a living human body," or by the use of a past tense, e.g., "I *have* had many experiences in the past" or "The earth *has* existed for many years," are, at least partially, false.

All the four expressions I have just introduced, namely, "Material things are not real," "Space is not real," "Time is not real," "The Self is not real," are, I think, unlike the expressions I used in (1), really ambiguous. And it may be that, in the case of each of them, some philosopher has used the expression in question to express some view he held which was not incompatible with (2). With such philosophers, if there are any, I am not, of course, at present concerned. But it seems to me that the most natural and proper usage of each of these expressions is a usage in which it does express a view incompatible with (2), and, in the case of each of them, some philosophers have, I think, really used the expression in question to express such a view. All such philosophers have, therefore, been holding a view incompatible with (2).

All such views, whether incompatible with *all* of the propositions in (1), or only with *some* of them, seem to me to be quite certainly false, and I think the following points are specially deserving of notice with regard to them:

(a) If any of the classes of propositions in (2) is such that no proposition of that class is true, then no philosopher has ever existed, and therefore none can ever have held with regard to any such class, that no proposition belonging to it is true. In other words, the proposition that some propositions belonging to each of these classes are true is a proposition which has the peculiarity, that, if any philosopher has ever denied it, it follows from the fact that he has denied it, that he must have been wrong in denying it. For when I speak of "philosophers" I mean, of course (as we all do), exclusively philosophers who have been human beings, with human bodies that have lived upon the earth, and who have at different times had many different experiences. If, therefore, there have been any philosophers, there have been human beings of this class; and if there have been human beings of this class, all the rest of what is asserted in (1) is certainly true too. Any view, therefore, incompatible with the proposition that many propositions corresponding to each of the propositions in (1) are true, can only be true, on the hypothesis that no philosopher has ever held any such view. It follows, therefore, that, in considering whether this proposition is true, I cannot consistently regard the fact that many philosophers whom I respect have, to the best of my belief, held views incompatible with it, as having any weight at all against it. Since, if I know that they have held such views, I am, *ipso facto*, knowing that they were mistaken, and, if I have no reason to believe that the proposition in question is true, I have still less reason to believe that they have held views incompatible with it, since I am more certain that they have existed and held *some* views, i.e., that the proposition in question is true, than that they have held any views incompatible with it.

(b) It is, of course, the case that all philosophers who have held such views have repeatedly, even in their philosophical works, expressed other views inconsistent with them: that is, no philosopher has ever been able to hold such views consistently. One way in which they have betrayed this inconsistency is by alluding to the existence of other philosophers. Another way is by alluding to the existence of the human race, and in particular by using "we" in the sense in which I have already constantly used it, in which any philosopher who asserts that "we" do so and so, e.g., that "*we* sometimes believe propositions that are not true," is asserting not only that he himself has done the thing in question, but that *very many other human beings, who have had bodies and lived upon the earth*, have done the same. The fact is, of course, that all philosophers have belonged to the class of human beings which exists only if (2) be true: that is to say, to the class of human beings who have frequently *known* propositions corresponding to each of the propositions in (1). In holding views incompatible with the proposition that propositions of all these classes are true, they have, therefore, been holding views inconsistent with propositions which they themselves knew to be true, and it was, therefore, only to be expected that they should sometimes betray their knowledge of such propositions. The strange thing is that philosophers should have been able to hold sincerely, as part of their philosophical creed, propositions inconsistent with what they themselves *knew* to be true, and yet, so far as I can make out, this has really frequently happened. My position, therefore, on this first point, differs from that of philosophers belonging to this group A, not in that I hold anything which they don't hold, but only in that I don't hold, as part of my philosophical creed, things which they do hold as part of theirs—that is to say, propositions inconsistent with some which they and I both hold in common. But this difference seems to me to be an important one.

(c) Some of these philosophers have brought forward, in favor of their position, arguments designed to show, in the case of some or all of the propositions in (1), that no propositions of that type can possibly be wholly true, because every such proposition entails both of two incompatible propositions. And I admit, of course, that if any of the propositions in (1) did entail both of two incompatible propositions it could not be true. But it seems to me I have an absolutely conclusive argument to show that none of them does entail both of two incompatible propositions. Namely this: All of the propositions in (1) are true; no true proposition entails both of two incompatible propositions; therefore, none of the propositions in (1) entails both of two incompatible propositions.

(d) Although, as I have urged, no philosopher who has held with regard to any of these types of proposition that no propositions of that type are true, has failed to hold also other views inconsistent with his view in this respect, yet I do not think that the view, with regard to any or all of these types, that no proposition belonging to them is true, is *in itself* a self-contradictory view, i.e., entails both of two incompatible propositions. On the contrary, it seems to me quite clear that it might have been the case that Time was not real, material things not real, Space not real, and selves not real.

And in favor of my view that none of these things, which might have been the case, *is* in fact the case, I have, I think, no better argument than simply this—namely, that all the propositions in (1) are, in fact, true.

B. This view, which is usually considered a much more modest view than A, has, I think, the defect that, unlike A, it really is self-contradictory, i.e., entails both of two mutually incompatible propositions.

Most philosophers, who have held this view, have held, I think, that though each of us knows propositions corresponding to *some* of the propositions in (1), namely to those which merely assert that *I* myself have had in the past experiences of certain kinds at many different times, yet none of us knows *for certain* any propositions either of the type (a) which assert the existence of *material things* or of the type (b) which assert the existence of *other* selves, beside myself, and that they also have had experiences. They admit that we do in fact *believe* propositions of both these types, and that they *may* be true: some would even say that we know them to be highly probable, but they deny that we ever know them, *for certain*, to be true. Some of them have spoken of such beliefs as "beliefs of Common Sense," expressing thereby their conviction that beliefs of this kind are very commonly entertained by mankind: but they are convinced that these things are, in all cases, only *believed*, not known for certain, and some have expressed this by saying that they are matters of Faith, not of Knowledge.

Now the remarkable thing which those who take this view have not, I think, in general duly appreciated, is that, in each case, the philosopher who takes it is making an assertion about "us"—that is to say, not merely about himself, but about *many other human beings as well*. When he says "No human being has ever known of the existence of other human beings," he is saying: "There have been many other human beings beside myself, and none of them (including myself) has ever known of the existence of other human beings." If he says: "These beliefs are beliefs of Common Sense, but they are not matters of *knowledge*," he is saying: "There have been many other human beings, beside myself, who have shared these beliefs, but neither I nor any of the rest has ever known them to be true." In other words, he asserts with confidence that these beliefs *are* beliefs of Common Sense, and seems often to fail to notice that, *if* they are, they must be true, since the proposition that they are beliefs of Common Sense is one which logically entails propositions both of type (a) and of type (b); it logically entails the proposition that many human beings, beside the philosopher himself, have had human bodies, which lived upon the earth, and have had various experiences, including beliefs of this kind. This is why this position, as contrasted with positions of group A, seems to me to be self-contradictory. Its difference from A consists in the fact that it is making a proposition about *human knowledge* in general, and therefore is actually asserting the existence of many human beings, whereas philosophers of group A in stating their position are not doing this: they are only contradicting *other* things which they hold. It is true that a philosopher who says "There have existed many human beings beside myself, and none of us has ever known of the existence of any human beings beside himself" is only contradicting himself if what he holds is "There have *certainly* existed many human beings beside myself" or, in other words, "*I know* that there have existed other human beings beside myself." But this, it seems to me, is what such philosophers have in fact been generally doing. They seem to me constantly to betray the fact that they regard the proposition that those beliefs are beliefs of Common Sense, or the proposition that they themselves are not the only members of the human race, as not merely true, but *certainly* true, and *certainly* true it cannot be, unless one member, at least, of the human race, namely themselves, has *known* the very things which that member is declaring that no human being has ever known.

Nevertheless, my position that I *know*, with certainty, to be true all of the propositions in (1), is certainly not a position, the denial of which entails both of two incompatible propositions. If I do *know* all these propositions to be true, then, I think, it is quite certain that other human beings also have known corresponding propositions: that is to say (2) also *is* true, and *I* know it to be true. But do I really *know* all the propositions in (1) to be true? Isn't it possible that I merely believe them? Or know them to be highly probable? In answer to this question, I think I have nothing better to say than that it seems to me that I *do* know them, with certainty. It is, indeed, obvious that, in the case of most of them, I do not know them *directly*: that is to say, I only know them because, in the past, I have known to be true *other* propositions which were evidence for them. If, for instance, I do know that the earth had existed for many years before I was born, I certainly only know this because I have known other things in the past which were evidence for it. And I certainly do not know exactly what the evidence was. Yet all this seems to me to be no good reason for doubting that I do know it. We are all, I think, in this strange position that we do *know* many things, with regard to which we *know* further that we must have had evidence for them, and yet we do not know *how* we know them, i.e., we do not know what the evidence was. If there is any "we," and if we know that there is, this must be so: for that there is a "we" is one of the things in question. And that I do know that there is a "we," that is to say, that many other human beings, with human bodies, have lived upon the earth, it seems to me that I do know, for certain.

If this first point in my philosophical position, namely my belief in (2), is to be given any name, which has actually been used by philosophers in classifying the positions of other philosophers, it would have, I think, to be expressed by saying that I am one of those philosophers who have held that the "Common Sense view of the world" is, in certain fundamental features, *wholly* true. But it must be remembered that, according to me, *all* philosophers, without exception, have agreed with me in holding this: and that the real difference, which is commonly expressed in this way, is only a difference between those philosophers, who have *also* held views inconsistent with these features in "the Common Sense view of the world," and those who have not.

The features in question (namely, propositions of any of the classes defined in defining (2)) are all of them features, which have this peculiar property—namely, that *if we know that they are features in the "Common Sense view of the world," it follows that they are true*: it is self-contradictory to maintain that we know them to be features in the Common Sense view, and that yet they are not true, since to say that we know this is to say that they are true. And many of them also have the further peculiar property that, *if they are features in the Common Sense view of the world (whether "we" know this or not), it follows that they are true*, since to say that there is a "Common Sense view of the world," is to say that they are true. The phrases "Common Sense view of the world" and "Common Sense beliefs" (as used by philosophers) are, of course, extraordinarily vague, and, for all I know, there may be many propositions which may be properly called features in "the Common Sense view of the world" or "Common Sense beliefs," which are not true, and which deserve to be mentioned with the contempt with which some philosophers speak of "Common Sense beliefs." But to speak with contempt of those "Common Sense beliefs" which I have mentioned is quite certainly the height of absurdity. And there are, of course, enormous numbers of other features in "the Common Sense view of the world" which, if these are true, are quite certainly true too: for example, that there have lived upon the surface of the earth not only human beings, but also many different species of plants and animals, etc.

II

What seems to me the next in importance of the points in which my philosophical position differs from positions held by some other philosophers is one which I will express in the following way. I hold, namely, that there is no good reason to suppose either (A) that *every* physical fact is *logically* dependent upon some mental fact or (B) that *every* physical fact is *causally* dependent upon some mental fact. In saying this, I am not, of course, saying that there *are* any physical facts which are wholly independent (i.e., both logically and causally) of mental facts: I do, in fact, believe that there are, but that is not what I am asserting. I am only asserting that there is *no good reason* to suppose the contrary, by which I mean, of course, that none of the human beings, who have had human bodies that lived upon the earth, have, during the lifetime of their bodies, had any good reason to suppose the contrary. Many philosophers have, I think, not only believed either that *every* physical fact is *logically* dependent upon some mental fact ("physical fact" and "mental fact" being understood in the sense in which I am using these terms) or that *every* physical fact is *causally* dependent upon some mental fact, or both, but also that they themselves had good reason for these beliefs. In this respect, therefore, I differ from them.

In the case of the term "physical fact," I can only explain how I am using it by giving examples. I mean by "physical facts," facts *like* the following: "That mantelpiece is at present nearer to this body than that bookcase is," "The earth has existed for many years past," "The moon has at every moment for many years past been nearer to the earth than to the sun," and "That mantelpiece is of a light colour." But, when I say "facts *like* these," I mean, of course, facts like them *in a certain respect*, and what this respect is I cannot define. The term "physical fact" is, however, in common use, and I think that I am using it in its ordinary sense. Moreover, there is no need for a definition to make my point clear; since among the examples I have given there are some with regard to which I hold that there is no reason to suppose *them* (i.e., these particular physical facts) either logically or causally dependent upon any mental fact.

"Mental fact," on the other hand, is a much more unusual expression, and I am using it in a specially limited sense, which, though I think it is a natural one, does need to be explained. There may be many other senses in which the term can be properly used, but I am only concerned with this one, and hence it is essential that I should explain what it is.

There may, possibly, I hold, be "mental facts" of three different kinds. It is only with regard to the first kind that I am sure that there are facts of that kind, but if there were any facts of either of the other two kinds, they would be "mental facts" in my limited sense, and therefore I must explain what is meant by the hypothesis that there are facts of those two kinds.

(a) My first kind is this. I am conscious now, and also I am seeing something now. These two facts are both of the mental facts of my first kind, and my first kind consists exclusively of facts which resemble one or other of the two *in a certain respect*.

(α) The fact that I am conscious now is obviously, in a certain sense, a fact, with regard to a particular individual and a particular time, to the effect that that individual is conscious at that time. And every fact which resembles this in that respect is to be included in my first kind of mental fact. Thus the fact that I was also conscious at many different times yesterday is not itself a fact of this kind: but it entails that there *are* (or, as we should commonly say, because the times in question are past times, "were") many other facts of this kind, namely each of the facts, which, at each of times in question, I could have properly expressed by "I am conscious *now*." *Any* fact which is, in this sense, a fact with regard to an individual and a time (whether the individual be myself or another, and whether the time be past or present), to the effect that that individual is conscious at that time, is to be included in my first kind of mental fact: and I call such facts, facts of class (α).

(β) The second example I gave, namely the fact that I am seeing something now, is obviously related to the fact that I am conscious now in a peculiar manner. It not only *entails* the fact that I am conscious now (for from the fact that I am seeing something it *follows* that I am conscious: I *could* not have been seeing anything, unless I had been conscious, though I might quite well have been conscious without seeing anything), but it also is a fact, with regard to a *specific way* (or mode) of being conscious, to the effect that I am conscious in that way: in the same sense in which the proposition (with regard to any particular thing) "This is red" both entails the proposition (with regard to the same thing) "This is colored," and is also a proposition, with regard to a specific way of being colored, to the effect that that thing is colored in that way. And any fact which is related in this peculiar manner to any fact of class (α) is also to be included in my first kind of mental fact, and is to be called a fact of class (β). Thus the fact that I am hearing now is, like the fact that I am seeing now, a fact of class (β), and so is any fact, with regard to myself and a past time, which could at that time have been properly expressed by "I am dreaming now," "I am imagining now," "I am at present aware of the fact that ...," etc. In short, any fact, which is a fact with regard to a particular individual (myself or another), a particular time (past or present), and *any particular kind of experience*, to the effect that that individual is having at that time an experience of that particular kind, is a fact of class (β): and only such facts are facts of class (β).

My first kind of mental facts consists exclusively of facts of classes (α) and (β), and consists of all facts of either of these kinds.

(b) That there are many facts of classes (α) and (β) seems to me perfectly certain. But many philosophers seem to me to have held a certain view with regard to the *analysis* of facts of class (a), which is such that, if it were true, there would be facts of another kind, which I should wish also to call "mental facts." I don't feel at all sure that this analysis is true, but it seems to me that it *may* be true, and since we can understand what is meant by the supposition that it is true, we can also understand what is meant by the supposition that there are "mental facts" of this second kind.

Many philosophers have, I think, held the following view as to the analysis of what each of us knows, when he knows (at any time) "I am conscious now." They have held, namely, that there is a certain intrinsic property (with which we are all of us familiar and which might be called that of "being an experience") which is such that, at any time at which any man knows "I am conscious now," he is knowing, with regard to that property and himself and the time in question, "There is occurring now an event which has this property (i.e., 'is an experience') and which is an experience of mine," and such that this fact is what he expresses by "I am conscious now." And if this view is true, there must be many facts of each of three kinds, each of which I should wish to call "mental facts," viz., (1) facts with regard to some event, which has this supposed intrinsic property, and to some time, to the effect that that event is occurring at that time, (2) facts with regard to this supposed intrinsic property and some time, to the effect that *some* event which has that property is occurring at that time, and (3) facts with regard to some property, which is a *specific way* of having the supposed intrinsic property (in the sense above explained in which "being red" is a specific way of "being colored") and some time, to the effect that some event which has that specific property is occurring at that time. Of course, there not only are not, but *cannot* be, facts of any of these kinds, unless there is an intrinsic property related to what each of us (on any occasion) expresses by "I am conscious now," in the manner defined above, and I feel very doubtful whether there is any such property; in other words, although I know for certain both that I have had many experiences, and that I have had experiences of many different kinds, I feel very doubtful whether to say the first is the same thing as to say that there have been many events, each of which was an experience and an experience of mine, and whether to say the second is the same thing as to say that there have been many events, each of which was an experience of mine, and each of which also had a different property, which was a specific way of being an experience. The proposition that I have had experiences does not necessarily entail the proposition that there have been any events which were experiences, and I cannot satisfy myself that I am acquainted with any events of the supposed kind. But yet it seems to me possible that the proposed analysis of "I am conscious now" is correct: that I am really acquainted with events of the supposed kind, though I cannot see that I am. And *if* I am, then I should wish to call the three kinds of facts defined above "mental facts." Of course, if there are "experiences" in the sense defined, it would be possible (as many have held) that there can be no experiences which are not some individuals' experiences, and in that case any fact of any of these three kinds would be logically dependent on, though not necessarily identical with, some fact of class (α) or class (β). But it seems to me also a possibility that, if there are "experiences," there might be experiences which did not belong to any individual, and, in that case, there would be "mental facts" which were neither identical with nor logically dependent on any fact of class (α) or class (β).

(c) Finally, some philosophers have, so far as I can make out, held that there are or may be facts which are facts with regard to some individual, to the effect that he is conscious, or is conscious in some specific way, but which differ from facts of classes (α) and (β), in the important respect that they are not facts *with regard to any time*: they have conceived the possibility that there may be one or more individuals who are *timelessly* conscious, and timelessly conscious in specific modes. And others, again, have, I think, conceived the hypothesis that the intrinsic property defined in (b) may be one which does not belong only to *events*, but may also belong to one or more wholes, which do *not* occur at any time: in other words, that there may be one or more *timeless* experiences, which might or might not be the experiences of some individual. It seems to me very doubtful whether any of these hypotheses are even possibly true, but I cannot see for certain that they are not possible: and, if they are possible, then I should wish to give the name "mental fact" to any fact (if there were any) of any of the five following kinds, viz.:

1. to any fact which is the fact, with regard to any individual, that he is *timelessly* conscious,

2. to any fact which is the fact, with regard to any individual, that he is *timelessly* conscious in any specific way,

3. to any fact which is the fact with regard to a *timeless* experience that it exists,

4. to any fact which is the fact with regard to the supposed intrinsic property "being an experience," that something timelessly exists which has that property, and

5. to any fact which is the fact, with regard to any property, which is a specific mode of this supposed intrinsic property, that something timelessly exists which has that property.

I have, then, defined three different kinds of facts, each of which is such that, if there *were* any facts of that kind (as there certainly *are*, in the case of the first kind), the facts in question *would be* "mental facts" in my sense, and to complete the definition of the limited sense in which I am using "mental facts," I have only to add that I wish also to apply the name to one *fourth* class of facts: namely to any fact, which is the fact, with regard to any of these three kinds of facts, or any kinds included in them, *that there are facts of the kind in question*, i.e., not only will each individual fact of class (α) be, in my sense, a "mental fact," but also the general fact "that there are facts of class (α)," will itself be a "mental fact", and similarly in all other cases: for example, not only will the fact that I am now perceiving (which is a fact of class (β)) be a "mental fact," but also the general fact that *there are* facts, with regard to individuals and times, to the effect that the individual in question is perceiving at the time in question, will be a "mental fact."

A. Understanding "physical fact" and "mental fact" in the senses just explained, I hold, then, that there is no good reason to suppose that *every* physical fact is *logically* dependent upon some mental fact. And I use the phrase, with regard to two facts, F_1 and F_2, "F_1 is *logically dependent* on F_2," wherever and only where F_1 *entails* F_2, either in the sense in which the proposition "I am seeing now" *entails* the proposition "I am conscious now," or the proposition (with regard to any particular thing) "This is red" entails the proposition (with regard to the same thing) "This is coloured," or else in the more strictly logical sense in which (for instance) the conjunctive proposition "All men are mortal, and Mr. Baldwin is a man" entails the proposition "Mr. Baldwin is mortal."

To say, then, of two facts, F_1 and F_2, that F_1 is *not* logically dependent upon F_2, is only to say that F_1 *might* have been a fact, even if there had been no such fact as F_2, or that the conjunctive proposition "F_1 is a fact, but there is no such fact as F_2," is a proposition which is not self-contradictory, i.e., does not entail both of two mutually incompatible propositions.

I hold, then, that, in the case of *some* physical facts, there is no good reason to suppose that there is some mental fact, such that the physical fact in question could not have been a fact unless the mental fact in question had also been one. And my position is perfectly definite, since I hold that this is the case with all the four physical facts, which I have given as examples of physical facts. For example, there is no good reason to suppose that there is any mental fact whatever, such that the fact that that mantelpiece is at present nearer to my body than that bookcase could not have been a fact, unless the mental fact in question had also been a fact, and, similarly, in all the other three cases.

In holding this I am certainly differing from some philosophers. I am, for instance, differing from Berkeley, who held that that mantelpiece, that bookcase, and my body are, all of them, either "ideas" or "constituted by ideas," and that no "idea" can possibly exist without being perceived. He held, that is, that this physical fact is logically dependent upon a mental fact of my fourth class: namely a fact which is the fact that there is at least one fact, which is a fact with regard to an individual and the present time, to the effect that that individual is now perceiving something. He does not say that this physical fact is logically dependent upon any fact which is a fact of any of my first three classes, e.g., on any fact which is the fact, with regard to a particular individual and the present time, that *that* individual is now perceiving something: what he does say is that the physical fact couldn't have been a fact, unless it had been a fact that there was *some* mental fact of this sort. And it seems to me that many philosophers, who would perhaps disagree either with Berkeley's assumption that my body is an "idea" or "constituted by ideas," or with his assumption that "ideas" cannot exist without being perceived, or with both, nevertheless would agree with him in thinking that this physical fact is logically dependent upon *some* "mental fact": for example, they might say that it could not have been a fact, unless there had been, at some time or other, or, were timelessly, *some* "experience." Many, indeed, so far as I can make out, have held that *every* fact is logically dependent on every other fact. And, of course, they have held in the case of their opinions, as Berkeley did in the case of his, that they had good reasons for them.

B. I also hold that there is no good reason to suppose that *every* physical fact is *causally* dependent upon some mental fact. By saying that F_1 is *causally* dependent on F_2, I mean only that F_1 *wouldn't* have been a fact unless F_2 had been, *not* (which is what "logically dependent" asserts) that F_1 *couldn't conceivably* have been a fact, unless F_2

had been. And I can illustrate my meaning by reference to the example which I have just given. The fact that that mantelpiece is at present nearer to my body than that bookcase is (as I have just explained) so far as I can see, not *logically* dependent upon any mental fact; it *might* have been a fact, even if there had been no mental facts. But it certainly is *causally* dependent on many mental facts: my body *would* not have been here unless I had been conscious in various ways in the past, and the mantelpiece and the bookcase certainly *would* not have existed, unless other men had been conscious too.

But with regard to two of the facts, which I gave as instances of physical facts, namely the fact that the earth has existed for many years past, and the fact that the moon has for many years past been nearer to the earth than to the sun, I hold that there is no good reason to suppose that these are *causally* dependent upon any mental fact. So far as I can see, there is no reason to suppose that there is any mental fact of which it could be truly said: unless this fact had been a fact, the earth would not have existed for many years past. And in holding this, again, I think I differ from some philosophers. I differ, for instance, from those who have held that all material things were created by God, and that they had good reasons for supposing this.

III

I have just explained that I differ from those philosophers who have held that there is good reason to suppose that all material things were created by God. And it is, I think, an important point in my position, which should be mentioned, that I differ also from all philosophers who have held that there is good reason to suppose that there is a God at all, whether or not they have held it likely that he created all material things.

And similarly, whereas some philosophers have held that there is good reason to suppose that we, human beings, shall continue to exist and be conscious after the death of our bodies, I hold that there is no good reason to suppose this.

[...]

Chapter 3

From *On Certainty*

Ludwig Wittgenstein

The next reading consists of forty-four notes from a collection of observations that the Austrian philosopher Ludwig Wittgenstein wrote in the last months of his life, and that were published after his death, under the title *On Certainty*. Wittgenstein's observations are, in part, a response to the views of G. E. Moore, including the views we have encountered in the preceding reading, and also in another essay, entitled "Proof of an External World" (1939). In his "Proof," Moore presents his case that there is a world external to our senses by holding up his hand and saying, "here is a hand." He claims that his proof satisfies three requirements for any successful proof: the premises differ from the conclusion, the premises have been demonstrated, and the conclusion follows from the premises. In "Proof" and "A Defence," Moore tries to meet skepticism head-on. Wittgenstein, by contrast, tries to sidestep skepticism.

Wittgenstein claims that statements such as "here is a hand" or "the world has existed for more than five minutes" might seem to say something factual about the world, and hence be open to doubt, but in reality they serve as a kind of framework, without which empirical propositions cannot make sense in the first place. At one point (in a passage not included below), Wittgenstein compares these sorts of propositions to a riverbed, which must remain in place for the river of language to flow smoothly, and at another point, as we have noted, he compares them to the hinges of a door, which must remain fixed for the door of language to serve any purpose.

The key, then, is not to claim certain knowledge of propositions like "here is a hand," but rather to recognize that, within the larger context in which they ordinarily arise, these sorts of propositions must "stand fast"; we must hold them above questions of knowledge or doubt—and we must do this not because they possess in themselves a special indubitable character, but rather because of the role they play within a much larger field of activities, which Wittgenstein calls a *form of life*.

A particular set of activities that make up a form of life is a *language game*. Consider the simple language game played by a surgeon and her assistant: when the surgeon says "scalpel," the assistant hands her a certain object and says "scalpel," and similarly with "hemostat," "sponge," and "clamp." According to the author of *On Certainty*, the *meaning* of these words is the use to which they are put in the language game. In the surgery game, a single word constitutes a particular command. In keeping with the rule-governed character of language, language games are rule-governed activities; however, they are not all *strictly* rule-governed. (Consider the activity of improvising free verse, or engaging in comedic patter.) There are many different sorts of games: some are competitive, others are not; some involve more than one player, others do not; some have set durations, others do not, and so forth. So, according to Wittgenstein, one cannot profitably provide an essential definition of "game," a definition that consists of describing necessary and sufficient conditions of being a game. The best one can do when it comes to identifying an activity as a language game is to defer to one or another feature of the activity, a feature that bears a "family resemblance" to other language games.

A proposition only has meaning within a given language game. When one attempts to doubt such propositions as G. E. Moore's "here is a hand," one removes the formulation from any identifiable language game, stripping it of meaning and sweeping away the common ground upon which doubt can arise in the first place.

Ludwig J. J. Wittgenstein was one of the most original and influential philosophers of the twentieth century. The only book-length work of philosophy that he published during his lifetime was a seventy-five-page book entitled *Tractatus Logico-Philosophicus*. Published in German in 1921, much of the *Tractatus* was written during the First World War, while Wittgenstein, then in his late twenties, was an artillery officer in the Austro Hungarian army and a prisoner of war. His later book, the ground-breaking *Philosophical Investigations* (1953), was published after his death in 1951. The *Philosophical Investigations* was in large part a repudiation of the equally bold ideas he had presented decades earlier, in the *Tractatus*. Our reading from *On Certainty* is very much a development of ideas presented in the *Philosophical Investigations*.

1. If you do know that here is one hand, we'll grant you all the rest.

When one says that such and such a proposition can't be proved, of course that does not mean that it can't be derived from other propositions; any proposition can be derived from other ones. But they may be no more certain than it is itself. (On this a curious remark by H. Newman.)[1]

2. From its seeming to me—or to everyone—to be so, it doesn't follow that it is so. What we can ask is whether it can make sense to doubt it.

3. If for example someone says, "I don't know if there's a hand here," he might be told, "Look closer." This possibility of satisfying oneself is part of the language game. It is one of its essential features.
[...]

8. The difference between the concept of "knowing" and the concept of "being certain" isn't of any great importance at all, except where "I know" is meant to mean: I can't be wrong. In a law court, for example, "I am certain" could replace "I know" in every piece of testimony. We might even imagine it's being forbidden to say "I know" there.
[...]

18. "I know" often means: I have the proper grounds for my statement. So if the other person is acquainted with the language game, he would admit that I know. The other, if he is acquainted with the language game, must be able to imagine how one may know something of the kind.
[...]

32. It's not a matter of Moore's knowing that there's a hand there, but rather we should not understand him if he were to say, "Of course I may be wrong about this." We should ask, "What is it like to make such a mistake as that?" For example, what's it like to discover that it was a mistake?

33. Thus we expunge the sentences that don't get us any further.
[...]

69. I should like to say: "If I am wrong about this, I have no guarantee that anything I say is true." But others won't say that about me, nor will I say it about other people.
[...]

74. Can we say: a *mistake* doesn't only have a cause, it also has a ground? That is, roughly: when someone makes a mistake, this can be fitted into what he knows aright.
[...]

---

[1] The reference here might be to a remark from *Grammar of Assent* (1870), by the theologian, poet, and priest John Henry Newman (1801–1890), but it is not clear which remark—M. M.

79. That I am a man and not a woman can be verified, but if I were to say I was a woman, and then tried to explain the error by saying I hadn't checked the statement, the explanation would not be accepted.

80. The truth of my statements is the test of my understanding of these statements.

81. That is to say: if I make certain false statements, it becomes uncertain whether I understand them.

82. What counts as an adequate test of a statement belongs to logic. It belongs to the description of the language game.

83. The *truth* of certain empirical propositions belongs to our frame of reference.

84. Moore says he knows that the earth existed long before his birth. And put like that it seems to be a personal statement about him, even if it is in addition a statement about the physical world. Now it is philosophically uninteresting whether Moore knows this or that, but it is interesting that, and how, it can be known. If Moore had informed us that he knew the distance separating certain stars, we might conclude from that that he had made some special investigations, and we shall want to know what these were. But Moore chooses precisely a case in which we all seem to know the same as he does, and without being able to say how. I believe for example that I know as much about this matter (the existence of the earth) as Moore does, and if he knows that it is as he says, then I know it too. For it isn't, either, as if he had arrived at this proposition by pursuing some line of thought which, while it is open to me, I have not in fact pursued.
[…]

91. If Moore says he knows the earth existed, etc., most of us will grant him that it has existed all that time, and also believe him when he says he is convinced of it. But has he also got the right ground for this conviction? For if not, then after all he doesn't *know* (Russell).

92. However, we can ask: May someone have telling grounds for believing that the earth has only existed for a short time, say since his own birth? Suppose he had always been told that—would he have any good reason to doubt it? Men have believed that they could make the rain; why should not a king be brought up in the belief that the world began with him? And if Moore and this king were to meet and discuss, could Moore really prove his belief to be the right one? I do not say that Moore could not convert the king to his view, but it would be a conversion of a special kind; the king would be brought to look at the world in a different way.

Remember that one is sometimes convinced of the correctness of a view by its simplicity or symmetry, i.e., these are what induces one to go over to this point of view. One then simply says something like: "That's how it must be."

93. The propositions presenting what Moore "knows" are all of such a kind that it is difficult to imagine why anyone should believe the contrary. For example, the proposition that Moore has spent his whole life in close proximity to the earth. Once more I can speak of myself here instead of speaking of Moore. What could induce me to believe the opposite? Either a memory or having been told. Everything that I have seen or heard gives me the conviction that no man has ever been far from the earth. Nothing in my picture of the world speaks in favor of the opposite.

94. But I did not get my picture of the world by satisfying myself of its correctness; nor do I have it because I am satisfied of its correctness. No: it is the inherited background against which I distinguish between true and false.

[...]

108. "But is there then no objective truth? Isn't it true, or false, that someone has been on the moon?" If we are thinking within our system, then it is certain that no one has ever been on the moon. Not merely is nothing of the sort ever seriously reported to us by reasonable people, but our whole system of physics forbids us to believe it. For this demands answers to the questions "How did he overcome the force of gravity?" "How could he live without an atmosphere?" and a thousand others which could not be answered. But suppose that instead of all these answers we met the reply: "We don't know how one gets to the moon, but those who get there know at once that they are there, and even you can't explain everything." We should feel ourselves intellectually very distant from someone who said this.

109. "An empirical proposition can be tested" (we say). But how? and through what?

110. What counts as its test? "But is this an adequate test? And if so, must it not be recognizable as such in logic?" As if giving grounds did not come to an end sometime. But the end is not an ungrounded presupposition: it is an ungrounded way of acting.

111. "I know that I have never been on the moon." That sounds different in the circumstances which actually hold, to the way it would sound if a good many men had been on the moon, and some perhaps without knowing it. In this case one could give grounds for this knowledge. Is there not a relationship here similar to that between the general rule of multiplying and particular multiplications that have been carried out?

I want to say: my not having been on the moon is as sure a thing for me as any grounds I could give for it.

112. And isn't that what Moore wants to say, when he says he knows all these things? But is his knowing it really what is in question, and not rather that some of these propositions must be solid for us?

113. When someone is trying to teach us mathematics, he will not begin by assuring us that he knows that a + b = b + a.

114. If you are not certain of any fact, you cannot be certain of the meaning of your words either.

115. If you tried to doubt everything you would not get as far as doubting anything. The game of doubting itself presupposes certainty.

116. Instead of "I know …," couldn't Moore have said: "It stands fast for me that …"? And further: "It stands fast for me and many others …."

117. Why is it not possible for me to doubt that I have never been on the moon? And how could I try to doubt it?

First and foremost, the supposition that perhaps I have been there would strike me as idle. Nothing would follow from it, nothing be explained by it. It would not tie in with anything in my life. When I say "Nothing speaks for, everything against it," this presupposes a principle of speaking for and against. That is, I must be able to say what would speak for it.

118. Now would it be correct to say: So far no one has opened my skull in order to see whether there is a brain inside, but everything speaks for, and nothing against, its being what they would find there?

119. But can it also be said: Everything speaks for, and nothing against the table's still being there when no one sees it? For what does speak for it?

120. But if anyone were to doubt it, how would his doubt come out in practice? And couldn't we peacefully leave him to doubt it, since it makes no difference at all?

121. Can one say: "Where there is no doubt there is no knowledge either"?

122. Doesn't one need grounds for doubt?
[…]

141. When we first begin to believe anything, what we believe is not a single proposition; it is a whole system of propositions. (Light dawns gradually over the whole.)

142. It is not single axioms that strike me as obvious, it is a system in which consequences and premises give one another mutual support.

143. I am told, for example, that someone climbed this mountain many years ago. Do I always enquire into the reliability of the teller of this story, and whether the mountain did exist years ago? A child learns there are reliable and unreliable informants much later than it learns facts which are told it. It doesn't learn at all that that mountain has existed for a long time: that is, the question whether it is so doesn't arise at all. It swallows this consequence down, so to speak, together with what it learns.

144. The child learns to believe a host of things. That is, it learns to act according to these beliefs. Bit by bit there forms a system of what is believed, and in that system some things stand unshakably fast and some are more or less liable to shift. What stands fast does so, not because it is intrinsically obvious or convincing; it is rather held fast by what lies around it.
[...]

151. I should like to say: Moore does not know what he asserts he knows, but it stands fast for him, as also for me; regarding it as absolutely solid is part of our method of doubt and enquiry.

152. I do not explicitly learn the propositions that stand fast for me. I can discover them subsequently like the axis around which a body rotates. This axis is not fixed in the sense that anything holds it fast, but the movement around it determines its immobility.

153. No one ever taught me that my hands don't disappear when I am not paying attention to them. Nor can I be said to presuppose the truth of this proposition in my assertions, etc. (as if they rested on it), while it only gets sense from the rest of our procedure of asserting.
[...]

166. The difficulty is to realize the groundlessness of our believing.
[...]
191. Well, if everything speaks for a hypothesis and nothing against it—is it then certainly true? One may designate it as such. But does it certainly agree with reality, with the facts? With this question you are already going round in a circle.

192. To be sure there is justification, but justification comes to an end.
[...]

Chapter 4

The Plain Truth about Common Sense: Skepticism, Metaphysics, and Irony

Mark Kingwell

Kingwell explores the strange circumstance, already noted, that "common sense has been both a target and a source of skepticism." He wants to focus on the commonness of common sense, rather than the much rarer "sense" of it, as "sound judgment."[1] In the first section of his paper, he distinguishes between "ordinary, average understanding," or plain common sense, on the one hand, and philosophical common sense, on the other. The word *plain* in Kingwell's term means something like "non-philosophical," in a sense that he will explain. Notice that the five "common-sense propositions" that Kingwell lists early in his presentation resemble Moore's list of truisms; thus, for example, the first item on Kingwell's list is: "there is an objectively existing world eternal to me."

Plain common sense insists that "a thing is what it is and is not what it is not." As Kingwell observes in Section 2, however, this leads inescapably to *philosophical common sense*, which systematically distinguishes between *appearance* and *reality*. Philosophical common sense leads beyond itself, connecting common sense to philosophy and science.

Metaphysicians like Descartes and Berkeley demanded one hundred percent certainty for beliefs, and they believed that they could get it. As we have seen, G. E. Moore, "the inveterate plain man," also believed he could get it. But skeptics have proceeded to disappoint these demands. The American logician Benson Mates (1919–2009) may well have been right: skepticism will always win out in the end.[2] However, this should make no difference to common

---

[1] Which was the focus of our reading from Reid, above.
[2] Refer to the Benson Mates entry in the Further Readings for Part I section below.

sense, which, as Kingwell notes, will "leave the disputants to their own perverse devices and desires."

But this is not the end of the story. Common sense resists philosophical defense, but it also demands the quest for certainty, and this quest leads to doubt. Whenever the man of common sense thinks about it, he demands a philosophical response to the skeptic; however, that response will forever fall short of its aim. Thus, as Kingwell writes in Section 3, "common sense is, contrary to common sense, not immune from *doubt from its own standpoint*." As it turns out, then, the plain truth about common sense is the same as the philosophical truth about it, namely, that "the plain and the philosophical run together whenever we stop to speak of the plain, whenever common sense pauses to say anything about itself." In Section 4, Kingwell concludes that those of us who are cursed with philosophical curiosity can do no better than to assume an attitude of irony when it comes to the quest for certainty.

Mark Kingwell (b.1963) is a Professor of Philosophy at the University of Toronto. He has written extensively on politics and culture.

1 Plain Common Sense

What is the plain truth about common sense?[3] It is surprising, though perhaps not to philosophers, that this question has no easy answer. We all think we know what common sense is until we begin either (1) to reflect critically on it, in which case we have arguably ceased to be commonsensical, or (2) to conflict with others about certain elements of it, casting parts of our own common sense into question. This, of course, will not do, for, among other things, common sense must be common; it must also, I could add, be stable, and these disagreements appear to threaten

---

[3]This paper was prepared with the assistance of a postdoctoral research fellowship from the Social Sciences and Humanities Research Council of Canada. I would like to thank Christopher Dustin, Hayden Ramsay, and Alex Oliver for helpful discussion. Earlier versions of this paper were read at meetings of the Cambridge University Moral Sciences Club, the Edinburgh University Philosophy Colloquium, and the Canadian Philosophical Association. My thanks to all those who offered comments on those occasions, and especially to those who disagreed so usefully: Hugh Mellor, Peter Lewis, and Lynd Forguson.

that stability. Sometimes such disputes proceed from category mistakes[4] and a rather common (if not a sensible) unwillingness to draw distinctions. If it is true, as Timothy Sprigge suggests, that "we will only be able to articulate clearly what the common sense view of the world is when we do not have an inordinate respect for it,"[5] then a degree of justified violence is in the offing. To get at common sense, we must do some conceptual carving. Whether this will *ex hypothesi* bar us from speaking, later, of the plain truth about it is the central question I want to raise in this discussion.

Some distinctions may help immediately. A great deal of what we commonly speak of as common sense is better described as "common nonsense": the tenets of folk wisdom, fishwives' tales, traditional remedies, received lore, and the like. With no disrespect to fishwives, much of what passes for sense in this realm is, and has been shown to be, false, and whatever else is true about common sense, it must not be known to be false. In other words, it survives as sense only to the extent that its falsity does not arise. It is very possible that its truth does not come up either, in any verificationist sense,[6] but that does not pose a threat to sense—at least not yet. But beliefs on the order that colds are contracted by sitting in drafts, that butter is good for blistered bums, or that philosophers cannot master worldly tasks are false and yet elements of a certain kind of common sense. We need not trouble to distinguish here— though we surely could—among superstition, pseudoscience, delusion, prejudice, and sheer bloody-mindedness, all of which may be found represented in this realm. Nor am I suggesting that the realm is itself a stable one, presenting a unified face to the world. We all have our own stores of this common (non)sense, sometimes defined by family or group solidarity, usually determined by cultural background, and almost always of little lasting philosophical interest when we want to isolate common sense for bigger fish frying.

To do *that* we have to draw at least one more distinction, though I do not pretend it will deal decisively with the elastic nature of common sense. The

---

[4]A *category mistake* is a logical fallacy or error that occurs when a speaker assigns to something (such as items of common nonsense) a characteristic that should properly be assigned to things only of another category (such as an empirical generalization). The mistake occurs, in this case, when one fails to distinguish between commonly held generalizations and commonly repeated nonsense.—M. M.

[5]"Philosophy and Common Sense," *Revue Internationale de Philosophie* 40, no. 158 (3) (1986): 204.

[6]*Verificationism* is the view that a statement is meaningful only if it can be determined to be either true or false.—M. M.

distinction, borrowed from Marcus Singer, is between common sense as what we might call *basic knowledge* and common sense as *sound judgment*. In the first sense, common sense "is ordinary, normal, average understanding—common understanding—without which one is foolish or incompetent or insane. In the other, common sense is thought of as good, sound, practical sense."[7] The distinction, Singer adds, is among other things useful for showing that "it is one of the anomalies of common sense that, in one sense, common sense is something common, while in another sense, common sense is something uncommon." I propose to leave the uncommon sense of common sense aside[8] and concentrate now on those elements, or at least those we can easily isolate, of the sense without which we court folly or insanity.

Once more, here we normally think we know what common sense is, but our thinking so can rapidly lead us into trouble. *Common* common sense (which I will call, with [Thompson] Clarke,[9] "plain common sense") is thought to be something shared by all human agents. It is sense both in the sense of being based on sense (the sensory receptors through which we experience the world) and in the sense of being common (it does not depend on particular experience or background). So it would not, could not, make sense to cut against this common sense, at least in those realms we call the everyday or the ordinary or the plain. That is, we would make ourselves out to be fools or mad people if we did that. We would lack what Herbert Fingarette has called, with reference to insanity, a "grasp of essential relevance."[10] That much is clear enough, I think, to stand.

Yet it is possible that, from some points of view (both plain and philosophical), we have left common sense behind even in saying this small amount. That is, by speaking of something common to all, have we left the realm of plain common sense and ventured into the realm of philosophical prejudice, the marshaling of universal categories and the bending to them of already historicized experience? Perhaps. An even more pressing objection is that our small clearing of common-sense space is always going to be a false achievement, for we cannot ever fully specify what the elements of plain common sense must be. In other words, all talk of plain common sense becomes,

[7]Singer [refer to the item in the Further Readings for Part IV section below—M. M.], 227. I am also indebted to Singer's analysis in this paper of folklore as "common nonsense."

[8]I think, however, that Singer is convincing on the point that this species of common sense has a considerable moral significance. This is true of the "sensus communis" thinkers discussed, for example, by Gadamer in *Truth and Method* (l, I), namely, Vico and Shaftesbury; it may be equally true, in the guise of the virtue *phronesis* of Aristotle.

[9]The reference is to Thompson Clarke's paper, "The Legacy of Skepticism," *Journal of Philosophy* 69 (20) (1972).—M. M.

[10]Herbert Fingarette, "Insanity and Responsibility," *Inquiry* 15 (1972).

like it or not, talk of *philosophical* common sense—and, whatever its charms, that is not the plain truth that we wanted. The reason for this claim, which I think is not quite commonsensical, is that plain common sense will by its very plain nature defy strict determination. Because it is a basic feature of—or perhaps "background to"— experience, our normal methods of investigation will fail when we attempt to isolate its *general* features and state them clearly. The common-sense view of the world is, as L. T. Hobhouse said, "the result of thought acting on masses of experience too great to be perfectly articulated."[11] So any articulation will be partial (not whole) and therefore partial (prejudiced). Thus, the second objection really becomes a version of the first.

Yet I do not think these objections are entirely convincing, and for a fairly commonsensical reason, namely, that whatever difficulties we may observe in the prospect of giving a full description to plain common sense, we can, without inordinate difficulty, say what some of the *main* features of plain common sense are. If we could not do that, it would not, I think, remain common sense. It is true that it will, at a later stage, prove necessary to stop the investigation of the plain, but not for these reasons exactly, and certainly we will not stop before we have fairly begun. Therefore, with apologies to these qualifying warnings, and with a measure of awareness about the dangers courted, I want to claim that the essential features of plain common sense are the following: (1) that there is an objectively existing world external to me; (2) that it has existed for some long time in the past and will so exist in the future; (3) that I exist as both a subject and an object in this world; (4) that I existed in the past and will exist in the future; and, finally, (5) that there are numerous others like me, both subjects and objects, who exist in time and the external world.

There is a great deal more I could say about plain common sense, shadings of detail and complex relationships, with exceptions and qualifications of varying degrees of interest. I could, in addition, speak like William James of common sense's pragmatic value: "Common sense appears," he writes, "as a perfectly definite state in our understanding of things [...] satisfies in an extraordinarily successful way the purposes for which we think. [...] It suffices for the necessary practical ends of life."[12] To speak this way is not necessary, however, and it may be misleading, for all of these details may be seen either to follow from my

---

[11] *The Theory of Knowledge: A Contribution to Some Problems of logic and Metaphysics* (London: Methuen, 1896), 377.

[12] William James, *Pragmatism, A New Name for Some Old Ways of Thinking: Popular Lectures on Philosophy* (New York: Longmans, Green & Co., 1907), 181–2.

five common-sense propositions or to extend beyond them to our goals and actions. What is plain, I think, is that those goals and actions could not succeed without a view of the world as it is essentially described by my five propositions.

Stated *as propositions,* of course, they have an odd flavor: the oddness of the move from plain common sense to philosophical common sense. It is an oddness that can lead us to wonder for what reason, in what sense, or in response to what challenge such propositions would or could be relevantly uttered. More of that later. For now, I think it is plain that anyone who doubted the truth of any of these propositions would be, as Bradley once put it, either a fool or an advanced thinker. Let us consider the advanced thinker.

2 Metaphysics/Skepticism

Common sense has been both a source and a target of skepticism. It has also been both an enemy and a friend of certain metaphysical doctrines, sometimes at the same time. It is these varied uses that will show us, I think, just why the philosophical truth about common sense is that there is none, and the plain truth about it is that there is no more to say, except ironically. What do I mean?

I mean first that many uses of common sense are *tropic.* That is, they post an appeal to common sense as part of a rhetorical strategy or course of argumentation. Thomas Paine did it, and so did his pamphleteering opponent, and disagreement here no more indicates the incoherence of common sense in the plain sense than such appeals ever do. These opposing appeals can indicate genuine disagreement about a proposition, but it is not necessarily or even often a common-sense one. For example, I may think it is only common sense that taxation without representation is unfair. You counter that it is only common sense that colonies cannot have the full rights of a home nation. Neither of these views is common sense, let alone "only" common sense—as if to quibble indicates a troubled mind, or a foolish one. Both speakers want to appear realistic, hard-nosed, and sensible; both want to suggest that any opposing view courts incoherence, if not outright insanity. But this is not strictly speaking true, for sane people may disagree about certain matters, especially in politics.

The same rhetorical strategy is evident in what might be called common sense, or plain, skepticism. I say, for example, that I am skeptical of the efficacy of placing purple rock crystals in my pockets during a *viva voce* examination. Here the tropes are a little harder to untangle. Plain skeptical appeals are usually scientific ones, finding superstition and widespread delusion full of error. This is not, it goes without saying, what we think of as philosophical skepticism, but neither is it, and this may require saying, a straightforward appeal to plain common sense—though it is allied with it. We might say that science is systematic and reflective common sense, but it will therefore conflict with undifferentiated or truly plain common sense (as in, e.g., the heliocentric model of the universe, which seems to confound the solid common-sense perception that the sun rises and sets), as well as with what I called earlier common nonsense (as in, e.g., the nonfalsifiable nature of astrological claims).

Despite the close relationship between them, then, straightforwardly to call this scientific attitude "common sense" is no more than to attempt an argumentative stamp of approval. Hence the rhetoric is not very different from the political example, though the appeals may be more resistant to objection. Plain common sense and science do run on some kind of line: "the way things really are" and "the way we commonly see them" are linked together, but never simply or without further ado. For one thing, plain common sense appears to require and admit of no particular theory or paradigm, whereas science always will. (At the very least, there must be a theory of experimental proof.) Theory provides access to the reality described in the *really* of the phrase "the way things really are."

It is perhaps *this* link between common sense and science that leads a certain kind of philosopher to make an appeal to common sense. Indeed, as in politics and other spheres of conceptual dispute, the appeal is frequent and may even provide a master trope for philosophical argumentation. Because there is, as Montaigne reminded us, nothing so absurd that some philosopher has not thought it, it has long been the habit of philosophers to decry the excesses and absurdities of their predecessors. This is most commonly, and most easily, accomplished by showing (or saying) that the predecessor has deviated from common sense in some ridiculous manner.

"From Descartes onwards," says Jonathan Rée,

> the habit of decrying the wayward voyages of old philosophers who, as represented by Milton, "found no end, in wandering mazes lost," became a pervasive mannerism of philosophical writing; and it enabled philosophical authors to make an intriguing invitation to their readers, that they join a democratic, commonsensical alliance against the baseless, self-deceiving conspiracy by which philosophers had imposed upon an over-indulgent public opinion in the past.[13]

---

[13]Jonathan Rée, "The Story of Philosophy," in *Philosophical Tales: An Essay on Philosophy and Literature* (London: Methuen, 1987), 41.

The starting point Rée chooses ("from Descartes onwards") is not idle. It is characteristic of philosophy in the mood inaugurated by Descartes—a mood in which the possibility of perceptual error is a great enemy—that questions of doubt and certainty, partiality and generality, assume an awful importance. Appeals to common sense, then, assume an authoritative status in what can be called traditional epistemology, the branch—though mood, again, is better—of philosophy in which knowledge is thought to be (required to be) both certain and general. As we shall see shortly, to just the extent that this thought (or requirement) is present, so is the specter of skepticism: but not now of the plain or common-sense variety.

In my view, claims to accord with common sense really perform a theoretical role even greater than that suggested by Rée. In addition to distancing themselves (often, though not always, explicitly) from earlier or anyway other systems of firm knowledge, they also distance themselves (often, though not always, implicitly) from suggestions that firm knowledge cannot be had. Thus, to take one prominent example, we have Bishop Berkeley's much-quoted avowal: "I side in all things with the mob," he says, pledging himself "to eternally banishing Metaphisics, &c., and recalling Men to Common Sense." Lest this statement appear incongruous with Berkeley's celebrated idealism, one has only to recall that a thesis about the grounds or dependency of knowledge may, possibly should, in no way affect the contents of knowledge. The reader of Berkeley who doubts his sanity with respect to the presence of the table in front of us (as students are sometimes inclined to) has failed to see that the metaphysical claim he makes is not in conflict with the commonsensical claim, but is, in fact, dependent on it.

Hence, to the extent that they attempt to provide solid grounds for belief or knowledge, and not change or perhaps even challenge the content of it, all metaphysical claims revolve on appeals of greater or lesser degree to the status and authority of plain common sense. George Pappas[14] notes that both realism and idealism can therefore be of the common-sense variety, claiming (1) that common-sense propositions are, in their own sphere, true and certain, and (2) that common sense is a reliable criterion for assessing metaphysical theories, if not the sole or strongest criterion. Divergences in metaphysical commitment result not from variable views of common sense as such, but rather from variation on what to do with it, what to make of it, how to relate it to truth, or how things really are. In Berkeley's case, versions of the two claims are accepted. He

---

[14]"Common Sense in Berkeley and Reid," *Revue Internationale de Philosophie* 158 (1986): 292–303.

might, of course, quibble that it makes no sense to speak of truth or certainty within the common-sense sphere, but he certainly does not doubt the stability of the mob's view of things for their purposes. He might also add that, given this, common sense can be only a touchstone to metaphysical evaluation, not a strict determinant. In short, Berkeley's "weak" common-sense metaphysical view entails that philosophy should accord with common sense only if it is also already superior to its metaphysical rivals in offering greater explanatory ability. Put oppositely, metaphysics should only contradict common sense when it thereby provides superior explanation of the world's true nature.

"Strong" common-sense claims will argue by contrast that, given common sense's presumptive truth, anything that does not accord with common sense must be false and cannot be countenanced in a metaphysics. Thus the no-nonsense realism of Thomas Reid, the Scottish "common sense" philosopher who wished to tie all metaphysical judgments to the putative authority of common sense, is only the most extreme version of a philosophical strategy intrinsic to all metaphysical system building. That extremism is dangerous, though, for it can lead to contradictions: common sense may change or be effectively reformed by science. And a variable realism no longer looks so hard-nosed and sensible. Reid makes the mistake of thinking that common sense is a firm category and therefore a suitable sole basis for his philosophical position. But "the common-sense view of the world is a mass of contradictions," Sprigge reminds us, "and one who wants to know how things really are must move on from common sense, to some view of the world which will clash with it at points. Since common sense clashes with itself the requirement of consistency with common sense rules out common sense itself."[15] Like the scientist, the responsible metaphysician *begins* with how things appear and moves from there to how things really are, based on a theory that is, by degrees, more or less responsive to the imagined firmness of the original appearance. Or, put in a different philosophical vocabulary, the philosopher begins with the *contents* of common-sense beliefs and from there moves to query the *grounds* of those beliefs, hoping either to establish the firmness of those grounds or to discover the manner in which belief of some (any) kind could be firmly grounded.

Thus it has always been philosophically fair to claim that, though the table appears to be really out there in front of us, it is not (i.e., not really), or that, though we believe the table to be there, we do not know it (or know it justifiably). What it is *not* fair to claim is that the table does not even appear to be there, that we do not believe it to be. That claim is insane. Of course the table [appears to be] there; open your eyes and

---

[15]Sprigge, "Philosophy and Common Sense," 203.

look! Metaphysical systems may bring on themselves all manner of tortuous apparatus and system machinery in a drive to say how things really stand, but if they do not, at some level, begin with how things commonsensically stand, they are no good even as metaphysics.

The traditional appearance/reality distinction and the more nuanced contents/ grounds of belief distinction are, from this point of view, versions—perhaps the governing ones—of the move from the plain to the philosophical.

In sum, responsiveness to common sense, true to philosophical argumentation's governing strategy of claiming to side with the mob against absurdity, is a necessary condition of a successful metaphysics, though (as the example of Reid shows) it is not a sufficient condition.[16] Singer puts the matter this way: "Although a metaphysics too literally attached to [common sense] may be false as metaphysics, no metaphysics that contradicts it *in its context and about its proper business* can be true."[17] Still, metaphysics often invites misunderstanding as a result of its alleged responsiveness to common sense, and it may in addition be motivated by urges that can be (should be?) resisted. Common sense, it is commonly thought, remains unimpressed by, and shows no need of, the saving systems constructed by metaphysics to save or explain it. It has no desire to move outside itself, and consequently its impatient replies to the metaphysician are usually on the order that he or she is not an advanced thinker, but in fact, a fool. You argue that there is no table really there? I just told you there was. How do I know? I opened my eyes and there it was before me. What, of what peculiar kind, is your problem?

Speaking now diagnostically, the metaphysician's problem is a philosophical one, and like many others of the same kind, it has the peculiarity that it cannot be felt to be a problem unless one had already assumed the one and only odd position from which it can arise as a problem. Put another way: to get the plain person to see a

---

[16]A failure to appreciate this instance of necessity/sufficiency has led some metaphysicians to discard common sense too quickly. "Very little can be done with common sense," said C. D. Broad: "Any theory that can fit the facts is certain to shock common sense somewhere; and in face of the facts we can only advise common sense to follow the example of Judas Iscariot, and 'go out and hang itself'" (*The Mind and Its Place in Nature* [New York: Harcourt, Brace, 1925], 184–6). Or compare Bradley's pronouncement, "I see no way ... by which the clear thinking which calls itself 'Common Sense' and is satisfied with itself, can ever be reconciled with metaphysics. ... And for 'Common Sense' also it will remain that we shall be able to live only so far as, wherever we feel it to be convenient, we can forget to think" (F. H. Bradley, *Essays on Truth and Reality* [Oxford: Clarendon Press, 1914], 444). What is distinctive about these complaints is that they arise from the philosophical realm—where one is in possession of "the facts"—looking back on the plain from which they have only just come.

[17]Singer [refer to the entry in the Further Readings for Part IV section below—M. M.], 234; emphasis mine. This italicized phrase, I want to say, captures what the plainness of plain common sense is all about.

problem with common sense is already to demand a surrender of plainness in favor of the philosophical, a surrender the person will resist insofar as he or she has common sense. What is the problem with untutored common sense? The problem is that it does not see its own weakness—but therein lies also its strength. Common-sense metaphysics, and metaphysics of many other kinds, are from this vantage responses to a certain kind of vulnerability that is felt to exist in plain common sense—but felt only philosophically.

What is that vulnerability? It is that common sense is felt not to be immune from a skeptical challenge of Cartesian provenance—not the dubiety of our senses on certain occasions (for we have common-sense, and also scientific, ways of dealing with that), but rather the dubiety that can arise even in cases of otherwise perfectly clear knowledge, namely, that I might be dreaming, or might be a brain in a vat.[18] It is understanding the true force of this doubt, understanding it in a sense in which it cannot simply be waved impatiently away, that motivates the metaphysician.

Yet here, as it has often been remarked, especially in the recent diagnostic moods of philosophy, the metaphysician cannot succeed. In order to refute the doubt introduced by Descartes, the metaphysician must resort to just the sort of system that common sense will find hard to countenance. Berkeley siding with the mob is all very well, but they will want none of him and his principled antirealism. The low opinion of the common-sense world would be a small price to pay in exchange for certain knowledge of that world. But it is the worse fate of the metaphysician to find that all quests for certainty will of necessity fail to rid themselves of the doubt introduced by Descartes. Any degree of knowledge that falls short of laying to rest the dreaming doubt cannot be called certain, and that doubt cannot, in the sense imagined by Descartes (i.e., under conditions of perfect knowledge, while I otherwise think myself clearheaded and with eyes peeled), be laid to rest.[19] The ingenuity of metaphysicians in seeking this good riddance of doubt may know no bounds, but their efforts are Sisyphean.

---

[18]Rée says, of the latter possibility, that, of course, we *are* brains in vats. Our vats happen to be bodies situated in the world. I take it that the point of saying this is to show that the force of the Cartesian doubt does not depend on a peculiar science-fiction imagination, or the "intuition-pumping" efficiency of some ingenious thought experiment.

[19]This dilemma of certain knowledge has been much remarked on, and it is, among other things, what Barry Stroud means by *the significance of philosophical skepticism* (*The Significance of Philosophical Scepticism* [Oxford: Clarendon Press, 1984]), especially Chapter I. Stroud's study is a book-length reply and commentary on Thompson Clarke's paper, "The Legacy of Skepticism." See also Stanley Cavell, *The Claim of Reason: Wittgenstein, Skepticism, Morality and Tragedy* (New York: Oxford University Press, 1979), Chapters 6 and 8.

Metaphysician and skeptic are locked in eternal struggle, a dance to the death that shall consume them both in claim and counterclaim.

It is no wonder, then, that the common-sense response to these disputes of traditional epistemology has been to leave the disputants to their own perverse devices and desires. There are, after all, lives to be led, houses to be built, meals to be savored, warm afternoons to be enjoyed in good company. And who, in his right mind anyway, could doubt that the world is right where it appears to be; moreover, that it is *really* there and requires no defense and succumbs to no challenge? Who could doubt that I am here, and so are others like me? That we have been in the past and will continue to be, though not for long, in the future? Although common sense might not put it this way, traditional epistemology is language on extended holiday, a long and fruitless journey to a world other than this one, a fanciful Club Med of the mind.

3 The Plain Person

This plain impatience with the traditional philosopher becomes the plain patience of Moore in his "Defence" and "Proof."[20] But here the complications of plain and philosophical proceed in a reverse direction: not the metaphysician who claims plain authority for his or her system (like Berkeley or Reid) but the system-busting plain person who inexplicably writes as a philosopher.

Moore convincingly shows that common sense of the plain variety is immune from the skeptical challenge, and concomitantly is uninterested in the system building of the metaphysician. For Moore, as for common sense generally, these two warring figures are two sides of the same foreign coin. And yet Moore's defense, and his proof, are generated by a philosophical intelligence, given philosophical window dressing of the usual kind (rigor, argumentation, plodding qualification), and ultimately thought to be philosophically worth saying. He says his "philosophical position" is that certain common-sense propositions are ones he "knows, with certainty, to be true."[21] These are, with some variation, the propositions I enumerated earlier. Moore's "defense" of these propositions is to point out what we might call a "performative contradiction" in those who persist in denying them. Any philosopher who has, for example, denied the existence of what are usually called "other minds" has at the same time assumed their existence in the people he or she is addressing. Moreover, because the

---

[20]The "Proof" is a reference to Moore's paper, "Proof of an External World," (refer to the G. E. Moore entry in the Further Readings for Part I section below).

[21]"A Defence of Common Sense" [refer to the reading above—M. M.].

propositions of common sense are known, with certainty, to be true, they cannot be consistently denied. "Some philosophers," he says, therefore find themselves in the unenviable position of affirming some (metaphysical) propositions that are incompatible with common sense, even while they *must* at the same time affirm the propositions of common sense.

Matters are likewise in Moore's "proof" of the external world. Here the existence of external objects is proven by demonstrating that we know that at least two external things exist, namely, my left hand and my right hand. I prove it by saying, "Here is one hand" (with a suitable gesture) and adding—though this is really philosophical overkill—"Here is another" (gesturing now with my other hand). Since we know this is a hand, to offer it to view is to *prove* its existence: that is, to generate a conclusion that is not contained in the premises, and goes beyond them.

It is with this "going beyond" the premises that the picture begins to get confusing. Our dissatisfaction with Moore's sleight of hand is the clue to this confusion, for it is only here that it is obvious just how Moore has failed to hit the mark in his remarks.[22] The problem, I take it, is not so much with him as with the status of the claim he thinks he is refuting. But Moore shares the blame in thinking that the skeptical claim (which may not be one) is even capable of refutation in the way assumed. In short, by ceasing for *even one moment* to be the plain person (the patience he displays is evidence of this ceasing), Moore succeeds only in giving his remarks a peculiar plain/philosophical status that is no better (though no worse) than the peculiar plain/philosophical character of the traditional epistemologist's remarks. Moore protests too much. Instead of offering a philosophical defense where one is neither needed nor possible, Moore might have been better advised to introduce his metaphysical foe to a skeptic and send them both off to another room.

I believe the picture of Moore is therefore relevantly as Clarke sees it. Moore, "the inveterate plain man," is fending off doubts that from the point of view of common sense are not serious: "These implained doubts are ignorable—either absurd, irrelevant, or out of place."[23] Yet Moore's foible is to attempt a defense of common sense in terms of very general propositions (that is, propositions of philosophical common sense). This attempt leads him beyond the security of the plain. He can—he must—be forgiven.

---

[22]Thomas Nagel (in *The View from Nowhere* [New York: Oxford University Press, 1986], 69) expresses this dissatisfaction by saying that Moore, confronted with the epistemological abyss between the content of belief and grounds of it, turned his back and announced he was on the other side.
[23]Clarke, 755.

It is not simply Moore's desire to philosophize that led him astray, but the nature of common sense itself. "Under a certain conception of common sense," says Clarke, "reality exceeds this daydream" of a plain person simply defeating always implained doubts. Our view from the plain extends past its limits, in other words, and this of necessity. Here we have not only the roots of the skeptical problem, but also the first indication that common sense is, contrary to common sense, not immune from *doubt from its own standpoint.*

How does reality exceed the plain, and in what sort of direction? Consider Clarke's misleading and misled plane spotters, who discern features of warplanes on the basis of partial information. From the position of greater information (knowledge of a little-used type similar in most respects to another), certain judgments of the spotters begin to appear doubtful. Although for practical (military) purposes, the spotters do not need to know of the additional possibility—the little-used plane is not as threatening as its near twin—it is nevertheless the case that grounds for doubt can be introduced, but only, of course, from the position that is detached from those practical purposes.

Clarke and Barry Stroud believe the skeptical doubt is like this: a function of a detachment view of objectivity. It is only in wanting to step back, and back again, and again, that Descartes' dreamer[24] enters the picture. As Clarke puts it, "We want to know not how things are *inside* the world, but how things are, absolutely. And the world itself is one of these things."[25] The desire to detach from practical purposes, and therefore from all imaginable contexts, is the engine that drives Cartesian doubt. (Certainty and doubt always come together, two modalities of the same desire.) It is the peculiar virulence of the skeptic's challenge that, though it arises only at the furthest reaches of the backward dance, appears to have an effect on all subordinate positions. That is, philosophical doubt casts aspersions on all knowledge, though not usually for practical purposes. Hence, drawing the line of doubt from context to context, and out of all context—the move from partial to general to universal—is tantamount to surrendering the certainty common sense led us to believe we had.

Is this a false trail, however? Is the line really connected, or is the philosopher instead doing something so different from the plane spotters that imagining the wider circles of possibility is a mug's game, the pathology of some few twisted

---

[24]Descartes' dreamer is a figure the French philosopher introduces in the first of his *Meditations on First Philosophy* (1641) to help demolish the edifice of doubtable belief, to clear the ground for the foundation of unshakable science. Because "there are no certain indications by which we may clearly distinguish wakefulness from sleep," I may doubt even that here is a hand.—M. M.

[25]Clarke, 762.

minds? We may be inclined to think so. If we just say no to objectivity (of the detached sort), can we not forestall doubt at just that point where we might otherwise threaten to tumble into the dreaming question? Then the question looks mad, or ill posed, or abusive of grammar, or falsely motivated, or excessively general—in short, a fetish of a strange minority of the population, deviant and ignorable. In Stroud's example, a party guest, told another guest has just seen a goldfinch in the garden, is moved to ask, "How does he know he's not dreaming?" We might take this as a feeble joke, of the kind often enough made at philosophy parties. If the guest were to persist in the question, however, past the point where we all laughed dutifully in recognition of the attempt at wit, we might begin to wonder just what was wrong. Was the guest ill? Tired? Or worse, gone mad?

Yet these responses will not do, ultimately, in laying the question to rest—though we may lay the guest to rest in a quiet corner. Certainly, the question is ill posed, perhaps pathological, in this context. But there is little question that we can pose the question otherwise, in other places, in a way that makes it immune from routine dismissal. Doing philosophy is one of these ways, perhaps the only one. For this reason, the impatience of some ordinary-language philosophy, confronted with a skeptic, begins to look similar to Moore's patient hand waving. Yet, because it is still philosophical, ordinary-language philosophy is subject to the same limitations as Moore, ultimately locking itself in an eternal struggle of claim and counterclaim.

It is Stanley Cavell's genius to describe this moment in the struggle over common sense, to suggest that the recovery of the ordinary is more problematic than the brisk ordinary-language philosopher sometimes assumes. (Skepticism's legacy, as Clarke suggests, may lie in its ability to force us to come to grips with, give a better characterization to, the plain.) What, after all, is the basis of a claim to ordinariness? It is trivial, but true, to say that the ordinary-language claim is always already extraordinary, just as Moore's common sense is already too uncommon to avoid philosophical counter-charge. Hume argued that, to recover the world we all know, one had to work through the false metaphysics of his predecessors; it was not enough merely to start with the everyday and remain there. Why not? Why not, from another vantage, simply dispense with the quest for certainty, the drive to detach, that leads us down that well-trodden garden path of doubt?

The reason, I think, is clear. Common sense itself demands it, rests happy with nothing less. The line of back stepping is contained in the very claim to certainty of itself that makes common sense commonsensical. Do we know that the world is out there? Of course we do. Is it really there, are you certain? Of course I am. How do you know you are not dreaming? I may reply that I simply know, or that I have just awoken, or that I pinched myself: but these are all consistent with the dreaming possibility. It is possible, as Clarke argues, that "we are forced wine tasters of the conceivable" and will therefore reach the limits of what we can imagine, where the detached doubters will begin to collapse in on themselves. Stroud does not think so, partly because his hard objectivity is consistent with all of us being dreamers, with no one around to say so, or stand where one could say so. True detachment means never having to say (never having to have at least one agent who can say) the rest are dreamers. And that is precisely the version of objectivity contained in common sense. Common sense is a time bomb of certainty whose own desires set it always on autodestruct.

4 Irony

The plain truth about common sense, then, is that it cannot restrict itself to the plain. That is also, I think, the philosophical truth about common sense. Common sense is not, contrary to itself, immune from skeptical doubt in its own sphere, or from its own inbuilt instability. The plain and the philosophical run together whenever we stop to speak of the plain, whenever common sense pauses to say anything about itself. Moore's dilemma is therefore ours. Common sense appears to entail, in its nature, what Stroud calls "the conditional truth of skepticism": If the Cartesian question can be posed, it leads to doubt of a kind we cannot coherently master or defeat. Can the question be posed? Or better, must it be? Or is the real question ultimately, as Hume suggested, how to live with our (always inevitable) skepticism, given that we cannot live it? Is philosophy, and common sense, too, always about forging deals with doubt?

[…]

So I am moved to say, in conclusion, that the plain truth about common sense is that we have no way of talking philosophically about it. The recurring oddness and confusion of our attempts so to talk stem from the dual fact that the plain actively resists philosophical defense (indicating a decisive break between the two realms), and yet inevitably demands the philosophical whenever plain dwellers stop to think (indicating a continuity between them). The image of vertigo is well chosen: it is not simply that our heads spin when we pause to think about the world and our knowledge of it; more to the present point, we can only avoid that spinning by not looking down, not pausing to think about the status of our common-sense achievement, but instead walking blithely on, eyes front. It is true that for most people, most of the time, this blitheness comes naturally. They put one foot in front of another without apparent effort. Some of us, cursed with a peculiar kind of curiosity, will insist on gazing into the abyss. Our best hope, then, is that we can, though unavoidably dizzy, avoid falling into it—and do so in interesting ways. I hope, plainly, that this is one of them.

FOR DISCUSSION OR ESSAYS

- Reid claimed that we are naturally constituted to accept certain self-evident first principles, including the existence of mind-independent objects. But could it be that we are constituted to accept *wrong* first principles sometimes? Explain why this might be the case, or why it could not be so.

- G. E. Moore says that he certainly knows that earth existed before he was born, but he knows this *without knowing exactly what the evidence for his belief is*. He writes: "We are all, I think, in this strange position that we do *know* many things, with regard to which we *know* further that we must have had evidence for them, and yet we do not know *how* we know them, i.e. we do not know what the evidence was." Evaluate this claim, focusing on the question of knowledge and justification.

- Moore defends common sense propositions by pointing out that in the very act of denying the propositions, skeptics have involved themselves in what Kingwell, in the third section of his reading above, called "performative contradiction." In your own words, explain what this means. Do you agree?

- Wittgenstein observed that doubt itself must rest on what is beyond doubt. Consider what he had to say about *language games* and *statements that "stand fast"* for us. How might we use these terms to make sense of common sense?

- Reid held that any judgment that conflicts with common sense must be false and cannot be countenanced in metaphysics. Kingwell observes that, since common sense is full of contradictions, Reid's "strong common sense" view is untenable. With whom do you agree more (assuming you agree with either)? Explain. (Consider whether Reid and Kingwell agree when it comes to their respective definitions of *common sense*.)

- At the end of Section 3, Kingwell writes that, "Common sense is a time bomb of certainty whose own desires set it always on autodestruct." What did he mean by this?

- What is a common sense understanding of common sense? After reading the General Introduction and the selections from Part I, are you convinced that a common sense understanding of common sense is inadequate, inaccurate, or misleading? In your own words, explain why or why not. (Keep in mind that this prompt is about the adequacy of a common-sense understanding of common sense, not the adequacy of each and every common-sense belief.)

FURTHER READINGS FOR PART I

Armstrong, A. MacC. "Philosophy and Common Sense." In *Philosophy and Phenomenological Research* 22, no. 3 (March 1962), 354–359. This short article begins with a discussion of Berkeley's seemingly strange claim that his immaterialism reflects "the plain dictates of nature and common sense." In the course of a brief historical discussion, Armstrong offers the following definition: "common sense is the complement of convictions held without question by the members of a certain generation of a certain society, with which they test the truth of knowledge and the morality of actions." "The essential defect of common sense," he writes, "is its sketchiness, or, more precisely [...] its vagueness, meagerness, and bias."

Geertz, Clifford. "Common Sense as a Cultural System." In *The Antioch Review* 33, no. 1 (Spring 1975), 5–26. The American anthropologist Geertz (1926–2006) describes common sense as one of many "cultural systems," including myth, painting, and religion, that characterizes a wide variety of societies, including tribal societies. Focusing on the Zande people of north-central Africa, he describes their witchcraft (*mangu*) as a kind of common sense, standing against a background of shared experience of "a familiar world, one everyone can, and should, recognize, and within which everyone stands or should, on his own feet." According to this use of the term, then, common sense is not distinctively modern.

Grave, Selwyn A. "Common Sense." In *The Encyclopedia of Philosophy*, edited by Paul Edwards. New York: Collier Macmillan, 1967. This is a handy introductory survey on the topic of philosophy and common sense, from Berkeley to Wittgenstein. In it we find the following insight: "... common sense does not declare itself in advance of attack upon it."

Hume, David. *A Treatise of Human Nature*, in various editions. First published in 1738. This work, especially Book I, exemplifies the sort of skepticism that Reid and other champions of "common sense" found so objectionable.

Mates, Benson. *Skeptical Essays*. Chicago and London: The University of Chicago Press, 1981. In this book, the late professor of logic argues that the traditional philosopher's task of refuting the skeptic must fail. The skeptical challenge, including the problem of what G. E. Moore formulated as the question "How do I know that there is anything other than *these* perceptions?" (Mates, 105), is both *intelligible* and *unsolvable*: the problem of skepticism cannot be solved, nor can it be "dissolved" without begging the skeptic's question.

Moore, G. E. "Proof of an External World." Originally published in *Proceedings of the British Academy* 25 (1939), 273–300; also included in *Philosophical*

Papers (London: Allen & Unwin, 1959), 127–150. In his famous "here is a hand" paper, Moore persists in his defense of the common-sense belief in "things outside of us," against skepticism and philosophical idealism. In one of the final lines of his "Proof," he writes, "I can know things, which I cannot prove." Among these, he writes, he certainly knows the premises of his argument for the existence of the "external world," even if he has provided no proof for them that meets the skeptic's challenge.

Reid, Thomas. *An Inquiry into the Human Mind on the Principles of Common Sense*. London: Forgotten Books, 2012. First published in 1764. In the forty odd pages of the introductory first chapter of *An Inquiry*, Reid argues that modern philosophy, from Descartes to Hume, leads to a skepticism that only common sense can cure.

Wittgenstein, Ludwig. *Philosophical Investigations*, edited by G. E. M. Anscombe and R. Rhees and translated by G. E. M. Anscombe. Oxford: Blackwell, 1953. This is a reading that more advanced students may profitably study, preferably after first having read Wittgenstein's earlier book, the *Tractatus Logico-Philosophicus* (1922).

Part II

Common Sense and Science

Introduction to Part II:
Common Sense and Science

As we have seen in the last reading in Part I, questions of skepticism lead to questions about the relationship between common sense and science. The topic of this relationship has filled enough paper to cover a landscape, and yet questions persist. Is common sense a background from which science emerges, or is it an obstacle to science? We all agree that science is a corrective to the uncritical prejudices of common sense, but does common sense have a role to play when it comes to assessing competing scientific claims? Is it a *foundation* of science, in some crucial sense of that word? *Science* and *common sense* are both terms that we use in distinctively modern ways, and one of the benefits of exploring the relationship between them is to gain a firmer and more nuanced understanding of what we mean by "science."

Albert Einstein is supposed to have quipped that common sense is the collection of prejudices acquired by age eighteen.[1] The point, presumably, is that innovative science must part ways with these prejudices. The British biologist Lewis Wolpert pressed the point further, declaring that, "if an idea fits with common sense, scientifically it is bound to be false."[2] In a similar vein, in our selection by Scott O. Lilienfeld, we will read that, "The foremost obstacle standing in the way of the public's acceptance of evolutionary theory is not a dearth of common sense. Instead, it is the public's erroneous belief that common sense is a dependable guide to evaluating the natural world."

By contrast, some recent philosophers, notably the late Harvard professor W. V. O. Quine and his followers, have emphasized the continuity of common sense and the sciences. In the General Introduction above, Richard W. Miller (who happens to have been a student of Quine's) illustrated his point that common sense is inseparable from science by noting that a scientific researcher who did not assume the reliability of eyesight under near-optimal conditions of observation could not

---

[1] Although the attribution is common, I have been unable to confirm that Einstein actually said it. The internet is awash with dubious "quotes" from Albert Einstein. He is also supposed to have said that "The whole of science is nothing more than a refinement of everyday thinking" (cited in Lewis Vaughn, *The Power of Critical Thinking*, 2nd edn. [Oxford and New York: Oxford University Press, 2007], 388). Whatever their accuracy, these two attributions do not sit well together.

[2] Lewis Wolpert, "Mind over Matter of Fact," *The Guardian of London*, March 15, 1997, 21.

confidently read a thermometer. Empirical scientists, including even those in the weirdly counterintuitive field of quantum physics, rely on pragmatically confirmed assumptions and truisms.

So common sense (or at least the most practically confirmed items of common sense that have sometimes gone by the name of *good sense*) is necessary to the practice of the sciences. Still, Wolpert's view has traction: when we try to describe the universe in both its smallest and its largest scales, we soon discover that our ordinary intuitions and ways of thinking are woefully inadequate. Where ordinary intuitions and common sense have failed, scientists have had to set them aside to arrive, often through the use of mathematics and formal methods, at entirely new conceptions, such as Einstein's four-dimensional elastic space-time; the infinite-dimensional Hilbert space of quantum mechanics; the abstruse mathematics of string theory, and perhaps multiple universes. Indeed, this may well be the case with medium-sized objects, too, including the objects of evolutionary biology and genuinely scientific social science. As the great German thinker Friedrich Engels noted, "sound common sense, respectable fellow that he is in the homely realm of his own four walls, has very wonderful adventures as soon as he ventures out into the wide world of research."[3]

In our first reading below, Professor Quine offers his defense of common-sense realism, arguing that, contrary to the fallacious reasoning of philosophical skeptics, we know "in a general way what the world is like." "We imbibe an archaic natural philosophy with our mother's milk," he writes, and part of that natural philosophy involves the notion of a reality independent of language. In denying that we know in a general way what the world is like, he writes, the skeptic has committed "a peculiarly philosophical fallacy," which consists in failing to recognize that:

> We cannot significantly question the reality of the external world, or deny that there is evidence of external objects in the testimony of our senses; for, to do so is simply to dissociate the terms *reality* and *evidence* from the very applications which originally did most to invest those terms with whatever intelligibility they may have for us.

Toward the end of his paper, Quine presents a "tentative ontology of physical objects and classes," to which the sciences should limit themselves.

In the reading after that, Austrian-British philosopher Karl R. Popper (1902–1994) argues that, when it comes to science and philosophy, "our starting point is common

---

[3]Introduction to *Anti-Dühring*, in *Karl Marx, Frederick Engels, Collected Works*, vol. 25 (London: Lawrence & Wishart, 1987), 22. First published in 1880.

sense, and our great instrument of progress is criticism." Although science, philosophy, and all rational thought must start from common sense, it is not a *secure* starting point. Popper acknowledges that skepticism with reference to mind-independent objects "is irrefutable; and this means of course that realism is indemonstrable." Still, there are arguments that tip the scale in favor of metaphysical realism. Popper presents five such arguments and concludes that, "all science, and all philosophy, are enlightened common sense"—at least when it comes to common-sense metaphysical realism. This is the first face of common sense, the smiling face.

When it comes to the theory of knowledge, though, things are different. The common-sense view of knowledge (the blank slate, or *tabula rasa* view, or what Popper calls the "bucket theory") holds that immediate experiences are the secure basis of all knowledge. This is the second face of common sense, the face with the sour expression. Popper has little trouble showing that this theory is "a naïve muddle," and in the course of doing so, he defends the view that knowing does not consist of passively receiving "given" sense perceptions; rather, it is an active, rapid, and increasingly efficient process of decoding environmental messages.

Popper contrasts his own *fallibilist* theory of knowledge to the common-sense theory. *Fallibilism* is the doctrine that (1) most or all beliefs are uncertain and possibly mistaken, and so a completely secure starting point of knowledge is not possible; fortunately, however, (2) such a starting point is not necessary for philosophy and science.[4] Popper argues that if we reject the attempt to build an unshakable foundation upon which to base all subsequent knowledge, then it is possible for common sense to serve as a starting point of philosophy and science. In the course of making his case, he surveys the relevant views of Rene Descartes, John Locke, David Hume, Immanuel Kant, Alfred Tarksi, and other illustrious philosophers who have grappled with questions of common sense and truth.

In the last reading in Part II, psychologist Scott O. Lilienfeld casts doubt on the optimistic view, voiced by Popper, Quine, and others, that science and common sense, more often than not, support each other. Focusing on one of the hottest flashpoints in the "culture wars" today, Lilienfeld suggests that, when it comes to popular acceptance of contemporary biological science, prevailing common sense is an obstacle, not an ally.

---

[4]This is not an uncommon view among recent philosophers. Quine, for example, was a fallibilist, and so was Wittgenstein. The latter point should become clear from a review of Wittgenstein's discussion of "the concept of 'knowing' and the concept of 'being certain'" (as in remarks 8 and 18 in our reading from *On Certainty*, above).

Chapter 5

The Scope and Language of Science

W. V. O. Quine

Beginning in the 1920s, a group of philosophers and philosophically minded physicists in Central Europe attempted to construct a new language of science that would, by its very structure, prevent confusions rooted in unclear language and unverifiable claims. Those who undertook this project were called "logical positivists," and several of their leading lights, including the German-born philosopher Rudolf Carnap (1891–1970), were greatly influenced by Ludwig Wittgenstein's earlier views, presented in his *Tractatus*.[1] In the course of pursuing this project for two decades, though, many of Carnap's collaborators came to the conclusion that the project had failed. In his mid-twenties, W. V. O. Quine (1908–2000) studied with Carnap. After the failure of the positivist project Quine turned his attention to reforming natural language (such as English), to make it more useful to scientists. In the following reading, we can see some of the distance that he had taken, in this respect, from his logical positivist predecessors.

In section I of Quine's paper, he takes up the now-familiar skeptical doubt that there is a world outside of our heads, and he discusses our related conviction that, in addition to the world of language, there exists a world *outside* of language, to which it refers. We are, writes Quine, "recipients and carriers of the evolving lore of the ages," and we might as well admit it. Part of this lore is "an archaic natural philosophy" that we have imbibed with our mother's milk.[2] Here we see at work Quine's emphasis on "conservatism" as a virtue of theories—how a good theory, in its main contentions, coheres with the theories

---

[1] In the introductory remarks for the Wittgenstein reading in Part I above, it was noted that he later repudiated the account of language presented in the *Tractatus*. As we know, our excerpts from *On Certainty* are in part a critical rejection of his earlier views.

[2] But not much *before* imbibing our mothers' milk: Quine rejects the possibility of *a priori* ideas, innate knowledge, or inborn lore.

adjacent to it, within our vast, ever-changing "webs of belief." Here we also see Quine's pragmatism at work: "our initially uncritical hypothesis of a physical world," he writes, "gains pragmatic support from whatever it contributes towards a coherent account of lore-bearing or other natural phenomena."

The logical positivists distinguished sharply between science and common sense, but Quine begs to differ: "Science," he writes, "is not a substitute for common sense, but an extension of it": "The scientist is indistinguishable from the common man in his sense of evidence except that the scientist is more careful." When it comes to the question *How does science get ahead of common sense?* Quine's answer, "in a word, is 'system.'"

In keeping with Quine's theme of the priority of the nonlinguistic to the linguistic, he devotes section II to the question *Whence the insistence on a world of external objects?* Beginning with remarks on the learning of language, he connects this to "scholarship"—the kind of learning that depends on the prior learning of words. In this way, "the notion of reality independent of language is carried over by the scientist from his earliest impressions."

In section III, after noting that "thought, if of any considerable complexity, is inseparable from language," Quine provides several broad suggestions as to how scientists can enhance objectivity and diminish confusions that careless language produces among scientists and philosophers. Like Carnap, Quine is concerned to provide a more useful "language of science," but by the end of section III (the last section of our excerpt), this appears to consist of stripping down and modifying a natural language by eliminating indicator words ("here," "now," "you," "we," and the like), using verb tenses more precisely, and minimizing ambiguity (as in the sentence "Your mothers bore you").

Willard Van Orman Quine was one of the most prominent American philosophers and logicians of the last century. Our excerpt consists of the first three sections of the six sections that make up his original paper.

I

I am a physical object sitting in a physical world.[3] Some of the forces of this physical world impinge on my surface. Light rays strike my retinas; molecules bombard my eardrums and fingertips. I strike back, emanating concentric airwaves. These waves take the form of

[3]Presented as an invited address in one of the Bicentennial Conferences at Columbia University, October 1954, and published with the editor's revisions in Lewis Leary, ed., *The Unity of Knowledge* (New York: Doubleday, 1955). My original text appeared afterward in the *British Journal for the Philosophy of Science*, 1957, and that is what is reprinted here, with negligible emendations, with the permission of the Columbia trustees and with the approval of the editor of the *British Journal.*

a torrent of discourse about tables, people, molecules, light rays, retinas, air waves, prime numbers, infinite classes, joy and sorrow, good and evil.

My ability to strike back in this elaborate way consists in my having assimilated a good part of the culture of my community, and perhaps modified and elaborated it a bit on my own account. All this training consisted in turn of an impinging of physical forces, largely other people's utterances, upon my surface, and of gradual changes in my own constitution consequent upon these physical forces. All I am or ever hope to be is due to irritations of my surface, together with such latent tendencies to response as may have been present in my original germ plasm. And all the lore of the ages is due to irritation of the surfaces of a succession of persons, together, again, with the internal initial conditions of the several individuals.

Now how is it that we know that our knowledge must depend thus solely on surface irritation and internal conditions? Only because we know in a general way what the world is like, with its light rays, molecules, men, retinas, and so on. It is thus our very understanding of the physical world, fragmentary though that understanding be, that enables us to see how limited the evidence is on which that understanding is predicated. It is our understanding, such as it is, of what lies beyond our surfaces, that shows our evidence for that understanding to be limited to our surfaces. But this reflection arouses certain logical misgivings: for is not our very talk of light rays, molecules, and men then only sound and fury, induced by irritation of our surfaces and signifying nothing? The world view which lent plausibility to this modest account of our knowledge is, according to this very account of our knowledge, a groundless fabrication.

To reason thus is, however, to fall into fallacy: a peculiarly philosophical fallacy, and one whereof philosophers are increasingly aware. We cannot significantly question the reality of the external world, or deny that there is evidence of external objects in the testimony of our senses; for, to do so is simply to dissociate the terms *reality* and *evidence* from the very applications which originally did most to invest those terms with whatever intelligibility they may have for us.

We imbibe an archaic natural philosophy with our mother's milk. In the fullness of time, what with catching up on current literature and making some supplementary observations of our own, we become clearer on things. But the process is one of growth and gradual change: we do not break with the past, nor do we attain to standards of evidence and reality different in kind from the vague standards of children and laymen. Science is not a substitute for common sense, but an extension of it. The quest for knowledge is properly an effort simply to broaden and deepen the knowledge which the man in the street already enjoys, in moderation, in relation to the commonplace things around him. To disavow the very core of common sense, to require evidence for that which both the physicist and the man in the street accept as platitudinous, is no laudable perfectionism; it is a pompous confusion, a failure to observe the nice distinction between the baby and the bath water.

Let us therefore accept physical reality, whether in the manner of unspoiled men in the street or with one or another degree of scientific sophistication. In so doing we constitute ourselves recipients and carriers of the evolving lore of the ages. Then, pursuing in detail our thus accepted theory of physical reality, we draw conclusions concerning, in particular, our own physical selves, and even concerning ourselves as lore bearers. One of these conclusions is that this very lore which we are engaged in has been induced in us by irritation of our physical surfaces and not otherwise. Here we have a little item of lore about lore. It does not, if rightly considered, tend to controvert the lore it is about. On the contrary, our initially uncritical hypothesis of a physical world gains pragmatic support from whatever it contributes toward a coherent account of lore-bearing or other natural phenomena.

Once we have seen that in our knowledge of the external world we have nothing to go on but surface irritation, two questions obtrude themselves—a bad one and a good one. The bad one, lately dismissed, is the question whether there is really an external world after all. The good one is this: Whence the strength of our notion that there is an external world? Whence our persistence in representing discourse as somehow about a reality, and a reality beyond the irritation?

It is not as though the mere occurrence of speech itself were conceived somehow as *prima facie* evidence of there being a reality as subject matter. Much of what we say is recognized even by the man in the street as irreferential: "Hello," "Thank you," "Ho hum," these make no claims upon reality. These are physical responses on a par, semantically, with the patellar reflex. Whence then the idea of scientific objectivity? Whence the idea that language is occasionally descriptive in a way that other quiverings of irritable protoplasm are not?

This is a question for the natural science of the external world: in particular, for the psychology of human animals. The question has two not quite separate parts: whence the insistence on a world of reference, set over against language? and whence the insistence on a world of external objects, set over against oneself? Actually we can proceed to answer this twofold question plausibly enough, in a general sort of way, without any very elaborate psychologizing.

II

Let us suppose that one of the early words acquired by a particular child is *red*. How does he learn it? He is treated to utterances of the word simultaneously with red presentations; further, his own babbling is applauded when it approximates to "red" in the presence of red. At length he acquires the art of applying the word neither too narrowly nor too broadly for his mother's tastes. This learning process is familiar to us under many names: association, conditioning, training, habit formation, reinforcement, and extinction, induction.

Whatever our colleagues in the laboratory may discover of the inner mechanism of that process, we may be sure of this much: the very possibility of it depends on a prior tendency on the child's part to weight qualitative differences unequally. Logically, as long as *a, b,* and *c* are three and not one, there is exactly as much difference between *a* and *b* as between *a* and *c;* just as many classes, anyway, divide *a* from *b* (i.e., contain one and not the other) as *a* from *c.* For the child, on the other hand, some differences must count for more than others if the described process of learning "red" is to go forward at all. Whether innately or as a result of prelinguistic learning, the child must have more tendency to associate a red ball with a red ball than with a yellow one; more tendency to associate a red ball with a red ribbon than with a blue one; and more tendency to dissociate the ball from its surroundings than to dissociate its parts from one another. Otherwise no training could mold the child's usage of the word *red*, since no future occasion would be more strongly favored by past applications of the word than any other. A working appreciation of something like "natural kinds,"[4] a tendency anyway to respond in different degrees to different differences, has to be there before the word *red* can be learned.

At the very beginning of one's learning of language, thus, words are learned in relation to such likenesses and contrasts as are already appreciated without benefit of words. No wonder we attribute those likenesses and contrasts to real stuff, and think of language as a superimposed apparatus for talking *about* the real.

The likenesses and contrasts which underlie one's first learning of language must not only be preverbally appreciable, they must, in addition, be intersubjective. Sensitivity to redness will avail the child nothing, in learning "red" from the mother, except insofar as the mother is in a position to appreciate that the child is confronted with something red. Hence, perhaps, our first glimmerings of an external world. The most primitive sense of externality may well be a sense of the mother's reinforcement of likenesses and contrasts in the first phases of word learning. The real is thus felt, first and foremost, as prior to language and external to oneself. It is the stuff that mother vouches for and calls by name.

This priority of the nonlinguistic to the linguistic diminishes as learning proceeds. *Scholarship* sets in, i.e., the kind of learning which depends on prior learning of words. We learn "mauve" at an advanced age, through a verbal formula of the form "the color

---

[4]A *natural kind* is a grouping that corresponds to parts or aspects of the passing scene that do not consist of artifacts. The common textbook examples of natural kinds are (most of?) the chemical elements represented on the periodic table. Quine accepts natural classifications into kinds as *sets*, on the basis of *similarity* between instances.—M. M.

of" or "a color midway between." And the scholarly principle takes hold early; the child will not have acquired many words before his vocabulary comes to figure as a major agency in its own increase. By the time the child is able to sustain rudimentary conversation in his narrow community, his knowledge of language and his knowledge of the world are a unitary mass.

Nevertheless, we are so overwhelmingly impressed by the initial phase of our education that we continue to think of language generally as a secondary or superimposed apparatus for talking about real things. We tend not to appreciate that most of the things, and most of the supposed traits of the so-called world, are learned through language and believed in by a projection from language. Some uncritical persons arrive thus at a copy theory of language: they look upon the elements of language as names of elements of reality, and true discourse as a map of reality. They project vagaries of language indiscriminately upon the world, stuffing the universe with and's and or's, singulars and plurals, definites and indefinites, facts and states of affairs, simply on the ground that there are parallel elements and distinctions on the linguistic side.

The general task which science sets itself is that of specifying how reality "really" is: the task of delineating the structure of reality as distinct from the structure of one or another traditional language (except, of course, when the science happens to be grammar itself). The notion of reality independent of language is carried over by the scientist from his earliest impressions, but the facile reification[5] of linguistic features is avoided or minimized.

But how is it possible for scientists to be thus critical and discriminating about their reifications? If all discourse is mere response to surface irritation, then by what evidence may one man's projection of a world be said to be sounder than another's? If, as suggested earlier, the terms *reality* and *evidence* owe their intelligibility to their applications in archaic common sense, why may we not then brush aside the presumptions of science?

The reason we may not is that science is itself a continuation of common sense. The scientist is indistinguishable from the common man in his sense of evidence, except that the scientist is more careful. This increased care is not a revision of evidential standards, but only the more patient and systematic collection and use of what anyone would deem to be evidence. If the scientist sometimes overrules something which a superstitious layman might have called evidence, this may simply be because the scientist has other and contrary evidence which, if patiently presented to the layman

---

[5]*Reification* is the process of regarding a thought or idea (or as in this case, "linguistic features") as an entity independent of our minds.—M. M.

bit by bit, would be conceded superior. Or it may be that the layman suffers from some careless chain of reasoning of his own whereby, long since, he came wrongly to reckon certain types of connection as evidential: wrongly in that a careful survey of his own ill-observed and long-forgotten steps would suffice to disabuse him. (A likely example is the "gambler's fallacy"—the notion that the oftener black pays the likelier red becomes.)

Not that the layman has an explicit standard of evidence—nor the scientist either. The scientist begins with the primitive sense of evidence which he possessed as layman, and uses it carefully and systematically. He still does not reduce it to rule, though he elaborates and uses sundry statistical methods in an effort to prevent it from getting out of hand in complex cases. By putting nature to the most embarrassing tests he can devise, the scientist makes the most of his lay flair for evidence, and at the same time he amplifies the flair itself, affixing an artificial proboscis of punch cards and quadrille paper.

Our latest question was, in brief, how science gets ahead of common sense, and the answer, in a word, is "system." The scientist introduces system into his quest and scrutiny of evidence. System, moreover, dictates the scientist's hypotheses themselves: those are most welcome which are seen to conduce most to simplicity in the overall theory. Predictions, once they have been deduced from hypotheses, are subject to the discipline of evidence in turn, but the hypotheses have, at the time of hypothesis, only the considerations of systematic simplicity to recommend them. Insofar, simplicity itself—in some sense of this difficult term—counts as a kind of evidence, and scientists have indeed long tended to look upon the simpler of the two hypotheses as not merely the more likable, but the more likely. Let it not be supposed, however, that we have found at last a type of evidence that is acceptable to science and foreign to common sense. On the contrary, the favoring of the seemingly simpler hypothesis is a lay habit carried over by science. The quest of systematic simplicity seems peculiarly scientific in spirit only because science is what it issues in.

III

The notion of a reality independent of language is derived from earliest impressions, if the speculations in the foregoing pages are right, and is then carried over into science as a matter of course. The stress on externality is likewise carried over into science, and with a vengeance. For the sense of externality has its roots, if our speculations are right, in the intersubjectivity which is so essential to the learning of language, and intersubjectivity is vital not only to language but equally to the further enterprise, likewise a social one, of science. All men are to qualify as witnesses to the data of science, and the truths of science are to be true no matter who pronounces them. Thus it is that science has got on rather with masses and velocities than with likes and dislikes. And thus it is that when science does confront likes and dislikes it confronts them as behavior, intersubjectively observable. Language in general is robustly extravert, but science is more so.

It would be unwarranted rationalism to suppose that we can stake out the business of science in advance of pursuing science and arriving at a certain body of scientific theory. Thus consider, for the sake of analogy, the smaller task of staking out the business of chemistry. Having got on with chemistry, we can describe it *ex post facto* as the study of the combining of atoms in molecules. But no such clean-cut delimitation of the business of chemistry was possible until that business was already in large measure done. Now the situation is similar with science generally. To describe science as the domain of cognitive judgment avails us nothing, for the definiens here is in as urgent need of clarification as the definiendum.[6] Taking advantage of existing scientific work, however, and not scrupling to identify ourselves with a substantive scientific position, we can then delineate the scientific objective, or the cognitive domain, to some degree. It is a commonplace predicament to be unable to formulate a task until half done with it.

Thought, if of any considerable complexity, is inseparable from language—in practice surely and in principle quite probably. Science, though it seeks traits of reality independent of language, can neither get on without language nor aspire to linguistic neutrality. To some degree, nevertheless, the scientist can enhance objectivity and diminish the interference of language, by his very choice of language. And we, concerned to distill the essence of scientific discourse, can profitably purify the language of science beyond what might reasonably be urged upon the practicing scientist. To such an operation we now turn.

In a spirit thus not of practical language reform but of philosophical schematism, we may begin by banishing what are known as *indicator words* (Goodman) or *egocentric particulars* (Russell): "I," "you," "this," "that," "here," "there," "now," "then," and the like. This we clearly must do if the truths of science are literally to be true independently of author and occasion of utterance. It is only thus, indeed, that we come to be able to speak of sentences, i.e., certain linguistic forms, as true and false. As long as the indicator words are retained, it is not the sentence but only the several events of its utterance that can be said to be true or false.

Besides indicator words, a frequent source of fluctuation in point of truth and falsity is ordinary ambiguity. One and the same sentence, qua linguistic form, may be true in one occurrence and false in another because the ambiguity of a word in it is

---

[6]The *definiendum* is the word, term, or phrase that is defined; the *definiens* is the word, term, or phrase that is used to define it.—M. M.

differently resolved by attendant circumstances on the two occasions. The ambiguous sentence *Your mothers bore you* is likely to be construed in one way when it follows on the heels of a sentence of the form "*x* bore *y*," and in another when it follows on the heels of a sentence of the form "*x* bores *y*."

In Indo-European languages there is also yet a third conspicuous source of fluctuation in point of truth and falsity, viz., tense. Actually tense is just a variant of the phenomenon of indicator words; the tenses can be paraphrased in terms of tenseless verbs governed by the indicator word *now*, or by *before now*, etc.

How can we avoid indicator words? We can resort to personal names or descriptions in place of "I" and "you," to dates or equivalent descriptions in place of "now," and to place names or equivalent descriptions in place of "here." It may indeed be protested that something tantamount to the use of indicator words is finally unavoidable, at least in the teaching of the terms which are to be made to supplant the indicator words. But this is no objection; all that matters is the *subsequent* avoidability of indicator words. All that matters is that it be possible in principle to couch science in a notation such that none of *its* sentences fluctuates between truth and falsity from utterance to utterance. Terms which are primitive or irreducible, from the point of view of that scientific notation, may still be intelligible to us only through explanations in an ordinary language rife with indicator words, tense, and ambiguity. Scientific language is in any event a splinter of ordinary language, not a substitute.

Granted then that we can rid science of indicator words, what would be the purpose? A kind of objectivity, to begin with, appropriate to the aims of science: truth becomes invariant with respect to speaker and occasion. At the same time a technical purpose is served: that of simplifying and facilitating a basic department of science, viz., deductive logic. For, consider, for example, the very elementary canons of deduction which lead from "*p* and *q*" to "*p*," and from "*p*" to "*p* or *q*," and from "*p* and if *p* then *q*" to "*q*." The letter "*p*," standing for any sentence, turns up twice in each of these rules, and clearly the rules are unsound if the sentence which we put for "*p*" is capable of being true in one of its occurrences and false in the other. But to formulate logical laws in such a way as not to depend thus upon the assumption of fixed truth and falsity would be decidedly awkward and complicated, and wholly unrewarding.

In practice certainly one does not explicitly rid one's scientific work of indicator words, tense, and ambiguity, nor does one limit one's use of logic to sentences thus purified. In practice one merely *supposes* all such points of variation fixed for the space of one's logical argument; one does not need to resort to explicit paraphrase, except at points where local shifts of context *within* the logical argument itself threaten equivocation.

This practical procedure is often rationalized by positing abstract entities, "propositions," endowed with all the requisite precision and fixity which is wanting in the sentences themselves, and then saying that it is with propositions, and not their coarse sentential embodiments, that the laws of logic really have to do. But this posit achieves only obscurity. There is less mystery in imagining an idealized form of scientific language in which sentences are so fashioned as never to vacillate between truth and falsity. It is significant that scientific discourse actually does tend toward this ideal, in proportion to the degree of development of the science. Ambiguities and local and epochal biases diminish. Tense, in particular, gives way to a four-dimensional treatment of space-time.

Chapter 6

Two Faces of Common Sense: An Argument for Common-Sense Realism and against the Common-Sense Theory of Knowledge

Karl Popper

Our next reading is from a paper titled "Two Faces of Common Sense," by Austrian-British philosopher Karl R. Popper. In the first section of our excerpt, the author discusses a theme that we have encountered in Part I: although common sense is "vague and insecure," it must nevertheless be the starting point of science and philosophy: "All science, and all philosophy," Popper writes, "are enlightened common sense." We make scientific progress by building on insecure foundations, and our great instrument of progress is the criticism of always-provisional conjectures, notably those of common sense. This is a statement of a theory of knowledge called *fallibilism*.

In the course of making his case for fallibilism, Popper acknowledges that skepticism with reference to mind-independent objects cannot be refuted, "and this means, of course, that realism [belief in mind-independent reality] is indemonstrable." Since refutability or falsifiability is what differentiates a genuine science from a pseudoscience, common-sense realism does not count as a scientific theory any more than Berkeley's idealism does. Nevertheless, Popper says, there are arguments against idealism, and in the section titled Arguments for Realism, he presents five of them.

When it comes to the common-sense *theory of knowledge*, however, matters are very different. According to it, we acquire knowledge about the world directly, by observation. Starting at the section titled The Mistaken Common-Sense Theory of Knowledge, Popper shows that the common-sense theory of knowledge, which he dubs the "bucket view," is self-contradictory and "a naïve muddle." In the section after that, he juxtaposes the "utterly naive and completely mistaken" bucket view to his preferred view. According to his "evolutionary epistemology" approach, we are innately disposed (thanks to our inborn or environmentally and developmentally induced constitution) to quickly and efficiently decode messages of "a coherent and partly regular or ordered system," namely reality. This all takes place without anything in the way of sense impressions, direct knowledge, "immediately given" experiences, or any similar inventions of modern philosophy that have become part of the common sense view of knowledge.

In the section titled The Pre-Darwinian Character of the Common-Sense Theory of Knowledge, Popper asserts that knowledge in the subjective sense—that is to say, knowledge of the sort that the bucket view emphasizes—is the result of the aforementioned innate dispositions, and as such it is not subject to the sort of criticism that the modern philosophers have attempted to subject it to. Only knowledge in the objective sense, in the form of linguistically formulated expectations, is subject to critical discussion. Thus, only knowledge in the objective, public sense could count as genuine conjectures and as candidates for refutation.

Sir Karl Raimund Popper has been described as one of the twentieth century's greatest philosophers of science. In his influential book, *Conjectures and Refutations* (to which he repeatedly refers in this paper),[1] he presents his case for rejecting the prevailing empiricist and positivist views about the scientific method, in favor of empirical falsification.

The Insecure Starting-Point: Common Sense and Criticism

Science, philosophy, rational thought, must all start from common sense.[2]

Not, perhaps, because common sense is a secure starting point: the term *common sense* which I am using here is a very vague term, simply because it denotes a vague

---

[1] *Conjectures and Refutations*, 4th edn (Abingdon on Thames: Routledge and Kegan Paul, 1972).

[2] This long essay, so far unpublished, is a revised and expanded version of a talk I gave to my former Seminar early in 1970. It is intended as a fairly full answer to the critics of my views on science. I am indebted to John Watkins, who has read through an earlier version of the essay and who pointed out to me a serious error which fortunately proved to be not relevant to my main argument. David Miller has most generously given his time to reading the essay thoroughly and repeatedly and has saved me not only from at least three similar errors but also from countless minor muddles of matter and style. I am deeply indebted to him for this.

and changing thing—the often adequate or true and often inadequate or false instincts or opinions of many men.

How can such a vague and insecure thing as common sense provide us with a starting point? My answer is: because we do not aim or try to build (as did, say, Descartes or Spinoza or Locke, Berkeley, or Kant) a secure system on these "foundations." Any of our many common-sense assumptions—our common-sense background knowledge, as it may be called—from which we start can be challenged and criticized at any time; often such an assumption is successfully criticized and rejected (for example, the theory that the earth is flat). In such a case, common sense is either modified by the correction, or it is transcended and replaced by a theory which may appear to some people for a shorter or longer period of time as being more or less "crazy." If such a theory needs much training to be understood, it may even fail forever to be absorbed by common sense. Yet even then we can demand that we try to get as close as possible to the ideal: *All science, and all philosophy, are enlightened common sense.*

Thus we begin with a vague starting point, and we build on insecure foundations. But we can make progress: we sometimes can, after some criticism, see that we have been wrong: we can learn from our mistakes, from realizing that we have made a mistake.

(Incidentally, I shall try to show later that common sense has been particularly misleading in the theory of knowledge. For there seems to be a common-sense theory of knowledge: it is the mistaken theory that we acquire knowledge about the world by opening our eyes and looking at it, or, more generally, by observation.)

My first thesis is thus that our starting point is common sense, and that our great instrument for progress is criticism.

But this thesis raises at once a difficulty. It has been said that if we wish to criticize a theory, say T_1, whether or not it is of a common-sense character, then we need some other theory, T_2, which furnishes us with the necessary basis or starting point or background for criticizing T_1. Only in the very special case that we can show T_1 to be inconsistent (a case called "immanent criticism," where we use T_1 in order to show that T_1 is false) can we proceed differently; that is, by showing that absurd consequences follow from T_1.

I think that this criticism of the method of criticism is invalid. (What it alleges is that all criticism must be either "immanent" or "transcendent," and that in the case of "transcendent" criticism we do not proceed critically since we have to assume dogmatically the truth of T_2.) For what really happens is this. If we feel that we could produce some criticism of T_1, which we can assume to be a consistent theory, then we either show that T_1 leads to unintended and undesirable consequences (it does not matter so much whether they are logically inconsistent), or we show that there is a competing theory T_2 which clashes with T_1, and which, we try to show, has certain advantages over T_1. This is all that is needed: as soon as we have competing theories, there is plenty of scope for critical, or rational, discussion: we explore the consequences of the theories, and we try, especially, to discover their weak points—that is, consequences which we think may be mistaken. This kind of critical or rational discussion may sometimes lead to a clear defeat of one of the theories; more often it only helps to bring out the weaknesses of both, and thus challenges us to produce some further theory.

The fundamental problem with the theory of knowledge is the clarification and investigation of this process by which, it is here claimed, our theories may grow or progress.

Contrast with Other Approaches

What I have said so far may appear quite trivial. To give it a point, I shall very briefly contrast it with other approaches.

Descartes was perhaps the first to say that everything depends upon the security of our starting point. In order to render this starting point really secure, he suggested the method of doubt: accept only what is absolutely indubitable.

He then started from his own existence, which seemed to him indubitable, since even doubting our own existence seems to presuppose the existence of a doubter (a doubting subject).

Now I am no more skeptical about the existence of my own self than Descartes was of his. But I also think (as did Descartes) that I shall die soon and that this will make little difference to the world, except to myself and two or three friends. Obviously the issues of one's own life and death are of some significance, but I conjecture (and I think Descartes would agree) that my own existence will come to an end without the world's coming to an end too.

This is a common-sense view, and it is the central tenet of what may be termed "realism." (Realism will soon be discussed more fully.)

I admit that the belief in one's own existence is very strong. But I do not admit that it can bear the weight of anything resembling the Cartesian edifice; as a starting platform it is much too narrow. Nor do I think, incidentally, that it is as indubitable as Descartes (excusably) believed. In Hugh Routledge's wonderful book, *Everest 1933*, we read of Kipa, one of the Sherpas who went higher than was good for him: "Poor old Kipa's bewildered mind still held doggedly to the idea that he was dead."[3] I do not assert

---

[3]Hugh Routledge, *Everest 1933* (London: Hodder & Stoughton, 1934), 143. (I had, though perhaps only for a few seconds, a similar experience to Kipa's when I was once struck by lightning on the *Sonnblick* in the Austrian Alps.)

that poor old Kipa's idea was common sense, or even reasonable, but it throws doubt on that directness and indubitability which Descartes was claiming. In any case, I do not propose to make any similar claim for certainty, even though I gladly admit that it is good, sane common sense to believe in the existence of one's thinking self. It is not the truth of Descartes's starting point which I wish to challenge, but its sufficiency for what he tries to do with it and, incidentally, its alleged indubitability.

Locke, Berkeley, even the "skeptic" Hume, and their many successors, especially Russell and Moore,[4] shared with Descartes the view that subjective experiences were particularly secure and therefore suitable as a stable starting point or foundation, but they relied mainly on experiences of an observational character. And Reid, with whom I share adherence to realism and to common sense, thought that we had some very direct, immediate, and secure perception of external, objective reality.

In opposition to this, I suggest that there is nothing direct or immediate in our experience: we have to *learn* that we have a self, extended in time and continuing to exist even during sleep and total unconsciousness, and we have to learn about our own and others' bodies. It is all decoding, or interpretation. We learn to decode so well that everything becomes very "direct" or "immediate" to us, but so it is with the man who has learned the Morse Code, or, to take a more familiar example, who has learned to read a book: it speaks to him "directly," "immediately." Nevertheless, we know that there is a complicated process of decoding going on; the apparent directness and immediacy are the result of training, just as in piano playing or car driving.

We have reason to conjecture that there is a hereditary basis to our decoding skills. At any rate, we sometimes do make mistakes in decoding, especially during the learning period, but also later, especially if unusual situations occur. The immediacy or directness of the well-learned decoding process does not guarantee faultless functioning; there is no absolute certainty, though certainty enough for most practical purposes. The quest for certainty, for a secure basis of knowledge, has to be abandoned.

Thus I see the problem of knowledge in a way different from that of my predecessors. Security and justification of claims to knowledge are not my problem. Instead, my problem is the growth of knowledge. In which sense can we speak of the growth or the progress of knowledge, and how can we achieve it?

---

[4]G. E. Moore was a great realist because he had a strong love for truth and felt clearly that idealism was false. Unfortunately, he believed in the common-sense subjectivist theory of knowledge, and thus throughout his whole life he hoped, in vain, that a proof of realism based on perception could be found—a thing that cannot exist. Russell relapsed from realism into positivism for the same reason.

Realism

Realism is essential to common sense. Common sense, or enlightened common sense, distinguishes between appearance and reality. (This may be illustrated by examples such as, "Today the air is so clear that the mountains appear much nearer than they really are." Or perhaps, "He appears to do it without effort, but he has confessed to me that the tension is almost unbearable.") But common sense also realizes that appearances (say, a reflection in a looking glass) have a sort of reality, or in other words, that there can be a surface reality—that is, an appearance—and a depth reality. Moreover, there are many sorts of real things. The most obvious sort is that of foodstuffs (I conjecture that they produce the basis of the feeling of reality), or more resistant objects (*objectum* = what lies in the way of our action) like stones, and trees, and humans. But there are many sorts of reality which are quite different, such as our subjective decoding of our experiences of foodstuffs, stones, and trees, and human bodies. The taste and weight of foodstuffs and of stones is again another sort of reality, and so are the properties of trees and human bodies. Examples of other sorts in this many-sorted universe are: a toothache, a word, a language, a highway code, a novel, a governmental decision; a valid or invalid proof; perhaps forces, fields of forces, propensities, structures, and regularities. (My remarks here leave it entirely open whether, and how, these many sorts of objects can be related to each other.)

Arguments for Realism

My thesis is that realism is neither demonstrable nor refutable. Realism like anything else outside logic and finite arithmetic is not demonstrable, but while empirical scientific theories are refutable,[5] realism is not even refutable. (It shares this irrefutability with many philosophical or "metaphysical" theories, in particular also

---

[5]This, of course, is one of my oldest theories. See, for example, Chapter 1 of my *Conjectures and Refutations*, especially pp. 37f. I disagree with those critics of my views who assert, for example, that Newton's theory is no more refutable than Freud's. A refutation of Newton's theory would be, for example, if all the planets except the earth continue to move as at present, while the earth moves on its present orbit but with constant acceleration even when moving away from its perihelion. (Of course, against this refutation and all others any theory whatever can be "immunized"—to use a term due to Hans Albert; this was stressed by me as long ago as 1934, and it is emphatically not the point at issue here.) I should say that the refutability of Newton or Einstein's theory is a fact of elementary physics and of elementary methodology. Einstein, for example, said that if the red shift effect (the slowing down of atomic clocks in strong gravitational fields) was not observed in the case of white dwarfs, his theory of general relativity would be refuted. No description whatsoever of any logically possible human behavior can be given which would turn out to be incompatible with the psychoanalytic theories of Freud, or of Adler, or of Jung.

with idealism.) But it is arguable, and the weight of the arguments is overwhelmingly in its favor.

Common sense is unquestioningly on the side of realism; there are, of course, even before Descartes—in fact ever since Heraclitus—a few hints of doubt whether or not *our ordinary world is perhaps just our dream*. But even Descartes and Locke were realists. A philosophical theory competing with realism did not seriously start before Berkeley, Hume, and Kant.[6] Kant, incidentally, even provided a proof for realism. But it was not a valid proof, and I think it important that we should be clear why no valid proof of realism can exist.

In its simplest form, idealism says: the world (which includes my present audience) is just my dream. Now it is clear that this theory (though you will know that it is false) is not refutable: whatever you, my audience, may do to convince me of your reality—talking to me, or writing a letter, or perhaps kicking me—it cannot possibly assume the force of a refutation, for I would continue to say that I am dreaming that you are talking to me, or that I received a letter, or felt a kick. (One might say that these answers are all, in various ways, immunizing stratagems. This is so, and it is a strong argument against idealism. But again, that it is a self-immunizing theory does not refute it.)

Thus idealism is irrefutable, and this means, of course, that realism is indemonstrable. But I am prepared to concede that realism is not only indemonstrable but, like idealism, irrefutable also; that no describable event, and no conceivable experience, can be taken as an effective refutation of realism.[7] Thus there will be in this issue, as in so many, no

---

[6]Positivism, phenomenalism, and also phenomenology are all of course infected by the subjectivism of the Cartesian starting point.

[7]The irrefutability of realism (which I am prepared to concede) may be questioned. The great Austrian authoress Marie Ebner von Eschenbach (1830–1916) tells in some memoirs of her childhood that she suspected realism to be mistaken. Perhaps things do disappear when we look away. So she tried to catch the world in its disappearing trick by suddenly turning round, half expecting that she would see how out of nothingness things try quickly to reassemble themselves, and she was both disappointed and relieved whenever she failed. Several comments may be made on this story. First, it is conceivable that this report of childish experimentation is not untypical, but normal and typical, and plays a part in the development of the common-sense distinction of appearance from reality. Secondly (and I am slightly inclined to favor this view) it is conceivable that the report is untypical; that most children are naive realists, or become so before an age within their memory, and Marie von Eschenbach certainly was an untypical child. Thirdly, I have experienced—and not only in childhood but also as an adult—something not too far removed from it: for example, when finding something of which I had completely forgotten, I sometimes felt that if nature had let this thing disappear, nobody would have been the wiser. (There was no need for reality to show that it "really" existed; nobody would have noticed had it not done so.) The question arises whether, if Marie had succeeded, this would have refuted realism or whether it would not merely have refuted a very special form of it. I do not feel obliged to go into this question, but rather *concede* to my opponents that realism is irrefutable. Should this concession be wrong, then realism is even nearer to being a testable scientific theory than I originally intended to claim.

conclusive argument. *But there are arguments in favor of realism,* or, rather, *against idealism.*

(1) Perhaps the strongest argument consists of a combination of two: (a) that realism is part of common sense, and (b) that all the alleged *arguments* against it are not only philosophical in the most derogatory sense of this term, but are at the same time based upon an uncritically accepted part of common sense; that is to say, upon that mistaken part of the common-sense theory of knowledge which I have called the "bucket theory of the mind"; see below, the section entitled The Mistaken Common-Sense Theory of Knowledge, and the section following that.

(2) Although science is a bit out of fashion today with some people, for reasons which are, regrettably, far from negligible, we should not ignore its relevance to realism, despite the fact that there are scientists who are not realists, such as Ernst Mach or, in our own time, Eugene P. Wigner;[8] their arguments fall very clearly in the class just characterized in (1). But let us for a moment forget about atomic physics (quantum mechanics). We can then assert that almost all, if not all, physical, chemical, or biological theories imply realism, in the sense that if they are true, realism must also be true. This is one of the reasons why some people speak of "scientific realism." It is quite a good reason. Because of its (apparent) lack of testability, I myself happen to prefer to call realism "metaphysical" rather than "scientific."[9]

However one may look at this, there are excellent reasons for saying that *what we attempt in science is to describe and (so far as possible) explain reality.* We do so with the help of conjectural theories; that is, theories which we hope are true (or near the truth), but which we cannot establish as certain or even as probable (in the sense of the probability calculus), even though they are the best theories which we are able to produce, and may therefore be called "probable" as long as this term is kept free from any association with the calculus of probability.

There is a closely related and excellent sense in which we can speak of "scientific realism": the procedure we adopt involves (as long as it does not break down, for

---

[8]For Wigner see especially his contribution to *The Scientist Speculates*, ed. I. J. Good (London: Heinemann, 1962), 284–302. For a criticism see especially Edward Nelson, *Dynamical Theories of Brownian Motion* (Princeton, NJ: Princeton University Press, 1967), §§ 14–16. See also my contributions in Mario Bunge, ed., *Quantum Theory and Reality* (Berlin: Springer, 1967), and in W. Yourgrau and A. van der Werde, eds., *Perspectives in Quantum Theory, Essays in Honor of Alfred Landé* (Cambridge, MA: M.I.T. Press, 1971).

[9]See my *Logik der Forschung*, 1934 (L.d.F.) where, in Section 79 (p. 252 of the English translation *The Logic of Scientific Discovery*, 1975—L.Sc.D.) I describe myself as a metaphysical realist. In those days I identified wrongly the limits of science with those of arguability. I later changed my mind and argued that nontestable (i.e., irrefutable) metaphysical theories may be rationally arguable. (See, for example, my paper "On the Status of Science and Metaphysics," first published in 1958 and now in my *Conjectures and Refutations*, 1963; 4th edn, 1972.)

example because of antirational attitudes) success in the sense that our conjectural theories tend progressively to come nearer to the truth; that is, to true descriptions of certain facts, or aspects of reality.

(3) But even if we drop all arguments drawn from science, there remain the arguments from language. Any discussion of realism, and especially all arguments against it, has to be formulated in some language. But human language is essentially descriptive (and argumentative),[10] and an unambiguous description is always realistic: it is *of* something—of some state of affairs which may be real or imaginary. Thus if the state of affairs is imaginary, then the description is simply false, and its negation is a true description of reality, in Tarski's sense.[11] This does not logically refute idealism or solipsism, but it makes it at least irrelevant. Rationality, language, description, argument are all about some reality, and they address themselves to an audience. All this presupposes realism. Of course, this argument for realism is logically no more conclusive than any other, because I may merely dream that I am using descriptive language and arguments, but this argument for realism is nevertheless strong and *rational*. It is as strong as reason itself.

(4) To me, idealism appears absurd, for it also implies something like this: that it is my mind which creates this beautiful world. But I know I am not its Creator. After all, the famous remark "Beauty is in the eye of the beholder," though perhaps not an utterly stupid remark, means no more than that there is a problem of the *appreciation* of beauty. I know that the beauty of Rembrandt's self-portraits is not in my eye, nor that of Bach's Passions in my ear. On the contrary, I can establish to my satisfaction, by opening and closing my eyes and ears, that my eyes and ears are not good enough to take in all the beauty that is there. Also, there are other people who are better judges—better able than I to appreciate the beauty of pictures and of music. Denying realism amounts to megalomania (the most widespread occupational disease of the professional philosopher).

(5) Out of many other weighty though inconclusive arguments, I wish to mention only one. It is this. If realism is true—more especially, something approaching scientific realism—then the reason for the impossibility of proving

---

[10]Bühler (partly anticipated by W. von Humboldt) clearly pointed out the descriptive function of language. I have referred to this in various places and argued for the need to introduce the argumentative function of language. See, for example, my paper "Epistemology Without a Knowing Subject" (read in Amsterdam in 1967, and now reprinted as Chapter 3 in the present volume [not included here.—MM]).

[11]According to Alfred Tarski's semantic theory of truth, a sentence "P" is true if and only if it is the case that P ("The Semantic Conception of Truth and the Foundations of Semantics," *Philosophy and Phenomenological Research* 4, no.3 (1943): 341–76).—M. M.

it is obvious. The reason is that our subjective knowledge, even perceptual knowledge, consists of dispositions to act, and is thus a kind of tentative adaptation to reality, and that we are searchers, at best, and at any rate fallible. There is no guarantee against error. At the same time, the whole question of the truth and falsity of our opinions and theories clearly becomes pointless if there is no reality, only dreams or illusions.

To sum up, I propose to accept realism as the only sensible hypothesis—as a conjecture to which no sensible alternative has ever been offered. I do not wish to be dogmatic about this issue any more than about any other. But I think I know all the epistemological arguments—they are mainly subjectivist—which have been offered in favor of alternatives to realism, such as positivism, idealism, phenomenalism, phenomenology, and so on, and although I am not an enemy of the discussion of *isms* in philosophy, I regard all the philosophical *arguments* which (to my knowledge) have ever been offered in favor of my list of *isms* as clearly mistaken. Most of them are the result of the mistaken quest for certainty, or for secure foundations on which to build. And all of them are typical philosophers' mistakes in the worst sense of this term: they are all derivatives of a mistaken though commonsensical theory of knowledge which does not stand up to any serious criticism. (Common sense typically breaks down when applied to itself; see the section titled The Mistaken Common-Sense Theory of Knowledge, below.)

I will conclude this section with the opinion of the two men whom I regard as the greatest of our time: Albert Einstein and Winston Churchill.

"I do not see," writes Einstein, "any 'metaphysical danger' in our acceptance of things—that is, of the objects of physics ... together with the spatio-temporal structures which pertain to them."[12]

This was Einstein's opinion after a careful and sympathetic analysis of a brilliant attempt at refuting naive realism due to Bertrand Russell.

Winston Churchill's views are very characteristic and, I think, a very fair comment upon a philosophy which may since have changed its colors, crossing the floor of the house from idealism to realism, but which remains as pointless as ever it was: "Some of my cousins who had the great advantage of University education," Churchill writes, "used to tease me with arguments to prove that nothing has any existence except what we think of it ..." He continues:

---

[12]See Albert Einstein, "Remarks on Bertrand Russell's Theory of Knowledge," in *The Philosophy of Bertrand Russell*, ed. P. A. Schilpp, The Library of Living Philosophers V (Evanston, IL: Northwestern University Press, 1944), 290f. Schilpp's translation on p. 291 is very much closer than mine, but I felt that the importance of Einstein's idea justified my attempt at a *very* free translation, which, I hope, is still faithful to what Einstein wanted to say.

I always rested upon the following argument which I devised for myself many years ago ... here is this great sun standing apparently on no better foundation than our physical senses. But happily there is a method, apart altogether from our physical senses, of testing the reality of the sun ... astronomers ... predict by [mathematics and] pure reason that a black spot will pass across the sun on a certain day. You ... look, and your sense of sight immediately tells you that their calculations are vindicated ... *We have taken what is called in military map-making "a cross bearing."* We have got *independent testimony* to the reality of the sun. *When my metaphysical friends tell me that the data on which the astronomers made their calculations were necessarily obtained originally through the evidence of their senses, I say "No." They might, in theory at any rate, be obtained by automatic calculating machines set in motion by the light falling upon them without admixture of the human senses at any stage* ... I ... reaffirm with emphasis ... that the sun is real, and also that it is hot—in fact hot as Hell, and that if the metaphysicians doubt it they should go there and see.[13]

I may perhaps add that I regard Churchill's argument, especially the important passages which I have put in italics, not only as a valid criticism of the idealistic and subjectivistic arguments, but as the philosophically soundest and most ingenious argument against subjectivist epistemology that I know. I am not aware of any philosopher who has not ignored this argument (apart from some of my students whose attention I have drawn to it). The argument is highly original; first published in 1930 it is one of the earliest philosophical arguments making use of the possibility of automatic observatories and calculating machines (programmed by Newtonian theory). And yet, forty years after its publication, Winston Churchill is still quite unknown as an epistemologist: his name does not appear in any of the many anthologies on epistemology, and it is also missing even from the *Encyclopedia of Philosophy*.

Of course Churchill's argument is merely an excellent refutation of the specious arguments of the subjectivists: *he does not prove realism.* For the idealist can always argue that he, or we, is dreaming the debate, with calculating machines and all. Yet I regard this argument as silly, because of its universal applicability. At any rate, unless some philosopher should produce some entirely new argument, I suggest that subjectivism may in future be ignored.

[...]

---

[13]See Winston S. Churchill, *My Early Life—A Roving Commission*, first published October 1930; quoted by permission of the Hamlyn Publishing Group from the Odhams Press edition, London, 1947, Chapter IX, 115f. (The italics are not in the original.) See also the Macmillan edition, London, 1944, 131f.

The Mistaken Common-Sense Theory of Knowledge

Common sense, I said, is always our starting point, but it must be criticized. And, as might have been expected, it is not too good when it comes to reflect on itself. In fact the common-sense theory of common-sense knowledge is a naive muddle. Yet it has provided the foundation on which even the most recent philosophical theories of knowledge are erected.

The common-sense theory is simple. If you or I wish to know something not yet known about the world, we have to open our eyes and look round. And we have to raise our ears and listen to noises, and especially to those made by other people. Thus our various senses are our *sources of knowledge*—the sources or the entries into our minds.

I have often called this theory the bucket theory of the mind. The bucket theory of the mind is best represented by a diagram:

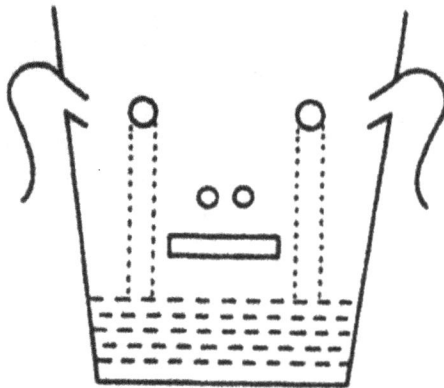

Figure 1 The Bucket.

Our mind is a bucket which is originally empty, or more or less so, and into this bucket material enters through our senses (or possibly through a funnel for filling or reaching it from above), and accumulates and becomes digested.

In the philosophical world this theory is better known under the more dignified name of the *tabula rasa* theory of the mind: our mind is *an empty slate* upon which the senses engrave their messages. But the main point of the *tabula rasa* theory goes beyond the common-sense bucket theory: I mean its emphasis on the perfect emptiness of the mind at birth. For our discussion this is merely a minor point of discrepancy between the two theories, for it does not matter whether we are or are not born with some "innate ideas" in our bucket—more perhaps in the case of intelligent children, fewer in the case of morons. The important thesis of the bucket theory is that we learn most, if not all, of what we do learn through the entry of experience into our sense openings, so that all experience consists of information received through our senses.

In this form, this thoroughly mistaken theory is still very much alive. It still plays a part in theories of teaching, or in "information theory," for example, though it is admitted now that the bucket is not empty at birth, but endowed with a computer program.

My thesis is that the bucket theory is utterly naive and completely mistaken in all its versions, and that unconscious assumptions of it in some form or other still exert a devastating influence especially upon the so-called behaviorists, suggesting the still powerful theory of the conditioned reflex and other theories which enjoy the highest reputations.

Among the many things which are wrong with the bucket theory of the mind are the following:

(1) Knowledge is conceived of as consisting of things, or thing-like entities in our bucket (such as ideas, impressions, *sensa*, sense data, elements, atomic experience, or—perhaps slightly better—molecular experiences or "*Gestalten*").

(2) Knowledge is, first of all, *in* us: it consists of information which has reached us, and which we have managed to absorb.

(3) There is *immediate* or *direct* knowledge; that is, the pure, unadulterated elements of information which have got into us and are still undigested. No knowledge could be more elementary and certain than this.

Point (3) can be elaborated as follows:

(3a) All error, all mistaken knowledge, according to the common-sense theory, comes from bad intellectual digestion which adulterates these ultimate or "given" elements of information by misinterpreting them, or by wrongly linking them with other elements; the sources of error are our subjective admixtures to the pure or given elements of information, which in their turn are not only free from error, but are the standards of all truth, so that it would be completely pointless even to raise the question whether they are perhaps erroneous.

(3b) Thus knowledge, so far as it is free from error, is essentially passively received knowledge, while error is always actively (though not necessarily intentionally) produced by us, either by interfering with "the given" or perhaps by some other mismanagement: the perfect brain would never err.

(3c) Knowledge which goes beyond the pure reception of the given elements is therefore always less certain than the given or elementary knowledge, which indeed constitutes the standard of certainty. If I doubt anything, I have just to open my eyes again and observe with a candid eye, excluding all prejudices: I have to purify my mind from sources of error.

(4) Nevertheless, we have a practical need of knowledge of a somewhat higher level: of knowledge which goes beyond the mere data or the mere elements. For what we need, especially, is knowledge that establishes expectations by connecting existing data with impending elements. This higher knowledge establishes itself by way of the *association of ideas or elements*.

(5) Ideas or elements are associated if they occur together, and, most important, *association is strengthened by repetition*.

(6) In this way, we establish *expectations* (if idea *a* is strongly associated with idea *b*, then the occurrence of *a* arouses a high expectation of *b*).

(7) In the same way, *beliefs* emerge. True belief is belief in an unfailing association. Erroneous belief is a belief in an association between ideas which, though they occurred together, perhaps sometime in the past, are not unfailingly repeated together. To sum up: what I call the common-sense theory of knowledge is something very close to the empiricism of Locke, Berkeley, and Hume and not far removed from that of many modern positivists and empiricists.

Criticism of the Common-Sense Theory of Knowledge

Almost everything is wrong in the common-sense theory of knowledge. But perhaps the central mistake is the assumption that we are engaged in what Dewey called the quest for certainty.

It is this which leads to the singling out of data or elements, or sense data or sense impressions or immediate experiences, as a secure basis of all knowledge. But far from being this, these data or elements do not exist at all. They are the inventions of hopeful philosophers, who have managed to bequeath them to the psychologists.

What are the facts? As children we learn to decode the chaotic messages which meet us from our environment. We learn to sift them, to ignore the majority of them, and to single out those which are of biological importance for us either at once, or in a future for which we are being prepared by a process of maturation.

Learning to decode the messages which reach us is extremely complicated. It is based upon innate dispositions. We are, I conjecture, innately disposed to refer the messages to a coherent and partly regular or ordered system: to "reality." In other words, our subjective knowledge of reality consists of maturing innate dispositions. (This, incidentally, is in my opinion too sophisticated a construction to be used as a strong independent argument in favor of realism.) However this may be, we learn the decoding by *trial and error elimination,* and although we become extremely good and quick at experiencing the decoded message as if it were "immediate" or "given," there are always some mistakes, usually corrected by special mechanisms of great complexity and considerable efficiency.

So the whole story of the "given," of true data, with certainty attached, is a mistaken theory, though part of common sense.

I admit that we experience much as if it were immediately given to us, and as if it were perfectly certain. This is thanks to our elaborate decoding apparatus, with its many built-in checking devices, taking what Winston Churchill would have called "crossbearings"; systems which manage to eliminate a great many of the mistakes we make in decoding, so that indeed in these cases in which we experience immediacy, we only seldom err. But I deny that these well-adapted experiences should be identified in any sense with "given" standards of reliability or truth. Nor in fact do these cases establish a standard of "directness," or of "certainty," or show that we can never err in our immediate perceptions; it is simply due to our incredible efficiency as biological systems. (A well-trained photographer will rarely make bad exposures. This is due to his training, and not to the fact that his pictures are to be taken as "data" or "standards of truth" or perhaps as "standards of correct exposure.")

Almost all of us are good observers and good perceivers. But this is a problem to be explained by biological theories, and not to be taken as the basis for any *dogmatism* of direct or immediate or intuitive knowledge. And after all, we do all fail sometimes; we must never forget our fallibility.

Criticism of the Subjectivist Theory of Knowledge

All this does not of course refute idealism or the subjectivist theory of knowledge. For all I have said about the psychology (or physiology) of perception, it may be merely a dream.

Yet there is a very good argument against the subjectivist and idealist theories which I have not yet used. It runs like this.

Most subjectivists assert with Berkeley that their theories agree in all practical respects with realism, and especially with the sciences; only, they say, the sciences do not reveal to us standards of truth but are nothing but perfect instruments of prediction. There can be no higher standards of certainty (save God-given revelation).[14] But then, physiology comes in and predicts that our "data" are fallible rather than standards of truth or of certainty. Thus if this form of subjective instrumentalism is true, then it leads to its own refutation. Therefore it cannot be true.

This, of course, does not refute an idealist who would reply that we are only dreaming that we have refuted idealism.

I may perhaps mention in passing that a formally similar argument of Russell's against "naive realism," an argument which greatly impressed Einstein, is unacceptable. It was this:

> The observer, when he seems to himself to be observing a stone, *is really, if physics* [physiology] *is to be believed, observing the effects of the stone upon himself.* Thus science seems to be at war with itself ... Naive realism leads to physics, and physics, if true, shows naive realism to be false. Therefore naive realism, if true, is false; therefore, it is false.[15]

Russell's argument is unacceptable, because the passage which I have italicized is mistaken. *When the observer observes a stone, he does not observe the effect of the stone upon himself* (though he might do so, say, by contemplating a wounded toe), even though he decodes some of the signals that reach him from the stone. Russell's argument is at the same level as the following: "When the reader seems to himself to be reading Russell, he is really observing the effects of Russell upon himself and therefore not reading Russell." The truth is, that reading (i.e., decoding) Russell is partly based upon observations of Russell's text, but there is no problem here worthy of analysis; we all know that reading is a complex process in which we do several sorts of things at once.

I do not think it worth pursuing these exercises in cleverness, and I repeat that, until some new arguments are offered, I shall naively accept realism.

---

[14]See my *Conjectures and Refutations*, Chapters 3 and 6.

[15]Cp. Bertrand Russell, *An Inquiry into Meaning and Truth* (London and New York: Allen & Unwin, 1940), 14f. (Italics not in the original.) See also Einstein's essay in P.A. Schilpp, ed., 282f. *The Philosophy of Bertrand Russell* (1944), 282f.

The Pre-Darwinian Character of the Common-Sense Theory of Knowledge

The common-sense theory of knowledge is radically mistaken in every point. Its fundamental mistakes can perhaps be cleared up as follows:

(1) *There is knowledge in the subjective sense, which consists of dispositions and expectations.*

(2) *But there is also knowledge in the objective sense, human knowledge, which consists of linguistically formulated expectations submitted to critical discussion.*

(3) The common-sense theory fails to see that *the difference between* (1) *and* (2) *is of the most far-reaching significance.* Subjective knowledge is not subject to criticism, although it can be changed by various means—for example, by the elimination (killing) of the carrier of the subjective knowledge or disposition in question. Thus knowledge in the subjective sense grows or achieves better adjustments by the Darwinian method of mutation and elimination of the organism. As opposed to this, objective knowledge can change and grow by the elimination (killing) of the linguistically formulated conjecture: the "carrier" can survive—he can, if he is a self-critical person, even eliminate his own conjecture.

The difference is that linguistically formulated theories can be *critically discussed.*

(4) Apart from this all-important mistake, the common-sense theory is mistaken in different places. It is, essentially, a theory of the genesis of knowledge: the bucket theory is a theory of our acquisition of knowledge—our largely passive acquisition of knowledge—and thus it is also a theory of what I call the *growth of knowledge. But as a theory of the growth of knowledge it is utterly false.*

(5) The *tabula rasa* theory is pre-Darwinian: to every man who has any feeling for biology it must be clear that most of our dispositions are inborn, either in the sense that we are born with them (for example, the dispositions to breathe, to swallow, and so on) or in the sense that in the process of maturation, the development of the disposition is elicited by the environment (for example, the disposition to learn a language).

(6) But even if we forget all about *tabula rasa* theories[16] and assume that the bucket is half full at birth, or that it changes its structure with the process of

---

[16]Some comments about the history of the *tabula rasa* theory will be found in the new addendum on Parmenides in the third edition of my *Conjectures and Refutations,* 1969 and 1972.

maturation, the theory is still most misleading. This is not only because all subjective knowledge is dispositional, but mainly because it is not a disposition of the associative type (or the conditioned reflex type). To put my position clearly and radically: *there is no such thing as association or conditioned reflex.* All reflexes are unconditioned; the supposedly "conditioned" reflexes are the results of modifications which partially or wholly eliminate the false starts, that is to say the errors in the trial-and-error process.

Sketch of an Evolutionary Epistemology

So far as I know, the term evolutionary epistemology is due to my friend Donald T. Campbell. The idea is post-Darwinian and goes back to the end of the nineteenth century—to such thinkers as J. M. Baldwin, C. Lloyd Morgan, and H. S. Jennings.

My own approach has been somewhat independent of most of these influences, though I read with great interest not only Darwin, of course, but also Lloyd Morgan and Jennings during the years before writing my first book. However, like many other philosophers I laid great stress upon the distinction between two problems of knowledge: its genesis or history on the one hand, and the problems of its truth, validity, and "justification" the other. (Thus I stressed, for example, at the Congress in Prague in 1934: "Scientific theories can never be 'justified', or verified. But in spite of this, a hypothesis *A* can under certain circumstances achieve more than a hypothesis *B* ...")[17] I even stressed very early that questions of truth or validity, not excluding *the logical justification off the preference for one theory over another* (the only kind of "justification" which I believe possible), must be *sharply distinguished from all genetic, historical, and psychological questions.*

However, already when writing my *Logik der Forschung* I came to the conclusion that we epistemologists can claim precedence over the geneticists: logical investigations of questions of validity and approximation to truth can be of the greatest importance for genetic and historical and even for psychological investigations. They are in any case logically prior to the latter type of question, even though investigations in the history of knowledge can pose many important problems to the logician of scientific discovery.[18]

---

[17]See *Erkenntnis* 5 (1935): 170ff; see also my *Logic of Scientific Discovery*, 315.
[18]I sometimes speak of the "principle of transference" when referring to the fact that what holds in logic must hold in genetics or in psychology, so that results may have psychological or, more generally, biological applications. See Section 4 of my paper "Conjectural Knowledge," Chapter 1 in this volume, 37f [not included here—M. M.].

Thus I speak here of evolutionary epistemology, even though I contend that the leading ideas of epistemology are logical rather than factual; despite this, all of its examples, and many of its problems, may be suggested by studies of the genesis of knowledge.

This attitude is indeed the precise opposite of that of the common-sense theory and of the classical epistemology of, say, Descartes, Locke, Berkeley, Hume, and Reid: for Descartes and Berkeley, truth is guaranteed by the origin of the ideas, which is ultimately supervised by God. Traces of the view that ignorance is sin are to be found not only in Locke and Berkeley but even in Hume and Reid. For there it is the directness or immediacy of our ideas, or impressions, or perceptions which is their divine seal of truth and which offers the best security for the believer, while in my view we sometimes regard theories as true, or even "immediately" true, because they are true *and our mental outfit is well adapted* to their level of difficulty. But we are never "justified" or "entitled" to claim the truth of a theory, or of a belief, by reason of the alleged immediacy or directness of the belief. This, in my view, is putting the cart before the horse: immediacy or directness may be the result of the biological fact that a theory is true and also (partly for this reason) very useful for us. But to argue that immediacy or directness establishes truth, or is a criterion of truth, is *the fundamental mistake of idealism.*[19]

Starting from scientific realism it is fairly clear that if our actions and reactions were badly adjusted to our environment, we should not survive. Since "belief" is closely connected with expectation and with readiness to act, we can say that many of our more practical beliefs are likely to be true, as long as we survive. They become the more dogmatic part of common sense which, though not by any means reliable, true, or certain, is always a good starting point.

However, we also know that some of the most successful animals have disappeared, and that past success is far from ensuring future success. This is a fact, and, clearly, although we could do something about it, we cannot do much. I mention this point in order to make it quite clear that past biological success never ensures future biological success. Thus, for the biologist, the fact that theories were successful in the past carries no guarantee whatever of success in the future.

---

[19]The epistemological idealist is right, in my view, in insisting that all knowledge, and the growth of knowledge—the genesis of the mutation of our ideas—stem from ourselves, and that without these self-begotten ideas there would be no knowledge. He is wrong in failing to see that without elimination of these mutations through our clashing with the environment there would not only be no incitement to new ideas, but no knowledge of anything. (Compare to *Conjectures and Refutations*, especially 117.) Thus Kant was right that it is our intellect which imposes its laws—its ideas, its rules—upon the inarticulate mass of our "sensations" and thereby brings order into them. Where he was wrong is that he did not see that we rarely succeed with our imposition, that we try and err again and again, and that the result—our knowledge of the world—owes as much to the resisting reality as to our self-produced ideas.

What is the situation? A theory refuted in the past may be retained as useful in spite of its refutation. Thus we can use Kepler's laws for many purposes. But a theory refuted in the past will be *untrue*. And we do not only look for biological or instrumental success. In science we *search for truth*.

A central problem of evolutionary theory is the following: according to this theory, animals which are not well adapted to their changing environment perish; consequently, those which survive (up to a certain moment) must be well adapted. This formula is little short of tautological, because "for the moment well adapted" means much the same as "has those qualities which made it survive so far." In other words, a considerable part of Darwinism is not of the nature of an empirical theory, but is a *logical truism*.

Let us make clear what is empirical in Darwinism and what is not. The existence of an environment with a certain structure is empirical. That this environment changes, but not too fast for long periods of time, and not too radically, is empirical; if it is too radical, the sun might explode into a *nova* tomorrow, and all life on earth and all adaptation will come to an end. In brief, there is nothing whatever in logic which explains the existence of conditions in the world under which life and slow (whatever "slow" may mean here) adaptation to the environment are possible.

But given living organisms, sensitive to environmental changes and changing conditions, and assuming that there is no pre-established harmony between the properties of the organisms and those of the changing environment,[20] we can say something like the following. Only if the organisms produce mutations, some of which are adjustments to impending changes, and thus involve mutability, can they survive, and in this way we shall find, as long as we find living organisms in a changing world, that those which happen to be alive are pretty well adjusted to their environment. If the process of adjustment has gone on long enough, then the speed, finesse, and complexity of the adjustment may strike us as miraculous. And yet, the method of trial and of the elimination of errors, which leads to all this, can be said not to be an empirical method but to belong to the *logic of the situation*. This, I think, explains (perhaps a little too briefly) the logical or *a priori* components in Darwinism.

---

[20]The following remark is here perhaps of interest. Konrad Lorenz writes in *Evolution and Modification of Behaviour* (London: Methuen, 1966), 103f: "Any modifiability which regularly proves adaptive, as learning indubitably does, presupposes a programming based on phylogenetically acquired information. To deny this necessitates the assumption of a prestabilized harmony between organism and environment."

The tremendous biological advance of the invention of a *descriptive and argumentative* language[21] can now be seen more precisely than before: the linguistic formulation of theories allows us to criticize and to eliminate them without eliminating the race which carries them. This is the first achievement. The second achievement is the development of a conscious and systematic attitude of criticism toward our theories. With this begins the method of science. The difference between the amoeba and Einstein is that, although both make use of the method of trial and error elimination, the amoeba dislikes to err while Einstein is intrigued by it: he consciously searches for his errors in the hope of learning by their discovery and elimination. The method of science is the critical method.

Thus evolutionary epistemology allows us to understand better both evolution and epistemology so far as they coincide with scientific method. It allows us to understand these things better on logical grounds.

[...]

---

[21]For the various functions of human language, see, for example, my *Conjectures and Refutations*, 134f.

Chapter 7

Why Scientists Shouldn't Be Surprised by the Popularity of Intelligent Design

Scott O. Lilienfeld

"Nothing in biology makes sense except in the light of evolution." So wrote the eminent Ukrainian-American geneticist Theodosius Dobzhansky (1900–1975) in 1973.[1] More than forty years later, the Gallup polling company reported that twice as many American respondents agreed that "God created humans in present form" than believed that "Humans evolved, God had no part."[2] The poll results appeared in a country that, we are regularly assured, is the most technologically advanced on Earth.

In our next reading, psychologist Scott O. Lilienfeld addresses this curious circumstance. He argues that the main obstacle standing in the way of the public's acceptance of evolutionary theory is not a lack of common sense; rather, it is the public's erroneous belief that common sense is at all a reliable guide to evaluating the natural world.

Scott O. Lilienfeld is Associate Professor of Psychology at Emory University and editor of *The Scientific Review of Mental Health Practice* (https://www. srmhp.org).

---

[1] The quote is the title of a paper by Dobzhanksy, published in *The American Biology Teacher* 35, no. 3 (March 1973): 125–9.

[2] "Evolution, Creationism, Intelligent Design," May 2017, https://news.gallup.com/poll/21814/evolution-creationism-intelligent-design.aspx. The reported results were as follows: "Humans evolved, with God guiding": 38 percent; "Humans evolved, God had no part": 19 percent; "God created humans in present form": 38 percent; "No opinion": 5 percent. It should be mentioned that, according to the same poll, Darwinian evolution has been faring better in recent years, especially among younger Americans: Gallup reported that the overall proportion of Americans who believe in secular evolution has doubled since 1999, from 9 percent to 19 percent. (Note that in the second paragraph of his article, Lilienfeld refers to an earlier Gallup poll.)

The growing popularity of intelligent design (ID) has left most scientists baffled, even exasperated. From their perspective, the match-up between Darwin's theory of natural selection and ID would be laughable were it not so worrisome. It pits one theory backed by tens of thousands of peer-reviewed articles and consistent with multiple lines of converging genetic, physiological, and paleontological evidence against an armchair conjecture that has flown under the radar of peer review and has yet to generate a single confirmed scientific prediction. If the contest were a boxing match, the referee would surely have stopped the fight seconds after the opening bell.

Yet, to the dismay of most scientists, large swaths of the American public not only harbor serious doubts about Darwinian theory but also believe that ID should be taught in science classes. In a 2005 *Gallup* poll, 34 percent of Americans said they believed that Darwinian theory was false and 31 percent favored ID as an explanation for the development of species. As of this writing, at least forty states are considering initiatives to include ID in public school science curricula. Early this past November, the Kansas Board of education voted to adopt standards mandating teachers to raise questions about Darwinian theory. Echoing the language of ID advocates, these standards refer to unexplained gaps in the fossil record and other purported challenges to the scientific status of this theory. (Shortly after this article was written, U.S. District Judge John Jones ruled that ID could not be taught as an alternative to Darwinian theory in Dover, Pennsylvania, public schools. It is too early to tell whether this ruling will affect popular support for ID across the country.)

In response to such developments, many scientists have expressed disdain—even ridicule—for believers in ID. Nobel Prize winner James D. Watson, codiscoverer of the structure of DNA, was quoted recently in *The New York Times* as saying that only people who "put their common sense on hold" doubt evolutionary theory.[3] Still other scientists have attributed malevolent intent to ID advocates. Expressing bewilderment at the ascendance of ID among the American public, one of my academic psychology colleagues abroad recently asked me, "What has happened to good sense and decency in the USA?"

Nevertheless, from the standpoint of psychological science, the only thing about ID's popularity that should surprise us is that so many scientists are surprised by it. Of course, much of the resistance to Darwinian theory is theological, and media coverage of ID proponents has accorded nearly exclusive emphasis to the intimate connection

---

[3]Nicholas Wade, "Darwin's Disciples, Now Friendly Rivals," *The New York Times*, October 27, 2005, https://www.nytimes.com/2005/10/27/health/darwins-disciples-now-friendly-rivals.html.

between ID and fundamentalist Christianity. Nevertheless, religion doesn't tell the whole story.

The other reason for the public's embrace of ID is its compatibility with intuition. Contra Watson, it is Darwinian evolution, not ID, that is glaringly inconsistent with common sense. Political commentator Patrick J. Buchanan's recent statements[4] are illustrative in this regard. Invoking "common sense," "experience," and "reason," Buchanan asked rhetorically, "How can evolution explain the creation of that extraordinary instrument, the human eye?"

Indeed, from the vantage point of commonplace intuition, it is far more plausible to believe that complex biological structures like the peacock's tail and elephant's trunk were shaped by a teleological force than by purposeless processes of mutation and natural selection operating over millions of years. To many laypeople, the latter explanation seems hopelessly farfetched. ID theorists have capitalized on this "argument from personal incredulity," as biologist Richard Dawkins terms it,[5] using the sculpted presidential faces on Mount Rushmore as a thought experiment. If an alien visiting the earth were to happen upon these faces, they ask, would it regard them as the outcome of intentional design or of unguided physical processes? The answer is obvious.

The foremost obstacle standing in the way of the public's acceptance of evolutionary theory is not a dearth of common sense. Instead, it is the public's erroneous belief that common sense is a dependable guide to evaluating the natural world. Even some prominent scientists and science writers have missed this crucial point. In a widely discussed article, psychologists Joaquim Krueger of Brown University and David Funder of the University of California-Riverside recently urged their colleagues to accord more credence to common sense notions of human nature.[6] And in a *New York Times* op-ed this past August, science writer John Horgan[7] called for a heightened emphasis on common sense in the evaluation of scientific theories.

Yet natural science is replete with hundreds of examples demonstrating that common sense is frequently misleading. The world seems flat rather than round. The

---

[4]P. J. Buchanan, "What Are Darwinists Afraid Of?" *Commentary*, August 7, 1995, https://www.realclearpolitics.com/commentary/com-8_7_05_pb.html.

[5]R. Dawkins, "Where'd You Get Those Peepers?" *New Statesman & Society* 8 (June 16, 1995): 29.

[6]J. L. Kreuger and D. C. Funder, "Towards a Balanced Social Psychology: Causes, Consequences, and Cures for the Problem-Seeking Approach to Social Behavior and Cognition," *Behavioral and Brain Sciences* 27 (2004): 313–27.

[7]J. Horgan, "In Defense of Common Sense," *The New York Times*, August 12, 2005. https://www.edge.org/conversation/john_horgan-in-defense-of-common-sense—M. M.

sun seems to revolve around Earth rather than vice versa. Objects in motion seem to slow down on their own accord, when in fact they remain in motion unless opposed by a countervailing force.

In my own discipline of psychology, striking violations of our intuitions abound.[8] Memory seems to operate like a video camera or tape recorder, but research demonstrates that memory is fallible and reconstructive. Most people believe that shifty eyes are good indicators of lying, but research reveals otherwise. Many people believe that opposites attract in relationships, but research shows that opposites tend to repel. The same goes for scores of other common sense claims regarding human nature, such as the belief that expressing anger is typically better than holding it in, that raising children in similar ways leads to marked similarities in their personalities, that most physically abused children grow up to become abusers themselves, and that the levels of psychiatric hospital admissions, crimes, and suicides increase markedly during full moons.

Of course, none of this demonstrates that common sense is worthless. When it comes to gauging our long-term emotional preferences for people and products, research suggests that we are often better off trusting our gut hunches than engaging in dry, objective analyses of the pros and cons.[9] Yet when it comes to discerning the workings of the outside world or the three-pound world inside of our cranial cavities, common sense is an exceedingly undependable barometer of the truth.

Ironically, if scientists took the implications of evolutionary theory more seriously, they would understand why. The human brain evolved to increase the probability that the genes of the body it inhabits make their way into subsequent generations. It did not evolve to infer general principles about the operation of the natural world, let alone to understand itself. It also did not evolve to comprehend vast expanses of time, such as the unimaginable tens or hundreds of millions of years over which biological systems evolved. Consequently, it is hardly surprising that many intelligent individuals, like Patrick Buchanan, glance at the remarkably intricate biological world and conclude that it must have been produced by a designer.

To a substantial extent, the fault in the current ID wars lies not with the general public, but with scientists and science educators themselves. Generations of biology, chemistry, and physics instructors have taught their disciplines largely as collections

---

[8] S. O. Lilienfeld, "Challenging Mind Myths in Introductory Psychology Courses," *Psychology Teacher Network* 15, no. 3 (2005): 1, 4, 6.

[9] Malcolm Gladwell, *Blink: The Power of Thinking without Thinking* (New York: Little, Brown, 2005); D. Myers, *Intuition: Its Powers and Perils* (New Haven, CT: Yale University Press), 2002.

of disembodied findings and facts. Rarely have they emphasized the importance of the scientific method as an essential toolbox of skills designed to prevent us from fooling ourselves. As Alan Cromer and Lewis Wolpert have noted,[10] science does not come naturally to any of us, because it often requires us to think in ways that run counter to our common sense.[11] Mark Twain observed that education requires us to unlearn old habits at least as much as learn new ones. Nowhere is Twain's maxim truer than in effective science education, which asks us to unlearn our reflexive inclination to uncritically trust our perceptions.

Moreover, scientists and the skeptical community at large have long been waging the battle against pseudoscience on only a single front. They have treated each dubious claim, whether it is ID, astrology, or the latest quack herbal remedy, as an isolated thinking error to be combated. In doing so, they have forgotten that the popularity of ID is merely one example of a far broader problem, namely the American public's embrace of pseudoscience in its myriad incarnations. This one-claim-at-a-time approach helps to explain why scientists are losing not only the ID wars, but also the broader war against public belief in pseudoscience. About a quarter of Americans believe that astrology is scientific and about half believe in extrasensory perception despite the virtually wholesale absence of evidence for either assertion. Public acceptance of alternative medicine continues to mount despite controlled studies showing that most popular alternative remedies are ineffective. Slaying each pseudoscientific dragon as it emerges is laudable and at times necessary, but as a long-term strategy against irrationality it is destined to fail.

Indeed, to win the long-term battle against pseudoscience, scientists must look beyond the narrow battles against ID. The real war they must wage is in the classroom. Specifically, scientists need to effect a sea change in how science is taught at the junior high, high school, and college levels. They must teach students not merely the core knowledge of their subject matter, but also an understanding of why researchers developed scientific methods in the first place, namely as an essential safeguard against human error.

To do so, they must inculcate in students a profound sense of humility regarding their own perceptions and interpretations of the world. They should teach students about optical illusions, which demonstrate that our perceptions can mislead us. They

---

[10]A. Cromer, "Uncommon Sense: The Heretical Nature of Science," *Science* 265 (1994): 688; Lewis Wolpert, *The Unnatural Nature of Science* (refer to the entry in the Further Readings for Part II section). — M. M.

[11]See also R.N. McCauley, "The Naturalness of Religion and the Unnaturalness of Science," in *Explanations and Cognitions*, ed. F. Keil and R. Wilson (Cambridge, MA: MIT Press, 2000), 68–85.

should show students how their common sense notions regarding the movements of physical objects, like the trajectory of a ball emerging from a spiral, are often incorrect. They should teach students that even highly confident eyewitness reports are frequently inaccurate. Most broadly, they must counteract what Stanford psychologist Lee Ross calls "naïve realism"—the deeply ingrained notion that what we see invariably reflects the true state of nature.[12] Scientists may well emerge victorious from the current ID battles. Given that the research evidence is overwhelmingly on their side, they certainly deserve to. Yet as Dawkins[13] reminds us, ideas can mutate at least as readily as genes. Unless scientists institute a fundamental change in how science is taught, it may be only a matter of time before a new and even more virulent variant of Intelligent Design emerges. Then scientists will again be surprised at the public's uncritical embrace of it, while shaking their heads in disbelief at the average American's lack of common sense.

---

[12]Lee Ross and Andrew Ward, "Naïve Realism: Implications for Social Conflict and Misunderstanding," in *Values and Knowledge*, ed. T. Brown, E. Reed, and E. Turiel (Hillsdale, NJ: Lawrence Erlbaum Associates, 1996), 103–135.

[13]Richard Dawkins, "Viruses and the Mind," *Free Inquiry* 13 (1993): 34–41.

FOR DISCUSSION OR ESSAYS

In our Part II readings, we have encountered three different descriptions of the relationship between common sense and the sciences: Quine argued that science is, in an important sense, an extension of common sense; Karl Popper argued that common sense and science agree on the crucial issue of metaphysical realism, but should part ways when it comes to their respective theories of knowledge, and Lilienfeld made the case that at least one science, namely evolutionary biology, "is glaringly inconsistent with common sense." A cautionary note: From these three readings, presented in a chronological sequence like this, you should *not* conclude that more recent philosophers, on the whole, have been converging on the view that common sense and the sciences conflict. For one thing, as we know, intellectual trends change and sometimes reverse direction; moreover, these trends—from logical positivism to postmodernism to evolutionary psychology and beyond—have never embraced quite all of the best thinkers of a given generation. At any rate, as far as some of us can discern, the broad question of the compatibility of common sense and the sciences remains as contested today as it has ever been.

- In our reading above, Quine wrote that, "The scientist is indistinguishable from the common man in his sense of evidence, except that the scientist is more careful." In our reading from Part I, by contrast, Mark Kingwell wrote that, "We might say that science is systematic and reflective common sense, but it will therefore conflict with undifferentiated or truly plain common sense [… as well as with …] common nonsense." Discuss the similarities and differences between Quine and Kingwell when it comes to their respective views on science and common sense.

- In an influential paper published several years before "The Scope and Language of Science," Quine wrote that, "Science is a continuation of common sense, and it continues the common-sense expedient of swelling ontology to simplify theory."[14] The word *ontology* in this passage refers to a field of philosophy that describes the most general or "fundamental" categories of reality or being, including alleged entities (such as substances, atoms and void, ideas, or minds), properties (such as red, solubility, polarity, and sourness), and the relations between them. Why might it be more

---

[14]"Two Dogmas of Empiricism," in *From a Logical Point of View* (Cambridge, MA: Harvard University Press, 1953), 45.

commonsensical to prefer a simpler *theory* to a simpler *ontology*, and not vice versa? (Quine provides a hint in our reading above.)

- Compare, contrast, and evaluate what Popper has to say about the common-sense theory of knowledge with G. E. Moore's defense of common sense.

- Quine and Popper had much in common. Each in his own way claimed to defend common sense, and each—again, in his own way—claimed to champion a "naturalized" or evolutionary approach to epistemology. But the two philosophers also differed sharply on key points of orientation. As we have seen, Quine emphasized "conservatism" (or the *coherence* of a particular theory or belief with other well-established theories within a web of beliefs) as one of several virtues of a scientific theory. Meanwhile, Popper emphasized *falsifiability* as the distinctive property of a genuinely scientific theory. Is falsifiability compatible with Quine's picture of a web of beliefs? Explain.

- In his paper in Part I (toward the beginning of Section 2), Mark Kingwell wrote that "plain common sense appears to require and admit of no particular theory or paradigm, whereas science always will." Popper, however, critically discusses (in the section of his paper titled The Mistaken Common-Sense Theory of Knowledge) "the common-sense theory of common-sense knowledge," and this "theory" would appear to qualify as an instance of Kingwell's plain common sense. Could it be that, despite its characteristic incoherence, common sense does after all admit of one or another "theory or paradigm"? Explain why or why not.

- Scott O. Lilienfeld made the case that common sense is an obstacle to science. Is there any way to reconcile this claim with Quine's claim that common sense is continuous with science?

- Lilienfeld is worried about "waging the battle against pseudoscience." What is pseudoscience? (Surely it isn't just any theory that has claimed to be scientific but is false. That would make great scientists of the past, including Isaac Newton and the chemist John Dalton, purveyors of pseudoscience.) Where is Lilienfeld's battle against pseudoscience to be waged? On public school boards? In the laboratory and university biology departments? In courts and state legislatures? In the court of public opinion? In all of the above? Somewhere else?

- A related prompt. Many commentators have lamented the lack of a vibrant and widespread culture of popular science in the United States. Discuss the relationship between popular science and common sense.

FURTHER READINGS FOR PART II

Bacon, Francis. *Novum Organum*. In *Works*, edited by J. M. Robertson. London: Routledge, 1905. First published in 1620, this work includes the English philosopher's discussion of the "Idols of the Mind," with reference to his claim that human thinking normally is biased toward believing in falsehoods.

Descartes, Rene. *Discourse on Method*. In various translations and editions. First published in 1637. Everybody has sufficient *bon sens*, but few use it well, and then only rarely; hence, the need for a skeptical, logical method. Common sense (or at least the common sense of a particular time and place) is unreliable.

Dewey, John. "Common Sense and Science: Their Respective Frames of Reference." In *The Journal of Philosophy* 45, no. 8 (April 8, 1948), 197–208. Neither science nor common sense should be viewed as distinct powers of the mind (or mental faculties), Dewey (1859–1952) writes, but rather as *transactions*, or processes of active adaptation to our environment. In this respect, common sense resembles commerce and even language use. Dewey rejects the assumption that science provides us with a truer or more accurate representation of "reality" than common sense can provide. What distinguishes the two sorts of transactions, rather, has to do with the purposes and uses of these respective sorts of transactions. In the case of common sense, knowing takes place "in order that the necessary affairs of everyday life be carried on," while "the relation is reversed in science as a concern."

Musgrave, Alan. *Common Sense, Science, and Scepticism*. Cambridge: Cambridge University Press, 1993. This is a historical survey, focusing on the arguments of best-known philosophers. Musgrave examines logic, semantics, and the theory of knowledge from the "critical rationalist" position of his former teacher, Karl Popper.

Quine, W. V. O., and Ullian, J. S. *The Web of Belief*. New York: McGraw-Hill, 1970, 1978. This little book was written for nonspecialists, as part of the authors' attempt to provide an overview of Quine's holistic and pragmatic view of belief and science. "The scientific community," the authors write, "is no private club." True, "much that we know does not count as science," our authors write, "but this is often less due to its subject matter than to its arrangement." (Both quoted passages from *Web of Belief*, 3.)

Wolpert, Lewis. *The Unnatural Nature of Science: Why Science Does Not Make (Common) Sense*. Cambridge: Harvard University Press, 1992. Wolpert presents a picture of science (a word he associates with well-known ancient Greek "precursors," as well as with the moderns), as "unnatural," in the sense of counterintuitive. He contrasts the salutary "unnaturalness" of science to supernaturalism, of course, but also to "naturalism," in a special sense of the word, which he associates with misleading common-sense beliefs. (A more standard philosophical definition of the word *naturalism* appears in the introductory section for the Baron d'Holbach reading, in Part III.)

Part III

Common Sense and Religion

Introduction to Part III: Common Sense and Religion

Our readings from G. E. Moore in Part I[1] and from Scott O. Lilienfeld in Part II underscore the remarkable fact that common sense has been summoned to testify for *both* sides in arguments for and against the claims of classical theism.[2] We will now examine this fact at closer quarters.

Whether or not science is compatible with common sense, relations between science and religion have become increasingly uneasy, as have relations between common sense and religion. Over the course of the past four centuries, the sciences have dealt common-sense defenders of classical theism some hard knocks. Astronomy, geology, and evolutionary biology have removed our species step-by-giant-step from the center of the cosmos and the moment of creation, and have battered the old common-sense notion that nature is God's creation.

But as Lilienfeld has noted, scientific thought is one thing, and widespread acceptance of scientific conclusions is something else entirely. If the sciences have dramatically parted ways with classical theism, it would appear that common sense has not done so—at least not as dramatically, and at least as far as the "common" or shared aspect of common sense is concerned. For the past several decades until just recently,[3] public opinion polls have reported that religious belief in America has been more prevalent than it was decades earlier, and that similar trends have appeared in other countries, too.

Our Part III readings might provide some insights. The first one is a version of a widely accepted proof of God's existence. Samuel Clarke's argument proceeds from (1) the observation that *things come into existence*, and (2) the commonsensical generalization (a tautology really) that *every effect has a cause*, and the argument

---

[1]Refer to the brisk Section III of Moore's "Defense of Common Sense."

[2]*Classical theism* is the belief in a personal God who is the creator of the world and is perfect in knowledge, power, and goodness. Instances of classical theism include Judaism, Christianity, and Islam, in their orthodox interpretations.

[3]The Pew Research Center reports that, in the second decade of the twenty-first century, religious belief has declined somewhat, especially among young adults ("U.S. Public Becoming Less Religious," November 3, 2015, https://www.pewforum.org/2015/11/03/u-s-public-becoming-less-religious, accessed March 18, 2019).

concludes that (3) the ultimate cause, or the first cause, of all change must be an unchanging, eternal, and self-existent being. This is a version of a type of proof of God's existence that has been called a *cosmological argument*. The argument, as we will see, is more complicated and interesting than one might think at first.

In the reading after that, English clergyman and utilitarian philosopher William Paley (1743–1805) argues that God's existence can be inferred from empirical evidence of the purposeful, *means-ends ordering* of the passing scene. We have already encountered this view in Part II, when Lilienfeld described the conclusions of proponents of intelligent design in the presence of the peacock's tail and the elephant's trunk. Paley's famous argument from design is observational (or *a posteriori*) in character and draws from what he takes to be an obvious analogy between a pocket watch and the intricately structured human eye.

The third reading consists of twenty-seven sections from the total 206 sections that comprise the main body of *Le Bon Sens*, a book published anonymously in 1772. The author, the German-French writer Paul-Henri Thiry, Baron d'Holbach (1723–1789), pummels belief in God with one objection after another. The barrage, d'Holbach's supporters have assured us, has been launched from the impregnable heights of *le bon sens*—good sense.

In our final reading from Part III, we encounter Alvin Plantinga's argument to the effect that, under certain circumstances that he describes, belief in the existence of God does not need justification in order to count as genuine *knowledge*, and that under the right conditions, such a belief can be held *rationally*, too. The argument is tricky, but at its center is the notion of a *properly basic belief*. He will endeavor to explain.

Chapter 8

A Cosmological Argument for the Existence of God

Samuel Clarke

Clarke believes that the existence of God can be demonstrated conclusively, and he tries to do so in the reading that follows. His argument is short but dense, and it might appear simple at first, but it is not. A few words of explanation are in order.

Clarke begins his argument with the eminently commonsensical assertion that *something exists*. A second premise, for which Clarke will provide a sub-argument, is the equally commonsensical claim that *nothing comes from nothing*. Since nothing comes from nothing, "it is absolutely and undeniably certain," he writes, "that something has existed from all eternity." This, he says, is "one of the most certain and evident truths in the world, acknowledged by all men and disputed by no one": atheists hold that *the world* has always existed, while believers hold that *God* has always existed.

But how could thought lead even one step beyond Clarke's claims in the previous paragraph? After all, the ancient Greek philosopher Parmenides claimed that, from the premise that something exists, he could reason no farther than the claim that *All is One*: that which has always existed is undifferentiated and unchanging. All appearance of change, he said, is an illusion; thus, the problem of the creation of the cosmos never arises.

For Clarke, though, change is not an illusion. Notice that his observation is not merely that something exists; rather, it is that something exists *that changes*: that is to say, something comes into existence—or, to say the same thing, something goes out of existence. (This is clear, for example, from Clarke's reference, in the first paragraph of Section II, to "a series of dependent beings.")

He then invokes the equally commonsensical observation that *whatever comes into existence must have a cause*. In view of these seemingly incontrovertible claims, one of two possibilities must follow: either (1) an *actual infinite regression* of cause and effect[1] has preceded us in time, or (2) the original and ultimate cause of the long series of causes and effects that have preceded us must be a "self-existent being"—a being that has existed eternally, that is uncaused, and is ultimately the cause of everything else. But hypothesis (1), Clarke claims, is "an express contradiction and impossibility": it is impossible, he claims, to conceive of the present state of affairs as the effect of a regression of causes stretching backwards infinitely in time.

Thus, by disjunctive syllogism, Clarke concludes that hypothesis (2) must be the case: "there has existed from eternity some one unchangeable and independent being," a self-existing reality that is not the world, but is rather the first uncaused cause, God.

Samuel Clarke (1675–1729) was an English philosopher, preacher, and theologian. Not included in our reading is Clarke's further argument that God will reward the just and punish the wicked, and that knowing this assures us of the existence of a "future state" (an afterlife) of rewards and punishments.[2]

I

First, then, it is absolutely and undeniably certain that something has existed from all eternity. This is so evident and undeniable a proposition, that no atheist in any age has ever presumed to assert the contrary, and therefore there is little need of being particular in the proof of it. For since something now is, it is evident that something always was, otherwise the things that now are must have been produced out of nothing, absolutely and without a cause, which is a plain contradiction in terms. For, to say a

---

[1] In his writings entitled *Physics* and *Metaphysics*, Aristotle distinguished between *actual* and *potential* infinity. A *potential infinity* is never complete: more and more elements can always be added, but at any given point in time there are never infinitely many of them. The passage of moments forever into the future is an example of a potential infinity. An *actual infinity*, by contrast, is complete and definite, and consists of infinitely many elements. In the philosophy of mathematics, the set of all natural numbers and the infinite sequence of rational numbers are actual infinities. A chain of causes and effects stretching from the present moment backwards in time forever would be another example of an actual infinite regression.

[2] It might be noted that Thomas Reid, whom we met in Part I, also subscribed to the cosmological argument for God's existence (*Essays on the Intellectual Powers of Man*, 6.6, 497, in *The Works of Thomas Reid*, listed in the Readings That Appear in This Book section below), as well as to the argument from design, which we will encounter in our Paley reading below (*Essays on the Intellectual Powers of Man*, 6.6, 508–9).

thing is produced and yet that there is no cause at all for that production, is to say that something is affected when it is affected by nothing, that is, at the same when it is not affected at all. Whatever exists has a cause, a reason, a ground of its existence, a foundation on which its existence relies, a ground or reason why it does exist rather than not exist, either in the necessity of its own nature (and then it must have been of itself eternal), or in the will of some other being (and then that other being must, at least in the order of nature and causality, have existed before it).

That something, therefore, has really existed from eternity, is one of the most certain and evident truths in the world, acknowledged by all men and disputed by no one. Yet, as to the manner how it can be, there is nothing in nature more difficult for the mind of men to conceive than this very first plain and self-evident truth. For how anything can have existed eternally, that is, how an eternal duration can be now actually past, is a thing utterly as impossible for our narrow understandings to comprehend, as anything that is not an express contradiction can be imagined to be. And yet, to deny the truth of the proposition, that an eternal duration is now actually past, would be to assert something still far more unintelligible, even a real and express contradiction. […]

II

There has existed from eternity some one unchangeable and independent being. For since something must needs to have been from eternity, as has been already proved and is granted on all hands, either there has always existed some one unchangeable and independent being from which all other beings that are or ever were in the universe have received their original, or else there has been an infinite succession of changeable and dependent beings produced one from another in an endless progression without any original cause at all. Now this latter supposition is so very absurd that, though all atheism must in its accounts of most things (as shall be shown hereafter) terminate in it, yet I think very few atheists ever were so weak as openly and directly to defend it. For it is plainly impossible and contradictory to itself. I shall not argue against it from the supposed impossibility of infinite succession, barely and absolutely considered in itself, for a reason which shall be mentioned hereafter. But, if we consider such an infinite progression as one entire endless series of dependent beings, it is plain this whole series of beings can have no cause from without of its existence because in it are supposed to be included all things that are, or ever were, in the universe. And it is plain it can have no reason within itself for its existence because no one being in this infinite succession is supposed to be self-existent or necessary (which is the only ground or reason of existence of anything that can be imagined within the thing itself, as will presently more fully appear), but every one dependent on the foregoing. And where no part is necessary, it is manifest the whole cannot be necessary—absolute necessity of existence not being an extrinsic, relative, and accidental denomination but an inward and essential property of the nature of the thing which so exists.

An infinite succession, therefore, of merely dependent beings without any original independent cause is a series of beings that has neither necessity, nor cause, nor any reason or ground at all of its existence either within itself or from without. That is, it is an express contradiction and impossibility. It is a supposing something to be caused (because it is granted in every one of its stages of succession not to be necessarily and of itself), and yet that, in the whole, it is caused absolutely by nothing, which every man knows is a contradiction to imagine done in time, and because duration in this case makes no difference, it is equally a contradiction to suppose it done from eternity. And consequently there must, on the contrary, of necessity have existed from eternity some one immutable and independent being. […]

Otherwise, thus: either there has always existed some unchangeable and independent being from which all other beings have received their original, or else there has been an infinite succession of changeable and dependent beings, produced one from another in an endless progression without any original cause at all. According to this latter supposition, there is nothing in the universe self-existent or necessarily existing. And if so, then it was originally equally possible that from eternity there should never have existed anything at all, as that there should from eternity have existed a succession of changeable and dependent beings. Which being supposed, then, what is it that has from eternity determined such a succession of beings to exist, rather than that from eternity there should never have existed anything at all? Necessity it was not because it was equally possible, in this supposition, that they should not have existed at all. Chance is nothing but a mere word, without any signification. And other being it is supposed there was none, to determine the existence of these. Their existence, therefore, was determined by nothing, neither by any necessity in the nature of the things themselves, because it is supposed that none of them are self-existent, nor by any other being, because no other is supposed to exist. That is to say, of two equally possible things, viz., whether anything or nothing should from eternity have existed, the one is determined rather than the other absolutely by nothing, which is an express contradiction. And consequently, as before, there must on the contrary of necessity have existed from eternity some one immutable and independent being. Which, what it is, remains in the next place to be inquired.

III

That unchangeable and independent being which has existed from eternity, without any external cause of its existence, must be self-existent, that is, necessarily existing. For whatever exists must either have come into being out of nothing, absolutely without cause, or it must have been produced by some external cause, or it must be self-existent. Now to arise out of nothing absolutely without any cause has been already shown to be a plain contradiction. To have been produced by some external cause cannot possibly be true of everything, but something must have existed eternally and independently, as has likewise been shown already. Which remains, therefore, that that being which has existed independently from eternity must of necessity be self-existent. Now to be self-existent is not to be produced by itself, for that is an express contradiction, but it is (which is the only idea we can frame of self-existence, and without which the word seems to have no signification at all)—it is, I say, to exist by an absolute necessity originally in the nature of the thing itself.

Chapter 9

An Argument from Design

William Paley

English clergyman William Paley, like his older contemporary Samuel Clarke, emphasized reason and ordinary experience—two alleged sources or concomitants of common sense. In the next reading, Paley uses analogy and metaphors, many of them drawn from medicine and natural history, to argue that the world is designed and sustained by God. In his day, the timepiece represented the culmination of technological innovation. It is not surprising, then, that his most famous device is the "watchmaker analogy." (Philosophers today similarly draw analogies from digital computers, robotics, artificial intelligence, and genetic engineering.) Arguing by analogy, he insists that those who describe the intricate functional organization of animals as the result of an undirected "principle of order" are providing an entirely unsatisfactory explanation of their function and form.

Paley makes his case intelligently and forcefully; however, he had the misfortune to be writing only a few decades before the publication of Charles Darwin's masterpiece, *The Origin of Species by Means of Natural Selection* (1859). In that book, Darwin describes a thoroughly materialist "principle of order" that provides an elegant explanation for a vast array of natural diversity, and that does so without any reference to a supernatural designer.

William Paley (July 1743–May 25, 1805) was a Christian apologist, a natural theologian, and minister in the Church of England. In the following reading, your editor has occasionally modernized spelling and punctuation, in keeping with contemporary usage.

Chapter I. State of the Argument

In crossing a heath, suppose I pitched my foot against a stone and were asked how the stone came to be there. I might possibly answer that, for anything I knew to the contrary, it had lain there for ever: nor would it perhaps be very easy to show the absurdity of this answer. But suppose I had found a *watch* upon the ground, and it should be enquired how the watch happened to be in that place. I should hardly think of the answer which I had before, given that, for anything I knew, the watch might have always been there. Yet why should not this answer serve for the watch, as well as for the stone? Why is it not as admissible in the second case as in the first? For this reason, and for no other, viz., that, when we come to inspect the watch we perceive (what we could not discover in the stone) that its several parts are framed and put together for a purpose, e.g., that they are so formed and adjusted as to produce motion, and that motion, so regulated as to point out the hour of the day; that, if the several parts had been differently shaped from what they are, of a different size from what they are, or placed after any other manner, or in any other order, than that in which they are placed, either no motion at all would have been carried on in the machine, or none which would have answered the use, that is now served by it. To reckon up a few of the plainest of these parts, and of their offices, all tending to one result: We see a cylindrical box containing a coiled elastic spring, which, by its endeavor to relax itself, turns round the box. We next observe a flexible chain (artificially wrought for the sake of flexure) communicating the action of the spring from the box to the fusee. We then find a series of wheels, the teeth of which catch in, and apply to, each other, conducting the motion from the fusee to the balance, and from the balance to the pointer. And at the same time, by the size and shape of those wheels so regulating that motion as to terminate in causing an index by an equable and measured progression, to pass over a given space in a given time. We take notice that the wheels are made of brass, in order to keep them from rust; the springs of steel, no other metal being so elastic; that over the face of the watch there is placed a glass, a material employed in no other part of the work, but, in the room of which, if there had been any other than a transparent substance, the hour could not be seen without opening the case. This mechanism being observed (it requires indeed an examination of the instrument, and perhaps some previous knowledge of the subject, to perceive and understand it, but being once, as we have said, observed and understood), the inference, we think, is inevitable: that the watch must have had a maker; that there must have existed, at some time and at some place or other, an artificer or artificers who formed it for the purpose which we find it actually to answer, who comprehended its construction and designed its use.

I. Nor would it, I apprehend, weaken the conclusion, that we had never seen a watch made; that we had never known an artist capable of making one; that we were altogether incapable of executing such a piece of workmanship ourselves, or of understanding in what manner it was performed: all this being no more than what is true of some exquisite remains of ancient art, of some lost arts, and, to the generality of mankind, of the more curious productions of modern manufacture. Does one man in a million know how oval frames are turned? Ignorance of this kind exalts our opinion of the unseen and unknown artist's skill, if he be unseen and unknown, but raises no doubt in our minds of the existence and agency of such an artist, at some former time, and in some place or other. Nor can I perceive that it varies at all the inference, whether the question arise concerning a human agent, or concerning an agent of a different species, or an agent possessing, in some respects, a different nature.

II. Neither, secondly, would it invalidate our conclusion that the watch sometimes went wrong, or that it seldom went exactly right. The purpose of the machinery, the design, and the designer might be evident, and in the case supposed would be evident, in whatever way we accounted for the irregularity of the movement, or whether we could account for it or not. It is not necessary that a machine be perfect in order to show with what design it was made: still less necessary, where the only question is whether it were made with any design at all.

III. Nor, thirdly, would it bring any uncertainty into the argument, if there were a few parts of the watch, concerning which we could not discover or had not yet discovered, in what manner they conduced to the general effect; or even some parts, concerning which we could not ascertain, whether they conduced to that effect in any manner whatever. For, as to the first branch of the case: if, by the loss, or disorder, or decay of the parts in question, the movement of the watch were found in fact to be stopped, or disturbed, or retarded, no doubt would remain in our minds as to the utility or intention of these parts, although we should be unable to investigate the manner according to which, or the connection by which, the ultimate effect depended upon their action or assistance, and the more complex is the machine, the more likely is this obscurity to arise. Then, as to the second thing supposed, namely, that there were parts which might be spared without prejudice to the movement of the watch, and that we had proved this by experiment, these superfluous parts, even if we were completely assured that they were such, would not vacate the reasoning which we had instituted concerning other parts. The indication of contrivance remained, with respect to them, nearly as it was before.

IV. Nor, fourthly, would any man in his senses think the existence of the watch, with its various machinery, accounted for by being told that it was one out of possible combinations of material forms; that whatever he had found in the place where he found the watch, must have contained some internal configuration or other, and that this configuration might be the structure now exhibited, viz., of the works of a watch, as well as a different structure.

V. Nor, fifthly, would it yield his enquiry more satisfaction to be answered, that there existed in things a principle of order, which had disposed the parts of the watch into their present form and situation. He never knew a watch made by the principle of order, nor can he even form to himself an idea of what is meant by a principle of order, distinct from the intelligence of the watchmaker.

VI. Sixthly, he would be surprised to hear that the mechanism of the watch was no proof of contrivance, only a motive to induce the mind to think so.

VII. And not less surprised to be informed that the watch in his hand was nothing more than the result of the laws of *metallic* nature. It is a perversion of language to assign any law as the efficient, operative cause of any thing. A law presupposes an agent, for it is only the mode according to which an agent proceeds: it implies a power, for it is the order, according to which that power acts. Without this agent and this power, which are both distinct from itself, the *law* does nothing, is nothing. The expression "the law of metallic nature" may sound strange and harsh to a philosophic ear, but it seems quite as justifiable as some others which are more familiar to him, such as "the law of vegetable nature," "the law of animal nature," or indeed as "the law of nature" in general, when assigned as the cause of phenomena, in exclusion of agency and power, or when it is substituted into the place of these.

VIII. Neither, lastly, would our observer be driven out of his conclusion, or from his confidence in its truth, by being told that he knew nothing at all about the matter. He knows enough for his argument. He knows the utility of the end: he knows the subserviency and adaptation of the means to the end. These points being known, his ignorance of other points, his doubts concerning other points, affect not the certainty of his reasoning. The consciousness of knowing little need not beget a distrust of that which he does know.

Chapter II. State of the Argument Continued

Suppose, in the next place, that the person who found the watch should, after some time, discover that in addition to all the properties which he had hitherto observed in it, it possessed the unexpected property of producing, in the course of its movement, another watch like itself (the thing is conceivable); that it contained within it a mechanism, a system of parts, a mold for instance, or a complex adjustment of laths, files, and other tools, evidently and separately calculated for this purpose. Let us enquire what effect ought such a discovery to have upon his former conclusion?

I. The first effect would be to increase his admiration of the contrivance, and his conviction of the consummate skill of the contriver. Whether he regarded the object of the contrivance, the distinct apparatus, the intricate, yet in many parts intelligible, mechanism by which it was carried on, he would perceive in this new observation nothing but an additional reason for doing what he had already done, for referring the construction of the watch to design and to supreme art. If that construction *without* this property, or which is the same thing, before this property had been noticed, proved intention and art to have been employed about it, still more strong would the proof appear, when he came to the knowledge of this further property, the crown and perfection of all the rest.

II. He would reflect that though the watch before him were *in some sense* the maker of the watch, which was fabricated in the course of its movements, yet it was in a very different sense from that in which a carpenter, for instance, is the maker of a chair; the author of its contrivance, the cause of the relation of its parts to their use. With respect to these, the first watch was no cause at all to the second: in no such sense as this was it the author of the constitution and order, either of the parts which the new watch contained, or of the parts by the aid and instrumentality of which it was produced. We might possibly say, but with great latitude of expression, that a stream of water ground corn: but no latitude of expression would allow us to say, no stretch of conjecture could lead us to think, that the stream of water built the mill, though it were too ancient for us to know who the builder was. What the stream of water does in the affair is neither more nor less than this: by the application of an unintelligent impulse to a mechanism previously arranged, arranged independently of it, and arranged by intelligence, an effect is produced, viz., the corn is ground. But the effect results from the arrangement. The force of the stream cannot be said to be the cause or author of the effect, still less of the arrangement. Understanding and plan in the formation of the mill were not the less necessary for any share which the water has in grinding the corn: yet is this share the same as that which the watch would have contributed to the production of the new watch, upon the supposition assumed in the last section. Therefore:

III. Although it is now no longer probable that the individual watch which our observer had found was made immediately by the hand of an artificer, yet doesn't this alteration in any way affect the inference that an artificer had been originally employed and concerned in the production? The argument from design remains as it was. Marks of design and contrivance are no more accounted for now than they were before. In the same thing we may ask for the cause of different properties. We may ask for the cause of the color of a body, of its hardness, of its heat, and these causes may be all different. We are now asking for the cause of that subserviency to a use, that relation to an end which we have remarked in the watch before us. No answer is given to this question by telling us that a preceding watch produced it. There cannot be design without a designer; contrivance without a contriver; [...] arrangement without anything capable of arranging; subserviency and relation to a purpose, without that which could intend a purpose; means suitable to an end, and executing their office in accomplishing that end, without the end ever having been contemplated, or the means accommodated to it. Arrangement, disposition of parts, subserviency of means to an end, and relation of instruments to a use imply the presence of intelligence and mind. No one, therefore, can rationally believe that the insensible, inanimate watch, from which the watch before us issued, was the proper cause of the mechanism we so much admire in it; could be truly said to have constructed the instrument, disposed its parts, assigned their office, determined their order, action, and mutual dependency, combined their several motions into one result, and that also a result connected with the utilities of other beings. All these properties, therefore, are as much unaccounted for as they were before.

IV. Nor is anything gained by running the difficulty further back, i.e., by supposing the watch before us to have been produced from another watch, that from a former, and so on indefinitely. Our going back ever so far brings us no nearer to the least degree of satisfaction upon the subject. Contrivance is still unaccounted for. We still want a contriver. A designing mind is neither supplied by this supposition, nor dispensed with. If the difficulty were diminished the further we went back, by going back indefinitely we might exhaust it. And this is the only case to which this sort of reasoning applies. Where there is a tendency, or as we increase the number of terms, a continual approach toward a limit, *there,* by supposing the number of terms to be what is called infinite, we may conceive the limit to be attained: but where there is no such tendency or approach, nothing is effected by lengthening the series. There is no difference as to the point in question (whatever there may be as to many points) between one series and another, between a series which is finite and a series which is infinite. A chain, composed of an infinite number of links, can no more support itself, than a chain composed of a finite number of links. And of this we are assured (though we never *can* have tried the experiment) because, by increasing the number of links from ten for instance to a hundred, from a hundred to a thousand, &c. we make not the smallest approach, we observe not the smallest tendency, toward self-support. There is no difference in this respect (yet there may be a great difference in several respects), between a chain of a greater or less length, between one chain and another, between one that is finite and one that is indefinite. This very much resembles the case before us. The machine, which we are inspecting, demonstrates, by its construction, contrivance and design. Contrivance must have had a contriver, design a designer, whether the machine immediately proceeded from another machine or not. That circumstance alters not the case: that other machine may, in like manner, have proceeded from a former machine. Nor does that alter the case: contrivance must have had a contriver. That former one from one preceding it: no alteration still: a contriver is still necessary. No tendency is perceived, no approach toward a diminution of this necessity. It is the same with any and every succession of these machines: a succession of ten, of a hundred, of a thousand; with one series as with another; a series which is finite, as with a series which is infinite. In whatever other respects they may differ, in this they do not. In all equally, contrivance and design are unaccounted for.

The question is not simply How came the first watch into existence? Which question, it may be pretended, is done away by supposing the series of watches thus produced from one another to have been infinite, and consequently to have had no such first, for which it was necessary to provide a cause. This, perhaps, would have been nearly the state of the question if nothing had been before us but an unorganized, unmechanized, substance, without mark or indication of contrivance. It might be difficult to show that such substance could not have existed from eternity, either in succession (if it were possible, which I think it is not, for unorganized bodies to spring from one another), or by individual perpetuity. But that is not the question now. To suppose it to be so is to suppose that it made no difference whether we had found a watch or a stone. As it is, the metaphysics of that question have no place; for, in the watch which we are examining, are seen contrivance, design; an end, a purpose; means for the end, adaptation to the purpose. And the question, which irresistibly presses upon our thoughts, is whence this contrivance and design. The thing required is the intending mind, the adapting hand, the intelligence by which that hand was directed. This question, this demand, is not shaken off by increasing a number or succession of substances, destitute of these properties; nor the more, by increasing that number to infinity. If it be said that, upon the supposition of one watch being produced from another in the course of that other's movements and by means of the mechanism within it, we have a cause for the watch in my hand, viz., the watch from which it proceeded, I deny that for the design, the contrivance, the suitableness of means to an end, the adaptation of instruments to an use (all which we discover in the watch), we have any cause whatever. It is in vain, therefore, to assign a series of such causes, or to allege that a series may be carried back to infinity, for I do not admit that we have yet any cause at all of the phenomena, still less any series of causes either finite or infinite. Here is contrivance, but no contriver; proofs of design, but no designer.

V. Our observer would further also reflect that the maker of the watch before him was, in truth and reality, the maker of every watch produced from it; there being no difference (except that the latter manifests a more exquisite skill) between the making of another watch with his own hands by the mediation of files, laths, chisels, etc., and the disposing, fixing, and inserting of these instruments, or of others equivalent to them, in the body of the watch already made, in such a manner as to form a new watch in the course of the movements which he had given to the old one. It is only working by one set of tools, instead of another.

The conclusion which the *first* examination of the watch, of its works, construction, and movement suggested was that it must have had, for the cause and author of that construction, an artificer, who understood its mechanism, and designed its use. This conclusion is invincible. A *second* examination presents us with a new discovery. The watch is found, in the course of its movement, to produce another watch similar to itself: and not only so, but we perceive in it a system of organization, separately calculated for that purpose. What effect would this discovery have, or ought it to have, upon our former inference? What, as hath already been said, but to increase, beyond measure, our admiration of the skill, which had been employed in the formation of such a machine? Or shall it, instead of this, all at once turn us round to an opposite conclusion, viz., that no art or skill whatever has been concerned in the business, although all other evidences of art and skill remain as they were, and this last and supreme piece of art be now added to the rest? Can this be maintained without absurdity? Yet this is atheism.

Chapter 10

Good Sense without God: Or Free Thoughts Opposed to Supernatural Ideas

Baron d'Holbach

Paul-Henri Thiry, Baron d'Holbach (1723–1789), is best known as the chief editor of the *Encyclopédie*, a vast, alphabetically organized compendium of many fields of human knowledge. Volume I of this first modern encyclopedia appeared in 1751, and by 1772 twenty-eight volumes had been published. The *Encyclopédie* was a sprawling panorama of the passing scene, often quirky, but supposedly stripped of religious dogma.

Baron d'Holbach was an early modern proponent of a position we may call *ontological naturalism*. This is the view that "nature" is just another name for *whatever is real*. Nature happens "of its own accord," without the assistance of the spirits, supernatural forces, or occult agencies that religions specialize in conjuring. Naturalists believe that the sciences are the best way of describing the passing scene, including our own species: the sciences tell us that humans are part of nature, thoroughly and inextricably connected to the rest of it. We do not enjoy a special cosmic status, we are not exempt from physical laws, and we should not expect a fate different from that of any other mortal beings. In d'Holbach's version of naturalism, humans do not have free will: we may feel strongly that we sometimes could have done otherwise, but this, he says, is an illusion.

Baron d'Holbach published his best-known book, *Systeme de la Nature*, anonymously, in 1770. It caused a great stir, and opponents dubbed it "the Atheists' Bible." Two years later, the author privately published a shorter version of the book, titled *Le Bon Sens* ("Good Sense"), and again he kept his name secret. Our selection is from an undated English translation of *Le Bon Sens*. No translator is credited, but it is thought to be a reprint of an English edition published in 1826 by one Richard Carlile.

[...]

§4. The principles of every religion are founded upon the idea of a God. Now, it is impossible to have true ideas of a being who acts upon none of our senses. All our ideas are representations of sensible objects. What then can represent to us the idea of God, which is evidently an idea without an object?[1] Is not such an idea as impossible as an effect without a cause? Can an idea without an archetype be anything, but a chimera? There are, however, divines, who assure us that the idea of God is innate, or that we have this idea in our mother's womb. Every principle is the result of reason; all reason is the effect of experience; experience is acquired only by the exercise of our senses; therefore, religious principles are not founded upon reason, and are not innate.

§5. Every system of religion can be founded only upon the nature of God and man, and upon the relations, which subsist between them. But to judge of the reality of those relations, we must have some idea of the divine nature. Now, the world exclaims, the divine nature is incomprehensible to man, yet ceases not to assign attributes to this incomprehensible God and to assure us that it is our indispensable duty to find out that God, whom it is impossible to comprehend.

The most important concern of man is what he can least comprehend. If God is incomprehensible to man, it would seem reasonable never to think of him, but religion maintains man cannot with impunity cease a moment to think (or rather dream) of his God.

§6. We are told that divine qualities are not of a nature to be comprehended by finite minds. The natural consequence must be that divine qualities are not made to occupy finite minds. But religion tells us that the poor finite mind of man ought never to lose sight of an inconceivable being, whose qualities he can never comprehend. Thus, we see, religion is the art of turning the attention of mankind upon subjects they can never comprehend.

§7. Religion unites man with God, or forms a communication between them, yet do they not say, "God is infinite?" If God be infinite, no finite being can have communication or relation with him. Where there is no relation, there can be no union, communication, or duties. If there be no duties between man and his God, there is no religion for man. Thus, in saying God is infinite, you annihilate religion for man, who is a finite being. The idea of infinity is to us an idea without model, without archetype, without object.

[...]

---

[1]God is "an idea without an object"—that is to say, it is not an idea that we can imagine at all.—M. M.

§17. Can we imagine ourselves sincerely convinced of the existence of a being, whose nature we know not, who is inaccessible to all our senses, whose attributes, we are assured, are incomprehensible to us? To persuade me that a being exists or can exist, I must be first told what that being is. To induce me to believe the existence or the possibility of such a being, it is necessary to tell me things concerning him that are not contradictory, and do not destroy one another. In short, to fully convince me of the existence of that being, it is necessary to tell me things that I can understand.

§18. A thing is impossible, when it includes two ideas that mutually destroy one another, and which can neither be conceived nor united in thought. Conviction can be founded only upon the constant testimony of our senses, which alone give birth to our ideas, and enable us to judge of their agreement or disagreement. That which exists necessarily is that whose nonexistence implies a contradiction. These principles, universally acknowledged, become erroneous when applied to the existence of a God. Whatever has been hitherto said upon the subject is either unintelligible or perfect contradiction, and must therefore appear absurd to every rational man.

[...]

§28. To avoid all embarrassment, we are told "that it is not necessary to know what God is; that we must adore him; that we are not permitted to extend our views to his attributes." But before we know that we must adore a God, must we not know certainly, that he exists? But how can we assure ourselves that he exists, if we never examine whether the various qualities attributed to him do really exist and agree in him? Indeed, to adore God is to adore only the fictions of one's own imagination, or rather, it is to adore nothing.

§29. In view of confounding things the more, theologians have not declared what their God is; they tell us only what he is not. By means of negations and abstractions, they think they have composed a real and perfect being. Mind is that which is *not* body. An infinite being is a being who is *not* finite. A perfect being is a being who is *not* imperfect. Indeed, is there any one, who can form real ideas of such a mass of absence of ideas? That which excludes all idea, can it be any thing but nothing?

To pretend that the divine attributes are beyond the reach of human conception is to grant that God is not made for man. To assure us that in God all is infinite is to own that there can be nothing common to him and his creatures. If there be nothing common to God and his creatures, God is annihilated for man, or at least rendered useless to him. "God," they say, "has made man intelligent, but he has not made him omniscient," hence, it is inferred that he has not been able to give him faculties sufficiently enlarged to know his divine essence. In this case, it is evident that God has not been able nor willing to be known by his creatures. By what right then would God be angry with beings who were naturally incapable of knowing the divine essence? God would be evidently the most unjust and capricious of tyrants, if he should punish an Atheist for not having known what, by his nature, it was impossible he should know.

§30. To the generality of men, nothing renders an argument more convincing than fear. It is therefore, that theologians assure us, *we must take the safest part*; that nothing is so criminal as incredulity; that God will punish without pity every one who has the temerity to doubt his existence; that his severity is just, since madness or perversity only can make us deny the existence of an enraged monarch who without mercy avenges himself on Atheists. If we coolly examine these threatenings, we shall find they always suppose the thing in question. They must first prove the existence of a God, before they assure us it is safest to believe and horrible to doubt or deny his existence. They must then prove that it is possible and consistent that a just God cruelly punishes men for having been in a state of madness that prevented their believing the existence of a being whom their perverted reason could not conceive. In a word, they must prove that an infinitely just God can infinitely punish the invincible and natural ignorance of man with respect to the divine nature. Do not theologians reason very strangely? They invent phantoms, they compose them of contradictions; they then assure us, it is safest not to doubt the existence of these phantoms they themselves have invented. According to this mode of reasoning, there is no absurdity that would not be safer to believe than not to believe.

All children are born Atheists; they have no idea of God. Are they then criminal on account of their ignorance? At what age must they begin to believe in God? It is, you say, at the age of reason. But at what time should this age commence? Besides, if the profoundest theologians lose themselves in the divine nature, which they do not presume to comprehend, what ideas must man have of him?

[...]

§36. It is observed that the wonders of nature are sufficient to lead us to the existence of a God, and fully to convince us of this important truth. But how many are there in the world who have the time, capacity, or disposition, necessary to contemplate Nature and meditate her progress? Men, for the most part, pay no regard to it. The peasant is not struck with the beauty of the sun, which he sees every day. The sailor is not surprised at the regular motion of the ocean; he will never draw from it theological conclusions. The phenomena of nature prove the existence of a God only to some prejudiced men, who have been early taught to behold the finger of God in every thing whose mechanism could embarrass them. In the wonders of nature, the unprejudiced philosopher sees nothing but the power of nature, the permanent and various laws, the necessary effects of different combinations of matter infinitely diversified.

§37. Is there anything more surprising than the logic of these divines, who, instead of confessing their ignorance of natural causes, seek beyond nature, in imaginary regions, a cause much more unknown than that nature, of which they can form at least some idea? To say that God is the author of the phenomena of nature, is it not to attribute them to an occult cause? What is God? What is a spirit? They are causes of which we have no idea. O wise divines! Study nature and her laws, and since you can there discover the action of natural causes, go not to those that are supernatural, which, far from enlightening, will only darken your ideas and make it utterly impossible that you should understand yourselves.

§38. Nature, you say, is totally inexplicable without a God. That is to say, to explain what you understand very little, you have need of a cause which you understand not at all. You think to elucidate what is obscure, by doubling the obscurity, to solve difficulties by multiplying them. O enthusiastic philosophers! To prove the existence of a God, write complete treatises of botany; enter into a minute detail of the parts of the human body; launch forth into the sky, to contemplate the revolution of the stars; then return to the earth to admire the course of waters; behold with transport the butterflies, the insects, the polypi, and the organized atoms, in which you think you discern the greatness of your God. All these things will not prove the existence of God; they will prove only that you have not just ideas of the immense variety of matter, and of the effects, producible by its infinitely diversified combinations, that constitute the universe. They will prove only your ignorance of nature; that you have no idea of her powers when you judge her incapable of producing a multitude of forms and beings, of which your eyes, even with the assistance of microscopes, never discern but the smallest part. In a word, they will prove that, for want of knowing sensible agents, or those possible to know, you find it shorter to have recourse to a word, expressing an inconceivable agent.

§39. We are gravely and repeatedly told, that, *there is no effect without a cause*; that *the world did not make itself*. But the universe is a cause, it is not an effect; it is not a work; it has not been made, because it is impossible that it should have been made. The world has always been; its existence is necessary; it is its own cause.[2] Nature, whose essence is visibly to act and produce, requires not, to discharge her

---

[2]D'Holbach denies Samuel Clarke's claim that the world must be the creation of God: if there is a "being" that has existed from all eternity, he suggests, then that being must be the *world*, in the most comprehensive sense of that word.—M. M.

functions, an invisible mover, much more unknown than herself. Matter moves by its own energy, by a necessary consequence of its heterogeneity. The diversity of motion, or modes of mutual action, constitutes alone the diversity of matter. We distinguish beings from one another only by the different impressions or motions which they communicate to our organs.

§40. You see, that all is action in nature, and yet pretend that nature, by itself, is dead and without power. You imagine, that this all, essentially acting, needs a mover! What then is this mover? It is a spirit, a being absolutely incomprehensible and contradictory. Acknowledge then, that matter acts of itself, and cease to reason of your spiritual mover, who has nothing that is requisite to put it in action. Return from your useless excursions; enter again into a real world; keep to second causes, and leave to divines their first cause, of which nature has no need, to produce all the effects you observe in the world.

[...]

§42. Whence comes man? What is his origin? Did the first man spring, ready formed, from the dust of the earth? Man appears, like all other beings, a production of nature. Whence came the first stones, the first trees, the first lions, the first elephants, the first ants, the first acorns? We are incessantly told to acknowledge and revere the hand of God, of an infinitely wise, intelligent and powerful maker, in so wonderful a work as the human machine. I readily confess that the human machine appears to me surprising. But as man exists in nature, I am not authorized to say that his formation is above the power of nature. But I can much less conceive of this formation, when to explain it, I am told, that a pure spirit, who has neither eyes, feet, hands, head, lungs, mouth nor breath, made man by taking a little clay, and breathing upon it.

We laugh at the savage inhabitants of Paraguay, for calling themselves the descendants of the moon. The divines of Europe call themselves the descendants, or the creation, of a pure spirit. Is this pretension any more rational? Man is intelligent; thence it is inferred that he can be the work only of an intelligent being, and not of a nature, which is void of intelligence. Although nothing is rarer than to see man make use of this intelligence, of which he seems so proud, I will grant that he is intelligent, that his wants develop this faculty, that society especially contributes to cultivate it. But I see nothing in the human machine, and in the intelligence with which it is endued, that announces very precisely the infinite intelligence of the maker to whom it is ascribed. I see that this admirable machine is liable to be deranged; I see, that his wonderful intelligence is then disordered, and sometimes totally disappears; I infer, that human intelligence depends upon a certain disposition of the material organs of the body, and that we cannot infer the intelligence of God, any more from the intelligence of man, than from his materiality. All that we can infer from it is that God is material. The intelligence of man no more proves the intelligence of God, than the malice of man proves the malice of that God, who is the pretended maker of man. In spite of all the arguments of divines, God will always be a cause contradicted by its effects, or of which it is impossible to judge by its works. We shall always see evil, imperfection, and folly resulting from such a cause, that is said to be full of goodness, perfection, and wisdom.

[...]

§45. Upon supposition that God is the author and mover of nature, there could be no disorder with respect to him. Would not all the causes that he should have made, necessarily act according to the properties, essences, and impulses given them? If God should change the ordinary course of nature, he would not be immutable. If the order of the universe, in which man thinks he sees the most convincing proof of the existence, intelligence, power and goodness of God, should happen to contradict itself, one might suspect his existence, or, at least, accuse him of inconstancy, impotence, want of foresight and wisdom in the arrangement of things; one would have a right to accuse him of an oversight in the choice of the agents and instruments, which he makes, prepares, and puts in action. In short, if the order of nature proves the power and intelligence of the Deity, disorder must prove his weakness, instability, and irrationality.

You say that God is omnipresent, that he fills the universe with his immensity, that nothing is done without him, and that matter could not act without his agency. But in this case, you admit that your God is the author of disorder, that it is he who deranges nature, that he is the father of confusion, that he is in man, and he moves him at the moment he sins. If God is every where, he is in me, he acts with me, he is deceived with me, he offends God with me, and combats with me the existence of God! O theologians! you never understand yourselves, when you speak of God.

§46. In order to have what we call intelligence, it is necessary to have ideas, thoughts, and wishes; to have ideas, thoughts, and wishes, it is necessary to have organs; to have organs, it is necessary to have a body; to act upon bodies, it is necessary to have a body; and to experience disorder, it is necessary to be capable of suffering. Whence it evidently follows, that a pure spirit can neither be intelligent, nor affected by what passes in the universe.

[...]

§54. Common sense teaches that we cannot and ought not to judge of a cause but by its effects.[3] A cause can be reputed constantly good only when it constantly produces good. A cause which produces both good and evil is sometimes good and sometimes evil. But the logic of theology destroys all this. According to that, the phenomena of nature, or the effects we behold in this world, prove to us the existence of a cause infinitely good, and this cause is God. Although this world is full of evils, although disorder often reigns in it, although men incessantly repine at their hard fate, we must be convinced that these effects are owing to a beneficent and immutable cause, and many people believe it or feign believe.

Every thing that passes in the world proves to us, in the clearest manner, that it is not governed by an intelligent being. We can judge of the intelligence of a being only by the conformity of the means which he employs to attain his proposed object. The object of God is the happiness of a man. Yet, a like necessity governs the fate of all sensible beings, who are born only to suffer much, enjoy little, and die. The cup of man is filled with joy and bitterness; good is everywhere attended with evil; order gives place to disorder; generation is followed by destruction. If you say that the designs of God are mysterious and that his ways are impenetrable, I answer that, in this case, it is impossible to judge whether God be intelligent.

[…]

§57. When we ask why so many miserable objects appear under the government of a good God, we are told, by way of consolation, that the present world is only a passage, designed to conduct man to a happier one. The divines assure us that the earth we inhabit is a state of trial. In short, they shut our mouths, by saying that God could communicate to his creatures neither impossibility nor infinite happiness, which are reserved for himself alone. Can such answers be satisfactory? The existence of another life is guaranteed to us only by the imagination of man, who, by supposing it, have only realized the desire they have of surviving themselves, in order to enjoy hereafter a purer and more durable happiness. How can we conceive that a God who knows every thing, and must be fully acquainted with the dispositions of his creatures, should want so many experiments, in order to be sure of their dispositions? According to the calculations of their chronologists, our earth has existed six or seven thousand years. During that time, nations have experienced calamities. History exhibits the human

---

[3]D'Holbach's elder contemporary David Hume emphasized this point in Chapter XI of his book *An Enquiry Concerning Human Understanding*, first published in 1748: "When we infer any particular cause from an effect, we must proportion the one to the other, and can never be allowed to ascribe to the cause any qualities, but what are exactly sufficient to produce the effect" (David Hume, *An Inquiry Concerning Human Understanding* [Indianapolis: The Bobbs-Merrill Company, Inc., 1955], 145).—M. M.

species at all times tormented and ravaged by tyrants, conquerors, and heroes; by wars, inundations, famines, plagues, etc. Are such long trials then likely to inspire us with very great confidence in the secret views of the Deity? Do such numerous and constant evils give a very exalted idea of the future state, his goodness is preparing for us? If God is so kindly disposed, as he is asserted to be, without giving men infinite happiness, could he not at least have communicated the degree of happiness, of which finite beings are susceptible here below? To be happy, must we have an *infinite* or *divine* happiness? If God could not make men happier than they are here below, what will become of the hope of a *paradise*, where it is pretended that the elect will forever enjoy ineffable bliss? If God neither could nor would avert evil from the earth, the only residence we can know, what reason have we to presume, that he can or will avert evil from another world, of which we have no idea? Epicurus observed:

> [E]ither God would remove evil out of this world, and cannot; or he can, and will not; or he has neither the power nor will; or, lastly, he has both the power and will. If he has the will, and not the power, this shews weakness, which is contrary to the nature of God. If he has the power, and not the will, it is malignity; and this is no less contrary to his nature. If he is neither able nor willing, he is both impotent and malignant, and consequently cannot be God. If he be both willing and able (which alone is consonant to the nature of God) whence comes evil, or why does he not prevent it?

Reflecting minds are still waiting for a reasonable solution of these difficulties, and our divines tell us that they will be removed only in a future life.

[…]

§66. The inventors of the dogma of eternal hell-torments have made of that God, whom they call so good, the most detestable of beings. Cruelty in men is the last act of wickedness. Every sensible mind must revolt at the bare recital of the torments inflicted on the greatest criminal, but cruelty is much more apt to excite indignation, when void of motives. The most sanguinary tyrants, the Caligulas, the Neros, the Domitians, had, at least, some motives for tormenting their victims. These motives were either their own safety, or the fury of revenge, or the design of frightening by terrible examples, or perhaps the vanity of making a display of their power, and the desire of satisfying a barbarous curiosity. Can a God have any of these motives? In tormenting the victims of his wrath, he would punish beings who could neither endanger his immoveable power nor disturb his unchangeable felicity. On the other hand, the punishments of the other life would be useless to the living, who cannot be witnesses of them. These punishments would be useless to the damned, since in hell there is no longer room for conversion, and the time of mercy is past. Whence it follows, that God, in the exercise of his eternal vengeance, could have no other end than to amuse himself, and insult the weakness of his creatures. I appeal to the whole human race: is there a man who feels cruel enough coolly to torment, I do not say his fellow creature, but any sensible being whatever, without emolument, without profit, without curiosity, without having any thing to fear? Confess then, O theologians, that, even according to your own principles, your God is infinitely more malevolent than the worst of men.

Perhaps you will say that infinite offences deserve infinite punishments. I answer, that we cannot offend a God, whose happiness is infinite; that the offences of finite beings cannot be infinite; that a God, who is unwilling to be offended, cannot consent that the offences of his creatures should be eternal; that a God, infinitely good, can neither be infinitely cruel, nor grant his creatures an infinite duration, solely for the pleasure of eternal torments.

Nothing but the most savage barbarity, the most egregious roguery, or the blindest ambition could have imagined the doctrine of eternal punishments. If there is a God whom we can offend or blaspheme, there are not upon earth greater blasphemers than those who dare to say that this same God is a tyrant, perverse enough to delight, during eternity, in the useless torments of his feeble creatures.

[...]

§86. The Divinity is frequently compared to a king, whose revolted subjects are the greater part of mankind, and it is said, he has a right to reward the subjects who remain faithful to him, and to punish the rebellious. This comparison is not just in any of its parts. God presides over a machine, every spring of which he has created. These springs act agreeable to the manner in which God has formed them; he ought to impute it to his own unskillfulness, if these springs do not contribute to the harmony of the machine, into which it was his will to insert them. God is a created king, who has created to himself subjects of every description; who has formed them according to his own pleasure whose will can never find resistance. If God has rebellious subjects in his empire, it is because God has resolved to have rebellious subjects. If the sins of men disturb the order of the world, it is because it is the will of God that this order should be disturbed.

Nobody dares to call in question the divine justice, yet, under the government of a just God, we see nothing but acts of injustice and violence. Force decides the fate of nations; equity seems banished from the earth; a few men sport, unpunished, with the peace, property, liberty, and life of others. All is disorder in a world governed by a God who is said to be infinitely displeased with disorder.

[...]

§117. Is there any thing more contradictory, impossible, or mysterious, than the creation of matter by an immaterial being, who, though immutable, operates continual changes in the world? Is any thing more incompatible with every notion of common sense, than to believe that a supremely good, wise, equitable, and powerful being presides over nature, and by himself directs the movements of a world full of folly, misery, crimes, and disorders, which by a single word, he could have prevented or removed? In fine, whenever we admit a being as contradictory as the God of theology, how can we reject the most improbable fables, astonishing miracles, and profound mysteries?

[…]

§137. Men are persuaded that religion is to them of all things the most serious, while it is precisely what they least examine for themselves. In pursuit of an office, a piece of land, a house, a place of profit, in any transaction or contract whatever, every one carefully examines all, takes the greatest precaution, weighs every word of a writing, and is guarded against every surprise. Not so in religion; every one receives it at a venture and believes it upon the word of others, without ever taking the trouble to examine.

Two causes concur to foster the negligence and carelessness of men, with regard to their religious opinions. The first is the despair of overcoming the obscurity in which all religion is necessarily enveloped. Their first principles are only adapted to disgust lazy minds, who regard them as a chaos impossible to be understood. The second cause is that every one is averse to being too much bound by severe precepts, which all admire in theory, but very few care to practice with rigor.

[…]

§171. We are perpetually told that without a God there would be no *moral obligation*; that the people and even the sovereigns require a legislator powerful enough to constrain them. Moral constraint supposes a law, but this law arises from the eternal and necessary relations of things with one another, relations which have nothing common with the existence of a God. The rules of Man's conduct are derived from his own nature, which he is capable of knowing, and not from the Divine nature of which he has no idea. These rules constrain or oblige us; that is, we render ourselves estimable or contemptible, amiable or detestable, worthy of reward or of punishment, happy or unhappy, accordingly as we conform to, or deviate from these rules. The law, which obliges man not to hurt himself, is founded upon the nature of a sensible being, who, in whatever way he came into this world, is forced by his actual essence to seek good and shun evil, to love pleasure and fear pain. The law, which obliges man not to injure, and even to do good to others, is founded upon the nature of sensible beings, living in society, whose essence compels them to despise those who are useless, and to detest those who oppose their felicity.

Whether there exists a God or not, whether this God has spoken or not, the moral duties of men will be always the same, so long as they are sensible beings. Have men then need of a God whom they know not, of an invisible legislator, of a mysterious religion and of chimerical fears, in order to learn that every excess evidently tends to destroy them, that to preserve health they must be temperate; that to gain the love of others it is necessary to do them good, that to do them evil is a sure means to incur their vengeance and hatred? "Before the law there was no sin."[4] Nothing is more false than this maxim. It suffices that man is what he is, or that he is a sensible being, in order to distinguish what gives him pleasure or displeasure. It suffices that one man knows that another man is a sensible being like himself, to perceive what is useful or hurtful to him. It suffices that man needs his fellow creature, in order to know that he must fear to excite sentiments unfavorable to himself. Thus the feeling and thinking being has only to feel and think, in order to discover what he must do for himself and others. I feel, and another feels like me; this is the foundation of all morals.

§172. We can judge of the goodness of a system of Morals, only by its conformity to the nature of man. By this comparison, we have a right to reject it, if contrary to the welfare of our species. Whoever has seriously meditated Religion, whoever has carefully weighed its advantages and disadvantages, will be fully convinced, that both are injurious to the interests of Man, or directly opposite to his nature.

"To arms! The cause of your God is at stake! Heaven is outraged! The faith is in danger! Impiety! Blasphemy! Heresy!" The magical power of these formidable words, the real value of which the people never understand, have at all times enabled priests to excite revolts, to dethrone kings, to kindle civil wars, and to lay waste. If we examine the important objects which have produced so many ravages upon earth, it appears that either the foolish reveries and whimsical conjectures of some theologian who did not understand himself, or else the pretensions of the clergy, have broken every social bond and deluged mankind with blood and tears.

[...]

§182. Every man who reasons soon becomes an unbeliever, for reason shows that theology is nothing but a tissue of chimeras: that religion is contrary to every principle of good sense, that it tinctures all human knowledge with falsity. The sensible man is an unbeliever, because he sees that, far from making men happier, religion is the chief source of the greatest disorders, and the permanent calamities with which man is afflicted. The man who seeks his own welfare and tranquility examines and throws aside religion, because he thinks it no less troublesome than useless to spend his life in trembling before phantoms, fit to impose only upon silly women or children.

---

[4]This is a line from the New Testament book of *Romans*, 5:13. The "law" is the Commandments that God is said to have given to the prophet Moses on Mount Sinai. Before then, according to one interpretation, all men sinned as they do today, and they paid the wages of sin, namely, death; nevertheless, they were not "charged" with breaking God's Commandment. Baron d'Holbach's point is that humans do not need divine commandments to tell right from wrong.—M. M.

If licentiousness, which reasons but little, sometimes leads to irreligion, the man of pure morals may have very good motives for examining his religion and banishing it from his mind. Religious terrors, too weak to impose upon the wicked in whom vice is deeply rooted, afflict, torment, and overwhelm restless imaginations. Courageous and vigorous minds soon shake off the insupportable yoke. But those who are weak and timorous languish under it during life, and as they grow old their fears increase.

Priests have represented God as so malicious, austere, and terrible a being, that most men would cordially wish that there was no God. It is impossible to be happy while always trembling. Ye devout! You adore a terrible God! But you hate him; you would be glad if he did not exist. Can we refrain from desiring the absence or destruction of a master, the idea of whom destroys our happiness? The black colors in which priests paint the Divinity are truly shocking, and force us to hate and reject him.

[…]

§195. Perhaps it will be asked, *whether Atheism can be proper for the multitude?* I answer, that any system which requires discussion is not made for the multitude. *What purpose then can it serve to preach Atheism?* It may at least serve to convince all those who reason, that nothing is more extravagant than to fret one's self, and nothing more unjust than to vex others, for mere groundless conjectures. As for the vulgar who never reason, the arguments of an Atheist are no more fit for them than the systems of a natural philosopher, the observations of an astronomer, the experiments of a chemist, the calculations of a geometrician, the researches of a physician, the plans of an architect, or the pleadings of a lawyer, who all labor for the people without their knowledge.

Are the metaphysical reasonings and religious disputes, which have so long engrossed the time and attention of so many profound thinkers, better adapted to the generality of men than the reasoning of an Atheist? Nay, as the principles of Atheism are founded upon plain common sense, are they not more intelligible than those of a theology, beset with difficulties, which even the persons of the greatest genius cannot explain? In every country, the people have a religion, the principles of which they are totally ignorant, and which they follow from habit without any examination: their priests alone are engaged in theology, which is too dense for vulgar heads. If the people should chance to lose this unknown theology, they mighty easily console themselves for the loss of a thing not only perfectly useless, but also productive of dangerous commotions.

It would be madness to write for the vulgar, or to attempt to cure their prejudices all at once. We write for those only who read and reason; the multitude read but little, and reason still less. Calm and rational persons will require new ideas, and knowledge will be gradually diffused.

[…]

Chapter 11

Belief without Argument

Alvin Plantinga

In this paper, the American philosopher Alvin Plantinga does not argue that God exists. He happens to believe that God does exist, and in other writings he presents arguments to support this claim.[1] But in this paper he argues merely that the belief in God can be held rationally. Plantinga defends the reformed theology position, which holds that, under certain circumstances, the believer is within her intellectual rights to believe in God, and that the belief can (and should) proceed from a foundation other than argument. His point resembles a formulation of Thomas Reid's: just as a rational person must accept the existence of mind-independent objects as a first principle (that is to say, without argument), so also, when certain conditions are met, "a person is entirely within his epistemic rights, entirely rational, in believing in God, even if he has no argument for this belief and does not believe it on the basis of any other beliefs he holds."

Under a wide variety of conditions, Plantinga argues, Christian belief (and by easy extension, theistic belief more generally) is *properly basic*, in the sense that it is not derived from any other beliefs. Moreover, he argues, under a variety of conditions, including many instances of testimony, a person can be "warranted" in holding Christian beliefs. If those conditions are met, and if it is true that God exists, then the corresponding belief stands as an item of knowledge—of true, *justified* belief. One of these conditions is the alleged circumstance that, as Plantinga writes, quoting French theologian John Calvin, "there is within the human mind, and indeed by natural instinct, an awareness of divinity." Plantinga appeals to this innate instinct, or *nisus*, to make the case that a person could be "warranted" in believing in God, in a way that he could never be warranted in believing in the Great Pumpkin. "Were it not for the existence of sin in the world," Plantinga adds, "human beings would believe in God to the same degree and with the same natural spontaneity that we believe in the existence of other persons, an external world, or the past."

---

[1] Refer to the Plantinga item in the Further Readings section for Part III, below.

Alvin Plantinga, (b.1932), an American philosopher in the analytic style, is Professor of Philosophy at Calvin College in Grand Rapids, Michigan.

Suppose we think of natural theology as the attempt to prove or demonstrate the existence of God. This enterprise has a long and impressive history—a history stretching back to the dawn of Christendom and boasting among its adherents many of the truly great thinkers of the Western world. Chief among these is Thomas Aquinas, whose work, I think, is the natural starting point for Christian philosophical reflection, Protestant as well as Catholic. Here we Protestants must be, in Ralph McInerny's immortal phrase, Peeping Thomists. Recently—since the time of Kant, perhaps—the tradition of natural theology has not been as overwhelming as it once was: yet it continues to have able defenders both within and without officially Catholic philosophy.

Many Christians, however, have been less than totally impressed. In particular, Reformed or Calvinist theologians have for the most part taken a dim view of this enterprise. A few Reformed thinkers [...] endorse the theistic proofs, but for the most part the Reformed attitude has ranged from indifference, through suspicion and hostility, to outright accusations of blasphemy. And this stance is initially puzzling. It looks a little like the attitude some Christians adopt toward faith healing: it can't be done, but even if it could, it shouldn't be. What exactly, or even approximately, do these sons and daughters of the Reformation have against proving the existence of God? What *could* they have against it? What could be less objectionable to any but the most obdurate atheist?

Proof and Belief in God

[...] According to John Calvin, who is as good a Calvinist as any, God has implanted in us all an innate tendency, or nisus, or disposition to believe in him:

"There is within the human mind, and indeed by natural instinct, an awareness of divinity." This we take to be beyond controversy. To prevent anyone from taking refuge in the pretense of ignorance, God himself has implanted in all men a certain understanding of his divine majesty. Ever renewing its memory, he repeatedly sheds fresh drops. Since, therefore, men one and all perceive that there is a God and that he is their Maker, they are condemned by their own testimony because they have failed to honor him and to consecrate their lives to his will. If ignorance of God is to be looked for anywhere, surely one is most likely to find an example of it among the more backward folk and those more remote from civilization. Yet there is, as the eminent pagan says, no nation so barbarous, no people so savage, that it has not a deepseated conviction that there is a God. So deeply does the common conception occupy the minds of all, so tenaciously does it inhere in the hearts of all! Therefore, since from the beginning of the world there has been no region, no city, in short, no household, that could do without religion, there lies in this a tacit confession of a sense of deity inscribed in the hearts of all.[2]

Indeed, the perversity of the impious, who though they struggle furiously are unable to extricate themselves from the fear of God, is abundant testimony that this conviction, namely, that there is some God, is naturally inborn in all, and is fixed deep within, as it were in the very marrow ... From this we conclude that it is not a doctrine that must first be learned in school, but one of which each of us is master from his mother's womb and which nature itself permits no one to forget.[3]

Calvin's claim, then, is that God has created us in such a way that we have a strong propensity or inclination toward belief in him. This tendency has been in part overlaid or suppressed by sin. Were it not for the existence of sin in the world, human beings would believe in God to the same degree and with the same natural spontaneity that we believe in the existence of other persons, an external world, or the past. This is the natural human condition; it is because of our presently unnatural sinful condition that many of us find belief in God difficult or absurd. The fact is, Calvin thinks, one who doesn't believe in God is in an epistemically substandard position—rather like a man who doesn't believe that his wife exists, or thinks she is like a cleverly constructed robot and has no thoughts, feelings, or consciousness.

Although this disposition to believe in God is partially suppressed, it is nonetheless universally present. And it is triggered or actuated by widely realized conditions:

Lest anyone, then, be excluded from access to happiness, he not only sowed in men's minds that seed of religion of which we have spoken, but revealed himself and daily discloses himself in the whole workmanship of the universe. As a consequence, men cannot open their eyes without being compelled to see him.[4]

---

[2]*Institutes of the Christian Religion*, ed. J. T. McNeill and trans. Ford Lewis Battles (Philadelphia, PA: Westminster Press, 1960), Book I, Chap. iii, Sec. l.

[3]*Institutes,* I, iii, 3.

[4]*Institutes,* V, v, 1.

Like Kant, Calvin is especially impressed in this connection, by the marvelous compages of the starry heavens above:

> Even the common folk and the most untutored, who have been taught only by the aid of the eyes, cannot be unaware of the excellence of divine art, for it reveals itself in this innumerable and yet distinct and well-ordered variety of the heavenly host.[5]

And Calvin's claim is that one who accedes to this tendency and in these circumstances accepts the belief that God has created the world—perhaps upon beholding the starry heavens, or the splendid majesty of the mountains, or the intricate, articulate beauty of a tiny flower—is entirely within his epistemic rights in so doing. It isn't that such a person is justified or rational in so believing by virtue of having an implicit argument—some version of the teleological argument, say. No, he doesn't need any argument for justification or rationality. His belief need not be based on any other propositions at all; under these conditions he is perfectly rational in accepting belief in God in the utter absence of any argument, deductive or inductive. Indeed, a person in these conditions, says Calvin, *knows* that God exists, has knowledge of God's existence, apart from any argument at all.

Elsewhere Calvin speaks of "arguments from reason" or rational arguments:

> The prophets and apostles do not boast either of their keenness or of anything that obtains credit for them as they speak; nor do they dwell upon rational proofs. Rather, they bring forward God's holy name, that by it the whole world may be brought into obedience to him. Now we ought to see how apparent it is not only by plausible opinion but also by dear truth that they do not call upon God's name heedlessly or falsely. If we desire to provide in the best way for our consciences—that they may not be perpetually beset by the instability of doubt or vacillation, and that they may not also boggle at the smallest quibbles—we ought to seek our conviction, in a higher place than human reasons, judgments, or conjectures, that is, in the secret testimony of the Spirit.[6]

Here the subject for discussion is not belief in the existence of God, but belief that God is the author of the Scriptures; I think it is clear, however, that Calvin would say the same thing about belief in God's existence. The Christian doesn't need natural theology, either as the source of his confidence or to justify his belief. Furthermore, the Christian *ought* not to believe on the basis of argument; if he does, his faith is likely

---

[5]*Institutes,* V, v, 2.
[6]*Institutes,* I, vii, 4.

to be unstable and wavering. From Calvin's point of view, believing in the existence of God on the basis of rational argument is like believing in the existence of your spouse on the basis of the analogical argument for other minds—whimsical at best and not at all likely to delight the person concerned.

Foundationalism

We could look further into the precise forms taken by the Reformed objection to Natural Theology; time is short, however; what I shall do instead is tell you what I think underlies these objections, inchoate and unfocused as they are. The reformers mean to say, fundamentally, that belief in God can properly be taken as basic. That is, a person is entirely within his epistemic rights, entirely rational, in believing in God, even if he has no argument for this belief and does not believe it on the basis of any other beliefs he holds. And in taking belief in God as properly basic, the reformers were implicitly rejecting a whole picture or way of looking at knowledge and rational belief; call it *classical foundationalism*. This picture has been enormously popular ever since the days of Plato and Aristotle; it remains the dominant way of thinking about knowledge, justification, belief, faith, and allied topics. Although it has been thus dominant, Reformed theologians and thinkers have, I believe, meant to reject it. What they say here tends to be inchoate and not well articulated; nevertheless the fact is they meant to reject classical foundationalism. But how shall we characterize the view rejected? The first thing to see is that foundationalism is a *normative* view. It aims to lay down conditions that must be met by anyone whose system of beliefs is *rational*, and here "rational" is to be understood normatively. According to the foundationalist, there is a right way and a wrong way with respect to belief. People have responsibilities, duties and obligations with respect to their believings just as with respect to their (other) actions. Perhaps this sort of obligation is really a special case of a more general moral obligation, or perhaps, on the other hand, it is *sui generis*.[7] In any event there are such obligations: to conform to them is to be rational and to go against them is to be irrational. To be rational, then, is to exercise one's epistemic powers *properly*—to exercise them in such a way as to go contrary to none of the norms for such exercise.

Foundationalism, therefore, is in part a normative thesis. I think we can understand this thesis more fully if we introduce the idea of a *noetic structure*. A

---

[7] "in a class by itself"—M. M.

person's noetic structure is the set of propositions he believes, together with certain epistemic relations that hold among him and these propositions. Thus some of his beliefs may be *based on* other things he believes; it may be that there is a pair of propositions A and B such that he believes A *on the basis of* B. Although this relation isn't easy to characterize in a revealing and nontrivial fashion, it is nonetheless familiar. I believe that the word "umbrageous" is spelled u-m-b-r-a-g-e-o-u-s: this belief is based on another belief of mine, the belief that that's how the dictionary says it's spelled. I believe that $72 \times 71 = 5112$. This belief is based upon several other beliefs I hold—such beliefs as that $1 \times 72 = 72, 7 \times 2 = 14, 7 \times 7 = 49, 49 + 1 = 50$, and others. Some of my beliefs, however, I accept but don't accept on the basis of any other beliefs. I believe that $2 + 1 = 3$, for example, and don't believe it on the basis of other propositions. I also believe that I am seated at my desk, and that there is a mild pain in my right knee. These too are basic for me; I don't believe them on the basis of any other propositions.

An account of a person's noetic structure, then, would include a specification of which of his beliefs are basic and which are nonbasic. Of course it is abstractly possible that *none* of his beliefs are basic; perhaps he holds just three beliefs, A, B, and C, and believes each of them on the basis of the other two. We might think this improper or irrational, but that is not to say it couldn't be done. And it is also possible that *all* of his beliefs are basic; perhaps he believes a lot of propositions, but doesn't believe any of them on the basis of any others. In the typical case, however, a noetic structure will include both basic and nonbasic beliefs.

Second, an account of a noetic structure will include what we might call an index of degree of belief. I hold some of my beliefs much more firmly than others. I believe both that $2 + 1 = 3$ and that London, England, is north of Saskatoon, Saskatchewan, but I believe the former more resolutely than the latter [...]

Third, a somewhat vaguer notion; an account of *S*'s noetic structure would include something like an index of *depth of ingression*. Some of my beliefs are, we might say, on the periphery of my noetic structure. I accept them, and may even accept them quite firmly, but if I were to give them up, not much else in my noetic structure would have to change. I believe there are some large boulders on the top of the Grand Teton. If I come to give up this belief, however (say by climbing it and not finding any), that change wouldn't have extensive reverberations throughout the rest of my noetic structure; it could be accommodated with minimal alteration elsewhere. So its depth of ingression into my noetic structure isn't great. On the other hand, if I were to come to believe that there simply is no such thing as the Grand Teton, or no mountains at all, or no such thing as the state of Wyoming, that would have much greater reverberations. And if, *per impossible*,[8] I were to come to think that there hadn't been much of a past (that the world was created just five minutes ago, complete with all its apparent memories and traces of the past), or that there weren't any other persons, that would have even greater reverberations; these beliefs of mine have great depth of ingression into my noetic structure.

Now classical foundationalism is best construed, I think, as a thesis about *rational* noetic structures. A noetic structure is rational if it could be the noetic structure of a person who was completely rational. To be completely rational, as I am here using the term, is not to believe only what is true, or to believe all the logical consequences of what one believes, or to believe all necessary truths with equal firmness, or to be uninfluenced by emotion; it is, instead, to do the right thing with respect to one's believings. As we have seen, the foundationalist holds that there are responsibilities and duties that pertain to believings as well as to actions, or other actions; these responsibilities accrue to us just by virtue of our having the sorts of noetic capabilities we do have. There are norms or standards for beliefs. To criticize a person as irrational, then, is to criticize her for failing to fulfill these duties or responsibilities, or for failing to conform to the relevant norms or standards. From this point of view, a rational person is one whose believings meet the appropriate standards. To draw the ethical analogy, the irrational is the impermissible; the rational is the permissible.

A rational noetic structure, then, is one that could be the noetic structure of a perfectly rational person. And classical foundationalism is, in part, a thesis about such noetic structures. The foundationalist notes, first of all, that some of our beliefs are based upon others. He immediately adds that a belief can't properly be accepted on the basis of just *any* other belief; in a rational noetic structure, *A* will be accepted on the basis of *B* only if *B supports A,* or is a member of a set of beliefs that together support *A*. It isn't clear just what this supports relation is; different foundationalists propose different candidates. One candidate, for example, is *entailment; A* supports *B* only if *B* is entailed by *A,* or perhaps is self-evidently entailed by *A,* or perhaps follows from *A* by an argument where each step is a self-evident entailment. Another and more permissive candidate is probability; perhaps *A* supports *B* if *B* is likely or probable with respect to *A*. And of course there are other candidates.

More important for present purposes, however, is the following claim: in a rational noetic structure, there will be some beliefs that are not based upon others: call these its *foundations*. If every belief in a rational noetic structure were based upon other beliefs, the structure in question would contain infinitely many beliefs. However things

---

[8]"although impossible"—M. M.

may stand for more powerful intellects—angelic intellects, perhaps—human beings aren't capable of believing infinitely many propositions. Among other things, one presumably doesn't believe a proposition one has never heard of, and no one has had time, these busy days, to have heard of infinitely many propositions. So every rational noetic structure has a foundation.

Suppose we say that *weak* foundationalism is the view that (1) every rational noetic structure has a foundation, and (2) in a rational noetic structure, nonbasic belief is proportional in strength to support from the foundations. When I say Reformed thinkers have meant to reject foundationalism, I do not mean to say that they intended to reject weak foundationalism. On the contrary, the thought of many of them tends to support or endorse weak foundationalism. What then do they mean to reject? Here we meet a further and fundamental feature of classic varieties of foundationalism: they all lay down certain conditions of proper or rational basicality. From the foundationalist point of view, not just any kind of belief can be found in the foundations of a rational noetic structure; a belief, to be properly basic (i.e., basic in a rational noetic structure) must meet certain conditions. It is plausible to see Thomas Aquinas, for example, as holding that a proposition is properly basic for a person only if it is self-evident to him (such that his understanding or grasping it is sufficient for his seeing it to be true) or "evident to the senses," as he puts it. By this latter term I think he means to refer to propositions whose truth or falsehood we can determine by looking or listening or employing some other sense—such propositions as:

(1) There is a tree before me

(2) I am wearing shoes

and

(3) That tree's leaves are yellow

Many foundationalists have insisted that propositions basic in a rational noetic structure must be *certain* in some important sense. Thus it is plausible to see Descartes as holding that the foundations of a rational noetic structure don't include such propositions as (1), (2), and (3) but more cautious claims—claims about one's own mental life, for example:

(4) It seems to me that I see a tree

(5) I seem to see something green

or, as Professor Chisholm puts it,

(6) I am appeared greenly to

Propositions of this latter sort seem to enjoy a kind of immunity from error not enjoyed by those of the former. I could be mistaken in thinking I see a pink rat; perhaps I am hallucinating or the victim of an illusion. But it is at the least very much harder to see that I could be mistaken in believing that I *seem* to see a pink rat, in believing that I am appeared pinkly (or pink ratty) to. Suppose we say that a proposition with respect to which I enjoy this sort of immunity from error is *incorrigible* for me; then perhaps Descartes means to hold that a proposition is properly basic for S only if it is either self-evident or incorrigible for S.

Aquinas and Descartes, we might say, are *strong* foundationalists; they accept weak foundationalism and add some conditions for proper basicality. Ancient and medieval foundationalists tended to hold that a proposition is properly basic for a person only if it is either self-evident or evident to the senses; modern foundationalists— Descartes, Locke, Leibniz and the like—tended to hold that a proposition is properly basic for S only if either self-evident or incorrigible for S. Of course this is a historical generalization and is thus subject to contradiction by scholars, such being the penalty for historical generalization, but perhaps it is worth the risk. And now suppose we say that *classical foundationalism* is the disjunction of ancient and medieval with modern foundationalism.

The Reformed Rejection of Classical Foundationalism

These Reformed thinkers, I believe, are best understood as rejecting classical foundationalism. They were inclined to accept weak foundationalism, I think, but they were completely at odds with the idea that the foundations of a rational noetic structure can at most include propositions that are self-evident or evident to the senses or incorrigible. In particular, they were prepared to insist that a rational noetic structure can include belief in God as basic. […]

In the passages I quoted earlier on, Calvin claims the believer doesn't need argument— doesn't need it, among other things, for epistemic respectability. We may understand him as holding, I think, that a rational noetic structure may perfectly well contain belief in God among its foundations. Indeed, he means to go further, and in two separate directions. In the first place, he thinks a Christian *ought* not believe in God on the basis of other propositions; a proper and well-formed Christian noetic structure will *in fact* have belief in God among its foundations. And in the second place Calvin claims that one who takes belief in God as basic can nonetheless know that God exists. Calvin holds that one can *rationally accept* belief in God as basic; he also claims that one can *know* that God exists even if he has no argument, even if he does not believe on the basis of other propositions. A weak foundationalist is likely to hold that some properly basic beliefs are such that anyone who accepts them *knows* them. More exactly, he is likely to hold that among the beliefs properly basic for a person *S,* some are such that if *S* accepts them *S* knows them. A weak foundationalist could go on to say that *other* properly basic beliefs can't be known, if taken as basic, but only rationally believed, and he might think of the existence of God as a case in point. Calvin will have none of this; as he sees it, one needs no arguments to know that God exists.

Among the central contentions of these Reformed thinkers, therefore, are the claims that belief in God is properly basic, and the view that one who takes belief in God as basic can also *know* that God exists.

The Great Pumpkin Objection

Now I enthusiastically concur in these contentions of Reformed epistemology, and by way of conclusion I want to defend them against a popular objection. It is tempting to raise the following sort of question. If belief in God is properly basic, why can't just any belief be properly basic? Couldn't we say the same for any bizarre aberration we can think of? What about voodoo or astrology? What about the belief that the Great Pumpkin returns every Halloween? Could I properly take that as basic? And if I can't, why can I properly take belief in God as basic? Suppose I believe that if I flap my arms with sufficient vigor, I can take off and fly about the room; could I defend myself against the charge of irrationality by claiming this belief is basic? If we say that belief in God is properly basic, won't we be committed to holding that just anything, or nearly anything, can properly be taken as basic, thus throwing wide the gates to irrationalism and superstition?

Certainly not. What might lead one to think that the Reformed epistemologist is in this kind of trouble? The fact that he rejects the criteria for proper basicality purveyed by the classical foundationalist? But why should *that* be thought to commit him to such tolerance of irrationality? [...]

[C]riteria for proper basicality must be reached from below rather than above; they should not be presented as *obiter dicta,*[9] but argued to and tested by a relevant set of examples. But there is no reason to assume, in advance, that everyone will agree on the examples. The Christian will of course suppose that belief in God is entirely proper and rational; if he doesn't accept this belief on the basis of other propositions, he will conclude that it is basic for him and quite properly so. Followers of Bertrand Russell and Madalyn Murray O'Hair may disagree, but how is that relevant? Must my

---

[9]"remarks in passing"—M. M.

criteria, or those of the Christian community, conform to their examples? Surely not. The Christian community is responsible to its set of examples, not to theirs.

Accordingly, the Reformed epistemologist can properly hold that belief in the Great Pumpkin is not properly basic, even though he holds that belief in God is properly basic and even if he has no full-fledged criterion of proper basicality. Of course he is committed to supposing that there is a relevant *difference* between belief in God and belief in the Great Pumpkin, if he holds that the former but not the latter is properly basic. But this should be no great embarrassment; there are plenty of candidates. Thus the Reformed epistemologist may concur with Calvin in holding that God has implanted in us a natural tendency to see his hand in the world around us; the same cannot be said for the Great Pumpkin, there being no Great Pumpkin and no natural tendency to accept beliefs about the Great Pumpkin.

By way of conclusion then, the Reformed objection to natural theology, unformed and inchoate as it is, may best be seen as a rejection of classical foundationalism. As the Reformed thinker sees things, being self-evident, or incorrigible, or evident to the senses is not a necessary condition of proper basicality. He goes on to add that belief in God is properly basic. He is not thereby committed, even in the absence of a general criterion of proper basicality, to suppose that just any or nearly any belief—belief in the Great Pumpkin, for example—is properly basic. Like everyone should, he begins with examples, and he may take belief in the Great Pumpkin as a paradigm of irrational basic belief.

FOR DISCUSSION OR ESSAYS

- Clarke posed the dilemma: either there has always existed an unchanging and independent being, "or else there has been an infinite succession of changeable and dependent beings produced one from another in an endless progression without any original cause at all." Explain in your own words why Clarke rejected the second horn of this dilemma: what did he mean when he wrote that an actual infinite regression of causes and effects is "an express contradiction and impossibility"? Do you agree? Why or why not?

- Clarke held that every event is an *effect* and a *cause*. But consider the following formulation: the universe (multiverse, megaverse, or whatever) is a singular "thing," namely, *that without which causes and effects would not exist in the first place*, and as such, it is not itself either a cause or an effect. If one were to accept this formulation, then how might it impact Clarke's Cosmological Argument?

- Paley wrote that, "There cannot be [...] arrangement, without anything capable of arranging; subserviency and relation to a purpose, without that which could intend a purpose." This seemed obvious to him and his readers. What do you think?

- A related question. Referring to a law of nature, Paley wrote that it "presupposes an agent: for it is only the mode according to which an agent proceeds." An agent, he writes, "implies a power; for it is the order according to which that power acts. Without this agent, without this power, which are both distinct from itself, the law does nothing, is nothing ..." Is he convincing here? Why or why not? (Think of different uses of the word *law*.)

- Baron d'Holbach claimed that the very notion of an infinite and inscrutable God is "incomprehensible to man," and thus we cannot even make sense of the formulation *God exists*, let alone believe it. Plantinga, by contrast, argued that under certain circumstances belief in God can be held rationally, even in the absence of arguments. Compare and contrast these conflicting views.

- Describe Plantinga's account of the Reformed epistemologists' rejection of "strong" or classical foundationalism. Are you convinced by his response to the Great Pumpkin objection? Why or why not?

- More than one reviewer has noted that, if believers may take belief in God as properly basic, then by the same argument atheists may take *disbelief* as basic. Belief in the existence of a spouse might be basic because, in view of the evidence, no clear alternatives seem plausible; however, this is not the case when it comes to belief in God. What do you think? Explain.

FURTHER READINGS FOR PART III

Mounds of literature accumulate annually, with titles like *Common Sense Religion, Common Sense Spirituality*, and *Common Sense Catechesis*. There is even a book in print entitled *Sense & Nonsense about Angels and Demons*, which promises to "cut through the clutter" and sort out this supernatural menagerie in a trustworthy way. Since this sort of literature is unlikely to convince a readership beyond the choir, very little of it is useful for our purposes. Of course, there is a great deal of literature written by champions of atheism, too, and it, too, is growing. Much of the latter body of literature could be described as updated versions of arguments we have encountered in d'Holbach. Here are several accessible titles by well-known authors on both sides of the topic of common experience and faith:

Dewey, John. *A Common Faith*. New Haven, CT: Yale University Press, 1934, 1962. In this short book, the American pragmatist philosopher proposes to dissociate "the religious" from "the supernatural." The latter has to do with "the necessity for a Supernatural Being and for an immortality that is beyond the power of nature." Dewey, of course, recommends that we scrap the supernatural. Thus unencumbered, he writes, "for the first time, the religious aspect of experience will be free to develop freely on its own account."

Hume, David. *Dialogues Concerning Natural Religion*. In various editions. The work was completed in 1776 and first published in 1779. Hume throws into doubt William Paley's assumptions about natural law and agency, analogical reasoning with reference to the causes of observed regularities in nature, and the very idea of raising thinking to the status of a cosmic principle of order.

John Paul II. *Fides et Ratio*. Encyclical Letter to the Bishops of the Catholic Church on the Relationship between Faith and Reason. Delivered on September 14, 1998. Available at: http://w2.vatican.va/content/john-paul-ii/en/encyclicals/documents/hf_jp-ii_enc_14091998_fides-et-ratio.html. The late Bishop of Rome revisits the relationship between faith, on the one hand, and philosophy and science, on the other. There is, he says, an "implicit philosophy" held by all, one that provides a reference point for rival philosophical traditions. He does not explicitly mention common sense, but the notion is there by implication in the encyclical. Christianity, he writes, is consistent with this "implicit philosophy": it is a rational religion and can defend itself.

Mackie, John L. *The Miracle of Theism: Arguments for and against the Existence of God*. Oxford: Clarendon Press, 1982. The book includes Mackie's "Critique of the Cosmological Argument."

Martin, Michael. *Atheism: A Philosophical Justification*. Philadelphia, PA: Temple University Press, 1990. Martin, a Professor of Philosophy at Boston University, has written a clear, brief response to Plantinga's paper, "Belief without Argument."

Plantinga, Alvin. *The Nature of Necessity*. Oxford: The Clarendon Press, 1974. Plantinga presents his "modal ontological argument" for the existence of God. The argument, in (overly?) simplified outline, may be represented as follows: *(i) it is possible that God exists; (ii) either it is not possible that God exists, or it is necessary that God exists; (iii) therefore, it is necessary that God exists; (iv) so God exists.* Premise (ii) is the heart of this ontological argument, and, unsurprisingly, it has been the target of skeptical attack. (Premise (i) has been the target of skeptical attack, too, including the first six or seven of d'Holbach's remarks, in our reading above.)

Part IV

Common Sense and Morality

Introduction to Part IV:
Common Sense and Morality

The anthropologist Clifford Geertz once wrote that, "common sense, or some kindred conception, has become a central category, almost *the* central category, in a wide range of modern philosophical systems."[1] We have seen that this is true, for example, when it comes to the field of philosophy of science. As we will see, it is especially true of ethics, the philosophical consideration of morality. So much has been written on the topic of common sense and morality that it is a hopeless task to try, by selecting a few readings, to survey the leading views. For our purposes, though, it will be enough if the following three readings give the reader a feel for one or two of the main approaches to the topic. The Further Readings section for Part IV will provide interested readers with a slightly broader range of views.

The author of our first reading, "The Evolution of the Moral Sense," is Charles Darwin, the founder of modern evolutionary biology. The reading is from *The Descent of Man, and Selection in Relation to Sex* (1871). Here, the great English naturalist is not presenting us with a moral theory, properly speaking; rather, he is presenting us with a theory about the origins of morality. He is not mainly concerned with the question *what should I do?* Rather, he is concerned with the question: *where do moral values come from?* He is not doing ethics, then; rather, he is doing *metaethics*.[2] According to Darwin, our common-sense notions of right and wrong, and our moral behavior, too, are rooted in a social instinct that predates our species.

In the rich and suggestive reading after that, the American philosopher Stanley Rosen sets himself the now-familiar task of considering whether common sense could or should regulate philosophical discourse, and he undertakes to do this commonsensically. Rosen first examines the role that practical intelligence (or prudence) plays when it comes to determining the "fundamental ends" of human behavior. This leads to reflections on the relationship between common sense on the one hand and technical and historical knowledge on the other, and to the crucial question of how to order and rank "basic motives" or "fundamental ends of human

---

[1]Geertz (see the item in the Further Readings section for Part I).

[2]The *Internet Encyclopedia of Philosophy* provides a nice distinction between *metaethics* and *ethics* proper: "Whereas the fields of applied ethics and normative theory focus on *what is moral*, metaethics focuses on *what morality itself is*."

behavior," to determine, in case of conflict, which overrides which. After noting defects of common sense, he concludes that providing a clear and self-consistent commonsensical explanation of common sense is impossible, and therefore that "common sense is altogether incapable of regulating philosophy."

Our third and last reading in Part IV is a long extract from Mortimer Adler's paper, "The Common-Sense View Philosophically Developed: A Teleological Ethics." Following Aristotle, Adler makes the case that there is one ultimate purpose or "end" for humans, namely, to seek that which makes for a really good life as a whole. With this end in view, Adler says, we recognize a corresponding duty, namely, to achieve a life that is really good as a whole. Thus, his common-sense moral philosophy is both a duty-centered ethics, and at the same time, an ethics of means and ends. Adler then considers several "insights that express the moral wisdom of a teleological ethics." In this connection, he discusses "moral virtue" and prudence, as well as freedom in more than one meaning of the word, before winding up the discussion by inspecting the goods that bring about the happiness that makes up such an important part of the good life.

Chapter 12

The Evolution of the Moral Sense: Concluding Remarks

Charles Darwin

Darwin's book *The Descent of Man, and Selection in Relation to Sex*, published twelve years after *The Origin of Species* (1859), focuses on the evolution of one particular social species, namely humans. In our selection from the book, Darwin attempts to give a naturalistic or nonsupernatural answer to the German philosopher Immanuel Kant's question: Where does the common moral sense of duty come from? As we will see, Darwin's answer has much to do with his notion of *sympathy*, a notion that, he writes, "forms an essential part of the social instinct, and is indeed its foundation-stone." He then describes how this social instinct is itself a result of evolution by natural selection, and concludes that, "the so-called moral sense is aboriginally derived from the social instincts."

   In the final section of our reading, Darwin contrasts his account of the origin of the "moral sense" to the ideas of certain influential thinkers of his day. The *utilitarian* philosophers held that an action is right or wrong depending on its consequences: if it promotes the greatest happiness of the greatest number of people, then it is right. Darwin does not deny the greatest happiness principle as a *standard* of conduct, but he rejects it as a *motive*, and he denies that it could account for the origin of our common moral sense. Rather, he says, the deeply rooted "social instinct" accounts for much of our conduct, in which no anticipation of consequences, whether narrowly hedonistic or more broadly utilitarian, appears to play a role. Darwin advises us to take "the general good," or the welfare of the community, as the standard of morality, rather than the greatest happiness—but this, he adds without elaboration, "would perhaps require some limitation on account of political ethics."

   To some readers today, Darwin's account—with its homey observations of the behavior of animals, its anecdotes about the "immorality of savages," and its armchair psychology—might sound like common sense in the worst sense of the term. In Darwin's day, though, it did not sound like any kind of common sense at all. Darwin broke with some of the most basic assumptions of his predecessors: "man," he insisted, is not a cosmically distinct half animal, and humans did not begin as isolated nuclear families in the forest, who later came together to form societies. The opinions of paleontologists and anthropologists have changed greatly in the century and a half since *The Descent of Man*; nevertheless, Darwin's influence on biology is as strong as ever. These days, as Theodosius Dobzhansky has noted in a passage quoted earlier, nothing in biology makes sense except in light of evolution by natural selection.

Man a Social Animal

Every one will admit that man is a social being. We see this in his dislike of solitude, and in his wish for society beyond that of his own family. Solitary confinement is one of the severest punishments which can be inflicted. Some authors suppose that man primevally lived in single families, but at the present day, though single families, or only two or three together, roam the solitudes of some savage lands, they always, as far as I can discover, hold friendly relations with other families inhabiting the same district. Such families occasionally meet in council, and unite for their common defense. It is no argument against savage man[1] being a social animal, that the tribes inhabiting adjacent districts are almost always at war with each other, for the social instincts never extend to all the individuals of the same species. Judging from the analogy of the majority of the Quadrumana[2] it is probable that the early ape-like progenitors of man were likewise social, but this is not of much importance for us. Although man, as he now exists, has few special instincts, having lost any which his early progenitors may have possessed, this is no reason why he should not have retained from an extremely remote period some degree of instinctive love and sympathy for his fellows. We are indeed all conscious that we do possess

---

[1] In the terminology of Darwin's day, a "savage society" would correspond roughly to the sort of communal society that we today would call a hunter-gatherer band. The next rung "up" on the cultural ladder was "barbarism," which appeared with animal husbandry, agriculture, and rigid political authority. The third rung, "civilization," appeared with writing systems, and we are assured that it is with us today.—M. M.

[2] Nonhuman primates that have hand-shaped feet.—M. M.

such sympathetic feelings,[3] but our consciousness does not tell us whether they are instinctive, having originated long ago in the same manner as with the lower animals, or whether they have been acquired by each of us during our early years. As man is a social animal, it is almost certain that he would inherit a tendency to be faithful to his comrades, and obedient to the leader of his tribe, for these qualities are common to most social animals. He would consequently possess some capacity for self-command. He would from an inherited tendency be willing to defend, in concert with others, his fellow men, and would be ready to aid them in any way, which did not too greatly interfere with his own welfare or his own strong desires.

The social animals which stand at the bottom of the scale are guided almost exclusively, and those which stand higher in the scale are largely guided, by special instincts in the aid which they give to the members of the same community, but they are likewise in part impelled by mutual love and sympathy, assisted apparently by some amount of reason. Although man, as just remarked, has no special instincts to tell him how to aid his fellow men, he still has the impulse, and with his improved intellectual faculties would naturally be much guided in this respect by reason and experience. Instinctive sympathy would also cause him to value highly the approbation of his fellows for, as Mr. Bain has clearly shown,[4] the love of praise and the strong feeling of glory, and the still stronger horror of scorn and infamy, "are due to the workings of sympathy." Consequently man would be influenced in the highest degree by the wishes, approbation, and blame of his fellow men, as expressed by their gestures and language. Thus the social instincts, which must have been acquired by man in a very rude state, and probably even by his early ape-like progenitors, still give the impulse to some of his best actions, but his actions are in a higher degree determined by the expressed wishes and judgment of his fellow men, and unfortunately very often by his own strong selfish desires. But as love, sympathy and self-command become strengthened by habit, and as the power of reasoning becomes clearer, so that man can value justly the judgments of his fellows, he will feel himself impelled, apart from any transitory pleasure or pain, to certain lines of conduct. He might then declare—not that any barbarian or uncultivated man could thus think—I am the supreme judge of my own conduct, and in the words of Kant, I will not in my own person violate the dignity of humanity.

---

[3] Hume remarks, "There seems a necessity for confessing that the happiness and misery of others are not spectacles altogether indifferent to us, but that the view of the former ... communicates a secret joy; the appearance of the latter ... throws a melancholy damp over the imagination" (*An Enquiry Concerning the Principles of Morals*, 1751 edition, 132).

[4] *Mental and Moral Science* (1868), 254.

The More Enduring Social Instincts Conquer the Less Persistent Instincts

We have not, however, as yet considered the main point, on which, from our present point of view, the whole question of the moral sense turns. Why should a man feel that he ought to obey one instinctive desire rather than another? Why is he bitterly regretful, if he has yielded to a strong sense of self-preservation, and has not risked his life to save that of a fellow creature? Or why does he regret having stolen food from hunger?

It is evident in the first place, that with mankind the instinctive impulses have different degrees of strength; a savage will risk his own life to save that of a member of the same community, but will be wholly indifferent about a stranger: a young and timid mother urged by the maternal instinct will, without a moment's hesitation, run the greatest danger for her own infant, but not for a mere fellow creature. Nevertheless many a civilized man, or even boy, who never before risked his life for another, but full of courage and sympathy, has disregarded the instinct of self-preservation, and plunged at once into a torrent to save a drowning man, though a stranger. In this case man is impelled by the same instinctive motive, which made the heroic little American monkey, formerly described, save his keeper, by attacking the great and dreaded baboon. Such actions as the above appear to be the simple result of the greater strength of the social or maternal instincts rather than that of any other instinct or motive, for they are performed too instantaneously for reflection, or for pleasure or pain to be felt at the time; though, if prevented by any cause, distress or even misery might be felt. In a timid man, on the other hand, the instinct of self-preservation might be so strong, that he would be unable to force himself to run any such risk, perhaps not even for his own child.

I am aware that some persons maintain that actions performed impulsively, as in the above cases, do not come under the dominion of the moral sense, and cannot be called moral. They confine this term to actions done deliberately, after a victory over opposing desires, or when prompted by some exalted motive. But it appears scarcely possible to draw any clear line of distinction of this kind.[5] As

---

[5] I refer here to the distinction between what has been called *material* and *formal* morality. I am glad to find that Professor Huxley (*Critiques and Addresses* [1873], 287) takes the same view on this subject as I do. Mr. Leslie Stephen remarks, "the metaphysical distinction between material and formal morality is as irrelevant as other such distinctions" (*Essays on Freethinking and Plain Speaking* [1873], 83).

[Darwin, then, rejects the distinction between, on the one hand, moral actions based on a decision procedure (such as, say, "follow your conscience," or "do what promotes the greatest happiness"), and on the other hand, moral actions undertaken "impulsively," without deliberation. The former would be instances of *formal morality*; the latter would be instances of *material morality*.—M. M.].

far as exalted motives are concerned, many instances have been recorded of savages, destitute of any feeling of general benevolence toward mankind, and not guided by any religious motive, who have deliberately sacrificed their lives as prisoners, [6]rather than betray their comrades, and surely their conduct ought to be considered as moral. As far as deliberation and the victory over opposing motives are concerned, animals may be seen doubting between opposed instincts, in rescuing their offspring or comrades from danger; yet their actions, though done for the good of others, are not called moral. Moreover, anything performed very often by us will at last be done without deliberation or hesitation, and can then hardly be distinguished from an instinct; yet surely no one will pretend that such an action ceases to be moral. On the contrary, we all feel that an act cannot be considered as perfect, or as performed in the most noble manner, unless it be done impulsively, without deliberation or effort, in the same manner as by a man in whom the requisite qualities are innate. He who is forced to overcome his fear or want of sympathy before he acts deserves, however, in one way higher credit than the man whose innate disposition leads him to a good act without effort. As we cannot distinguish between motives, we rank all actions of a certain class as moral, if performed by a moral being. A moral being is one who is capable of comparing his past and future actions or motives, and of approving or disapproving of them. We have no reason to suppose that any of the lower animals have this capacity; therefore, when a Newfoundland dog drags a child out of the water, or a monkey faces danger to rescue its comrade, or takes charge of an orphan monkey, we do not call its conduct moral. But in the case of man, who alone can with certainty be ranked as a moral being, actions of a certain class are called moral, whether performed deliberately, after a struggle with opposing motives, or impulsively through instinct, or from the effects of slowly gained habit.

But to return to our more immediate subject, although some instincts are more powerful than others, and thus lead to corresponding actions, yet it is untenable, that in man the social instincts (including the love of praise and fear of blame) possess greater strength, or have, through long habit, acquired greater strength than the instincts of self-preservation, hunger, lust, vengeance, etc. Why then does man regret, even though trying to banish such regret, that he has followed the one natural impulse rather than the other, and why does he further feel that he ought to regret his conduct? Man in this respect differs profoundly from the lower animals.

---

[6]I have given one such case, namely of three Patagonian Indians who preferred being shot, one after the other, to betraying the plans of their companions in war (*Journal of Researches* [1845], 103).

Nevertheless we can, I think, see with some degree of clearness the reason of this difference.

Man, from the activity of his mental faculties, cannot avoid reflection: past impressions and images are incessantly and clearly passing through his mind. Now with those animals which live permanently in a body, the social instincts are ever present and persistent. Such animals are always ready to utter the danger signal, to defend the community, and to give aid to their fellows in accordance with their habits; they feel at all times, without the stimulus of any special passion or desire, some degree of love and sympathy for them; they are unhappy if long separated from them, and always happy to be again in their company. So it is with ourselves. Even when we are quite alone, how often do we think with pleasure or pain of what others think of us—of their imagined approbation or disapprobation, and this all follows from sympathy, a fundamental element of the social instincts. A man who possessed no trace of such instincts would be an unnatural monster. On the other hand, the desire to satisfy hunger, or any passion such as vengeance, is in its nature temporary, and can for a time be fully satisfied. Nor is it easy, perhaps hardly possible, to call up with complete vividness the feeling, for instance, of hunger; nor indeed, as has often been remarked, of any suffering. The instinct of self-preservation is not felt except in the presence of danger, and many a coward has thought himself brave until he has met his enemy face to face. The wish for another man's property is perhaps as persistent a desire as any that can be named, but even in this case the satisfaction of actual possession is generally a weaker feeling than the desire: many a thief, if not a habitual one, after success has wondered why he stole some article.[7]

---

[7]Enmity or hatred seems also to be a highly persistent feeling, perhaps more so than any other that can be named. Envy is defined as hatred of another for some excellence or success, and [Francis] Bacon insists (Essay ix.), "Of all other affections envy is the most importune and continual." Dogs are very apt to hate both strange men and strange dogs, especially if they live near at hand, but do not belong to the same family, tribe, or clan; this feeling would thus seem to be innate, and is certainly a most persistent one. It seems to be the complement and converse of the true social instinct. From what we hear of savages, it would appear that something of the same kind holds good with them. If this be so, it would be a small step in any one to transfer such feelings to any member of the same tribe if he had done him an injury and had become his enemy. Nor is it probable that the primitive conscience would reproach a man for injuring his enemy; rather it would reproach him, if he had not revenged himself. To do good in return for evil, to love your enemy, is a height of morality to which it may be doubted whether the social instincts would, by themselves, have ever led us. It is necessary that these instincts, together with sympathy, should have been highly cultivated and extended by the aid of reason, instruction, and the love or fear of God, before any such golden rule would ever be thought of and obeyed.

A man cannot prevent past impressions often repassing through his mind; he will thus be driven to make a comparison between the impressions of past hunger, vengeance satisfied, or danger shunned at other men's cost, with the almost ever-present instinct of sympathy, and with his early knowledge of what others consider as praiseworthy or blamable. This knowledge cannot be banished from his mind, and from instinctive sympathy is esteemed of great moment. He will then feel as if he had been baulked in following a present instinct or habit, and this with all animals causes dissatisfaction, or even misery.

The above case of the swallow affords an illustration, though of a reversed nature, of a temporary though for the time strongly persistent instinct conquering another instinct, which is usually dominant over all others. At the proper season these birds seem all day long to be impressed with the desire to migrate; their habits change; they become restless, are noisy, and congregate in flocks. Whilst the mother bird is feeding, or brooding over her nestlings, the maternal instinct is probably stronger than the migratory, but the instinct which is the more persistent gains the victory, and at last, at a moment when her young ones are not in sight, she takes flight and deserts them. When arrived at the end of her long journey, and the migratory instinct has ceased to act, what an agony of remorse the bird would feel, if, from being endowed with great mental activity, she could not prevent the image constantly passing through her mind, of her young ones perishing in the bleak north from cold and hunger.

At the moment of action, man will no doubt be apt to follow the stronger impulse, and though this may occasionally prompt him to the noblest deeds, it will more commonly lead him to gratify his own desires at the expense of other men. But after their gratification when past and weaker impressions are judged by the ever-enduring social instinct, and by his deep regard for the good opinion of his fellows, retribution will surely come. He will then feel remorse, repentance, regret, or shame; this latter feeling, however, relates almost exclusively to the judgment of others. He will consequently resolve more or less firmly to act differently for the future, and this is conscience, for conscience looks backwards, and serves as a guide for the future.

The nature and strength of the feelings which we call regret, shame, repentance or remorse, depend apparently not only on the strength of the violated instinct, but also partly on the strength of the temptation, and often still more on the judgment of our fellows. How far each man values the appreciation of others depends on the strength of his innate or acquired feeling of sympathy, and on his own capacity for reasoning out the remote consequences of his acts. Another element is most important, although not necessary, the reverence or fear of the Gods, or Spirits believed in by each man: and this applies especially in cases of remorse. Several critics have objected that though some slight regret or repentance may be explained by the view advocated in this chapter, it is impossible thus to account for the soul-shaking feeling of remorse. But I can see little force in this objection. My critics do not define what they mean by remorse, and I can find no definition implying more than an overwhelming sense of repentance. Remorse seems to bear the same relation to repentance, as rage does to anger, or agony to pain. It is far from strange that an instinct so strong and so generally admired, as maternal love, should, if disobeyed, lead to the deepest misery, as soon as the impression of the past cause of disobedience is weakened. Even when an action is opposed to no special instinct, merely to know that our friends and equals despise us for it is enough to cause great misery. Who can doubt that the refusal to fight a duel through fear has caused many men an agony of shame? Many a Hindoo, it is said, has been stirred to the bottom of his soul by having partaken of unclean food. Here is another case of what must, I think, be called remorse. Dr. Landor acted as a magistrate in West Australia, and relates[8] that a native on his farm, after losing one of his wives from disease, came and said that:

> [H]e was going to a distant tribe to spear a woman, to satisfy his sense of duty to his wife. I told him that if he did so, I would send him to prison for life. He remained about the farm for some months, but got exceedingly thin, and complained that he could not rest or eat, that his wife's spirit was haunting him, because he had not taken a life for hers. I was inexorable, and assured him that nothing should save him if he did.

Nevertheless the man disappeared for more than a year, and then returned in high condition, and his other wife told Dr. Landor that her husband had taken the life of a woman belonging to a distant tribe, but it was impossible to obtain legal evidence of the act. The breach of a rule held sacred by the tribe, will thus, as it seems, give rise to the deepest feelings—and this quite apart from the social instincts, excepting in so far as the rule is grounded on the judgment of the community. How so many strange superstitions have arisen throughout the world we know not; nor can we tell how some real and great crimes, such as incest, have come to be held in an abhorrence (which is not however quite universal) by the lowest savages. It is even doubtful whether in some tribes incest would be looked on with greater horror, than would the marriage of a man with a woman bearing the same name, though not a relation.

---

[8]*Insanity in Relation to Law* (Ontario, The United States, 1871), 14.

To violate this law is a crime which the Australians hold in the greatest abhorrence, in this agreeing exactly with certain tribes of North America. When the question is put in either district, is it worse to kill a girl of a foreign tribe, or to marry a girl of one's own, an answer just opposite to ours would be given without hesitation.[9]

We may, therefore, reject the belief, lately insisted on by some writers, that the abhorrence of incest is due to our possessing a special God-implanted conscience. On the whole it is intelligible that a man urged by so powerful a sentiment as remorse, though arising as above explained, should be led to act in a manner, which he has been taught to believe serves as an expiation, such as delivering himself up to justice.

Man prompted by his conscience will through long habit acquire such perfect self-command, that his desires and passions will at last yield instantly and without a struggle to his social sympathies and instincts, including his feeling for the judgment of his fellows. The still hungry, or the still revengeful, man will not think of stealing food, or of wreaking his vengeance. It is possible, or as we shall hereafter see, even probable, that the habit of self-command may, like other habits, be inherited. Thus at last man comes to feel, through acquired and perhaps inherited habit, that it is best for him to obey his more persistent impulses. The imperious word *ought* seems merely to imply the consciousness of the existence of a rule of conduct, however it may have originated. Formerly it must have been often vehemently urged that an insulted gentleman *ought* to fight a duel. We even say that a pointer *ought* to point, and a retriever to retrieve game. If they fail to do so, they fail in their duty and act wrongly.

If any desire or instinct leading to an action opposed to the good of others still appears, when recalled to mind, as strong as, or stronger than, the social instinct, a man will feel no keen regret at having followed it, but he will be conscious that if his conduct were known to his fellows, it would meet with their disapprobation, and few are so destitute of sympathy as not to feel discomfort when this is realized. If he has no such sympathy, and if his desires leading to bad actions are at the time strong, and when recalled are not overmastered by the persistent social instincts, and the judgment of others, then he is essentially a bad man, [10]and the sole restraining motive left is the fear of punishment, and the conviction that in the long run it would be best for his own selfish interests to regard the good of others rather than his own.

---

[9]E. B. Tylor, in *Contemporary Review*, April 1873, 707.

[10]Dr. Prosper Despine, in his *Psychologie Naturelle* (1868) (tom. i., 243; tom. ii., 169), gives many curious cases of the worst criminals who apparently have been entirely destitute of conscience.

It is obvious that every one may with an easy conscience gratify his own desires, if they do not interfere with his social instincts, that is with the good of others, but in order to be quite free from self-reproach, or at least of anxiety, it is almost necessary for him to avoid the disapprobation, whether reasonable or not, of his fellow men. Nor must he break through the fixed habits of his life, especially if these are supported by reason, for if he does, he will assuredly feel dissatisfaction. He must likewise avoid the reprobation of the one God or gods in whom, according to his knowledge or superstition, he may believe, but in this case the additional fear of divine punishment often supervenes.

The Strictly Social Virtues at First Alone Regarded

The above view of the origin and nature of the moral sense, which tells us what we ought to do, and of the conscience which reproves us if we disobey it, accords well with what we see of the early and undeveloped condition of this faculty in mankind. The virtues which must be practiced, at least generally, by rude men, so that they may associate in a body, are those which are still recognized as the most important. But they are practiced almost exclusively in relation to the men of the same tribe, and their opposites are not regarded as crimes in relation to the men of other tribes. No tribe could hold together if murder, robbery, treachery, etc., were common; consequently, such crimes within the limits of the same tribe "are branded with everlasting infamy,"[11] but excite no such sentiment beyond these limits. A North American Indian is well pleased with himself, and is honored by others, when he scalps a man of another tribe, and a Dyak cuts off the head of an unoffending person, and dries it as a trophy. The murder of infants has prevailed on the largest scale throughout the world,[12] and has met with no reproach, but infanticide, especially of females, has been thought to be good for the tribe, or at least not injurious. Suicide during former times was not generally considered as a crime,[13] but rather, from the courage displayed, as an honorable act, and

---

[11]See an able article in the *North British Review*, 1867, 395. See also Mr. W. Bagehot's articles on the Importance of Obedience and Coherence to Primitive Man, in the *Fortnightly Review*, 1867, 529, and 1868, 457, etc.

[12]The fullest account which I have met with is by Dr. Gerland, in his *Ueber das Aussterben der Naturvölker*, 1868, but I shall have to recur to the subject of infanticide in a future chapter.

[13]See the very interesting discussion on suicide in Lecky's *History of European Morals*, vol. i. (1869), 223. With respect to savages, Mr. Winwood Reade informs me that the Negroes of west Africa often commit suicide. It is well known how common it was amongst the miserable aborigines of South America, after the Spanish conquest. For New Zealand, see the voyage of the "Novara," and for the Aleutian Islands, Müller, as quoted by Houzeau, *Les Facultés Mentales*, etc., tom. ii, 136.

it is still practiced by some semi-civilized and savage nations without reproach, for it does not obviously concern others of the tribe. It has been recorded that an Indian Thug conscientiously regretted that he had not robbed and strangled as many travelers as did his father before him. In a rude state of civilization the robbery of strangers is, indeed, generally considered as honorable.

Slavery, although in some ways beneficial during ancient times,[14] is a great crime, yet it was not so regarded until quite recently, even by the most civilized nations. And this was especially the case, because the slaves belonged in general to a race different from that of their masters. As barbarians do not regard the opinion of their women, wives are commonly treated like slaves. Most savages are utterly indifferent to the sufferings of strangers, or even delight in witnessing them. It is well known that the women and children of the North American Indians aided in torturing their enemies. Some savages take a horrid pleasure in cruelty to animals[15] and humanity is an unknown virtue. Nevertheless, besides the family affections, kindness is common, especially during sickness, between the members of the same tribe, and is sometimes extended beyond these limits. Mungo Park's touching account of the kindness of the Negro women of the interior to him is well known. Many instances could be given of the noble fidelity of savages toward each other, but not to strangers; common experience justifies the maxim of the Spaniard, "Never, never trust an Indian." There cannot be fidelity without truth, and this fundamental virtue is not rare between the members of the same tribe: thus Mungo Park heard the Negro women teaching their young children to love the truth. This, again, is one of the virtues which becomes so deeply rooted in the mind, that it is sometimes practiced by savages, even at a high cost, toward strangers, but to lie to your enemy has rarely been thought a sin, as the history of modern diplomacy too plainly shows. As soon as a tribe has a recognized leader, disobedience becomes a crime, and even abject submission is looked at as a sacred virtue.

As during rude times no man can be useful or faithful to his tribe without courage, this quality has universally been placed in the highest rank, and although in civilized countries a good yet timid man may be far more useful to the community than a brave one, we cannot help instinctively honoring the latter above a coward, however benevolent. Prudence, on the other hand, which does not concern the welfare of others, though a very useful virtue, has never been highly esteemed. As no man can practice the virtues necessary for the welfare of his tribe without self-sacrifice, self-command, and the power of endurance, these qualities have been at all times highly and most

---

[14]See Mr. W. Bagehot, *Physics and Politics* (1872), 72.

[15]See, for instance, Mr. Hamilton's account of the Kaffirs, *Anthropological Review*, 1870, xv.

justly valued. The American savage voluntarily submits to the most horrid tortures without a groan, to prove and strengthen his fortitude and courage, and we cannot help admiring him, or even an Indian Fakir, who, from a foolish religious motive, swings suspended by a hook buried in his flesh.

The other so-called self-regarding virtues, which do not obviously, though they may really, affect the welfare of the tribe, have never been esteemed by savages, though now highly appreciated by civilized nations. The greatest intemperance is no reproach with savages. Utter licentiousness and unnatural crimes prevail to an astounding extent.[16] As soon, however, as marriage, whether polygamous, or monogamous, becomes common, jealousy will lead to the inculcation of female virtue, and this, being honored, will tend to spread to the unmarried females. How slowly it spreads to the male sex, we see at the present day. Chastity eminently requires self-command; therefore, it has been honored from a very early period in the moral history of civilized man. As a consequence of this, the senseless practice of celibacy has been ranked from a remote period as a virtue.[17] The hatred of indecency, which appears to us so natural as to be thought innate, and which is so valuable an aid to chastity, is a modern virtue, appertaining exclusively, as Sir G. Staunton remarks,[18] to civilized life. This is shewn by the ancient religious rites of various nations, by the drawings on the walls of Pompeii, and by the practices of many savages.

We have now seen that actions are regarded by savages, and were probably so regarded by primeval man, as good or bad, solely as they obviously affect the welfare of the tribe—not that of the species, nor that of an individual member of the tribe. This conclusion agrees well with the belief that the so-called moral sense is aboriginally derived from the social instincts, for both relate at first exclusively to the community. The chief causes of the low morality of savages, as judged by our standard, are, firstly, the confinement of sympathy to the same tribe. Secondly, powers of reasoning insufficient to recognize the bearing of many virtues, especially of the self-regarding virtues, on the general welfare of the tribe. Savages, for instance, fail to trace the multiplied evils consequent on a want of temperance, chastity, etc. And, thirdly, weak power of self-command, for this power has not been strengthened through long-continued, perhaps inherited, habit, instruction, and religion.

---

[16]Mr. M'Lennan has given (*Primitive Marriage* [1865], 176) a good collection of facts on this head.

[17]Lecky, *History of European Morals*, vol. i, 1869, 109.

[18]*Embassy to China*, vol. ii, 348.

I have entered into the above details on the immorality of savages,[19] because some authors have recently taken a high view of their moral nature, or have attributed most of their crimes to mistaken benevolence.[20] These authors appear to rest their conclusion on savages possessing those virtues which are serviceable, or even necessary, for the existence of the family and of the tribe—qualities which they undoubtedly do possess, and often in a high degree.

Concluding Remarks

It was assumed formerly by philosophers of the derivative school of morals[21] that the foundation of morality lies in a form of Selfishness, but more recently the "greatest happiness principle" has been brought prominently forward. It is, however, more correct to speak of the latter principle as the standard, and not as the motive of conduct. Nevertheless, all the authors whose works I have consulted, with a few exceptions,[22] write as if there must be a distinct motive for every action, and that this must be associated with some pleasure or displeasure. But man seems often to act impulsively, that is from instinct or long habit, without any consciousness of pleasure, in the same manner as does probably a bee or ant, when it blindly follows its instincts. Under circumstances of extreme peril, as during a fire, when a man endeavors to save a fellow creature without a moment's hesitation, he can hardly feel pleasure, and still less has he time to reflect on the dissatisfaction which he might subsequently experience if he did not make the attempt. Should he afterwards reflect over his own conduct,

---

[19]See on this subject copious evidence in Chapter vii of Sir J. Lubbock, *Origin of Civilisation* (1870).

[20]For instance Lecky, *History of European Morals*, vol. i, 124.

[21]This term is used in an able article in the *Westminster Review*, Oct., 1869, 498, for the "greatest happiness principle." See J. S. Mill, *Utilitarianism*, 17. [The school, then, would include the utilitarian philosophers Jeremy Bentham and John Stuart Mill.—M. M.].

[22]Mill recognizes in the clearest manner that actions may be performed through habit without the anticipation of pleasure (*System of Logic*, vol. ii, 422). Mr. H. Sidgwick also, in his "Essay on Pleasure and Desire" (*The Contemporary Review*, April 1872, 671), remarks: "To sum up, in contravention of the doctrine that our conscious active impulses are always directed toward the production of agreeable sensations in ourselves, I would maintain that we find everywhere in consciousness an extra-regarding impulse, directed toward something that is not pleasure; that in many cases the impulse is so far incompatible with the self-regarding that the two do not easily coexist in the same moment of consciousness." A dim feeling that our impulses do not by any means always arise from any contemporaneous or anticipated pleasure has, I cannot but think, been one chief cause of the acceptance of the intuitive theory of morality, and of the rejection of the utilitarian or "greatest happiness" theory. With respect to the latter theory the standard and the motive of conduct have no doubt often been confused, but they are really in some degree blended.

he would feel that there lies within him an impulsive power widely different from a search after pleasure or happiness, and this seems to be the deeply planted social instinct.

In the case of the lower animals it seems much more appropriate to speak of their social instincts, as having been developed for the general good rather than for the general happiness of the species. The term, *general good*, may be defined as the rearing of the greatest number of individuals in full vigor and health, with all their faculties perfect, under the conditions to which they are subjected. As the social instincts both of man and the lower animals have no doubt been developed by nearly the same steps, it would be advisable, if found practicable, to use the same definition in both cases, and to take as the standard of morality, the general good or welfare of the community, rather than the general happiness, but this definition would perhaps require some limitation on account of political ethics.

When a man risks his life to save that of a fellow creature, it seems also more correct to say that he acts for the general good, rather than for the general happiness of mankind. No doubt the welfare and the happiness of the individual usually coincide, and a contented, happy tribe will flourish better than one that is discontented and unhappy. We have seen that even at an early period in the history of man, the expressed wishes of the community will have naturally influenced to a large extent the conduct of each member, and as all wish for happiness, the "greatest happiness principle" will have become the most important secondary guide and object; the social instinct, however, together with sympathy (which leads to our regarding the approbation and disapprobation of others), having served as the primary impulse and guide. Thus the reproach is removed of laying the foundation of the noblest part of our nature in the base principle of selfishness; unless, indeed, the satisfaction which every animal feels, when it follows its proper instincts, and the dissatisfaction felt when prevented, be called selfish.

The wishes and opinions of the members of the same community, expressed at first orally, but later by writing also, either form the sole guides of our conduct, or greatly reinforce the social instincts; such opinions, however, have sometimes a tendency directly opposed to these instincts. This latter fact is well exemplified by the *Law of Honor*, that is, the law of the opinion of our equals, and not of all our countrymen. The breach of this law, even when the breach is known to be strictly accordant with true morality, has caused many a man more agony than a real crime. We recognize the same influence in the burning sense of shame which most of us have felt, even after the interval of years, when calling to mind some accidental breach of a trifling, though fixed, rule of etiquette. The judgment of the community will generally be guided by some rude experience of what is best in the long run for all the members, but this judgment will not rarely err from ignorance and weak powers of reasoning. Hence the strangest customs and superstitions, in complete opposition to the true welfare and happiness of mankind, have become all-powerful throughout the world. We see this in the horror felt by a Hindoo who breaks his caste, and in many other such cases. It would be difficult to distinguish between the remorse felt by a Hindoo who has yielded to the temptation of eating unclean food, from that felt after committing a theft, but the former would probably be the more severe.

How so many absurd rules of conduct, as well as so many absurd religious beliefs, have originated, we do not know; nor how it is that they have become, in all quarters of the world, so deeply impressed on the mind of men, but it is worthy of remark that a belief constantly inculcated during the early years of life, whilst the brain is impressible, appears to acquire almost the nature of an instinct, and the very essence of an instinct is that it is followed independently of reason. Neither can we say why certain admirable virtues, such as the love of truth, are much more highly appreciated by some savage tribes than by others,[23] nor, again, why similar differences prevail even amongst highly civilized nations. Knowing how firmly fixed many strange customs and superstitions have become, we need feel no surprise that the self-regarding virtues, supported as they are by reason, should now appear to us so natural as to be thought innate, although they were not valued by man in his early condition.

Notwithstanding many sources of doubt, man can generally and readily distinguish between the higher and lower moral rules. The higher are founded on the social instincts, and relate to the welfare of others. They are supported by the approbation of our fellow men and by reason. The lower rules, though some of them when implying self-sacrifice hardly deserve to be called lower, relate chiefly to self, and arise from public opinion, matured by experience and cultivation, for they are not practiced by rude tribes.

As man advances in civilization, and small tribes are united into larger communities, the simplest reason would tell each individual that he ought to extend his social instincts and sympathies to all the members of the same nation, though personally unknown to him. This point being once reached, there is only an artificial barrier to prevent his sympathies extending to the men of all nations and races. If, indeed, such men are separated from him by great differences in appearance or habits, experience unfortunately shews us how long it is, before we look at them as our fellow creatures. Sympathy beyond the confines of man, that is, humanity to the lower animals, seems to be one of the latest moral acquisitions. It is apparently unfelt by savages, except toward their pets. How little the old Romans knew of it is shewn by their abhorrent gladiatorial exhibitions. The very idea of humanity, as far as I could observe, was new

---

[23]Good instances are given by Mr. Wallace in *Scientific Opinion*, September 15, 1869, and more fully in his *Contributions to the Theory of Natural Selection* (1870), 353.

to most of the Gauchos of the Pampas. This virtue, one of the noblest with which man is endowed, seems to arise incidentally from our sympathies becoming more tender and more widely diffused, until they are extended to all sentient beings. As soon as this virtue is honored and practiced by some few men, it spreads through instruction and example to the young, and eventually becomes incorporated in public opinion.
[…]

Finally the social instincts, which no doubt were acquired by man as by the lower animals for the good of the community, will from the first have given to him some wish to aid his fellows, some feeling of sympathy, and have compelled him to regard their approbation and disapprobation. Such impulses will have served him at a very early period as a rude rule of right and wrong. But as man gradually advanced in intellectual power, and was enabled to trace the more remote consequences of his actions; as he acquired sufficient knowledge to reject baneful customs and superstitions; as he regarded more and more, not only the welfare, but the happiness of his fellow men; and as from habit, following on beneficial experience, instruction and example, his sympathies became more tender and widely diffused, extending to men of all races, to the imbecile, maimed, and other useless members of society, and finally to the lower animals—so would the standard of his morality rise higher and higher. And it is admitted by moralists of the derivative school and by some intuitionists that the standard of morality has risen since an early period in the history of man.[24]

As a struggle may sometimes be seen going on between the various instincts of the lower animals, it is not surprising that there should be a struggle in man between his social instincts, with their derived virtues, and his lower, though momentarily stronger impulses or desires. This, as Mr. Galton[25] has remarked, is all the less surprising, as man has emerged from a state of barbarism within a comparatively recent period. After having yielded to some temptation we feel a sense of dissatisfaction, shame, repentance, or remorse, analogous to the feelings caused by other powerful instincts or desires, when left unsatisfied or baulked. We compare the weakened impression of a past temptation with the ever-present social instincts, or with habits gained in early youth and strengthened during our whole lives, until they have become almost as strong as instincts. If with the temptation still before us we do not yield, it is because either the social instinct or some custom is at the moment predominant, or because we have learnt that it will appear to us hereafter the stronger, when compared with the

---

[24]A writer in the *North British Review* (July, 1869, 531), well capable of forming a sound judgment, expresses himself strongly in favor of this conclusion. Mr. Lecky (*History of European Morals*, vol. i., 143) seems to a certain extent to coincide therein.

[25]See his remarkable work on *Hereditary Genius* (1869), 349. The Duke of Argyll (*Primeval Man* [1869], 188) has some good remarks on the contest in man's nature between right and wrong.

weakened impression of the temptation, and we realize that its violation would cause us suffering. Looking to future generations, there is no cause to fear that the social instincts will grow weaker, and we may expect that virtuous habits will grow stronger, becoming perhaps fixed by inheritance. In this case the struggle between our higher and lower impulses will be less severe, and virtue will be triumphant.

Chapter 13

Common Sense and Human Nature

Stanley Rosen

In our next reading, Cleveland-born philosopher Stanley Rosen defines common sense as "the ordinary language of common experience." With a definition this broad it is a safe bet that, as he writes, "In every age about which we are informed, there have been men of common sense."[1] He proposes to examine common sense commonsensically, to see if it can serve as a self-consistent and complete basis for the estimation of human behavior.

Common sense operates by relying on order and regularity: it tells us that "men are always the same." At the same time, it also tells us that people are different, that men and women are variable, incautious, and unreliable. How are we to reconcile the regularity of people with their variability and unreliability? This question has an obvious bearing on ethics, the philosophical examination of morality.

Common sense tells us that, in order to evaluate the actions of men—in order to determine not only whether the actions are rational or effective, but also whether they are right or wrong—one must have in hand a notion of human nature. When we speak commonsensically about human nature, we take for granted that there are enduring "basic motives" or "fundamental ends," such as self-preservation, personal security, glory, power, self-realization, moral virtue, or spiritual perfection.

Common sense also tells us that when it comes to determining how to achieve any of these "fundamental ends," we must already know the ways of the world. So the question arises, "[H]ow much does a man of common sense

---

[1]In a passage not included in our excerpt, however, Rosen offers the following unsettling remark: "The world of common experience is not an objective, fully defined entity, but a rather murky and ambiguous concatenation of partially determined forms and partially achieved possibilities." (See the Rosen entry in the Readings That Appear in This Book section at the end of this book.)

have to know in order to act in a commonsensical way?" If we are to follow commonsensical reasoning, the answer is *quite a lot*. Indeed, "One cannot fix the limit of things which the man of common sense needs to know." This observation is as true of philosophy and science as it is of morality. Men of common sense think of themselves as eminently practical.[2] But detailed practical, technical, and scientific knowledge lies outside the purview of common sense. Thus, "Common sense transcends itself in its very exercise; in crucial cases, its activity amounts to a replacement of common sense by technical knowledge."

"Fundamental ends" often conflict, and when they do, we take it for granted that there is a correct and accessible way to order and rank them. Unfortunately, Rosen observes, common sense is of little use when it comes to ranking "fundamental ends," or establishing once and for all a "hierarchy of needs," to adjudicate their conflicts as they arise. The pursuit of glory often trumps considerations of moral virtue; the quest for salvation sometimes comes at the cost of personal security; the pursuit of happiness might require relinquishing power, and so on. In this way, too, people differ, and we evaluate their actions from case to case.

Because a universalizable hierarchy of ends is not in the offing, Rosen writes, "the most one could say is that common sense, when faced with its shortcomings, must admit that its own explanations of itself are inadequate, but not that they are altogether mistaken." In this and other ways, "one might say that the inadequacy of common sense lies in its inability to explain itself." However, Rosen writes, "This inability is not necessarily a defect." "Common sense appears to be defective only when it is expected to fulfill the function of philosophy," but fortunately, it provides a remedy for its own defect: "common sense tells us when we are in a predicament from which common sense alone, or in conjunction with technical knowledge, cannot extricate us."

The late Stanley Rosen (1929–2014) was Professor of Philosophy at Boston University. A frequent claim in his work is that philosophical discussions have no other basis than the intelligent understanding of the features of what he called "ordinary experience." This should become clearer as we read on.

[...] Let us examine the evidence of common sense from its own point of view, if and for so long as this proves to be possible, and see whether common sense is as

---

[2]Why *men* of common sense? Because, as (male) champions of common sense have assured us, men are more commonsensical than women (Rosenfeld, 31–2).

commonly recognizable as is claimed. It is well to take our bearings by a preliminary survey of some kinds of experience in which we say, "that is a matter of common sense," or, "every sensible man knows *that*." In so doing, we shall remain as innocent as possible of technical devices imported from philosophy. This will require us to be simple, but not, I trust, simple-minded. For common sense is not regarded as simple-mindedness. On the contrary, the latter is a pejorative term, often used as virtually synonymous with "a lack of common sense." For example, if X believes that all men are virtuous in their daily actions, or that justice always triumphs in this world, or that one must always say exactly what he thinks, he is called "simple-minded," not on the ground that he is ignorant of moral philosophy, theology, or psychology, but because he is held to have misunderstood something about human nature which is accessible to us from everyday experience. Whether or not common sense is really common, it surely is not universal, since there are always some men like X who plainly lack it.

The example calls our attention to one of the most obvious areas in which common sense is held to apply: the assessment of human nature. Indeed, it might be argued that this area is sufficiently inclusive to contain the entire domain of common sense. In accord with this argument, we not infrequently refer to common sense as *prudence*. Prudence, or, in the old-fashioned phrase, practical intelligence or wisdom, is the ability to assess human conduct, to regulate oneself in accord with this assessment, and to persuade others to follow suit. I have purposely begun with a rather abstract definition of prudence (although not so abstract as to fall outside the domain of common sense). I do so in order to suggest that every attempt to put flesh on the bare bones of the definition leads to an ambiguity which suggests the limitations of common sense. The prudent man is one who possesses some kind of experience, understanding, and knowledge. This is clear from the fact that he is said to know or understand human nature; it is also apparent from the fact that not all men, but only relatively few, are prudent. The scarcity of prudent men also suggests that "prudence" is a narrower term than "common sense." The prudent man knows how to gain desired ends, to avoid failure and disaster, to ensure security and survival. Prudence is very close to, if not identical with, political wisdom or statesmanship. It seems to be a specialized form or development of common sense, a species rather than the genus as a whole. For example, it takes common sense to recognize which of several political candidates possesses prudence, but the ability to distinguish the prudent man is not itself a sign that he who possesses it is sufficiently gifted to hold office.

Prudence and common sense cannot be precisely, but only approximately, distinguished. The two are closely related; even if prudence be a specialized form of common sense, it must still conform to the standards of common sense. Prudent men would not be held in such esteem if they could not be recognized by a wider audience. But this audience is not simply equivalent to the people as a whole. Many men are themselves imprudent and praise the imprudence of others. The people as a whole may in extreme cases recognize the difference between a prudent and an imprudent statesman after the fact, but there are all too many instances in which it can be seen that the majority do not "learn from experience," an ability which is essential to men of common sense. If men of common sense form a larger class than prudent men, they are still less than the whole of mankind. So much seems relatively straightforward, nor do we need to define precisely, and therefore precipitously, the difference between prudence and common sense. But it is necessary for us to ask what the standards of common sense are, and how or to what degree they are accessible to common sense itself.

Since everyone admits the existence of common sense and can cite instances of its employment, it would be absurd or the reverse of commonsensical to deny that such standards are *somehow* accessible. Did we not speak a moment ago of human nature? Surely we decide whether an act is commonsensical by measuring it against the standard of our knowledge of human nature. By "human nature" we presumably mean something like "how people behave." As the word "common" implies, common sense would be impossible unless there were a certain regularity in human behavior, and unless this regularity were apparent to the nonspecialist. That is, the term "nature" in the phrase "human nature" is not analogous to the nature studied by the molecular biologist or astronomer, but rather to the nature which is observed by the "naturalist," as for example the birdwatcher or student of insect behavior. This analogy is at best inexact, but it is not altogether unhelpful in guiding us to the "sense" of "commonly" accessible knowledge about human nature.

What qualities of human nature can we specify as recognized by common sense? Our example of the simple-minded man gives us a clue, however distasteful to those who admire moral virtue. The man of prudence or common sense tells us that men are selfish, vain, variable, thoughtless, and so *incautious*. The idea of caution is inseparable from common sense or prudence: given a fundamental wariness or mistrust, there follows the sobering recognition that men are not trustworthy. We are now speaking of human nature, of regularly observable behavior, and not of individuals, or of particular moments in their lives. There are surely circumstances in which common sense advises us that a man *is* trustworthy; otherwise there would be no prudent men. And sometimes, under certain conditions, common sense may tell us that it is reasonable to trust a man upon whom, in other conditions, we could not rely. Inseparable from the unreliability of men as a whole, then, is the notion of their variability, and this in turn is related to the matter of conditions. The variability of men makes it possible for the sensible man to decide upon, perhaps even to bring about, conditions making for reliability (to use a weaker term than trustworthiness). But how then are we to reconcile the regularity of men with their variability? Common sense seems to tell us that "men are always the same" and that "mankind is infinitely variable."

If we consult common sense, I believe the answer it gives us is that regular patterns are discernible within the ostensibly infinite changes. Even the disagreement of men of common sense about the fundamental motive of human behavior occurs within a relatively restricted domain: the pursuit of physical pleasure, the love of glory, wealth, power, moral virtue, wisdom. Perhaps this list is not complete; perhaps it is the nature of such an investigation that no list of fundamental ends could be proven to be complete, in the sense that we "prove" results in mathematics. And yet the list is both specific and general enough for practical purposes. For common sense is eminently practical; it does not strive for a precision which is alien to its domain. Our list represents those ends which are most commonly held to move men to action. The means men use are variable; the end which governs an individual's conduct may change in the course of his life, but with respect to mankind as a whole, the ends remain the same. As men of common sense are inclined to say, "so long as men remain men" their motives will be much the same. Of course, it is possible to argue, on the basis of contemporary genetics and modern political theory, that human nature is radically mutable, that the ends themselves can be changed, or that some apparently eternal ends may be eliminated. But to argue in this way is to transcend common sense, to insist upon the inadequacy of common sense as the standard for the theoretical understanding of man. Common sense might perhaps reply that if, thanks to the science of genetics, men become gods, they will still be motivated by the love of virtue and knowledge, as gods are said to be. But it is clear that, if common sense refers to "the human condition," its guidance will no longer be relevant when that condition has been transcended.

This last line of argument cannot be extended from within the viewpoint of common sense; insofar as it is a legitimate line of argument, it suggests, as I mentioned, the *limitation* of common sense. We shall have occasion in a while to pursue the problem which modern natural science poses for common sense in men who are *not* gods. But for the time being, I should like to continue our discussion of commonsensical estimations of human behavior in the moral and political dimensions. We should gain nothing by establishing prematurely the limitations of common sense, even if by means of a position which sometimes seems to wish to deny any such limitations, at least when faced with examples of philosophy which it dislikes. The example of science is useful in conjunction with commonsensical reflections on morality and politics, especially with respect to the issue of *conditions*. The prudent or commonsensical man may know the ends by which men are generally motivated, but will he know the conditions which may induce men to act by one end rather than another? If it is held that common sense does include knowledge of these conditions, it soon becomes obvious that it does not include the knowledge of how to obtain or produce those conditions. To take a simple example, common sense tells us that widespread poverty is undesirable, at least in ages of great wealth and power (a qualification to which I shall return). But it does not tell us, in precisely such an age, when social life is a function of complex economic, political, and scientific developments, how to *remove* poverty. In a time such as our own, common sense tells us that "commonsensical" notions like thrift, individual initiative, even good will, are inadequate means for the achievement of the end in view. This suggests that common sense is irrelevant in complex situations, a suggestion that does not seem to be borne out by experience. Instead, it is evident that in complex situations common sense, or at least prudence, seems to be most desirable.

The man of common sense is he who can reduce a complex situation to its simplest components. In the example of the fight against poverty, to reduce the problem to its simplest components is not to remove poverty but to decide what must be done. More specifically, it means deciding upon the kind of special knowledge that is needed. Common sense fulfills its task in this situation by deciding to whom it must turn over the responsibility for achieving the remedy or goal which it has itself prescribed. In this way, the commonsensical (or perhaps prudent) man needs to be, if not a scholar or scientist, at least well informed. One's prudence must extend to the ability to decide *what one must know* in order to act prudently. The prudent man must know which experts, which technicians are needed to accomplish the desired purpose. One element in the elimination of poverty might be to prevent the destruction of crops by insects or other pests. No one would say that knowledge of chemistry is a necessary prerequisite of common sense, and yet it is quite clear that there is something about chemistry (in addition to the fact of its existence) that the man of common sense ought to know. He need not be aware of the formula for insect spray or possibly poison gas, but he must know that such products exist and whom to consult about them should the need arise. This raises a serious problem in the effort to define common sense, not to mention preserving its authority in human affairs. There were men of common sense prior to the existence of chemistry. But once such a science has emerged, it seems to be the duty of the commonsensical man to be informed about it, at least to the extent that it impinges upon or is a component of common experience. To combat illness with prayer alone when a physician is readily available would be absurd: absurd, that is, if common sense is our guide. The difficulty arises: how much does a man of common sense have to know in order to act in a commonsensical way? If it is his duty to consult experts in specific situations, then it must also be his duty to be an expert about experts. He must, as it were, know everything, or at least something about everything. This duty is not discharged nor the problem avoided by talk about the limitations of human nature. Whatever may be the case with human nature, our example shows only the limitations of common sense. One cannot fix the limit of things which the man of common sense needs to know. Common sense transcends itself in its very exercise; in crucial cases, its activity amounts to a replacement of common sense by technical knowledge.

I think we can now easily see that the problem touches upon the issue of history generally, and not just upon science. If the man of common sense relies upon nothing but his "good sense,"[3] he runs the risk, or rather the certain risk, of becoming parochial, out of touch, of acting foolishly or *senselessly*. On the other hand, if common sense is equivalent to knowledge of history, then there is no such thing as common sense, or else only and all historians must be men of common sense. I very much doubt that even professional historians would claim that much. We must admit that there is no sensible way to define the degree to which knowledge is a precondition or a part of common sense, but we must also admit that common sense without any knowledge is an impossibility. Common sense requires knowledge, both of means and ends, but it requires something else which is at least as important as such knowledge. A few paragraphs ago I said, "Common sense tells us that widespread poverty is undesirable, at least in ages of great wealth and power." Let me now explain the significance of the qualifying phrase. There are those who maintain, whether rightly or not, that an "economics of scarcity" is a necessary condition for the preservation of political and mental virtue. They say that poverty can be eliminated only through highly developed technology, which in turn demands the subordination of the whole texture of human life to the unrestricted development of science. I do not wish to expand this argument, and I am certainly not endorsing it; I merely mention it as an illustration of the problem at hand. Thus far we have talked about common sense (and prudence) in essentially "utilitarian" terms. It was taken for granted that the fundamental ends of human behavior are accessible to common sense, but nothing was said about deciding their rank or order. We can no longer conceal from ourselves, I believe, that herein lies the most serious task faced by common sense.

The most trivial, and so most widely experienced, instances of the application of common sense give the impression that there is no question of ranking the ends of activity. This ranking is taken for granted as somehow already settled, namely, as

---

[3]In a reading in Part VI, it will be noted that Antonio Gramsci uses the term *good sense* in a very different way from Rosen.—M. M.

the ranking in which self-preservation, and then a secure and even comfortable self-preservation, predominate. "Use your common sense" is too frequently taken to mean "do what is best for you," and this in turn suggests to us, "protect yourself," or "get what you can." I call these interpretations frequent; I do not say that they are universal. Even if the translations I have given of "use your common sense" are excessively frank or brutal, I ask the reader if his experience does not confirm the pervasive influence of the "evaluations" mentioned. The preservation of interest, whether personal or public, tends to be interpreted, when we appeal to common sense (as distinct from religion or old fashioned philosophy), in terms of physical security. As we have noted, the very notion of prudence (and so at least in part of common sense) entails the idea of caution, and therefore implies the hostility or dangerousness of mankind, against which we must constantly be on our guard. "Be sensible" or "be reasonable," in their commonsensical context, usually mean "watch out for danger!" as when a gunman says, "Be sensible; give me your money or I'll shoot!"

I do not wish to enter here into a topic from the history of philosophy, and so will merely allude to the fact that modern political philosophy begins by restricting the classical imperative "live well" to the harsher and theoretically briefer "stay alive." To discuss this point properly would require a lengthy and at present unnecessary digression. Whether or not the reader accepts my capsule comment on the history of political thought, the fact remains that there are a variety of ways in which the most generally recognized ends may be ranked. The ranking which we make determines our whole conception of life, and accordingly, it determines our conception of common sense. When we speak in everyday language about common sense, we do so in a way which takes it for granted that there *are* enduring ends (and so that there is something called human *nature*). But even further, we take it for granted that there is a correct and accessible ordering of these ends. Sometimes philosophers argue as though common sense itself supports a repudiation of "human nature" as an abstract generalization for which there are no verifying facts. They claim, too, that ends are "in fact" man-made wishes or expressions of desire, called "values," and as such dependent upon "conditions" which change from one time, society, or group to another. Whether or not this argument is sound, I do not believe that it is supported by common sense. We believe, as men of common sense, that the community of that sense lies in the general accessibility of a standard by which actions and opinions may be certified as "sensible." No man of common sense believes common sense to be equivalent to sociology, cultural anthropology, or a "scientific" knowledge of historical relativity. Even the view that "all truth is relative" rests upon the commonsensical assumption of stability in human nature, not with respect to the facts of behavior or means, but rather with respect to the ends.

For what could it mean to say that, "common sense tells us there is no such thing as human nature"? Nothing other, I believe, than the senseless assertion that "common sense tells us there is no such thing as common sense." In every specific situation when we judge the sensibility of men, or decide that some statement "makes sense," we assess the man or his words by means of knowledge (or belief) concerning how men act, or "what things are *really* like." To "make sense" is not to invent something unique, like a poem, but to behave or speak in accord with "reality." However questionable words like "nature" or "reality" may be from a philosophical viewpoint, they lie at the core of common sense's self-confidence. Common sense operates by reliance upon order or regularity. But it is not a codified technique or method, because to each general proposition of common sense, there are always exceptions. "Men" may be selfish, but X may act for altruistic reasons. Psychological analyses of altruism which reduce it to selfishness are in part a rejection of common sense, as being unable to explain human behavior, in part an expression of the common sense view that people behave in a regular or orderly way. Such analyses say in effect: we must be "realistic" in interpreting human behavior, and "realism" means awareness of the properties of things (*res*). A *realistic* assessment of man rests upon the interpretation of man as a *res,* and so as possessing properties which define his nature. Our common-sense experience shows us that such properties exist, and that empirical science depends upon the prior observation (and not simply observability) of these properties. On the other hand, common sense is unable to define these properties completely or precisely. Similarly, common sense rests upon the objective nature of ends, but it cannot define or evaluate completely or precisely what these ends are.

From this defect of common sense, it does not follow *as a conclusion of common sense* that there are no objective ends, or that there is no hierarchy of ends. So far as I can see, the most one could say is that common sense, when faced with its shortcomings, must admit that its own explanations of itself are inadequate, but not that they are altogether mistaken. Or rather, one might say that the inadequacy of common sense lies in its inability to explain itself. This inability is not necessarily a defect. We would never say that chemistry is defective because it is unable to produce lyric poems. An inability is a defect only if the corresponding ability is a virtue intrinsic to the object in question. Common sense appears to be defective only when it is expected to fulfill the function of philosophy. It is soon seen to be defective if we expect it to serve as a measure for evaluating theories. The theoretical man does not lose his common sense; *qua* theoretician, he goes beyond it. Having gone beyond common sense, he is able to see it clearly, and therefore to reflect about it. No such reflection is possible from within common sense itself. This is the decisive weakness of attempts to construct a "common sense" philosophy, or to rely implicitly upon a commonsensical approach to philosophy. When common sense is taken for philosophy, it is treated as a self-consistent and selfexplanatory theory or theoretical method. But this goes directly against common sense experience, as we have now seen. What counts as commonsensical is to a large extent dependent upon extra-commonsensical theoretical interpretations of experience. If we deny this, then we are unable to explain the fact that evaluations or estimates differ depending upon different conceptions of what is valuable or estimable. To repeat: these differences do not do away with common sense altogether, but exhibit its intrinsic limitations. There *is* something about our experience which is always the same, which underlies the mutability of particular experiences or circumstances, and so makes possible the exercise of common sense in any age, under almost any circumstances. Common sense can "use" this sameness, but it cannot "explain" it. If then we say that common sense is the ability to come to the best possible conclusion under *any* circumstances, that goes much too far. In deciding which of several possible procedures to employ within a biological experiment, we cannot merely be acting in accord with common sense, but we need knowledge of biology. On the other hand, the knowledge of biology is not always (perhaps never) sufficient. We seem to need common sense, or something indistinguishable from it, to decide how best to employ our knowledge under the circumstances. A man may possess vast technical knowledge, and yet the way in which he employs this knowledge may be vitiated by a lack of common sense. There are some circumstances in which the possession of both technical knowledge and common sense is still inadequate, as for example when deciding what to do about poverty from the point of view of society or civilization as a whole.

Let me put this last point as clearly as I can. I believe that common sense tells us when we are in a predicament from which common sense alone, or in conjunction with technical knowledge, cannot extricate us. The man of common sense, when face to face with an uncommon or extraordinary experience, does not simply condemn it as absurd, but recognizes that it cannot be evaluated simply by the exercise of common sense. He is therefore prepared to have recourse to "uncommon sense," whether in himself or in another, and he sees that this is the only sensible thing to do. The decisive instance of such an experience occurs when we ask ourselves: "what is common sense?" There is no entirely adequate commonsensical answer to this question, because the crucial conditions which determine what we mean by "commonsensical" at any time always partially transcend the exercise of common sense at that time.

The first tentative results of our inspection of common sense support at least the suspicion that philosophical thinking, even when it must employ common sense, is different from and broader than common sense. Let us approach the issue from a slightly different angle and consider what we mean by "ordinary" or "common experience," to which common sense apparently applies for counsel when exercising its judgment. The term "ordinary" contains the notion of ordering, and the standard by which we order is that of the regular or of what is common. In this sense an ordinary experience is regulative; we assess and evaluate situations with respect to the "rules" (even if only "rules of thumb") which are general summations of what commonly or regularly occurs. But these remarks, although commonplace in one sense, are excessively abstract in another. By giving the impression of a well-known definition, they combine the psychological effects of custom and "scientific rigor" to lull us into security. Do we actually know what sensible men mean by common experience? To begin with, it seems to refer to an experience which is accessible to everyone. But this initial impression is obviously not adequate in itself. For example, nothing would seem to be more obvious than that we exist, that we have bodies, that we are conscious, that the world includes us rather than we it, and so on. And yet there are individuals for whom none of these facts—if they are facts—is obvious. I am not referring to philosophers, as for example those who find it necessary to "demonstrate" their own or the external world's existence; although a genuinely sensible man would surely do well to be impressed by the fact that extremely intelligent men require demonstrations for what seems to be obvious. I think we are arguing from a philosophical position, rather than from common sense itself, when we assert that men who try to demonstrate common sense facts of common experience are certified *by* common sense as absurd or senseless. For instance, we tacitly assume in some of these cases that "common sense" is the same as naive materialism. But naive materialism is, for better or worse, a "sophisticated" philosophical interpretation of immediate experience. If most unphilosophical men are today naive materialists in the sense that they regard only extended bodies as real things, is this guaranteed by prephilosophical common sense, or is it the result of the widely accepted theoretical *interpretation* of experience, which has been so disseminated throughout our civilization that all "sensible" men accept it unthinkingly? In some ages, in some societies, men believe in spirits, transmigration of souls, psychic phenomena, and they are able to act very sensibly on the basis of their beliefs. If it is generally accepted in a given community that the gods will be appeased by the sacrifice of an ox, or that spiritual perfection is enhanced by standing upon one's head or by *not* killing oxen under any circumstances, by what right do we say that men who believe these things are lacking in common sense? To say this is merely to illustrate the fact that, in our civilization, "common sense" has come to take its meaning from the sensing of physical entities. On the basis of this philosophical step, we tend to take it for granted that no sensible man ever senses anything but bodies.

When a man holds up his hand and says, "common sense tells me—indeed guarantees—that this corporeal hand really exists," why should we believe him? To insist upon the corporeal existence of a hand is after all a theoretical interpretation of experience. Another man might claim that what we call a "hand" is really an imaginary being, an *image* of the incorporeal reality of consciousness. I do not suggest that this statement is certified by common sense, either. It, too, is an interpretation. My point is that immediate experience does not guarantee information about the nature of existence, whether as corporeal or mental. Common sense is not the immediate recognition of the mode of existence of an immediately experienced phenomenon. It is an interpretation, and so a *mediation,* of "immediate" experience. As such, it necessarily employs general categories or ideas which have properties and implications that cannot be circumscribed by what we commonly call "common sense." Prephilosophical man undoubtedly used or was used by bodies, and came to some general conclusions about effective ways for dealing with bodies of various kinds, without ever coming to the clear-cut theoretical conclusion: "that lion is a body, and not a malevolent spirit; the hand with which I hold my spear is an extended body, and not a psychic manifestation of my own spirit." Does this mean that such a man was unable to possess common sense, or to act in ways which we should have to call commonsensical? In a philosophical environment, or in a scientific environment, or in environments which have been colored by the pervasive effects of philosophy and science, we may well be able to exercise our common sense in more complex or subtle ways. But how would we behave differently from prephilosophical man if a lion were charging us and we held a spear? I am not speaking here of instinctive response; suppose that we are talking about such a case. What does common sense tell us to do? The answer is obvious: we may run, or climb a tree, or throw our spear, just as the prephilosophical man would have done, depending upon the circumstances, none of which requires a decision concerning the mode of existence of lion, spear, or hand.

Common sense may tell us that we exist, but it does not supply us with a philosophical or scientific interpretation of the fact that we exist. At the most, we might say that it supplies us with a *common sense* interpretation of that fact. I do not for a moment believe that it is possible to isolate such an interpretation from all philosophical and scientific interpretations, or elements of such interpretations, to hold up a clearly defined "common sense interpretation" as that which is *prior* to theory and to which theory must conform. Every such clear-cut definition of "common sense interpretation," and so of "common experience," is itself a theoretical interpretation, fundamentally philosophical but perhaps secondarily what is now called "scientific." I hasten to repeat that this does not mean a denial of common sense. What I deny is that common sense can give an adequate description or explanation of itself without the assistance of philosophy. There is either no such thing as "common sense philosophy," or *every* philosophy is a common sense philosophy in that it offers an interpretation of what we commonly call "common experience." Common experience is not self-explanatory, however satisfactory unspeculative men may find the term. To prove this, we have only to try to define or explain "common experience" in a non- or prephilosophical manner. [...]

Chapter 14

The Ethics of Common Sense

Mortimer J. Adler

In our next selection, philosopher Mortimer Adler attempts to "refine common-sense opinions into philosophical insights," to "set forth the ethics of common sense." Alder's discussion is strongly influenced by Aristotle, and this paper will provide an entry of sorts into the ancient philosopher's ethics. The discussion covers a lot of ground, so it might be helpful to preview the main points.

In Section 2 (the first section of our reading selection), Adler writes that, in view of our rational nature as humans, making "a whole life that is really good for us" is "the one and only end we ought to seek." It is self-evident, he says, that this good life as a whole is the single ultimate end that we desire and that we ought to seek. All other ends—whether self-preservation, health, wealth, power, moral virtue, spiritual perfection, or anything else—must promote this purpose.

Right off the bat, then, by setting up an ultimate purpose or end to be achieved, Adler is presenting us with a *teleological* ethics—that is, an ethics that aims for that ultimate end. The moral problem of determining the means to that end is also a *practical* problem; how do we distinguish between real goods (that is, to say, objects of desire) and merely apparent goods? And how do we then go about pursuing the goods necessary for a life that is really good as a whole? Thus, for Adler as for Aristotle, the field of ethics is a field of practical knowledge.

It should not come as a surprise that from this one single end, a basic moral duty follows, namely, to "seek that which is really good for us." Thus, Adler's common-sense ethics is also an ethics of duty—a *deontological ethics*. Since the system that he describes is both teleological and deontological, it spans two approaches to ethics that have often been seen as distinct: in much of modern ethics, a focus on *duty* (as in Kant)[1] has often been contrasted to a focus on the *consequences of actions* (as in utilitarianism). Adler, however, combines these two approaches. "Moral philosophy," he writes, "not only *can*

---

[1]Refer to the Kant entry in the Further Readings for Part IV section.

be both teleological and deontological at the same time, it also *must* be both" if it is to be both moral and practical.

In Section 3, Adler lays out six "insights that express the moral wisdom of a teleological ethics." In the course of doing this, he mention various "partial goods" that are means to the ultimate end (or *totum bonum*) of a good life as a whole. These include wealth, pleasure, virtue, treating others justly, and acquiring knowledge.

In Section 4, Adler describes these real goods further, and the types of activity by which they are obtained. Some of them (like health, wealth, pleasure, friendship, and knowledge), are wholly or partly within our power of choice; others, like peace and just government, are not. Adler mentions goods for the improvement of oneself and one's community, and he discusses two additional goods that are constitutive of a good life, namely, *idling* and *rest*. He distinguishes the former from the latter, and from the important good of *leisure*, too.

In Section 5, Adler distinguishes *limited* goods (goods of which there can be too much) from *unlimited* goods, notably leisure time for self-improvement. He touches on a number of other topics, too, including how to rank goods, and then concludes with the claim that, of the five basic types of human activity that he has described earlier, "only one calls for the maximum investment of our time, and that one is leisure-work."

Mortimer Adler (1902–2001) was influenced not only by Aristotle, but also by the great Christian writer, Thomas Aquinas. Although he taught for years at Columbia University and the University of Chicago, he wrote for a nonacademic audience, and produced more than one bestseller. "A general audience can read any book I write," he once said, "and they do." Our selection consists of most of Chapter 15 of the book *The Time of Our Lives: The Ethics of Common Sense*.

[Section (1) not included in this selection.]

(2)

When the common-sense man thinks practically, that is, when he thinks about how to act or what choices to make, he thinks in terms of end and means. As a matter of simple fact, there is no other way to think practically. One can act aimlessly and without reflection or deliberation, but if one acts purposefully and thoughtfully, one must do so, first, by having some goal or objective in view, and then by considering the steps that must be taken to achieve it. When, in any sphere of action or production, men set a goal or objective for themselves, the practical problem to be solved is one of discovering the best—the most effective—means for accomplishing it. And when the practical problem is solved, its solution is expressed in a set of normative judgments, such as "To reach the objective, A, that we have set for ourselves, we should do X, Y, and Z" where X, Y, and Z represent the most effective means for attaining the end.

Such normative judgments are hypothetical rather than categorical, because the practical problem arose as a result of a goal that an individual or a group of individuals set for himself or themselves. They did not have to set this goal for themselves; they elected to do so. The normative judgments involved, made more explicit, take the form, "If we wish to achieve A, we ought to do X, Y, and Z."

The man of common sense may think about the practical problem of making a good life for himself in the same way that he thinks about other practical problems: if one wants to make a good life for one's self, one ought to do this or that, so-and-so or such-and-such. It is at this point that the philosopher steps in to make one correction in common-sense thinking, a correction that converts the problem of making a good life from a practical problem like any other practical problem into a practical problem that is *also* a moral problem.

It becomes a moral problem as soon as it is seen that the end in view is set for us, rather than one that we do or do not set for ourselves, as we wish. The end is set for us by the recognition of the self-evident truth of the categorical normative judgment that we ought to seek what is really good for us, and nothing less than everything that is really good for us. With this recognition that the *totum bonum commune,* a whole life that is really good, is the ultimate end that we ought to seek, the solution of the practical problem that is also a moral problem takes the form of categorical ought judgments[2] concerning the means we ought to employ in order to achieve the one and only end we ought to seek.

By this one correction, common-sense thinking about the practical problem of achieving a good life is thus made philosophically sound, and as thus philosophically developed, it becomes a teleological ethics, but—and this is a point of the greatest importance—it does not cease to be a practical or pragmatic moral philosophy because it attaches categorical oughts to the end and to the means.

It is generally supposed by modern philosophers that if an ethical doctrine is deontological (one that is set forth in terms of categorical oughts), it is diametrically opposed to an ethical doctrine that is pragmatic and teleological (one that is set forth in terms of end and means). It is further supposed by the exponents of a deontological ethics that teleological thinking about a good life or happiness must be purely pragmatic

---

[2]"Categorical ought judgments" are *duties.*—M. M.

or practical, and cannot be moral or ethical because the only ought judgments it can make are hypothetical, not categorical. Both of these widespread suppositions are erroneous.

Moral philosophy not only *can* be both teleological and deontological at the same time; it also *must* be both if it is to be a sound ethical doctrine that is at once moral and practical. If it is teleological without being deontological, it is purely pragmatic or practical, as some forms of utilitarianism are, and so it is not moral philosophy. If it is deontological without being teleological, it is purely rationalistic and out of touch with the facts of life, and so, by ceasing to be practical or pragmatic, it becomes basically unsound. Although the moral philosophy based on common sense is both teleological and deontological, I shall refer to it simply as a teleological ethics because its first principle is an ultimate end that is the whole of real goods and because, given that first principle, all its conclusions are about means that ought to be employed because they are necessary for achieving the end.[3]

Only one controlling insight is needed to construct an ethics that is both teleological and deontological. It is that nothing can be either an end or a means for action unless it is also a good—an object of desire. When the end and the means are seen to be real, not apparent, goods, then these real goods, related as end and means, become objects of categorical moral obligation as well as objects of desire.

(3)

The philosophical development of the ethics of common sense adds a number of other fundamental insights that express the moral wisdom of a teleological ethics. They are as follows:

First, the most egregious moral error that anyone can make is to convert a means into the end. All misconceptions of the good life are examples of this error. They

---

[3] Although the ethics of common sense is both teleological and deontological, it is primarily teleological because the *totum bonum* as ultimate end is its first principle and the object of the one basic moral obligation—the obligation to make a life that is really good as a whole. Every other good is a means to this end; every other moral obligation, either in regard to the goods one ought to seek for one's self or in regard to the rights of others, derives from the one basic moral obligation that relates to the ultimate normative end of all our actions. In order to be both teleological and deontological, and, more than that, in order properly to subordinate the deontological to the teleological, deriving categorical oughts from the consideration of end and means, an ethics must (a) affirm the primacy of the good and (b) distinguish between real and apparent goods. That is why the ethics of Kant and of Mill only *appear* to be both, but under careful scrutiny are not. While Kant appears to be concerned with ends as well as duties, he makes duties—or the right, not the good—primary. And while Mill appears to be concerned with duties as well as with ends and means, his failure to recognize the distinction between real and apparent goods prevents him from making ends and means objects of categorical obligation.

substitute a part for the whole—identifying happiness or a whole life that is really good with one of the partial goods that is an element in the good life. To identify happiness with the possession of wealth without limit, or with the maximization of pleasure, is to misconceive happiness in this way. Wealth and pleasure are real goods, but only parts of happiness, not the whole of it. It is equally an error to identify the good life as a whole with being virtuous, with acting justly toward others, or even with acquiring as much knowledge as possible, for even though these are goods of which one cannot have enough, they are still only partial goods. None is the *totum bonum;* none is the end, but only a means. This error is, of course, compounded when happiness is identified with an apparent rather than a real good, such as power or domination over other men, for this is not even a means to the end of a good life.

Second, the means are the end in the process of becoming. As we have seen, when the end is a temporal whole, such as a good life, it is always a becoming, never a complete being. Strictly, we should not speak of human happiness as the "well-being" of a man, but rather as his "well-becoming." Nevertheless, since this process of well-becoming is a series of stages of development, the end exists to some extent at each stage of development, in the form of the means already acquired, the means now being acquired, and the means about to be acquired.

Third, a correct understanding of the end we ought to seek and of the means we ought to employ is not enough, practically, for achieving the end through the means. It is also necessary to desire the end we ought to seek, and to choose the means we ought to employ, and these represent noncognitive acts on our part. This is just another way of saying that knowledge, even in the form of moral wisdom, is not the same as moral virtue, which consists in desiring and choosing as we ought.

Moral virtue consists in a habitual disposition of appetite, desire, or will, which inclines a man in the direction of the end he ought to seek, and consequently also controls his choice of means in the same direction. Since it is frequently the case that several alternative means are available, all of them good because they serve the end, the man of moral virtue or good character also needs prudence or sound judgment to choose the better or the best—the more or most effective—of these means.

When it is said that as a man's moral character is, so does he conceive the end that he ought to seek, the point to be stressed is that a correct conception of the end is implicit in the disposition that constitutes a good moral character. Correspondingly, a mistaken view of the end is implicitly present in a man of bad moral character. In this sense, moral virtue by itself involves a form of knowledge—an implicit, nonintellectual acknowledgment of the end that ought to be sought. But the converse is not true: intellectual knowledge by itself does not involve moral virtue. A man can explicitly know the end he ought to seek, and not in fact desire it or choose the means for attaining it.

Fourth, when we understand that happiness or a whole life that is really good consists in the possession of all the things that are really good for a man to have, we can also see that this *totum bonum* or ultimate end cannot be achieved unless the partial goods that constitute it and are means to it are chosen in the right order and proportion. Some of the partial goods that enter into the constitution of a good life as a whole, such as health, wealth, and pleasure, can be sought to an extent that prevents or impedes the acquirement of other real goods that are indispensable elements of a good life as a whole. Furthermore, since partial goods are not all equally good, and since some of them are means to others, the pursuit of happiness can be frustrated or defeated by choices that do not conform to a right ordering of the partial goods.

Once again we see the role that moral virtue plays in the pursuit of happiness, for since the means are the end in the process of becoming, moral virtue, in disposing a man to seek the end that he ought to seek, also disposes him to seek it by choosing the means to it in the right order and the right proportion of the partial goods that constitute a good life as a whole. This is another way of saying what was said earlier: the moral problem we face from day to day is always one of choosing between what is really good in the long run of our life as a whole and what is really or only apparently good in the short run—here and now.

Fifth, in addition to distinguishing among partial real goods by seeing that some may serve as means to others, we must also make a more fundamental distinction between (i) the partial goods that are *constitutive* means to the end of a good life as a whole and (ii) partial goods that are *operative* or *instrumental* means to this end. The constitutive means are those partial goods that answer to natural needs, as health does, or wealth, pleasure, friendships, the peace of the civil community, or knowledge in any of its many forms. The operative or instrumental means are the actions we perform to obtain the real goods we need, or even more basically, they are the means whereby we are disposed to choose real goods in the right order and proportion, and to choose the better or the best among available goods.

Moral virtue or a good moral character and prudence or sound judgment are thus seen to be the principal operative or instrumental means to happiness. Although the primary real goods are those that satisfy natural needs, and although moral virtue and prudence are good only because they are indispensable or necessary factors in the process of satisfying all of our natural needs, it is nevertheless the case that the operative or instrumental means are of primary importance in the pursuit of happiness.

A human life is good through the possession of all the real goods that constitute the *totum bonum,* but it becomes good through the choices that are made from moment to moment, and so in the process of becoming happy, the goods that are the instrumental means to happiness are the primary factors.[4]

I just said that moral virtue and prudence are the principal operative or instrumental means to happiness. There is at least one other, and that is freedom.

---

[4]The instrumentality of moral virtue as an operative means to happiness or a good life should be clear to anyone who realizes that, in the course of living, we are required to choose from day to day, and from moment to moment, how we shall use our time, what activities we shall engage in, what order we shall engage in them, and to which we shall give preference in the economy of our limited time and energy. Moral virtue is simply a good habit of willing and choosing—a *habit* because it is an acquired and stable disposition to will and choose in a certain way, and a *good disposition* because it is a habitual inclination of the will toward the *totum bonum* as ultimate end, and a habitual tendency to choose between alternative courses of action or alternative goods according to whether they are or are not means to the ultimate end.

On the indispensability of a rightly directed will for a good life, see my discussion of the primary role of moral virtue as an instrumental means in Mortimer Adler, *A Dialectic of Morals* (Notre Dame, IN: University of Notre Dame Press, 1941), 67–68, 97–102, 105–7. In commenting on Augustine's observation that happiness consists in having all our desires satisfied, provided that we desire nothing amiss, Aquinas points out that "desiring nothing amiss is needed for happiness, as a necessary disposition thereto" (*Summa Theologica,* Pt. 1–11, Q. 3, A. 4, Reply 5). *Moral virtue is simply the habitual disposition to desire nothing amiss;* that is why it is necessary for a good life.

Prudence or sound judgment enters into the picture only with respect to such alternative means as are directed to the ultimate end. One may be better—more effective—than another, and it requires prudence to select the better of the several means that are morally sound, any of which a man of moral virtue would be inclined to choose because it is a means to the end his will is habitually inclined toward. While moral virtue and prudence are distinct—one being a habit of willing the end that ought to be sought and of choosing the appropriate means that ought to be employed, the other being a habit of deliberating about and deciding between morally acceptable means to the end—they are also existentially inseparable. Only a man of good moral character can also be prudent. Lacking moral virtue, the miser, the profligate, or the libertine may be clever or cunning in his calculations about the most effective means for achieving the apparent goods he wants and that he has made into ends, but such cleverness or cunning is only a counterfeit of prudence.

Furthermore, when different moral virtues are distinguished and given such names as temperance, fortitude, and justice, as has been traditionally done by those moral philosophers who have correctly understood moral virtue as consisting in a good habit of willing and choosing, the distinction is purely analytical—a distinction of aspects. It does not signify the existential separateness of diverse good habits. If it did, it would be possible for a man to be temperate without having fortitude, to have fortitude without being temperate, and to be just without either temperance or fortitude. But this cannot be the case if a good moral character or the possession of moral virtue consists in the habitual inclination of a man to the one ultimate end that he ought to seek. The unity of that end implies the unity of moral virtue, and requires us to deny an existential plurality of moral virtues. It is still useful to employ such terms as "temperance," "fortitude," and "justice," in order to distinguish diverse aspects of a good moral character, but whenever these terms are used for analytical purposes, it is necessary to safeguard their use against the serious error of converting them into the names of existentially distinct habits or dispositions, capable of existing separately, one without the others.

One form of freedom, sometimes called internal freedom and sometimes moral freedom, is identical with moral virtue. It is the freedom possessed by the virtuous man who is able, by habitual disposition, to will as he ought, or, stated negatively, it is a freedom from the contrary pressure of immediate wants, which enables a man to seek what he needs in the long run.

Another form of freedom—the freedom to act as one desires or chooses, a freedom from coercion, duress, or the lack of enabling means—is not a freedom that is acquired with moral virtue, but is rather one that men possess only when the external circumstances of their lives confer it on them. Such freedom of action is clearly an operative or instrumental means to leading a good life, but it is also a real good that answers to a natural need, and as such it is a constitutive as well as an instrumental means.

The same holds true for still another form of freedom—political liberty, the freedom that men possess when they are governed with their own consent and with a voice in government. Like freedom of action, this, too, is a circumstantial freedom, and one that, answering to a natural need, is a constitutive as well as an instrumental means to happiness. That both freedom of action and political liberty are real goods that answer to natural needs is implied in the recognition of them as natural rights, which a just government should secure for all its people.[5]

Although for the most part both Aristotle and Aquinas make this error, they do, nevertheless, in certain crucial passages, reveal some understanding of the unity of moral virtue, as well as of the existential inseparability of prudence from a good moral character. See Aristotle, *Nichomachean Ethics*, Book IV, Chapter 12; and Aquinas, *Summa Theologica*, Pt. I–II, Q. 61, A. 4. Compare to Jacques Maritain, *Art and Scholasticism* (NY: Sheed and Ward, 1933), 15–17, 153–4; and John Dewey, *Human Nature and Conduct* (NY: Henry Holt and Company, 1922), Chapter III.

[5]For a dialectical analysis of the acquired freedom that is existentially inseparable from the possession of acquired moral virtue, see Mortimer Adler, *The Idea of Freedom* (NY: Doubleday, 1958), Vol. I, Chapters 1–6, 15–16; and Vol. II, Chapter 17. For a similar treatment of the circumstantial freedom that consists in freedom from coercion, duress, or the lack of enabling means, see ibid., Vol. I, Chapters 12–14; Vol. II, Chapter 14; and for the special form of circumstantial freedom that is political liberty, see ibid., Vol. I, Chapter 18; Vol. II, Chapter 6.

Man being by nature a political animal, having a natural capacity for participation in government, political liberty answers to a natural need and so is a real good and the basis of a natural right. To deprive a man of political liberty—the liberty of a citizen with suffrage, governed by his own consent and with a voice in government—is to deprive him of something he needs to make a good life for

Sixth and last, among the constitutive means of a good life, we must distinguish between the goods of choice and the goods of chance or fortune—on the one hand, the means that are wholly within our own power to employ or not employ according to our own choices, and on the other hand, the means that are made available or unavailable to us by the favorable or unfavorable circumstances that surround our lives. Some of the constitutive means to happiness are wholly goods of choice; some are wholly goods of chance, conferred or withheld by favorable or unfavorable circumstances, and some are mixed in character—partly gifts of fortune and partly within our own power of choice. With this distinction in mind, we can understand the meaning of the compact statement that the pursuit of happiness consists in choosing and acting

---

himself. Freedom from coercion, duress, or the lack of enabling means also corresponds to a natural need—the need that is implicit in man's capacity to choose this or that course of action, for when a man is prevented by circumstances from carrying out his choice, his natural tendency to execute his choice in overt action is frustrated or unfulfilled. Therefore, such freedom from coercion, duress, or the lack of enabling means is also a real good and the basis of a natural right.

While freedom of choice and the freedom that is acquired with moral virtue are both instrumental or operative means to happiness, they do not fulfill natural needs and so they are not constitutive means, or parts of a good life, as political liberty and freedom from coercion are. Either man's freedom of choice is an element in his specific constitution, or it does not exist at all. It cannot be acquired; it is not conferred upon him by outward circumstances. Whether one affirms or denies man's natural possession of freedom of choice, one cannot say that man has a natural right to such freedom. Similarly, one cannot say that man has a natural right to the freedom acquired with moral virtue. He needs such freedom just as he needs moral virtue—as an indispensable instrumental or operative means to making a good life—but his having it or not having it depends solely on how he uses his own freedom of choice, not upon any external circumstances or the actions of other men that might deprive him of it.

To sum up, of the four forms of freedom, two—the circumstantial freedom of action and that special form of circumstantial freedom which is political liberty—are constitutive parts of the good life as well as instrumental means to becoming happy, and these two alone are involved in man's natural right to liberty. One of the remaining two—the acquired freedom of the virtuous man—is only an instrumental means to becoming happy, but not a constitutive part of the good life, except perhaps as one of the many ways in which, through leisure activities, a man improves himself—his character as well as his mind. In any case, this freedom is not involved in man's natural right to liberty. Finally, the fourth form of freedom—freedom of the will or of choice—either exists as a species-specific property of human nature, or it does not exist at all. If it does exist, and all men have this freedom as a native endowment, they cannot also claim it as a natural right. Nor can it be regarded as a good that answers to or fulfills a natural need. But can it be regarded as an instrumental means to happiness? If we understand a means to be something that we may or may not employ according to our choice, then freedom of choice cannot be a means. Nevertheless, it can be said that the moral problem of making a good life for one's self would not exist for us unless we had freedom of choice. This form of freedom is, therefore, even more fundamental than an indispensable instrumental means to happiness, for it is a condition prerequisite to there being any pursuit of happiness. See Chapter 17, Note 5, and further on [not included in our reading—M. M.].

in a manner that manifests a virtuous disposition, under favorable circumstances that confer a requisite minimum of the goods of fortune.[6]

(4)

The six points just stated outline the framework of a teleological ethics but do not exhaust its substance. Of the substantive points that remain, we need consider only two. The first concerns the enumeration of the real goods that are constitutive means

---

[6]The relation between happiness and moral virtue is often imprecisely stated. It is sometimes said that happiness consists in being virtuous, which is plainly false. If a man had moral virtue and none of the real goods that constitute the *totum bonum,* his life would not be a happy one, or good as a whole. While having some of the real goods that constitute the *totum bonum* may depend upon the exercise of moral virtue in the making of choices, this is certainly not true of all of them; some are wholly goods of chance or fortune, and some depend in part at least on chance or fortune.

It is also sometimes said that the happy life is the virtuous life. This is also plainly false. The happy life is a life made good by the possession, in the right order and proportion, of all the things that a man needs—all the things that are really good for him. Virtue enters into the picture as an instrumental means to a man's getting all the things that are really good for him, and perhaps also as one among many forms of self-improvement, which is the real good aimed at by the activities of leisure.

In addition, it is sometimes said that happiness consists in virtuous activity, which, if not false, is a very misleading way of stating the truth. We have seen that the five basic types of activity are sleeping, playing, working, leisuring, and idling. The adjective "virtuous" does not designate a type of activity, in any way commensurate or coordinate with the five basic types mentioned above. Each of these five basic types of activity can be engaged in in such a way or to such an extent that the result is good or bad for the individual, and if the result is good because a good choice has been made among alternative courses of action for the sake of the good life as a whole, then we should say of the activity that it was virtuously chosen, not that it was a virtuous activity.

The truth concealed in the misleading statement that happiness consists in virtuous activity begins to appear in the statement that a good life consists of activities "in accordance with virtue," which is to say, "chosen well, or virtuously, or as a man of good moral character would choose them." Even then the statement needs expansion to make it fully explicit and precise. Happiness, as the *totum bonum,* consists of, or is constituted by, the possession of all the real goods a man needs in the course of a whole life. In the definition of happiness, there need be no mention at all of moral virtue. Virtue becomes significant and relevant only when we turn from the constitution of happiness (the elements of a good life as achieved) to the pursuit of happiness (the process of making one's whole life good). It is only in the pursuit of happiness or in the process of making one's whole life good that moral virtue functions as an instrumental means. Hence it is precisely correct to say that the pursuit of happiness consists in choosing and acting in a manner that manifests a virtuous disposition, under favorable circumstances that confer a requisite minimum of the goods of fortune. If a man has moral virtue or a good moral character, he has one—*but only one*—of the things it takes to become happy, and while moral virtue is one of the principal means to becoming happy, it is by no means a principal part of being happy.

to happiness, and the types of activity by which they are obtained—activities that use up the time of our lives and that are thus the temporal parts of life.

The real goods that have so far been mentioned can be grouped under four heads. In naming them, I will also name the type of activity by which they are obtained, insofar as they are within our power of choice.

(1) *Bodily health and vigor*: all biologically necessary activities, such as sleeping, eating, cleansing, and sometimes playing when playing is therapeutic or recreational—for which I have used *sleep* as an omnibus term.

(2) *Wealth* (the means of subsistence and the comforts or conveniences of life): economically necessary activities such as working for a living or managing one's estate; which I have called *subsistence work*.

(3) *Pleasure* (in all its experienceable forms, sensual, aesthetic, and intellectual): all forms of activity engaged in wholly for their own sake, with no result beyond themselves—for which I have used *play* as an omnibus term.

(4) *The goods of self- or social improvement*: all forms of activity by which the individual improves himself and contributes to the improvement of his society and its culture—for which I have used the term *leisure* or *leisure work*. Among these goods are: (a) friendships, and (b) knowledge in all its forms—skills or arts, sciences, understanding, and wisdom.

In addition to these goods that are wholly or partly within our power of choice, there are all the goods that are conferred upon us by favorable external circumstances and that are nonetheless constitutive means to the end of a good life. Among these goods are: (a) the good of communal life, which is peace, and (b) a good society and a just government, one that promotes the general welfare and treats all men equally by securing the natural right of each, including his right to life and his right to a decent livelihood, his right to freedom of action, and his right to political liberty.

Is this enumeration exhaustive? I think it is exhaustive of the real goods that are constitutive means to a good life as a whole. But on the side of the activities that can occupy the times of our lives, the foregoing enumeration fails to mention two.

One of these has been referred to in earlier chapters. It is *idling*. I have not included it here because it does not appear to aim at the acquirement of any type of real good that answers to a natural need. Yet it should not be lightly dismissed as of no importance, in view of the fact that many men, perhaps all of us, consume many hours in idling. Let me appeal to a machine metaphor in order to explain idling. We say that an automobile engine idles when it runs while the auto remains in place, going nowhere. The engine turns over, but the usual appropriate result—locomotion—is not achieved. So, when men idle, they are not asleep, or at work, or at play, or engaged in leisure. They are awake but doing nothing productive of a desired result. Nevertheless, idling may produce results not consciously or intentionally planned, as when, in the course of idling, thoughts or decisions spring unpremeditated from the unconscious.

Another form of activity not yet mentioned goes by the name of rest, in that connotation of the term expressed in the meaning of the Sabbath as a day of rest, or when it is said that after performing the work of creation in six days, on the seventh day God rested. Clearly, in this meaning of the term, rest is not to be confused with sleep, or recreational play, or even with leisuring. Also clearly, the term as thus used has a religious and theological connotation, which signifies a form of activity that is apart from or transcends our secular and worldly lives. Since I have restricted our discussion of the good life to one that is lived in this world, on the natural plane and in a secular fashion, the activity of rest cannot enter into our considerations. But, in passing, I would like to suggest that on the secular plane, some forms of *idling,* which involve moments of quiet contemplation, reverie, or fantasy, may perform a function that is the secular equivalent of the function performed by *rest* in the religious life.

(5)

The second substantive point to be made concerns the order of goods, or what is sometimes called the scale of values. Among the constitutive means to happiness, some are limited and some are unlimited goods, and the latter are superior to and take precedence over the former. By an *unlimited good,* I mean one of which we cannot have enough, such as knowledge in any of its forms, or friendship and love. By a *limited good,* I mean one that is good only in some quantity, the kind of good about which it is true to say you can have too much of a good thing.[7]

Consider wealth, in the form of consumable goods. The quantity of wealth that is good, that is not excessive or superfluous, is obviously relative to our needs for the necessities and amenities of life. The same holds for the pleasures of play in all its forms. Although the principle of limitation is not as obvious here as it is in the case of consumable wealth, it is nevertheless clear that since play does not result in self-improvement, the devotion of all of one's free time to play would be

---

[7]Compare to Plato, *Philebus,* 27b–28e.

stultifying. In itself, health would appear to be an unlimited good, but on the side of the activities productive of health, it is certainly possible to devote more time than is necessary to the care of the body and to the development of its physical vigor.

Of the five basic types of human activity,[8] only one—the one that is productive of unlimited goods—calls for the maximum investment of our time, and that one is leisure work. The limitation to be imposed on the amount of time devoted to the other types of activity is solely for the sake of allowing as much time as possible for the pursuits of leisure. The goods of leisure are thus seen to be the highest goods among those that constitute a good life.

Biologically necessary activities are common to men and all other animals. While the effort we make to maintain health is characteristically a human undertaking, bodily health and vigor are not characteristically human goods. Health and wealth are functionally interdependent as goods. On the one hand, a sufficient degree of bodily health and vigor is needed as a means to the performance of subsistence work, and on the other hand, some degree of consumable wealth beyond the minimum necessities serves as a means to the maintenance of bodily health and vigor. Nevertheless, of these two, there is a sense in which health is the higher good. If we were compelled by circumstances to subordinate one to the other, we should give health priority or precedence in our scale of values. It contributes more, in the long run, to making a good life for ourselves.

Purely playful activities are good in themselves in that they provide us with immediately enjoyable pleasures; they do not serve as means to any other partial good, as wealth serves health, and as both of these serve as means to engagement in leisure and to the goods that leisure work produces. The immediately enjoyable pleasure of play satisfies a natural need and so is a part of or a constitutive means to a good life as a whole, but since the pleasures of play do not increase our human stature one cubit, play should be subordinated to the activities of leisure, which do.

Only leisure activities—activities that are creative in the primary sense of being self-creative, not productive of other things—contribute, first of all, to the growth of a human being as specifically human and, second, to the improvement of human society and the advancement of human culture. It is for this reason that the goods of leisure are the highest goods in the scale of partial goods, and that among the parts of life—the

---

[8]Recall that Adler's five sorts of "activities that use up our time" are: sleeping, playing, working, leisuring, and idling.—M. M.

activities that use up our time—the activities of leisure make the greatest contribution to a good life as a whole.[9]

Hence, in the choices that we make from day to day in the use of our time, we ought to subordinate all other activities to leisure work. We ought to engage in the others only to an extent that is based on our natural needs, or in a way that is limited by the consideration that nothing we do should unnecessarily consume the time left for the pursuits of leisure.

---

[9]To say that the activities of leisure make the greatest contribution to a good life as a whole is not to say that, of the five basic types of activity, leisure and leisure alone should be engaged in without limit. Every type of activity, even leisure work must be limited in the amount of time devoted to it, in order to allow sufficient time for other types of activity, such as sleep and play, that are also indispensable to the making of a good life. Nevertheless, in terms of the order of the real goods that result from the various types of activity, the other indispensable types of activity should be subordinated to leisuring, not leisuring to them. Of the goods that result from different types of activity, the goods of self-improvement are the only ones that are unlimited goods—goods of which we cannot have too much. Self-improvement, in all its aspects, thus represents the *summum bonum*, the highest in the order of all the real goods that constitute the *totum bonum*, and leisuring is the highest type of human activity because it aims at and results in the highest type of good.

However, in one respect, play, together with the pleasure intrinsic to it, is more like the *totum bonum* than leisure, together with the self-improvement that results from it. If a man at play forgets or ignores his life as a whole, he is for the moment engaged in an activity the pleasure of which satisfies him without reference to anything beyond itself. Just as a good life as a whole is not a means to anything beyond itself, so the pleasure of play is not a means to any other good *except a good life as a whole*. In contrast, the goodness of leisuring is always and only that of a means to a good life as a whole, and in the scale of goods that constitute the *totum bonum*, the goods of self-improvement resulting from leisure are more valuable—make a greater contribution—than the pleasure intrinsic to play.

FOR DISCUSSION OR ESSAYS

- In our reading, Darwin wrote that, "To do good in return for evil, to love your enemy, is a height of morality to which it may be doubted whether the social instincts would, by themselves, have ever led us." Thomas Reid, in his *Essays on the Active Powers of Man*[10] (not included in this book), described the Golden Rule as a "rule of conduct [that] is self-evident to every man who hath a conscience." According to Reid, what hinders us from discerning what we owe to others is self-love and a lack of honesty with ourselves. But in view of Darwin's remark, could we say the same about the Christian maxims to turn the other cheek and to love one's enemy?

- In our reading, Darwin described how the more enduring social instincts, such as sympathy, conquer the less persistent instincts. Did he thereby provide an answer to Stanley Rosen's question of how to order and rank "basic motives" or "fundamental ends of human behavior"? Explain.

- Rosen wrote that, "Even the view that 'all truth is relative' rests upon the commonsensical assumption of stability in human nature, not with respect to the facts of behavior or means, but rather with respect to the ends." What did he mean by this? Do you agree? Explain.

- In a passage from "Common Sense and Human Nature" that is not included in our selection, Rosen wrote that: "Common sense does not in itself adjudicate between the rival philosophical positions of materialism and idealism, except in the sense that it rejects both, or would reject them if it could conceive of them." Discuss this claim, with reference to Reid and Moore's contention that common sense certifies the falsehood of the idealist view that *all that exists are minds and their ideas*.

- By Adler's lights, Rosen's conflicting "fundamental ends" are not really fundamental at all, but are rather, "constitutive means of a good life," some of which, properly, are prior to others. Compare and contrast Adler's ethics to Rosen's, when it comes to the former's *totum bonum* and the latter's "fundamental ends."

- Adler claims that the ethical system that he describes is not only teleological, but it is also deontological, because it holds that all rational humans have

---

[10]Thomas Reid, *Essays on the Active Powers of Man* (London: John Bell and G. G. J and J. Robinson, 1788), 375.

a categorical (unqualified) *duty* to seek that which is really good for us. Do you agree that humans have a duty to pursue genuine happiness? What about self-improvement? Why or why not?

FURTHER READINGS FOR PART IV

As with the topic of religion and common sense, so also with the topic of morality and common sense, mounds and mounds of books and articles have been published. The items in the short list below were chosen with an eye to their usefulness to those who have completed the readings in Part IV.

Adler, Mortimer J. "The Good Life and the Good Society." In *The Common Sense of Politics*, 18–29. New York: Holt, Rinehart and Winston, 1971. This piece, which comprises Chapter 2 of *The Common Sense of Politics*, is a companion piece to the earlier book from which our Adler selection was drawn. As the author sees it, political philosophy is one half of moral philosophy, the other half of which is ethics. In this book, too, Adler shows his debt to Aristotle: the question of what the main features of human society should be like comes down to the question *What sort of society is most conducive to a truly good life for men and women?*

Boulter, Stephen. *The Rediscovery of Common Sense Philosophy*. Basingstoke, UK and New York: Palgrave Macmillan, 2007. Boulter argues that "there is as yet no good reason not to believe that there are moral facts, and that these facts, like any facts, are independent of our representations of them" (Boulter, 177–8).

Butler, Joseph. "Upon the Social Nature of Man." This is Sermon 1 in Butler's book, *Fifteen Sermons*, published in 1726. Butler, a philosopher and bishop in the Church of England, presents his case against the widespread common-sense view that all human actions are selfishly motivated (a view that we today call *psychological egoism*). Butler's target is the materialist philosopher Thomas Hobbes. He acknowledges that self-love is indeed a major factor in motivating human behavior, as Hobbes had claimed; however, Butler argues, it is not the only instinctive human motivation: there is also a "natural principle of benevolence" in men and women.

Kant, Immanuel. *Groundwork (or Foundations) of the Metaphysics of Morals* (1785). In this very influential work, the great German philosopher presents and illustrates what he takes to be the fundamental principle of morality, the Categorical Imperative. This imperative, he argues, is implicit in the moral thinking of ordinary men and women. Kant begins by reflecting on the concept of *good will* (we might say good intentions), and then explains the difference between a *hypothetical* imperative and a *categorical* one, the latter of which he takes to be distinctive of morality. After that, he provides two or three formulations of the Categorical Imperative, with illustrations.

Rachels, James and Stuart. *The Elements of Moral Philosophy* 6th edition. New York: McGraw-Hill, 1986, 2012. The late American philosopher James Rachels (1941–2003) takes aim at a common ethical view called *cultural relativism*. This is the view that "custom is king": there are no principles of right conduct that are applicable across-the-board to all individuals and societies at all times. Rachels points out that the indisputable fact that different cultures have different moral codes does not imply that right and wrong are just a matter of opinion. After observing that the differences among moral codes is less dramatic than it may seem at first, he explains in clear language why he does not subscribe to cultural relativism.

Singer, Marcus G. "Ethics and Common Sense." In *Revue Internationale de Philosophie* 40, no. 158(3) (1986), 221–258. Singer notes that common sense and morality both bear on "our intercourse with people," and he argues that ethics is essential to common sense. Thus, "Common sense is intrinsically and ineluctably ethical in character." Although common sense is essential to ethics, it is not *sufficient* for it, because it is basically conservative, not innovative, and it can be oppressive, too. "Moral progress" requires that common sense morality be supplemented and corrected by ethical thinking outside of common sense.

Part V

Common Sense and Economics

Introduction to Part V: Common Sense and Economics

Since early modern times, common sense has figured prominently in the "moral science" that we call economics. In contemporary economics, sophisticated formal techniques, including econometrics, applied statistics, and game theory play a prominent role. But this does not diminish the fact that mainstream economics takes a great deal for granted when it comes to human psychology and society, and that much of what it takes for granted goes by the name of common sense. Economic common sense includes such items as: "incentives matter," "there is no such thing as a free lunch," "trade promotes progress," "prices bring the choices of buyers and sellers into balance," and many other economic claims that have attained the status of uncontestable truths.[1]

The MIT economist Paul Samuelson (1915–2009) wrote one of the bestselling economics textbooks of all time. Simply titled *Economics,* the book has gone through at least nineteen editions and been translated into more than twenty languages. "I don't care who writes a nation's laws or crafts its advanced treaties," Samuelson once said, "if I can write its economics textbooks."[2] Economics is a weighty field and the stakes are high, so it is not surprising that pundits, policy wonks, and authors of economics textbooks so often invoke the authority of common sense to certify their claims. In the prologue to another textbook titled *Economics,* for example, we read:

> Economics is involved in all the things you've been doing all your life. So how have you been able to get along all these years without knowing any economics? You haven't. The fact is, you know quite a lot of basic economics already. Everybody does.

---

[1] See for example, "Twelve Key Elements of Economics," in *Common Sense Economics: What Everyone Should Know about Wealth and Prosperity*, ed. James D. Gwartney, Richard L. Stroup, Dwight R. Lee, and Tawni Ferrarini (New York: St. Martin's Press, 2010), 5–39.

[2] The quote appeared in the *New York Times*, October 12, 1986, Sec. 3. It has been quoted more recently in "The Puzzling Failure of Economics," *The Economist*, August 25, 1997, among other places.

You already know, right now, 40 or 50 or maybe 70 or 80 percent of the economics you will know when you get to the end of this [800-page] book. But right now you don't call it "economics." You call it "common sense."[3]

Introductory material in economics textbooks often creates the impression that the economic arrangements that prevail today differ from arrangements in the past only in the degree of complexity and efficiency. As one observer described it:

> There is a common-sense view of capitalism in which it really has no beginning. Capitalism's origins are traced back to the most primitive acts of exchange, in any form of trade or market activity; it is seen as an almost natural process of technological development that has characterized human progress from the earliest times. Capitalism, so to speak, is taken for granted, either as the outcome of some perennial tendencies in human nature, or of natural laws when and where they are given a chance. Laws of capitalist economy are treated as if they are universal laws of human behavior or production activity.[4]

Authors of textbooks, of course, must often summarize material and simplify their presentations. But there are many ways of summarizing and simplifying, and whether an author is aware of it or not, the way she goes about doing this reflects a great many commitments. If in the course of simplifying our survey of economic history we create the impression that the prevailing economic system *has always been with us*, then readers might reasonably conclude that it *always will be with us*. Whether or not the universalizing assertions about capitalism are true, they have proved useful when it comes to defending the status quo. If current economic arrangements are inscribed in human nature and common sense, then it is futile at best to try to change them.

Our next two readings are typical of the sort of literature that starts with economic principles that, it is claimed, all sensible people agree upon when they are reasonably informed. Harvard economist Gregory Mankiw submits for our consideration ten "central ideas" that describe how rational people make decisions, and that unify the study of economics. The reading after that will serve as an example of the vast and ever-expanding body of edifying literature that grounds capitalism in our common-sense assumptions about human nature, society, and the passing scene. The excerpt, written by Nobel Prize winning economist Gary Becker

---

[3]Elbert V. Bowden, *Economics: The Science of Common Sense*, fifth edn. (Cincinnati: South-Western Publishing Co., 1986), xiii.

[4]Randhir Singh, *What Was Built and What Failed in the Soviet Union: Crisis of Socialism—Notes in Defence of a Commitment*, vol. 2 (Delhi: Aakar Books, 2011), 197–8.

and U.S. Court of Appeals jurist Richard A. Posner, is a forceful piece of advocacy. It is not itself an instance of philosophy; nevertheless, it is included here because it exemplifies, in a clear and convincing way, a particular interpretation of economic history. According to this interpretation, the field of economics has unfolded as the gradual and ever-more-complete realization that capitalism is the best of all possible economic systems.

Mainstream economists typically avoid discussing the relationship between wealth and political power. This relationship, we are led to believe, is not a proper object of examination for the science of economics. From the classical political economist David Ricardo to Léon Walrus (the pioneer of general equilibrium theory) and beyond, economics has more and more completely been "devoted to analysis of enduring principles of economics, divorced from social, political and philosophical commentary."[5] The assumption is that a scientific economics—no longer *political economy*—can and should skirt "politics."

In the third and last reading in Part V, Jacinda Swanson, professor of political science at Western Michigan University, casts a critical eye on this assumption. She agrees with American economist Joseph Stiglitz, recipient of the 2001 Nobel Prize in Economics, who observed that "Macroeconomic policy can never be devoid of politics: it involves fundamental trade-offs and affects different groups differently."[6] Swanson describes the depoliticization of economics, explains why it takes place, and suggests how to re-politicize economics. In the course of doing this, she re-describes the relationship between common sense and partisan discourse. According to our commonsensical understanding of common sense, beliefs become items of common sense when the evidence of daily life weighs on their side. By contrast, Swanson suggests a reverse relationship: beliefs that somehow receive common sense status thereby receive immunity from the testimony of daily experience.

Once again, we see that common sense presents itself as *above controversy*, when in fact controversy and partisanship are the very occasion for it arising, and the very medium that sustains it. Common sense presents itself as a neutral and "non-ideological" referee in debates, when in fact its appearance more often marks an escalation of conflict.

Swanson's paper provides a smooth transition to the topic we will take up in Part VI.

---

[5]Thomas Sowell, *Basic Economics* (refer to the entry in the Further Readings for Part V section), 624. Attentive readers may judge for themselves the extent to which such discussions have been purged of social, political, and philosophical commentary.

[6]"Downsides of Fed Independence," *The Nation* (Thailand), November 14, 2005, n.p.

Chapter 15

Ten Principles of Economics

N. Gregory Mankiw

Economics textbooks and works of popular economics purport to deliver the cold, hard facts of life: trade-offs and opportunity cost, supply and demand, comparative advantage, marginal preferences, and much else in the way of "dismal" news. The authors of these books provide hard-nosed critiques of such common misconceptions as "needs" "fair price," "predatory pricing," and "involuntary unemployment."[1] Gregory Mankiw is exemplary in this respect. He begins with what is supposed to be obvious: "an economy is just a group of people interacting with one another as they go about their lives." The behavior of an economy, he writes, "reflects the behavior of the individuals who make up the economy." Economic activity, then, is the sum of the interactions of pre-given, self-regarding individuals, and one of the chief focuses of economics should be studying the behavior of these discrete individuals. By depicting an economy this way, as we will see, he elevates psychological considerations to the center of economics.

Nicholas Gregory Mankiw is a professor of economics at Harvard University. From 2003 to 2005, he served as chairman of the Council of Economic Advisors under former U.S. President George W. Bush. His book *Principles of Economics*, now in its eighth edition, is described in the promotional copy as "the most popular, widely-used economics textbook by students worldwide."

---

[1] Thomas Sowell provides an exemplary overview. (Refer to the entry in the Further Readings for Part V section.) Of course, none of this is particularly inaccurate, as far as it goes. Typically, though, these authors seldom get around to acknowledging other facts of life that might strike some people as important, too, including the reality of class stratification in modern societies, the role of the state in maintaining "free market economies," and the pervasiveness of political domination within the borders of "free market" countries, and beyond their borders, too.

How People Make Decisions

There is no mystery to what an "economy" is. Whether we are talking about the economy of Los Angeles, of the United States, or of the whole world, an economy is just a group of people interacting with one another as they go about their lives. Because the behavior of an economy reflects the behavior of the individuals who make up the economy, we start our study of economics with four principles of individual decision-making.

Principle #1: People Face Trade-Offs

The first lesson about making decisions is summarized in the adage: "There is no such thing as a free lunch." To get one thing that we like, we usually have to give up another thing that we like. Making decisions requires trading off one goal against another.

Consider a student who must decide how to allocate her most valuable resource—her time. She can spend all of her time studying economics, she can spend all of her time studying psychology, or she can divide her time between the two fields. For every hour she studies one subject, she gives up an hour she could have used studying the other. And for every hour she spends studying, she gives up an hour that she could have spent napping, bike riding, watching TV, or working at her part-time job for some extra spending money.

Or consider parents deciding how to spend their family income. They can buy food, clothing, or a family vacation. Or they can save some of the family income for retirement or the children's college education. When they choose to spend an extra dollar on one of these goods, they have one less dollar to spend on some other good.

When people are grouped into societies, they face different kinds of trade-offs. The classic trade-off is between "guns and butter." The more we spend on national defense (guns) to protect our shores from foreign aggressors, the less we can spend on consumer goods (butter) to raise our standard of living at home. Also important in modern society is the trade-off between a clean environment and a high level of income. Laws that require firms to reduce pollution raise the cost of producing goods and services. Because of the higher costs, these firms end up earning smaller profits, paying lower wages, charging higher prices, or some combination of these three. Thus, while pollution regulations give us the benefit of a cleaner environment and the improved health that comes with it, they have the cost of reducing the incomes of the firms' owners, workers, and customers.

Another trade-off society faces is between efficiency and equity. *Efficiency* means that society is getting the most it can from its scarce resources. *Equity* means that the benefits of those resources are distributed fairly among society's members. In other words, efficiency refers to the size of the economic pie, and equity refers to how the pie is divided. Often, when government policies are being designed, these two goals conflict.

Consider, for instance, policies aimed at achieving a more equal distribution of economic well-being. Some of these policies, such as the welfare system or unemployment insurance, try to help those members of society who are most in need. Others, such as the individual income tax, ask the financially successful to contribute more than others to support the government. Although these policies have the benefit of achieving greater equity, they have a cost in terms of reduced efficiency. When the government redistributes income from the rich to the poor, it reduces the reward for working hard; as a result, people work less and produce fewer goods and services. In other words, when the government tries to cut the economic pie into more equal slices, the pie gets smaller.

Recognizing that people face trade-offs does not by itself tell us what decisions they will or should make. A student should not abandon the study of psychology just because doing so would increase the time available for the study of economics. Society should not stop protecting the environment just because environmental regulations reduce our material standard of living. The poor should not be ignored just because helping them distorts work incentives. Nonetheless, acknowledging life's trade-offs is important because people are likely to make good decisions only if they understand the options that they have available.

Principle #2: The Cost of Something Is What You Give Up to Get It

Because people face trade-offs, making decisions requires comparing the costs and benefits of alternative courses of action. In many cases, however, the cost of some action is not as obvious as it might first appear.

Consider, for example, the decision whether to go to college. The benefit is intellectual enrichment and a lifetime of better job opportunities. But what is the cost? To answer this question, you might be tempted to add up the money you spend on tuition, books, room, and board. Yet this total does not truly represent what you give up to spend a year in college.

The first problem with this answer is that it includes some things that are not really costs of going to college. Even if you quit school, you would need a place to sleep and food to eat. Room and board are costs of going to college only to the extent that they are more expensive at college than elsewhere. Indeed, the cost of room and board at your school might be less than the rent and food expenses that you would pay living on your own. In this case, the savings on room and board are a benefit of going to college.

The second problem with this calculation of costs is that it ignores the largest cost of going to college—your time. When you spend a year listening to lectures, reading textbooks, and writing papers, you cannot spend that time working at a job. For most students, the wages given up to attend school are the largest single cost of their education.

The *opportunity cost* of an item is what you give up to get that item. When making any decision, such as whether to attend college, decision makers should be aware of the opportunity costs that accompany each possible action. In fact, they usually are. College-age athletes who can earn millions if they drop out of school and play professional sports are well aware that their opportunity cost of college is very high. It is not surprising that they often decide that the benefit is not worth the cost.

Principle #3: Rational People Think at the Margin

Decisions in life are rarely black and white but usually involve shades of gray. At dinnertime, the decision you face is not between fasting and eating like a pig, but whether to take that extra spoonful of mashed potatoes. When exams roll around, your decision is not between blowing them off or studying twenty-four hours a day, but whether to spend an extra hour reviewing your notes instead of watching TV. Economists use the term *marginal changes* to describe small incremental adjustments to an existing plan of action. Keep in mind that "margin" means "edge," so marginal changes are adjustments around the edges of what you are doing.

In many situations, people make the best decisions by thinking at the margin. Suppose, for instance, that you asked a friend for advice about how many years to stay in school. If he were to compare for you the lifestyle of a person with a Ph.D. to that of a grade school dropout, you might complain that this comparison is not helpful for your decision. You have some education already and most likely are deciding whether to spend an extra year or two in school. To make this decision, you need to know the additional benefits that an extra year in school would offer (higher wages throughout life and the sheer joy of learning) and the additional costs that you would incur (tuition and the forgone wages while you're in school). By comparing these *marginal benefits* and *marginal costs,* you can evaluate whether the extra year is worthwhile.

As another example, consider an airline deciding how much to charge passengers who fly standby. Suppose that flying a 200-seat plane across the country costs the airline $100,000. In this case, the average cost of each seat is $100,000 ÷ 200, which is $500. One might be tempted to conclude that the airline should never sell a ticket for less than $500. In fact, however, the airline can raise its profits by thinking at the margin. Imagine that a plane is about to take off with ten empty seats, and a standby passenger is waiting at the gate willing to pay $300 for a seat. Should the airline sell it to him? Of course it should. If the plane has empty seats, the cost of adding one more passenger is minuscule. Although the *average* cost of flying a passenger is $500, the *marginal* cost is merely the cost of the bag of peanuts and can of soda that the extra passenger will consume. As long as the standby passenger pays more than the marginal cost, selling him a ticket is profitable.

As these examples show, individuals and firms can make better decisions by thinking at the margin. A rational decision maker takes an action if and only if the marginal benefit of the action exceeds the marginal cost.

Principle #4: People Respond to Incentives

Because people make decisions by comparing costs and benefits, their behavior may change when the costs or benefits change. That is, people respond to incentives. When the price of an apple rises, for instance, people decide to eat more pears and fewer apples because the cost of buying an apple is higher. At the same time, apple orchards decide to hire more workers and harvest more apples, because the benefit of selling an apple is also higher. As we will see, the effect of price on the behavior of buyers and sellers in a market—in this case, the market for apples—is crucial for understanding how the economy works.

Public policymakers should never forget about incentives, for many policies change the costs or benefits that people face and, therefore, alter behavior. A tax on gasoline, for instance, encourages people to drive smaller, more fuel-efficient cars. It also encourages people to take public transportation rather than drive and to live closer to where they work. If the tax were large enough, people would start driving electric cars.

When policymakers fail to consider how their policies affect incentives, they often end up with results they did not intend. For example, consider public policy regarding auto safety. Today all cars have seat belts, but that was not true fifty years ago. In the 1960s, Ralph Nader's book *Unsafe at Any Speed* generated much public concern over auto safety. Congress responded with laws requiring seat belts as standard equipment on new cars.

How does a seat belt law affect auto safety? The direct effect is obvious: When a person wears a seat belt, the probability of surviving a major auto accident rises. But that's not the end of the story, for the law also affects behavior by altering incentives. The relevant behavior here is the speed and care with which drivers operate their cars. Driving slowly and carefully is costly because it uses the driver's time and energy. When deciding how safely to drive, rational people compare the marginal benefit from safer driving to the marginal cost. They drive more slowly and carefully when the benefit of increased safety is high. It is no surprise, for instance, that people drive more slowly and carefully when roads are icy than when roads are clear.

Consider how a seat belt law alters a driver's cost–benefit calculation. Seat belts make accidents less costly because they reduce the likelihood of injury or death. In other words, seat belts reduce the benefits to slow and careful driving. People respond to seat belts as they would to an improvement in road conditions—by faster and less careful driving. The end result of a seat belt law, therefore, is a larger number of accidents. The decline in safe driving has a clear, adverse impact on pedestrians, who are more likely to find themselves in an accident but (unlike the drivers) don't have the benefit of added protection.

At first, this discussion of incentives and seat belts might seem like idle speculation. Yet, in a 1975 study, economist Sam Peltzman showed that the auto-safety laws have had many of these effects. According to Peltzman's evidence, these laws produce both fewer deaths per accident and more accidents. The net result is little change in the number of driver deaths and an increase in the number of pedestrian deaths.[2]

Peltzman's analysis of auto safety is an example of the general principle that people respond to incentives. Many incentives that economists study are more straightforward than those of the auto-safety laws. No one is surprised that people drive smaller cars in Europe, where gasoline taxes are high, than in the United States, where gasoline taxes are low. Yet, as the seat belt example shows, policies can have effects that are not obvious in advance. When analyzing any policy, we must consider not only the direct effects but also the indirect effects that work through incentives. If the policy changes incentives, it will cause people to alter their behavior.

---

[2]"If an undergraduate handed in the seat belt research nowadays as a term paper, I would ask her to redo it. It was a primitive piece of work, but it came up with a provocative answer to a well-posed question. My critics don't quarrel with the basic theory of an offsetting response. There is a continuing debate about the magnitude of this response in specific cases." ("Sam Peltzman Thinks You Should Belt Up," *Chicago Booth Review*, November 27, 2017, http://review.chicagobooth.edu/economics/2016/article/sam-peltzman-thinks-you-should-belt.) —M. M.

How People Interact

The first four principles discussed how individuals make decisions. As we go about our lives, many of our decisions affect not only ourselves but other people as well. The next three principles concern how people interact with one another.

Principle #5: Trade Can Make Everyone Better Off

You have probably heard on the news that the Japanese are our competitors in the world economy. In some ways this is true, for American and Japanese firms do produce many of the same goods. Ford and Toyota compete for the same customers in the market for automobiles. Compaq and Toshiba compete for the same customers in the market for personal computers.

Yet it is easy to be misled when thinking about competition among countries. Trade between the United States and Japan is not like a sports contest, where one side wins and the other side loses. In fact, the opposite is true: Trade between two countries can make each country better off.

To see why, consider how trade affects your family. When a member of your family looks for a job, he or she competes against members of other families who are looking for jobs. Families also compete against one another when they go shopping, because each family wants to buy the best goods at the lowest prices. So, in a sense, each family in the economy is competing with all other families.

Despite this competition, your family would not be better off isolating itself from all other families. If it did, your family would need to grow its own food, make its own clothes, and build its own home. Clearly, your family gains much from its ability to trade with others. Trade allows each person to specialize in the activities he or she does best, whether it is farming, sewing, or home building. By trading with others, people can buy a greater variety of goods and services at lower cost.

Countries as well as families benefit from the ability to trade with one another. Trade allows countries to specialize in what they do best and to enjoy a greater variety of goods and services. The Japanese, as well as the French and the Egyptians and the Brazilians, are as much our partners in the world economy as they are our competitors.

Principle #6: Markets Are Usually a Good Way to Organize Economic Activity

The collapse of communism in the Soviet Union and Eastern Europe in the 1980s may be the most important change in the world during the past half century. Communist countries worked on the premise that central planners in the government were in the best position to guide economic activity. These planners decided what goods and services were produced, how much was produced, and who produced and consumed these goods and services. The theory behind central planning was that only the government could organize economic activity in a way that promoted economic well-being for the country as a whole.

Today, most countries that once had centrally planned economies have abandoned this system and are trying to develop market economies. In a *market economy*, the decisions of a central planner are replaced by the decisions of millions of firms and households. Firms decide whom to hire and what to make. Households decide which firms to work for and what to buy with their incomes. These firms and households interact in the marketplace, where prices and selfinterest guide their decisions.

At first glance, the success of market economies is puzzling. After all, in a market economy, no one is looking out for the economic well-being of society as a whole. Free markets contain many buyers and sellers of numerous goods and services, and all of them are interested primarily in their own well being. Yet, despite decentralized decision-making and self-interested decision makers, market economies have proven remarkably successful in organizing economic activity in a way that promotes overall economic well-being.

In his 1776 book *An Inquiry into the Nature and Causes of the Wealth of Nations*, economist Adam Smith made the most famous observation in all of economics: Households and firms interacting in markets act as if they are guided by an "invisible hand" that leads them to desirable market outcomes. One of our goals in this book is to understand how this invisible hand works its magic. As you study economics, you will learn that prices are the instrument with which the invisible hand directs economic activity. Prices reflect both the value of a good to society and the cost to society of making the good. Because households and firms look at prices when deciding what to buy and sell, they unknowingly take into account the social benefits and costs of their actions. As a result, prices guide these individual decision makers to reach outcomes that, in many cases, maximize the welfare of society as a whole.

There is an important corollary to the skill of the invisible hand in guiding economic activity: When the government prevents prices from adjusting naturally to supply and demand, it impedes the invisible hand's ability to coordinate the millions of households and firms that make up the economy. This corollary explains why taxes adversely affect the allocation of resources: Taxes distort prices and thus the decisions of households and firms. It also explains the even greater harm caused by policies that directly control prices, such as rent control. And it explains the failure of communism. In communist countries, prices were not determined in the marketplace but were dictated by central planners. These planners lacked the information that gets reflected in prices when prices are free to respond to market forces. Central planners failed because they tried to run the economy with one hand tied behind their backs—the invisible hand of the marketplace.

Principle #7: Governments Can Sometimes Improve Market Outcomes

If the invisible hand of the market is so great, why do we need government? One answer is that the invisible hand needs government to protect it. Markets work only if property rights are enforced. A farmer won't grow food if he expects his crop to be stolen, and a restaurant won't serve meals unless it is assured that customers will pay before they leave. We all rely on government-provided police and courts to enforce our rights over the things we produce.

Yet there is another answer to why we need government: Although markets are usually a good way to organize economic activity, this rule has some important exceptions. There are two broad reasons for a government to intervene in the economy—to promote efficiency and to promote equity. That is, most policies aim either to enlarge the economic pie or to change how the pie is divided.

Although the invisible hand usually leads markets to allocate resources efficiently, that is not always the case. Economists use the term *market failure* to refer to a situation in which the market on its own fails to produce an efficient allocation of resources. One possible cause of market failure is an *externality*, which is the impact of one person's actions on the well-being of a bystander. For instance, the classic example of an external cost is pollution. Another possible cause of market failure is *market power*, which refers to the ability of a single person (or small group) to unduly influence market prices. For example, if everyone in town needs water but there is only one well, the owner of the well is not subject to the rigorous competition with which the invisible hand normally keeps self-interest in check. In the presence of externalities or market power, well-designed public policy can enhance economic efficiency.

The invisible hand may also fail to ensure that economic prosperity is distributed equitably. A market economy rewards people according to their ability to produce things that other people are willing to pay for. The world's best basketball player earns more than the world's best chess player simply because people are willing to pay more to watch basketball than chess. The invisible hand does not ensure that everyone has sufficient food, decent clothing, and adequate health care. Many public policies, such as the income tax and the welfare system, aim to achieve a more equitable distribution of economic well-being.

To say that the government *can* improve on market outcomes at times does not mean that it always *will*. Public policy is made not by angels but by a political process that is far from perfect. Sometimes policies are designed simply to reward the politically powerful. Sometimes they are made by well-intentioned leaders who are not fully informed. One goal of the study of economics is to help you judge when a government policy is justifiable to promote efficiency or equity, and when it is not.

How the Economy as a Whole Works

We started by discussing how individuals make decisions and then looked at how people interact with one another. All these decisions and interactions together make up "the economy." The last three principles concern the workings of the economy as a whole.

Principle #8: A Country's Standard of Living Depends on Its Ability to Produce Goods and Services

The differences in living standards around the world are staggering. In 2000 the average American had an income of about $34,100. In the same year, the average Mexican earned $8,790, and the average Nigerian earned $800. Not surprisingly, this large variation in average income is reflected in various measures of the quality of life. Citizens of high-income countries have more TV sets, more cars, better nutrition, better health care, and longer life expectancy than citizens of lowincome countries.

Changes in living standards over time are also large. In the United States, incomes have historically grown about two percent per year (after adjusting for changes in the cost of living). At this rate, average income doubles every thirty-five years. Over the past century, average income has risen about eightfold.

What explains these large differences in living standards among countries and over time? The answer is surprisingly simple. Almost all variation in living standards is attributable to differences in countries' *productivity*—that is, the amount of goods and services produced from each hour of a worker's time. In nations where workers can produce a large quantity of goods and services per unit of time, most people enjoy a high standard of living; in nations where workers are less productive, most people must endure a more meager existence. Similarly, the growth rate of a nation's productivity determines the growth rate of its average income.

The fundamental relationship between productivity and living standards is simple, but its implications are far-reaching. If productivity is the primary determinant of living standards, other explanations must be of secondary importance. For example, it might be tempting to credit labor unions or minimum-wage laws for the rise in living standards of American workers over the past century. Yet the real hero of American workers is their rising productivity. As another example, some commentators have claimed that increased competition from Japan and other countries explained the slow growth in U.S. incomes during the 1970s and 1980s. Yet the real villain was not competition from abroad but flagging productivity growth in the United States.

The relationship between productivity and living standards also has profound implications for public policy. When thinking about how any policy will affect living standards, the key question is how it will affect our ability to produce goods and services. To boost living standards, policymakers need to raise productivity by ensuring that workers are well educated, have the tools needed to produce goods and services, and have access to the best available technology.

Principle #9: Prices Rise When the Government Prints Too Much Money

In Germany in January 1921, a daily newspaper cost 0.30 marks. Less than two years later, in November 1922, the same newspaper cost 70,000,000 marks. All other prices in the economy rose by similar amounts. This episode is one of history's most spectacular examples of *inflation*, an increase in the overall level of prices in the economy.

Although the United States has never experienced inflation even close to that in Germany in the 1920s, inflation has at times been an economic problem. During the 1970s, for instance, the overall level of prices more than doubled, and President Gerald Ford called inflation "public enemy number one." By contrast, inflation in the 1990s was about three percent per year; at this rate it would take more than twenty years for prices to double. Because high inflation imposes various costs on society, keeping inflation at a low level is a goal of economic policymakers around the world.

What causes inflation? In almost all cases of large or persistent inflation, the culprit turns out to be the same—growth in the quantity of money. When a government creates large quantities of the nation's money, the value of the money falls. In Germany in the early 1920s, when prices were on average tripling every month, the quantity of money was also tripling every month. Although less dramatic, the economic history of the United States points to a similar conclusion: The high inflation of the 1970s was associated with rapid growth in the quantity of money, and the low inflation of the 1990s was associated with slow growth in the quantity of money.

Principle #10: Society Faces a Short-Run Tradeoff between Inflation and Unemployment

When the government increases the amount of money in the economy, one result is inflation. Another result, at least in the short run, is a lower level of unemployment. The curve that illustrates this short-run trade-off between inflation and unemployment is called the *Phillips curve*, after the economist who first examined this relationship.

The Phillips curve remains a controversial topic among economists, but most economists today accept the idea that society faces a short-run trade-off between inflation and unemployment. This simply means that, over a period of a year or two, many economic policies push inflation and unemployment in opposite directions. Policymakers face this trade-off regardless of whether inflation and unemployment both start out at high levels (as they were in the early 1980s), at low levels (as they were in the late 1990s), or someplace in between.

The trade-off between inflation and unemployment is only temporary, but it can last for several years. The Phillips curve is, therefore, crucial for understanding many developments in the economy. In particular, it is important for understanding the business cycle—the irregular and largely unpredictable fluctuations in economic activity, as measured by the number of people employed or the production of goods and services.

Policymakers can exploit the short-run trade-off between inflation and unemployment using various policy instruments. By changing the amount that the government spends, the amount it taxes, and the amount of money it prints, policymakers can influence the combination of inflation and unemployment that the economy experiences. Because these instruments of monetary and fiscal policy are potentially so powerful, how policymakers should use these instruments to control the economy, if at all, is a subject of continuing debate.

Chapter 16

Income Inequality and Corporate Responsibility

Gary Becker and Richard A. Posner

These four short pieces are from a book on popular economics titled *Uncommon Sense: Economic Insights, from Marriage to Terrorism,* by economist Gary S. Becker and juror Richard A. Posner. Becker's first point is as dramatic as it is convincing: in recent decades, capitalism in China and India has created enormous wealth. As the authors of the *Communist Manifesto* emphasized 158 years earlier, "The bourgeoisie [that is to say, the capitalist class—M. M.], during its rule of scarce one hundred years, has created more massive and more colossal productive forces than have all preceding generations together."[1] After their observation about China and India, Becker and Posner arrive, from their shared free-market or laissez-faire perspective, at similar positions under the headings of rising income inequality and corporate responsibility.

Our selections were written in 2006 and 2005, and they appeared in print a couple of years before the 2008 financial crisis. Three or four years later, Posner wrote, in his book, *A Failure of Capitalism* (2009), that the Great Recession of late 2007 to 2009 had caused him to question the rational choice, *laissez faire* economic model that lies at the heart of his Law and Economics theory.

The late Gary Stanley Becker (1930–2014) was a professor of economics and sociology at the University of Chicago. In 1992 he won the Nobel Prize in Economics, "for having extended the domain of microeconomic analysis to a wide range of human behavior and interaction, including non-market behavior."

---

[1] Karl Marx and Friedrich Engels, *Manifesto of the Communist Party,* in *Marx Engels Collected Works,* vol. 6 (London: Lawrence and Wishart, 1976), 489. Indeed, as Marx and Engels uncommonsensically emphasized, thanks to capitalism there is "too much means of subsistence, too much industry, too much commerce" (Marx and Engels, 490). They were referring to devastating periodic downturns of the business cycle, but the statement has added poignancy today, in view of the effects of anthropogenic global warming.

Richard Allen Posner (b. 1939) was an economist, a Ronald Reagan appointee to the U.S. Court of Appeals for the Seventh Circuit in Chicago, and the prolific author of some forty books on a wide range of economic topics. *New York Times* interviewer Adam Liptak described him as "among the most provocative figures in American law in the last half-century."[2]

Is the Increased Earnings Inequality among Americans Bad?

Gary Becker April 23, 2006

Income inequality widened, particularly between urban and rural households after China began its rapid rate of economic development in 1980. At the same time, the fraction of Chinese men, women, and children who live on less than $2 a day—the World Bank's definition of poverty—greatly fell. Few would argue that the poor in China did not become much better off due to the rapid economic development, even though the gap between their incomes and those of the middle and richer classes widened by a lot. A similar conclusion would apply to India as the explosion in its general economic development during the past twenty years widened the gap between rich and poor, but raised the income levels of the very poor.

I make this observation in reaction to the great concern expressed by politicians and many others in the United States over the rather substantial increase during the past twenty-five years in earnings inequality among Americans. The China and India examples illustrate that whether rising inequality is considered good or bad depends on how it came about. I believe that the foundation of the growth in earnings inequality of Americans has mainly been beneficial and desirable.

The basic facts are these. There has been a general trend toward rising gaps between the earnings of more and less skilled persons. With regard to education, real earnings (that is, earnings adjusted for changes in consumer prices) of high school dropouts did not change much. Earnings of high school graduates grew somewhat more rapidly, so that the gap between dropout and graduate earnings expanded over time.

---

[2]Adam Liptak, "An Exit Interview with Richard Posner, Judicial Provocateur," *New York Times*, September 11, 2017, https://www.nytimes.com/2017/09/11/us/politics/judge-richard-posner-retirement.html.

The main action came in the earnings of college graduates and those with postgraduate education. They both increased at a rapid pace, with the earnings of persons with MBAs, law degrees, and other advanced education growing the most rapidly. All these trends produced a widening of earnings inequality by education level, particularly between those with college education and persons with lesser education. I should also note that while an upward trend in the earnings gap by education is found for both men and women, and for African Americans and whites, the earnings of college-educated women and African Americans increased more rapidly than did those of white males. As a result, inequality by sex and race, particularly among college-educated persons, narrowed by a lot.

As the education earnings gap increased, a larger fraction of high school graduates went on to get a college education. This trend toward greater higher education is found among all racial and ethnic groups, and for both men and women, but it is particularly important for women. The growth in the number of women going to and completing college has been so rapid that many more women than men are now enrolled as college students. Women have also shifted toward higher earnings fields, such as business, law, and medicine, and away from traditional occupations of women, such as K-12 teachers and nurses. The greater education achievement of women compared to men is particularly prominent among blacks and Latinos.

The widening earnings gap is mainly due to a growth in the demand for educated and other skilled persons. That the demand for skilled persons has grown rapidly is not surprising, given developments in computers and the Internet, and advances in biotechnology. Also, globalization increased the demand for products and services from the United States and other developed nations produced by college-educated and other highly skilled employees. Globalization also encouraged a shift to importing products using relatively low-skilled labor from China and other low-wage countries instead of producing them domestically.

Rates of return on college education shot up during the past several decades due to the increased demand for persons with greater knowledge and skills. These higher rates of return induced a larger fraction of high school graduates to get a college education, and increasingly to continue with postgraduate education.

Some of you might question whether rates of return on higher education did increase since tuition grew rapidly during the past twenty-five years. However, increases in tuition were mainly induced by the greater return to college education. Pablo Pena in a Ph.D. dissertation in progress at the University of Chicago argues convincingly that tuition rose in part because students want to invest more in the quality of their education. Increased spending per student by colleges is partly financed by higher tuition levels.

This brings me finally to the punch line. Should not an increase in earnings inequality due primarily to higher rates of return on education and other skills be considered a favorable rather than unfavorable development? Higher rates of return on capital are a sign of greater productivity in the economy, and that inference is fully applicable to human capital as well as to physical capital. The initial impact of higher returns to human capital is wider inequality in earnings (just as the initial effect of higher returns on physical capital is to widen income inequality), but that impact becomes more muted and may be reversed over time as young men and women invest more in their human capital.

I conclude that the forces raising earnings inequality in the United States are on the whole beneficial because they reflected higher returns to investments in education and other human capital. Yet, this is not a ground for complacency, for the responses so far to these higher returns is disturbingly limited. Why have not more high school graduates gone on for college education when the benefits are so apparent? And why did the fraction of American youth who drop out of high school, especially African American and Hispanic males, remain quite constant at about 25 percent of all high school students?

The answer to both questions lies partly in the breakdown of the American family, and the resulting low skill levels acquired by children in broken families. Cognitive skills tend to get developed at very early ages, while my colleague, James Heckman, has shown that noncognitive skills, such as study habits, getting to appointments on time, and attitudes toward work, get fixed at later, although still relatively young, ages. High school dropouts certainly appear to be seriously deficient in the noncognitive skills that would enable them to take advantage of the higher rates of return to greater investments in education and other human capital.

So instead of lamenting the increased earnings gap by education, attention should focus on how to raise the fraction of American youth who complete high school, and then go on for a college education. These pose tough challenges since the solutions are not cheap or easy. But it would be a disaster if the focus were on the earnings inequality itself. For that would lead to attempts to raise taxes and other penalties on higher earnings due to greater skills, which could greatly reduce the productivity of the world's leading economy by discouraging investments in human capital.

Why Rising Income Inequality in the United States Should Be a Nonissue

Richard A. Posner

Becker explains the rising income inequality in the United States persuasively; I would add only that as society becomes more competitive and more meritocratic, income inequality is likely to rise simply as a consequence of the underlying inequality—which is very great—between people that is due to differences in IQ, energy, health, social skills, character, ambition, physical attractiveness, talent, and luck. Public policies designed to reduce income inequality, such as highly progressive income taxation and middle-class subsidies, are likely to reduce the aggregate wealth of society, and therefore should not be adopted unless rising income inequality is a social problem.

Is it? That depends, I think, on average income (and hence on the wealth of society as a whole), on whether incomes are rising (at all levels), and on the particular way in which the income distribution is skewed. The higher the average income in a society, the less likely is inequality to cause envy or social unrest. The reason is that, given diminishing marginal utility of income, people who are well-off do not have a strong sense of deprivation by reason of their not having an even higher income. If, moreover, their income is rising, they are more likely to derive satisfaction from a comparison of their present income to their former income than to be dissatisfied by the fact that some other people's incomes have risen even more. In my book *Frontiers of Legal Theory*, Chapter 3 (2001), I present empirical evidence supporting a positive correlation between political stability on the one hand and average, and rising, income on the other hand.

It is true that progressive taxation and other income-equalizing policies are found in rich rather than poor countries. But that is partly because poor countries lack the governmental infrastructure for administering complex policies and partly because these societies have powerful social norms of equality. Studies of peasant societies find that "black" envy is widespread in them—that is, if your neighbor has a nicer barn than yours, you'd prefer to burn it down rather than to exert yourself to build an equally good barn. "White" envy, in contrast, better described as emulation, promotes economic growth.

As for the way in which a society's income distribution is skewed, if, though average income is high and rising, there is a very small, very wealthy, upper class, a tiny middle class, and a huge lower class, the society is likely to be unstable. Because the majority of the population will not be well-off, and the upper and middle classes small, there will be few defenders of the existing distribution.

The United States has a high average income, incomes are rising for most groups in the population—though more slowly than for the wealthiest—and most of the population is middle or upper class. It is therefore not surprising that rising income inequality has not generated noticeable social unrest or calls for return of heavy progressive taxation. Moreover, when nonpecuniary income is taken into account, there is less inequality than the income statistics suggest. In a democratic and rights-oriented society such as the United States, all citizens have a bundle of equal political rights (to the vote, to the free exercise of religion, to be free from unreasonable searches and seizures, and so forth) that are a form of income, and equal political duties that are a form of expense. Rich people as well as ordinary and poor are prosecuted for crime, and, as in the recent spate of corporate scandals, often punished very heavily.

What is more, income statistics do not record the enormous secular improvement in the quality of products and services, and hence in the utility that purchases confer on consumers. Think only of the extraordinary improvements in the quality of automobiles, medical care, and electronic products. Americans whose income has not increased faster than the rate of inflation are nevertheless living far better than they used to live. They know this, and it is one reason they are not clamoring for income redistribution.

A cultural factor that reduces the social tensions that might otherwise arise from a sharp and rising inequality of Americans' incomes is that the United States, unlike the countries of Europe, has no aristocratic tradition. There is no suite of tastes, accent, bearing, etc., that distinguishes the rich in America from the nonrich. The rich have more and better goods, but they do not act as if they were a "superior" sort of person, refined, well-bred, looking down on the average Joe. The rich play golf, but so do the middle class. The middle class follow sports, but so do the upper class.

Finally, rising income inequality in the United States is due in part to increased immigration, since immigrants, legal as well as illegal, tend to work for lower wages than citizens. Immigrants do not, however, compare themselves with wealthy citizens, but rather with the much lower wages they could expect to earn in their countries of origin. Rather than immigrants envying wealthy citizens, many citizens are hostile to poor immigrants!

The "problem" of income inequality should not be confused with the problem of poverty. The first, I have argued, is, at least in the United States at present, a pseudo-problem. Poverty is a genuine social problem, because by definition it signifies a lack of the resources necessary for a decent life. It is only tenuously if at all related to income inequality, since one could have zero poverty in a society in which the gap between the income of the worst-off members of society and the wealthiest members was huge— imagine if the poorest person in America earned $100,000 a year and the wealthiest $1 billion.

The more competitive and meritocratic a society, the more intractable the problem of poverty. The reason is that in such a society the poor tend to be people who are not productive because they simply do not have the abilities that are in demand by employers. It is unlikely that everybody (other than the severely disabled) can be trained up to a level at which there is a demand for his or her labor, and so there is likely to be an irreducible amount of poverty even in a wealthy society such as ours, unless we provide generous welfare benefits—which will discourage work.

Do Corporations Have a Social Responsibility beyond Stockholder Value?

Gary Becker July 24, 2005

Do corporations have any responsibilities beyond trying to maximize stockholder value, adhering to contracts, implicit as well as explicit, and obeying the laws of the different countries where they operate? My answer is "no," although maximizing value, meeting contracts, and obeying laws help achieve many of the goals by those claiming corporations should be "socially responsible" by taking care of the environment, considering the effects of their behavior on other stakeholders, and contributing to good causes. Still, laws and contracts, and individual use of their own resources, rather than corporate behavior, should be the way to implement various social goals.

References to the behavior of corporations really mean the behavior of top management who are in essence employed by stockholders through their representatives—boards of directors. In most cases, it is rather obvious that management should try to increase stockholder value through their pricing policies, the products they offer, where they locate plants, and so forth. CEOs who fail to do this are subject to termination either through takeovers or by being fired. In fact, the tenure of corporate heads seems to have become shorter over time.

In many other situations, apparent conflicts between maximizing stockholder value and social goals disappear on closer examination. A corporation may give money to local charities, play up its contributions to the environment, and do other things that only appear to reduce shareholder value because that behavior sufficiently improves the government regulations that affect their profitability. Or a company may give to various public causes, like Ben and Jerry's ice cream company did in the past, because this attracts customers who want to support these causes partly by buying the products of companies that contribute to these causes.

Treatment of employees that on the surface appear to reduce profitability often is in fact consistent with the criteria of maximizing stockholder value while respecting laws and contract. For example, a company may raise the value to shareholders by keeping on older workers beyond the age where their productivity is sufficiently high to justify their earnings. Keeping older workers on attracts younger workers at lower wages since they expect too that they will not be let go when they get older. Or employees may invest in their on the job training because of an explicit contract or implicit agreement with their employers that their earnings will rise with their tenure as their productivity rises because of their investments. It would be inconsistent with my criteria if a company did not raise wages appropriately of some employees when their tenure and productivity increased because the company realized that these employees did not have good opportunities at other companies. This behavior would violate my recommendation that a company maximize stockholder value, subject to obeying all laws and contracts, implicit as well as explicit.

To take an example of what I do not believe companies should do, a global company operating in a poor country should not pay higher wages for either adult or child labor, adjusted for the quality of the labor, than is the prevailing standard in the labor market of this country, as long as higher wages would lower the profits of the company. I am assuming the wages they pay do not violate any laws or contracts of the countries where they operate, and that they are not subject to such bad publicity that their profits actually would increase if they paid more. I should add that pressure to pay much higher wages in labor markets of developing nations reduces the number employed there by international companies, and would tend to worsen, not improve, the plight of the poor populations of these countries.

Even in cases where this does not contribute to profitability, top management may want to use company resources to promote environmental ends that are not required by law, give to local symphonies, promote fair trade coffee or other fair trade products, and engage in other acts that increase the managers' utility, prestige, and standing in their communities. In a competitive market for managers, management would have to take sufficiently lower earnings, bonuses, and options to in effect pay for the company assets and profits they use to boost their own welfare and community standing. So in such a competitive management market, management essentially engages in "socially responsible" behavior out of its own earnings. This would not lower stockholder value, and is consistent with my criteria.

If the management is entrenched, they might be able to give away resources to environmental and other groups without lowering their own earnings, but by lowering instead dividends and other payments to stockholders. Even this, however, would not affect stockholder returns if instead management could have taken higher earnings, bonuses, or stock options for themselves. Depending on what they would have done with their higher earnings, the use of company profits for particular social causes may or may not lead to better overall outcomes. But surely an important goal of any reform in corporate management is to reduce the entrenchment of management, and inject more competition into the market for CEOs and other top corporate leaders.

Whatever the degree of competition in the market for top management, the market for stock ownership is highly competitive. Those stockholders that want companies to use potential profits for environmental or other social causes might be willing to buy the stocks of companies that do this, even if that means lower monetary rate of return on their investments. If there are enough of these stockholders, then companies that engage in these practices would be maximizing stockholder values, and their behavior would be consistent with the criteria for corporate behavior that I advocate.

But such socially conscious stockholders are a small fraction of all owners of stocks, especially of large institutional funds and investors. These funds would avoid companies that are "socially responsible" until prices of the stock of these companies fell sufficiently to give the same risk-adjusted monetary rate of return provided by companies that do not engage in social behavior. This implies that new companies that are expected to contribute to various social goals beyond making profits and respecting laws and contracts will have lower initial public offering (IPO) prices if they issue stock than they otherwise would have. In that case, the founders of socially minded companies will bear the cost of their social responsibility. That is appropriate and not objectionable. I am bothered only when managers, founders, or others in control of corporations that behave in a "socially responsible" manner try to pass the cost of behaving in this way on to others rather than bearing the costs themselves.

The Social Responsibility of Corporations

Posner's Comment

I agree with almost everything that Becker says, but will suggest a few qualifications. I can think of one situation in which "pure" charitable donations by corporations, i.e., donations that do not increase profitability, could benefit shareholders. Assuming that most shareholders make some charitable donations, they might want the corporations they invest in to make modest charitable donations on the theory that a corporation will have more information about what are worthwhile charitable enterprises than an individual does. For example, charities differ greatly in the amount of money that they spend on their own administration, including salaries and perquisites for the employees of the charity, relative to the amount they give to the actual objects of charity. Presumably corporations are in a better position to determine which charities are efficient than individuals are; if so, then shareholders may impliedly consent to some amount of charitable giving by their corporations. But not much. The reason is that one person's charity is another person's deviltry: a shareholder who is opposed to abortion on religious grounds would be offended if his corporation contributed to Planned Parenthood. The practical significance of this point is that corporations avoid controversial charities, so that the issue of implied consent becomes whether the shareholder would like his corporation to make a modest contribution to some set of uncontroversial charities.

For the reason suggested above, the answer may be "yes"—and for the additional reason that there is a tax angle. If the shareholder receives a dividend, the corporation will have paid corporate income tax on the income from which the dividend is paid. Suppose the corporation and the shareholder are both in the 20 percent bracket. The corporation earns $10, pays $2 in tax, and gives the shareholder $8. The shareholder gives the $8 to charity, which costs him $6.40, since he gets a 20 percent tax deduction. If the shareholder wants the charity to have $10, it has to dig into his pockets for another $2, which costs him $1.60 (because of the 20 percent deduction), and so the total cost to him of giving the charity $10 is $8. Now suppose that, instead, the corporation gives the $10 to charity, a deductible expense, at a cost to it therefore of $8. Then the charity receives $10 rather than, as before, only $8. The shareholder loses his $2 deduction, which means that the total cost to him of the transfer is, as before, $8. But the corporation is better off to the tune of $2, since it avoids the corporate income tax on the $10 in income that it gave the charity. And anything that benefits the corporation benefits the shareholder.

Given product market as well as capital market competitive pressures, charitable spending that is not profit maximizing because the cost exceeds the private benefits that Becker lists (public relations, advertising, government relations, and so forth) is unlikely to be significant. Even if corporate managers are not effectively constrained to profit maximization by their shareholders, expenditures that do not reduce the cost or increase the quality of the corporation's products will place it a competitive disadvantage with firms that do not make such expenditures.

A more difficult question has to do with a corporation's policy on obeying laws. From a strict shareholder standpoint, it might seem that corporate managers should obey the law only when the expected costs of violating it would exceed the expected benefits, so that managers would have a duty to their shareholders to disobey the law, perhaps especially in countries in which law enforcement is very weak, a country, for example, that had a law against child labor but was unable to enforce the law. This would be a case of a pure dash between ethical and profit-maximization duties. My view is that, given external (i.e., social as distinct from private) benefits of compliance with law, the ethical argument should prevail, so that a shareholder would be precluded from complaining that corporate management, by failing to violate the law even when it could get away with it, was violating its fiduciary duty to shareholders.

Another argument based on an externality, an argument that lies behind the law that forbids U.S. firms to engage in bribery abroad, even in countries where bribery is extremely common, is that reducing the amount of bribery in those countries will benefit U.S. firms in the long run by making the markets in these countries more open, to the advantage of efficient firms.

The fact that it will sometimes be in the shareholder interest for management to violate the law provides, moreover, a ground for punishing corporate managers sufficiently severely for corporate crimes that the punishment is not offset by shareholder gains for which the managers could be expected to be rewarded.

Chapter 17

Economic Common Sense and the Depoliticization of the Economic

Jacinda Swanson

In the preceding reading, Gary S. Becker noted that, compared to the fact that so many hundreds of millions in China and India had risen out of poverty in recent decades, the growing gap between the rich and the poor in those countries is a "nonissue." Becker noted that "the China and India examples illustrate that whether rising inequality is considered good or bad depends on how it came about." One might add that, like all judgments of good and bad, it also depends on who does the "considering": for whom is rising inequality of income good or bad? Becker and Posner have a quick response: for almost everyone in China and India.

But there is an additional consideration when it comes to widening inequalities of income and wealth—a consideration that one rarely hears from mainstream economists. One might have thought that commonsensical grown-ups could agree that *big differences in wealth just are big differences in political power.* After all, in the highly stratified societies in which we live, wealth "obviously" is *power over* others. Yet, this seemingly obvious insight does not quite rank as common sense, if we put the emphasis on the word *common.* Indeed, when many mainstream "social scientists" do not dismiss this point outright, then as we have seen, they ignore it. The straightforward descriptive usefulness of the insight, as well as its practical value, seem to be inconsequential, at least at the level of popular discourse and for much of mainstream economics and "political science."

How to account for the strange selectivity of economic common sense? Our next reading, an excerpt from an academic paper by political science Professor Jacinda Swanson, might provide insight. Swanson describes how, in mainstream economics as well as in the popular imagination, "the economy" has come to be represented as a realm of activity that can be understood in isolation from politics.[1] In the course of what Swanson calls the *conceptual depoliticization* of economics, mainstream economists and commonsensical "thought leaders" also privatize politics, portraying citizens as consumers, for whom political participation is just another realm for the expression of private preferences. The latter process is what Swanson calls *practical depoliticization*.

Unlike many scholars in the humanities, Swanson does not try to conceal her political commitments. But like many of them, her paper is replete with citations and academic parlance, such as "antiessentialist Marxian economic theory," "voluntarist conceptions of human agency," and "depoliticized conceptualizations." Still, her point should be clear enough: it is a mostly unspoken assumption of both academics and of commonsensical nonspecialists, too, that modern economic relations can best be studied in isolation from power and politics, and that, so construed, these relations are eternal features necessary for any self-perpetuating and remotely attractive human society.

Swanson wishes to avoid any suggestion of *economic determinism* or *economism*—the prevailing notion that there is a one-way causal connection, or something close to it, between the character of economic practices in a society, and other social practices, including law, public institutions, religion, and so on. An especially widespread version of economic determinism is the commonsensical assumption that one particular aspect of economic practices, namely technological innovation, is the engine that drives an economy and history in general. Swanson opposes the sort of thinking that produces claims such as, for example, that social media—a consequence of fortuitous free market innovation[2]—has ushered in a new type of society and a new historical epoch.

There is, however, room to doubt the claim, which Swanson makes in her introductory remarks, that repoliticizing the economic involves accepting the belief that "citizens are able not only to freely regulate and redesign existing economic practices but also to create new ones." A broad survey of economic histories suggests that economic practices are not contingent and

---

[1] Compare to Evans Watkins, *Everyday Exchanges: Market Work and Capitalist Common Sense* (Stanford, CA: Stanford University Press), 1998. The author, a Professor of English, also challenges this common representation of economic activity.

[2] For a very different description of the genesis of social media, see: Yasha Levine, *Surveillance Valley: The Secret Military History of the Internet* (New York: Public Affairs, 2018).

interchangeable at will, as she claims: there are *just so many ways* that sustainable economic practices can be structured, and while the number of ways is greater than *one*, it is not large.

Swanson teaches in the Department of Political Science at Western Michigan University, Kalamazoo. Our excerpt does not include material in her original article, including long passages devoted to the ideas of Italian thinker Antonio Gramsci, whom we will meet in Part VI.

Economic practices in the United States are often *depoliticized* in at least two different, but related ways: (1) they are naturalized or essentialized conceptually,[3] and (2) political control over them is limited. In this article, I examine some of the ways in which popular and academic discourses implicitly or explicitly depoliticize economic relations in one or both of these manners.[4] This depoliticization is problematic not only philosophically but also politically. Feminist, poststructuralist, and Marxian theorists have long pointed out the philosophical problems with naturalized and essentialist conceptions of the individual and social practices, and the same problems hold for economically essentialist and determinist conceptions of economic practices.

In terms of its political impact, the conceptual depoliticization of economic practices, along with positive perceptions of market capitalism, leads many U.S. citizens, including many academics, to accept, or at least not to contest, existing economic relations, regardless of the problems and injustices they cause. As a result, such ways of thinking tend either deliberately or inadvertently to contribute to the reproduction and legitimacy of the economic status quo. In either case, alternative ways of organizing economic relations often appear not to exist—as inconceivable—or as illegitimate, unjust, or unwise.[5]

---

[3]*Naturalized*: that is to say, represented as eternal or transhistorical. *Essentialized*: represented as an intrinsic or necessary trait of something. In the case at hand, the social relations that prevail here and now are assumed to be necessary features of any tenable or desirable human community, and to be certified by an unchanging human nature. Swanson's target here is the common-sense claim that the operations of the market are the natural and "true" determinates of a society, and so any attempt to interfere with these operations, notably taxation, regulation, and other "government" interference, typically produces suboptimal results.—M. M.

[4]Author's Note: I would like to thank the anonymous reviewers, David Ruccio, Fred Dallmayr, Joe Buttigieg, Emily Hauptmann, and Neve Gordon for helpful comments on various versions of this article.

[5]J. K. Gibson-Graham, *The End of Capitalism (As We Knew It)* (Cambridge, MA: Blackwell, 1996); Watkins, *Everyday Exchanges*; Fred Block, *Postindustrial* Possibilities (Berkeley: University of California Press, 1990).

Discourse is, consequently, an important factor in whether existing economic practices continue to be reproduced or become politically contested.[6] The theoretical, normative, and political upshot of this article is that depoliticized conceptualizations need to be identified and criticized for both philosophical and political reasons. Academics and citizens who care about economic justice and democracy should therefore be attentive to how they conceptualize economic practices and the effects of their conceptualizations.

In the next section, I briefly indicate how economic practices in the United States have been depoliticized conceptually and/or practically (politically). In the following section, I draw on recent developments in antiessentialist Marxian economic theory, Antonio Gramsci's theory of hegemony, and poststructuralist theory to construct a framework for conceptualizing economic practices in a more politicized manner and for theorizing their relationship with political and cultural practices. The insights of these different theoretical approaches are rarely brought together within the fields of either political economy or political theory. Eschewing economistic and naturalized conceptions, the framework I develop conceives economic practices as contingent, historical, and thoroughly social, which means that citizens are able not only to freely regulate and redesign existing economic practices, but also to create new ones. This framework therefore aims at mitigating economic injustice as well as expanding the scope of democracy. In this way, my arguments for politicizing the economic contribute to theories of radical democracy, which have tended to undertheorize and/or to devote relatively little explicit attention to economic practices.

[...] In the final section, I provide examples of some of the specific ways in which discourses can be depoliticized, briefly sketching how such instances are economistic, limit political control over economic practices, or otherwise perpetuate the economic status quo and discourage political resistance. [...]

The Depoliticization of the Economic

In their influential book *The American Ethos*, Herbert McClosky and John Zaller[7] argued that Americans are committed to both democracy and capitalism and that

---

[6]It is also important to acknowledge less subtle social and institutional factors—for example, electoral laws and campaign financing—that hinder average citizens' ability to alter and to extend democratic control over economic practices, as well as their ability to participate in politics more generally (see, e.g., Sheldon S. Wolin, "What Revolutionary Action Means Today," in *Dimensions of Radical Democracy*, ed. Chantal Mouffe (New York: Verso, 1992), 240–53; Peter Bachrach and Aryeh Botwinick, *Power and Empowerment* (Philadelphia, PA: Temple University Press, 1992), Chapter 3).

[7]Herbert McClosky and John Zaller, *The American Ethos: Public Attitudes Toward Capitalism and Democracy* (Cambridge, MA: Harvard University Press, 1984).

these are the core values in American political culture. In addition to evidence provided by academic research and public opinion polls, public discourse and cultural representations constantly reveal that, for the vast majority of citizens, U.S.-style market capitalism is not only the best economic system in the world, but also an integral aspect, or even a precondition, of democracy.[8] The virtues of market capitalism and its compatibility with democracy are thus clearly deeply embedded forms of what Gramsci[9] called *common sense,* those ideas that are taken for granted or unquestioned in society.

Precisely because it is common sense for most U.S. citizens and academics that market capitalism is the fairest, most efficient, and only nontotalitarian economic system in the world, faith in existing economic practices and institutions remains largely unshaken by events such as the collapse of Enron and the financial troubles of WorldCom, the largest bankruptcies in U.S. history, or the stock market bubble and crash of the late 1990s. Such events do not prompt widespread public or academic debate about the underlying goals or organization of existing economic relations. Instead, these events are usually seen as caused by a handful of corporate "bad apples" and typically result only in public condemnations of the excesses of individual companies and, less often, in policies aimed at curbing corruption and increasing the accountability of individual economic actors. Nor does confidence in capitalism and markets seem to be shaken by the fact that more and more citizens believe that the political system is captured by big economic interests; the fact that significant portions of the population, especially minorities and female-headed families, live in poverty; or the fact that the income and wealth gaps between the rich and the

---

[8]See, for example, James M. Carlson, "Television Viewing," *Political Communication* 10, no. 3 (1993): 243–57; Robert A. Peterson, Gerald Albaum, and George Kozmetsky, *Modern American Capitalism* (New York: Quorum Books, 1990).

[Swanson's article, published in March 2008, must have been submitted to the *Political Research Quarterly* at least a couple of months earlier; thus, it did not register changing public perceptions of "socialism," especially among younger Americans, during and after the Great Recession. (In an August 14, 2018 article entitled "Most Young Americans Prefer Socialism to Capitalism," the Gallup organization reported that, according to their latest poll, 18- to 29-year-olds had more positive views of socialism (51 percent positive) than capitalism (45 percent positive); https://www.fastcompany.com/90246644/more-and-more-americans-believe-socialism-will-boost-equity. Of course, questions could be raised as to how respondents variously understood the words *socialism* and *capitalism* (https://news.gallup.com/opinion/polling-matters/243362/meaning-socialism-americans-today.aspx, accessed June 24, 2019).) — M.M.]

[9]Gramsci, "The Study of Philosophy" (see the item in the Readings That Appear in This Book section), 323–33, 419.

poor have returned to pre-Depression-era levels.[10] In this sense, existing economic practices are often *depoliticized conceptually,* that is, naturalized and treated as common sense.

Furthermore, over the past few decades many Republican—but, increasingly, also centrist and Democratic—politicians and citizens have sought to demonize government, especially government regulation of the economy and businesses, as well as government provision of social services. Such criticisms have motivated and/or justified attempts to reduce government's realm of activity.[11] They are often premised on the belief that government is (allegedly) less competent and efficient than the private sector and/or that government action curtails individual choice and thus freedom.[12] They are also frequently premised on the more general economistic notion that political involvement in "the economy" interferes with the smooth operation of the laws (supposedly) governing market and other economic behavior. This latter—*depoliticized,* that is, essentialist—notion is of course promoted by a variety of economistic popular conceptions and academic theories, such as neoclassical economics.[13]

Once issues or phenomena are portrayed as "economic" within this all-too-common economistic mindset, political control or regulation is deemed more or less inappropriate. The ways in which the boundary between "the economic" and "the political" is drawn therefore have enormous implications for politics, democracy, and justice. Economism can have even more far-reaching effects when it is argued that noneconomic phenomena must accommodate or even subordinate themselves to the "imperatives" of the economic sphere.[14]

In effect, these sorts of procapitalist, antigovernment or small-government, and economistic arguments and forms of common sense amount, I contend, to

---

[10]ABC *News/Washington Post* poll, October 26, 2003; *CBS/New York Times* poll, July 11, 2004; *Los Angeles Times* poll, January 15, 2005; U.S. Census Bureau, 2004; Kevin Phillips, *Wealth and democracy* (NY: Broadway Books, 2002).

[11]While some governmental programs can be justifiably criticized for being undemocratic and unjust in implementation and design, this is not the type of criticism most antigovernment or small-government critics typically or primarily have in mind (Bachrach and Botwinick; Nancy Fraser, *Unruly Practices* (Minneapolis: University of Minnesota Press, 1989)). It is nevertheless important not to conflate government with democracy, and thus to avoid characterizing all antigovernment discourse as antipolitical or antidemocratic.

[12]Joseph A. Buttigieg, "Pechino e Berlino," *Critica Marxista* 5 (September–October 1999): 20–7; Buttigieg, "Gramsci on Civil Society," *Boundary 2* 22, no. 3 (1995): 1–32.

[13]Stephen A. Resnick and Richard D. Wolff, *Knowledge and Class* (Chicago: University of Chicago Press, 1989); Gibson-Graham; Watkins, *Everyday Exchanges*; Jacinda Swanson, "The Economy and Its Relation to Politics," *Polity* 39, no. 2 (2007): 208–33; Swanson, *Politicizing the Economic* (Ph.D. thesis, Department of Political Science, University of Notre Dame, 2002).

[14]Teivo Teivainen, "Overcoming Economism," *Review* 25, no. 3 (2002): 317–42, citing 317–21; Teivainen, *Enter Economism, Exit Politics* (New York: Zed, 2002), xv–xvi, 1–2, 10, 25.

a concerted effort to scale back one particular form—yet, in the United States, possibly the predominant form—of political control over economic matters. They redraw the boundary between the political and the economic so that a vast sphere of "freedom" is reserved for economic activities and the operation of the economy's (allegedly) autonomous laws, while the scope of politics and democratic self-government is radically curtailed. In other words, such arguments and common senses, which are often depoliticized *conceptually,* discursively depoliticize economic practices in the second sense of the term, *practically* (politically). Conceptual depoliticization therefore can sometimes lead to practical depoliticization.

While a vulgar notion of false consciousness (particularly in its various orthodox and economistic Marxist formulations) has been rightly and widely criticized, in light of the inequalities and injustices accompanying market capitalism, it is not enough to claim—as most neoclassical economists, procedural liberal political theorists, and mainstream political scientists, for example, do—that U.S. citizens have freely chosen, or that they prefer, existing economic practices. Rather, one must also consider the cultural bases of capitalist hegemony, that is, the construction of consent—or, in Gramscian and Foucauldian terminology,[15] how certain ways of thinking become accepted or even normalized (i.e., naturalized or commonsensical). As that which is taken for granted, capitalist common sense narrows the scope of debate and thus plays a particularly important role in depoliticizing and perpetuating capitalist exploitation.

Politicizing the Economic

[...]

[I]argue that economic practices should be theorized as fundamentally *constituted* by—not just shaped or influenced by—the numerous "economic," "political," "cultural," and "natural" processes surrounding them.[16] Using this framework, economic relations are theorized as contingent, historical, and socially constituted, which means that citizens no longer have to accommodate themselves to oppressive economic relations or to see themselves as passive victims of an immutable economic system,

---

[15]That is to say, in the terminology of Antonio Gramsci and of French social theorist Michel Foucault (1926–1984).—M. M.

[16]*Capitalism* is defined here as an exploitative class process—in which laborers sell their labor power as a commodity to capitalists who appropriate and distribute the surplus produced by the laborers— rather than a process of exchange or commodification, a form of ownership, or a drive for profits. *Exploitation* refers specifically to those class processes in which laborers do not appropriate the surplus labor they have produced; rather, someone else does (Resnick and Wolff).

as academic and popular discourses all too often suggest.[17] This alternative theorization of economic practices is in part what I mean by *politicizing the economic*. *Politicizing* here refers to changing the way we *conceptualize* economic practices and thus rejecting naturalized, essentialist, or determinist, that is, depoliticized and common-sense conceptions.

For instance, *politicizing the economic* means analyzing and drawing attention to the many ways in which "political" practices and institutions—such as governmental regulation, democratic electoral procedures and accountability, party competition, lobbying of elected officials, and citizens' levels and types of political participation— constitute "economic" processes, and vice versa. For instance, politicized conceptions would acknowledge the ways in which capitalist appropriation of the surplus produced by exploited laborers enables appropriators, but not laborers, to utilize such surplus to influence elections and political party formation and activities. Politicized conceptions would also account for the many ways in which political processes facilitate capitalist exploitation: property rights and other laws that allow managers and/or owners, rather than producers, to appropriate surplus; antiunion laws and inadequate enforcement of worker rights that make worker activism and union organizing difficult and risky; and so on.

Within my alternative theorization, particular discourses, and their conceptualizations of social relations, are conceived as one of the many social processes that reproduce or subvert any given economic practice or institution. As a result, to confront forms of oppression like economic exploitation, the various popular and academic discourses that perpetuate it—either by legitimating or normalizing it—have to be thematized and altered.[18] Reconceptualizing the economics is an important step not only in transforming unjust economic practices but also in expanding the scope of democracy. In this sense, politicizing economic practices has much in common, I argue, with theories of radical democracy. Consistent with earlier politicizations of

---

[17]See, for example, Ernesto Laclau and Chantal Mouffe, *Hegemony and Socialist Strategy* (London: Verso, 1985); Anna Marie Smith, *Laclau and Mouffe* (New York: Routledge, 1998); Judith Butler, *Excitable Speech* (New York: Routledge, 1997). For a fuller elaboration of this framework, see J. Swanson, "Power and Resistance," *Contemporary Political Theory* 6, no. 1 (2007): 4–23; Swanson, "Recognition and Redistribution," *Theory, Culture & Society* 22, no. 4 (2005): 87–118; and Swanson, *Politicizing the Economic* (Ph.D. thesis, Department of Political Science, University of Notre Dame, 2002).

[18]Gibson-Graham; Evan Watkins, "Gramscian Politics and Capitalist Common Sense," *Rethinking Marxism* 11, no. 3, (1999), 83–90, Watkins, *Everyday Exchanges*; Antonio Gramsci, *Prison Notebooks*, vol. III, ed. Joseph A. Buttigieg (New York: Columbia University Press, 2007): n7, n83; Gramsci, "The Study of Philosophy," in *Selections from the Prison Notebooks* (refer to the Gramsci entry in the Readings That Appear in This Book section, at the end of this book), 330–1, 344–5; Antonio Gramsci, *Selections from the Cultural Writings*, ed. David Forgacs and Geoffrey Nowell-Smith (Cambridge, MA: Harvard University Press, 1995), 418–20.

economic and social relations by Marx, Engels, Gramsci, and [French philosopher Louis] Althusser, many radical democratic theorists rightly argue that politics cannot and should not be limited to a distinct sphere of society, both because such distinct spheres do not exist and because no political, economic, or cultural practice should be immune from political challenge.[19] At the same time, Marxian theory is useful for correcting the tendency of much democratic theory, including radical democratic theory, to neglect and/or to undertheorize economic processes, especially class processes.[20] As economist Richard Wolff observed,[21] Marxian theory's specific contribution to democratic theory is to make class an object of democracy, since its exclusion from the democratic agenda "can only work to sustain the existing class structures."

I therefore propose that, in its second meaning, *politicizing the economic* refers to increasing political, especially democratic, control—although not necessarily state or centralize control—over "economic" relations. Politicization here means putting unjust or disputed economic relations on the political agenda and subjecting them to public deliberation and reworking, that is, extending more forthright and purposeful public, as opposed to private or elite, control over those economic discourses and practices that affect a group of, or all, citizens. Contra liberalism and other voluntarist conceptions of human agency, politicizing economic practices does not mean, though, that they can be easily or quickly transformed or that the consequences of doing so can be fully predicted or controlled. Existing social relations, identities, and discourses, as well as existing technologies and natural conditions, may partly constrain social change, at least in the short term. Citizens thus need to be attentive to such potential limitations and unintended consequences.[22]

Relating the two senses of the terms, I maintain that the more "economic" (and other social) relations are politicized in the first sense (conceptually, ontologically), the more they can be politicized in the second (politically, practically). Otherwise, if economic relations were immutable or necessary, there would be no point in attempting to modify them. Consequently, politicization in the first sense might be

---

[19]See, for example, Laclau and Mouffe; Claude Lefort, *Democracy and Political Theory* (Minneapolis: University of Minnesota Press, 1988); Smith; Iris Marion Young, *Justice and the Politics of Difference* (Princeton, NJ: Princeton University Press, 1990).

[20]Jonathan Diskin and Blair Sandler, "Essentialism and the Economy in the Post-Marxist Imaginary," *Rethinking Marxism* 6, no. 3 (1993): 28–48; Lucinda Swanson, "Recognition and Redistribution," *Theory, Culture & Society* 22 (4) (2005): 87–118.

[21]"Marxism and Democracy," *Rethinking Marxism* 12, no. 1 (2000): 113, 115, 121.

[22]Karl Marx, *The Eighteenth Brumaire of Louis Bonaparte* (New York: International Publishers, 1852/1963); Swanson, "Power and Resistance"; Resnick and Wolff, 20–3; Timothy Mitchell, *Rule of Experts* (Berkeley: University of California Press, 2002), 10, 50–1.

seen as a precondition of a wide-ranging politicization of economic practices in the second sense. In this way, like theories of radical democracy, the philosophy of praxis'[23] theory of society, human activity, and knowledge makes possible its broad democratic commitments. Clearly, democratic practices do not depend, either historically or theoretically, on an antiessentialist theory of society, but the latter allows a more expansive form of democracy, wherein no social practice is immune from scrutiny and potential transformation.

By conceptualizing economic relations in a more politicized way, the common-sense belief among many U.S. academics and citizens that market capitalism is the best and/or only nontotalitarian economic system in the world can consequently begin to be challenged. If the cultural hegemony of market capitalism can be destabilized, citizens can begin to see that market capitalism is not necessarily the only way of organizing economic relationships and that noncapitalist and alternative, more just methods of "economic" production and distribution/allocation already exist in the United States.[24] A counterhegemonic struggle against the existing cultural bases of capitalist hegemony is thus an integral—although not the only—step in *democratically* transforming oppressive economic practices and increasing the scope of democracy in this country, in contrast to top-down strategies for doing so.[25]

I argue that critical analyses of political–economic discourses and forms of common sense are therefore needed to determine the extent to which particular discourses are capitalist or compatible with capitalism, as well as the extent to which they are transgressive of capitalism. Those moments within existing political–economic discourse and common sense that favor an expanded notion of the political, those that are resistant to capitalist practices, and those that are capitalist, but contradictory, may be some of the starting points for counterhegemonic efforts to reconceptualize capitalism and the political-economic nexus. For instance, blue collar suspicion and resentment of managers as unproductive and not deserving of their higher pay and status may provide an opening for raising questions about the appropriation of surplus labor and

---

[23]The "philosophy of praxis"—that is to say, Marxist philosophy. Swanson is here adopting the terminology of Antonio Gramsci, which we will encounter in our reading in Part VI.—M. M.

[24]Community Economies Collective, "Imagining and Enacting Noncapitalist Futures," *Socialist Review* 28, nos. 3–4 (2001): 93–135.

[25]Gramsci, "The Study of Philosophy"; Smith.

the internal control of economic enterprises.[26] Popular resentment of big business and distrust of concentrated power, reflected in some polling data, could also be mobilized for counterhegemonic purposes.[27]

[…]

Examples of Depoliticized and Procapitalist Discourses

As I argue above, many depoliticized conceptualizations of economic practices are rooted in economistic ways of thinking, which are problematic both philosophically and politically. Consequently, any academic or popular political–economic discourse that conceives "the economy," "the market," economic enterprises, and individual economic behavior in an economistic manner, whether explicitly or more subtly, must be thoroughly criticized. Based on the Gramscian framework outlined above, I argue that all these "economic" phenomena should be theorized as complexly socially and historically constituted and thus diverse in their organization, operation, and effects. Hence, the following types of conceptualizations need, I contend, to be identified, denounced, and replaced: those that see "the economy" or markets as self-constituting or self-regulating (e.g., governed by an "invisible hand"), separate from the rest of society with their own laws, types of behavior, motivations, forms of thinking (e.g., utility maximization, self-interest, or instrumental rationality), and predictable effects (e.g., growth, efficiency, social welfare, or equilibrium); and those that view various types of economic phenomena (e.g., markets or economic enterprises) as essentially the same in their basic structure, that is, similarly determined by a limited number of "economic" variables (e.g., supply and demand, free trade, laissez-faire, competition, or profitability) and therefore operating according to similar "laws," "imperatives," or "logics" and having similar outcomes.[28]

For example, deterministic, abstract, and highly simplified conceptions of economic phenomena such as "the market" "undermine the ability of citizens to understand how these institutions work and what new possibilities may be found

---

[26]Barbara Ehrenreich, *Fear of Falling* (New York: Harper Perennial, 1989), 136–7.

[27]See, for example, Peterson, Albaum, and Kozmetsky, 15.

[28]Richard D. Wolff and Stephen A. Resnick, *Economics: Marxian versus Neoclassical* (Baltimore: Johns Hopkins University Press, 1987); Gibson-Graham; Watkins, *Everyday Exchanges*; Jack Amariglio and David F. Ruccio, "Postmodernism, Marxism, and the Critique of Modern Economic Thought," *Rethinking Marxism* 7, no. 3 (1994): 7–35; Antonio Callari, "Economic Subjects and the Shape of Politics," *Review of Radical Political Economics* 23, nos. 1–2 (1991): 201–7; Barry Hindess, *Freedom, Equality, and the Market* (New York: Tavistock, 1987); Block; J. Swanson, "The Economy and Its Relation to Politics," *Polity* 39, no. 2 (2007): 208–33.

within them," that is, how particular markets differ concretely and can be organized to achieve different goals.[29] Furthermore, belief in economic or market laws can foster a kind of political abdication of responsibility for the design and outcomes of economic practices. Echoing Marx's and Gramsci's (nonvoluntaristic) insistence on humans' ability to change their world, Jason Myers, wrote, "What politics demands, above all else, is responsibility: at the end of the process, we will be the masters of our own fate. The opposite inclination—the desire to throw up our hands and let the market decide—looks suspiciously like the Sartrean fear of freedom."[30]

Academic and popular discourses may also depoliticize economic practices by limiting political control, regulation, or design of "economic" phenomena through a variety of arguments, tactics, and institutions. For instance, if economic phenomena are viewed as self-constituting or as behaving according to economic laws, interference in these laws must be more or less limited or even prohibited. Yet, as Gramsci pointed out:

> It must be made clear that laissez-faire too is a form of State "regulation," introduced and maintained by legislative and coercive means. It is a deliberate policy, conscious of its own ends, and not the spontaneous, automatic expression of economic facts.[31]

In other words, what is portrayed within some discourses as deregulation or laissez-faire still involves, among other things, political enforcement of certain rules, rights, contracts, and norms of behavior; not just anything goes. "Private" economic actors and enterprises may be given relatively wide latitude in their behavior and decision making, but there are still limits on what they are allowed to do—limits, namely, they expect the government to ensure others (e.g., competitors or employees) do not breach.

Moreover, the (alleged) complexity and esoteric nature of economic laws sometimes mean that political leaders, not to mention citizens, are deemed too inept or ignorant—or too selfish, which might cause them to ignore the economic laws—to make economic decisions. According to such thinking, institutions like independent central banks and balanced budget amendments are therefore needed to prudently insulate economic phenomena (and their laws of motion) from politics. Run by (so-called) experts trained

---

[29]Kenneth Hoover, *Economics as Ideology* (New York: Rowman & Littlefield, 2003), 259.
[30]"Ideology after the Welfare State," *Historical Materialism* 10, no. 2 (2002): 177.
[31]Gramsci, "The Study of Philosophy," 160.

in the economic Laws and Truths, for example, of neoclassical economics, institutions like independent central banks are furthermore often seen as knowledgeable, neutral, and objective, and thus above criticism.[32]

As a result, activists, scholars, and politicians who criticize policies advocated by these experts are often accused of being ignorant, irrational, or "narrow special interests," labels that attempt, sometimes successfully, to marginalize or to discredit such critics and their alternative economic discourses.[33] In addition, restricting political control of economic practices can have the perverse effect of further delegitimating politics: by constraining what political leaders can do, they are less able to achieve beneficial economic goals and to mitigate harmful economic events, making them and their political parties appear incompetent and incapable of managing economic matters.[34]

Political control of economic practices is also limited by discourses that argue that certain types of political policies should be minimized or eliminated because of the ways in which they might "interfere" with a variety of (allegedly) fundamental "economic" imperatives. For example, economies and economic enterprises are said to risk failure if they do not remain competitive. Enterprises must maintain or increase their profits (i.e., accumulate capital) if they are to stay in business. National and local governmental policies (e.g., concerning taxation, wages, infrastructure, the environment, labor conditions, international trade, etc.) and union negotiations (e.g., concerning pay, benefits, job security, workplace organization, etc.) must consequently defer to and respect such economic "imperatives." Otherwise, we are told, businesses will fail, workers will be laid off or forced to take pay or benefit cuts, governments will lose tax revenues, cities and property values will crumble, and so forth. In this way, economic "imperatives" like "competitiveness" and "profitability" function to restrict political debate and economic options, essentializing and naturalizing existing economic practices and *obscuring their diversity, complexity, and many other social conditions of existence.* Moreover, such imperatives are often treated as common sense.[35]

---

[32]Resnick and Wolff; Wolff and Resnick; Teivainen, "Overcoming Economism," 322–3; Teivainen, *Enter Economism*, 17–18, 27, 179.

[33]Mark Rupert, "(Re)Politicizing the Global Economy," *Review of International Political Economy* 2, no. 4 (1995): 664–9; 682–5.

[34]Teivainen, *Enter Economism*, 175.

[35]GibsonGraham; J. K. Gibson-Graham and Phillip O'Neill, "Exploring a New Class Politics of the Enterprise," in *Re/Presenting Class*, ed. J. K. Gibson-Graham, Stephen A. Resnick, and Richard D. Wolff (Durham, NC: Duke University Press, 2001), 56–80; James Rinehart, "The Ideology of Competitiveness," *Monthly Review* 47, no. 5 (1995): 14–23.

Unfortunately, it is not only explicitly political–economic discourses that perpetuate the notion of economic imperatives and givens. In his study of U.S. high school biology education during the early twentieth century, Eric Engles, for instance, argued that discourses within the natural sciences also reinforced (and naturalized) capitalism and existing economic relations by, among other things, asserting the "biological" and "natural" pervasiveness of competition, zero-sum games with winners and losers, conflicts of interests, scarcity, the need for constant effort, the clear utility of divisions of labor and thus hierarchy, and the need to adapt to given conditions. If such principles are "natural," then social practices should be organized accordingly, regardless of their unequal, unpleasant, and undemocratic consequences. In addition, Eric W. Engles worried that public schools (then and now) promulgate a positivist notion of scientific knowledge as neutral and objective, which tends to obscure the political effects and diversity of theories and conceptions.[36]

Clichés and stereotypes about existing economic relations and behavior (e.g., economic interests, motivations, work habits, supply and demand, wages, or union leadership) similarly strengthen and naturalize existing economic practices when they treat them as all-powerful, unalterable, or irreplaceable aspects of contemporary society. Appeals to "reasonableness" or obviousness can also, for instance, when they treat economic phenomena as unchanging and thus aspects of life to be accepted and accommodated (e.g., as found in assertions of unassailable, undeniable truths or "rules of the game"; requests to "let's be honest" or "let's face it"; or claims of "it's the society we're living in") or when they treat alternative economic arrangements as utopian or unrealistic.[37]

By obscuring the *social* nature of existing arrangements and problems, individualistic discourses promoting personal responsibility and individual effort depoliticize by deflecting attention from the organization and societal effects of economic practices and institutions. If, according to such discourses, individuals' decisions and efforts determine their individual well-being and position in society— that is, if individuals are responsible for their own personal fate—notions of collective responsibility and collective action to alter unjust social relations are either not particularly important or inappropriate. Such discourses therefore encourage people to work within, and to maximize their own individual well-being within, the

---

[36]Eric W. Engles, "Early Twentieth-Century High School Biology Education," *Capitalism, Nature, Socialism* 6, no. 2 (1995): 65, 72–3, 50–1.

[37]Charles Woolfson, "The Semiotics of Working Class Speech," *Working Papers in Cultural Studies* 9 (1976): 163–97.

economic status quo, regardless of others' fate and often in competition with others.[38] As Leo Howe (1994) noted:

> Such an ideology encourages division and isolation. For those who pride themselves on having risen up the economic ladder, by dint of hard work and effort, it sustains them in their repudiation of those left behind. In both cases, the possibilities of collective political action are inhibited and the prevailing system of inequalities is preserved and ratified.[39]

Unfortunately, U.S. culture contains many stories, maxims, and clichés that reinforce such individualistic, depoliticized conceptualizations: the notion of "pulling yourself up by your bootstraps"; "rags-to-riches" stories; and phrases like "you can do anything if you set your mind to it," "life is what you make it," and "where there's a will there's a way."[40]

The depoliticizing effects of individualistic discourses suggest that, insofar as discourses supporting welfare state programs may reflect a greater appreciation of social interdependence, collective responsibility, and the social factors affecting individuals' opportunities and fate, such discourses may be a starting point for politicizing social relations and countering individualistic explanations. In other words, acknowledging the need for "social provision and social responsibility" implies, on at least some level, awareness of the *social* nature of existing arrangements and relations, that is, that society is not just a collection of self-sufficient individuals and is "more than just the accidental collision of individual desires." Such conceptions may make citizens more susceptible to then recognizing their ability to collectively and deliberately alter existing social arrangements.[41]

[...]

---

[38]Leo Howe, "Ideology, Domination, and Unemployment," *Sociological Review* 42, no. 2 (1994): 315–40; Jason Myers, "Ideology after the Welfare State," *Historical Materialism* 10, no. 2 (2002): 171–89, citing 181; Rupert, 658–92; Jacinda Swanson, "Self Help," *Radical Philosophy* 101 (2000): 29–38. The closely related discourse of meritocracy is similarly individualistic and depoliticizing (Howe; Young, Chapter 7).

[39]Howe, 325.

[40]Ibid.

[41]Myers, 181–2; Yahya M. Madra, "Questions of Communism," *Rethinking Marxism* 18, no. 2 (2006): 205–24, 220–1.

FOR DISCUSSION OR ESSAYS

- As we have seen, many introductory economics textbooks and popular discussions of economics prominently invoke common sense. Some of these same sources also arrive at surprising and counter-intuitive conclusions: seat belt laws cause pedestrian deaths; rent control decimates neighborhoods; higher taxes reduce total tax revenue; labor unions harm workers, and so on. How does one reconcile the "counter-intuitive" conclusions of economists with their "commonsensical" starting points?

- To illustrate the point that there is no such thing as a free lunch, Gregory Mankiw first describes several instances of everyday decision-making by individuals, then he turns to policy decisions that involve such trade-offs as "a cleaner environment" versus "a higher level of income"; greater "efficiency" versus greater "equity," and guns versus butter. But compare the trade-offs we make in our everyday lives to trade-offs when it comes to determining a national budget. Are there differences between these two sorts of trade-offs that are significant enough to raise doubts that they are *relevantly* similar? (Hint: recall Joseph Stiglitz's observation that macroeconomic policy can never be devoid of politics because it affects different groups differently.)

- A related question, focusing on the much-discussed guns-or-butter trade-off. Clearly, the groups that benefit from expenditures on "national defense"[42] differ from those that benefit from expenditures on butter. In view of the enormous military spending by the United States over the course of decades when the country has faced no threats to its shores, and in view of lost opportunity costs when it comes to alternative uses of these revenues, what insights (if any) do we gain from Mankiw's claim that, when it comes to policy, the trade-off is between *the size of the pie* and *how the pie is divided*?

- Becker claims that college students are investing in their "human capital" (which presumably consists of education, training, intelligence,

---

[42]"To protect our shores from foreign aggressors," as Mankiw describes its purpose. Presumably, this includes maintaining 800 foreign military bases, and military budgets that amount to more than half of total federal discretionary spending (52 percent in 2019), as well as prosecuting a long series of far-flung bombing campaigns and trillion-dollar wars, which in retrospect seem never to have achieved their proclaimed goals.

skills, health, and other assets that employers value, such as loyalty and punctuality). According to this view, "human capital," an "intangible asset or quality not listed on a company's balance sheet" (Investopedia), would appear to consist of *job readiness*—something that almost all adults possess, at least to some degree. But what is the sense of speaking of job readiness as a kind of *capital*, in any familiar sense of the word? (Someone who has just graduated from college with large student debt cannot then turn around and sell the "human capital" that she supposedly owns; rather, she must work years, typically for an owner of "physical capital," to "realize her investment" in education. In the meantime, most of her income goes to purchase articles of *personal consumption*, such as rent, food, entertainment, and so on—not consumption to produce goods that she can then sell at a profit.) In view of these considerations, what is the advantage of speaking as though wage earners, even those that possess no "physical capital," are owners of a kind of capital?

- Swanson wrote that "conceptual depoliticization" can sometimes lead to "practical depoliticization." What is the difference between the two? In your own words, describe how the one can lead to the other.

- Swanson suggests that "depoliticizing discourse" helps explain why so many Americans accept existing economic relations. Mainstream economists like Mankiw and Becker, by contrast, might claim that, thanks to any of a number of *non*-discursive circumstances (including a relatively high standard of living), *Americans are, by and large, satisfied with their lives in a free market economy*, and this goes a long way to explain the prevalence of complacent, depoliticizing discourse. Compare and evaluate these two claims.

FURTHER READINGS FOR PART V

Friedman, Milton. *Capitalism and Freedom*. Chicago: University of Chicago Press, 1962, 2002. With more than one million copies sold in numerous translations over the course of more than fifty years, this encomium to capitalism is one of the most popular books on the topic ever.

Hahn, L. Albert. *Common Sense Economics*. New York: St. Martin's Press, 2005, 2010. In this accessible book, the author presents another anti-Keynesian defense of laissez-faire economics.

Hill, Rod and Myatt, Tony. *The Economics Anti-Textbook*. London: Zed Books, 2010. Mainstream textbooks often present economics as an objective science free from value judgments. The discipline, we hear, puts a settled body of principles to work on reliable data, to test hypotheses and thereby arrive at policy prescriptions supported by a consensus of specialists. Hill and Myatt's *Anti-Textbook* argues that this is a dangerously misleading myth.

Rescher, Nicholas. *Common Sense: A New Look at an Old Philosophical Tradition*. Milwaukee: Marquette University Press, 2005. In Chapter 4, entitled "Common Sense, Trust, and Communication," Rescher, a pragmatist philosopher, offers an economic rationale for our trust in common sense. Thus, he turns it around: economics underwrites common sense, not vice versa.

Smith, Adam. *An Inquiry into the Nature and Causes of the Wealth of Nations*. Chicago: The University of Chicago Press, 1976. First published in 1776, this book has been described as having done for economics what *The Origin of Species* did for biology. Much of what Smith has to say might surprise students who are used to hearing about this champion of free markets, but have not actually read his most famous work.

Sowell, Thomas. *Basic Economics: A Common Sense Guide to the Economy*. 4th edn. New York: Basic Books, 2011. The author, a conservative economist, columnist, and scholar in residence at the Hoover Institution at Stanford University, provides a nontechnical "common sense" introduction (of more than 600 pages in the latest edition) to topics from price theory to labor markets, the banking system, and international trade. *Basic Economics* is a compendium of the strongest arguments for *laissez-faire* economics, in the spirit of Milton Friedman.

Part VI

Common Sense and Politics

Introduction to Part VI: Common Sense and Politics

In our very first reading from Part 1, Thomas Reid wrote of common sense that, "We must have a certain degree of it if we are to be subjects of law and government, capable of managing our own affairs, and responsible for our conduct toward others." More than a century and a half later, the German-American philosopher Hannah Arendt drew an even stronger connection between self-government and common sense, describing the latter as "the political sense *par excellence*."[1] In our final readings we will consider whether Arendt's characterization is to the point, and if so in what respect.

Intellectual historian Sophia Rosenfeld described common sense as "political," too, but in a different, less appreciative sense. Over the course of the past two centuries, she noted, the record certainly seems to show that, "claims about common sense are, in public life, almost always polemical."[2] Until the middle of the nineteenth century, for example, common sense had overwhelmingly condemned democracy in its most familiar forms. To the rulers and also to many of their subjects, it seemed obvious beyond argument that the "rule of the many" would result in generalized chaos. Eventually, though, self-appointed representatives of common sense demanded the establishment of electoral democracy, which, it was hoped, would produce more common sense—and social stability.

More recently, champions of common sense have taken up positions for and against a wide range of causes, including immigration reform, school vouchers, national health insurance, and same-sex marriage. In these disputes and hundreds of others, the side that had an exclusive claim to common sense was the side that had its mouth open at the moment. As one student put it, when it comes to politics, "common sense is what the opposition is lacking."

No document better exemplifies the contentious political character of common sense than that watershed document of modern factional agitation, Thomas Paine's pamphlet, *Common Sense* (written in January 1776). In his tract, Paine laid out the main lines of his argument for the independence, sooner rather than later, of the

---

[1] Hannah Arendt, *The Human Condition* (Chicago: University of Chicago Press, 1958/1998), 318.
[2] Rosenfeld, 15.

American colonies from Great Britain. He brought much effort and skill to bear in order to convince his readers of what were supposed to be self-evident claims. But the first line of Paine's Introduction to *Common Sense* appears to belie the self-evidence and "commonness" of his reflections: "Perhaps," he wrote, "the sentiments contained in the following pages are not yet sufficiently fashionable to procure them general favor ..."

When Paine's pamphlet burst into print in January 1776, though, it did indeed gain favor throughout the thirteen colonies. Its message was simple: Britain had no right to govern America; the system of monarchy itself was basically corrupt, and Americans would be much better off on their own. Not everyone who read the pamphlet nodded with approval, though. Leaders of the large minority of pro-British loyalists in the colonies struck back. In March 1776, barely three months after the appearance of *Common Sense*, their rejoinder appeared, in the form of another pamphlet under the nearly synonymous title, *Plain Truth*. (As it turns out, Paine himself had originally considered titling his work *Plain Truth*; now his opponent took that title for the opposing argument.) The author of *Plain Truth*, who took the pseudonym "Candidus," was in fact a wealthy planter from the colony of Maryland, named James Chalmers.[3] He depicted Paine as a "quack," lacking in the common sense that so clearly pointed toward reconciliation with the English throne and King George III.

The confrontation between Paine and Chalmers illustrates Rosenfeld's position vividly: in public life, common sense is almost invariably polemical. As we will see in our final reading, populist appeals to common sense, whether launched from the left, the right, or anywhere in between, are convincing because they seem to come from nowhere at all on "the political spectrum" (another common-sense trope!). By the first decade of our century, though, the Tea Party and its right-wing descendants had appropriated common sense, and, as Thomas Frank will explain in our third reading below, the appeal to common sense has largely become the province of conservatives and right-wing populists.

Our first reading is from the essay "The Study of Philosophy," by the Italian Marxist Antonio Gramsci (1891–1937). Anticipating the views of Quine, Kingwell, and Wittgenstein in some respects, Gramsci distinguishes two levels here: (i) at the first level, any discourse or use of language at all brings with it an unconscious but specific

---

[3]James Chalmers (Candidus), *Plain Truth, Addressed to the Inhabitants of America* (Philadelphia, PA: R. Bell, 1776).

conception of the world; (ii) at the second level, there is awareness and criticism.[4] But when it comes to the unconscious truisms, on the one hand, and awareness and criticism, on the other, which will prevail from case to case when it comes to describing the passing scene and making evaluations on the basis of those descriptions? If, as Gramsci claimed, common sense does not have the final word when it comes to which truism or maxim to consult, then how is priority determined? Gramsci will offer his insights.

Hannah Arendt, the author of our second reading, agrees that we—or at least "true philosophers"—have conflicting priorities when it comes to common sense and speculative thought; however, she offers a very different definition of common sense, and a very different description of the relationship between philosophy, on the one hand, and politics on the other. Arendt was, among other things, a brilliant interpreter of Aristotle. If, as Aristotle claimed, man is in essence a civic or political animal (a *zoon politikon*), then common sense has been around as long as humans have. Even the true philosopher, "one who spends his whole life in thought," shares common sense with the "many." Typically, though, the philosopher reverses the verdicts of common sense. Nowhere is this more obvious than in the common-sense recognition of the affinity between philosophy and death. Common sense tells us that death is the worst misfortune that can befall us; nevertheless, since ancient times philosophers have professed to welcome death as a release of the mind from the cage of the body. For common sense, then, speculative thinking is "out of order." The intramural warfare between thought and common sense is the conflict within the philosopher's own mind, between solitary speculative thought, on the one hand, and on the other hand, the essentially political and practical common sense that pronounces philosophy useless.

Our third selection, an excerpt from journalist Thomas Frank's bestseller *What's the Matter with Kansas?*, echoes Arendt's theme of the suspicion that the "many" display toward specialists and "elites." But it also jibes with Gramsci's description of common sense as contentious, fragmented, and incoherent. Without using the term, Frank examines a striking instance of *cultural hegemony* in his home state. Native "common nonsense," he writes, trumps the most direct "economic self-interest" and refutes the commonsensical view of individuals as rational pleasure maximizers. If, as some economics textbooks assure us, common sense consists in the pursuit of rational self-interest, then the good people of Kansas have

---

[4]What Gramsci has to say about "spontaneous philosophy" applies first and foremost to level (i). Also note similarities here with Kingwell, who holds that what he calls *plain common sense* does not tolerate contradiction when it stumbles upon it, and that *philosophical common sense* explicitly distinguishes between appearance and reality.

demonstrated either that (i) common sense is not at all common in their home state, or (ii) the phrase *pursuit of self-interest* does not have much substance at all.

The last reading is another work of partisan journalism. The article, by the Jamaican sociologist Stuart Hall and the cultural theorist Alan O'Shea, is included here because it explores the role of common sense in contemporary political rhetoric, and because it exemplifies in a clear way some of the claims we have encountered in our Gramsci reading. Hall and O'Shea agree with Gramsci that common sense is contradictory and typically conservative in outlook, but they put special emphasis on the Italian thinker's observation that it also contains "utopian elements," pointing outside of the status quo. As such, common sense is "a site of political struggle." And because we in complex modern societies are simultaneously citizens, workers, and consumers, common sense has "become a contested arena" in our daily lives, too.

Chapter 18

The Study of Philosophy (1932)

Antonio Gramsci

Recall that in our reading from Part II, W. V. O. Quine wrote: "We imbibe an archaic natural philosophy with our mother's milk." More than twenty-five years earlier, an inmate in Turi Prison in southern Italy noted that "the personality is strangely composite: it contains Stone Age elements and principles of a more advanced science, prejudices from all past phases of history at the local level and intuitions of a future philosophy which will be that of a human race united the world over." Indeed, that prison inmate, the Italian Marxist Antonio Gramsci, believed that any given language itself contains "a specific conception of the world." In this sense, as Gramsci observed, "everyone is a philosopher, though in his own way and unconsciously."

Many of the authors we've read have emphasized the practical character of common sense,[1] but as we have heard, Gramsci described common sense as *inconsequential*: common sense certifies choices and preferences after the fact; it never decides the day. We describe a behavior or choice as commonsensical only *after* we have committed ourselves to it, not before. Common sense, then, is more an honorific than a guide to reasoning: it is a seal of approval on a choice already made.[2]

In his "Critical Notes on an Attempt at Popular Sociology," another essay included in the *Selections from the Prison Notebooks*, Gramsci describes common sense as the "philosophy of non-philosophers."[3] But in the same paragraph, he appears to acknowledge that in an important sense few people are philosophers, since a hallmark of *philosophy*, as opposed to *common sense*, is that the former is much more coherent than the later.

---

[1] Gramsci's emphasis on the contradictory nature of common sense contrasts to Reid's view. Reid acknowledged that common sense is fallible, but Gramsci went much further, holding that "it" cannot stand as an adequate justification of any particular factual assertion.

[2] Notice that if common sense is not a guide for evaluating beliefs or coming to decisions, then it seems unlikely that it issues from a special mental faculty.

[3] Gramsci, 419.

Common sense is not a single unique conception, identical in time and space. It is the "folklore" of philosophy, and, like folklore, it takes countless different forms. Its most fundamental characteristic is that it is a conception which, even in the brain of one individual, is fragmentary, incoherent, and inconsequential, in conformity with the social and cultural position of those masses whose philosophy it is.[4]

Individuals utilize common sense to cope with daily life and explain to themselves the small segment of the much larger social order that absorbs them in the course of their lives. Because it is by nature limited in focus, though, common sense obstructs our view of the greater systemic nature of socioeconomic reality, including exploitation and class domination. People concentrate their attention upon their immediate concerns and problems in their personal lives, rather than the systemic sources of their social and economic reality. This accounts in part for why common sense is "a chaotic aggregate of disparate conceptions and one can find there anything that one likes."[5]

It also accounts for the fact, as Gramsci sees it, that common sense is always the common sense of this or that particular social group, and that every social class has its own common sense.[6] He describes beliefs that make up parts of one or another common sense, tracking them to their reproduction in families, religious movements, schools, and other social institutions. The striking fact that common sense is so fragmented, jumbled, and malleable arises from the circumstance that every social stratum has its common sense, and in a class-divided society any given common sense is as disjointed and conflict-ridden as the prevailing social relations.

Gramsci connects common sense to *cultural hegemony*—the diffusion throughout society of values, attitudes, beliefs, and morality that bind the ruled to their rulers. "Hegemony" is his term for the largely nonviolent process by which class domination "spontaneously" reproduces the consent of the ruled by installing the presuppositions of the ruling class as the common sense of the society as a whole.[7] The contest for cultural hegemony is never

---

[4]Ibid.

[5]Ibid., 422.

[6]Ibid., 326.

[7]Nancy Fraser, "From Progressive Neoliberalism to Trump—and Beyond," *American Affairs* 1, no. 4 (Winter 2017), americanaffairsjournal.org, accessed August 27, 2018. Gramsci distinguishes between two distinct forms of political control: (i) *domination*, or direct physical coercion by police, army, courts, and other repressive state institutions, and (ii) *hegemony*, or ideological control and consent. No regime, no matter how repressive, can sustain itself by threat of violence alone: popular support and legitimacy are needed in order to maintain stability, and this is especially true when it comes to complex modern societies.

entirely one-sided, though, and through criticism of the prevailing common sense those at the bottom might arrive at a new, more coherent "conception of the world"—and potentially, under the right circumstances, an alternative hegemony.

As we will see, Gramsci puts great emphasis on the field of education, including the "popular education" of adults. In this connection, he distinguishes between, on the one hand, the wishful, magical thinking that constitutes a large part of the fragmentary and incoherent body of common sense (*senso comune*), and on the other hand, those parts of common sense that have been practically confirmed. He calls the latter "good sense" (*il buon senso*). If we are ever to sort out the jumble that is common sense, we have no choice but to start formal education from where we are, with our prevailing good sense, contrasting it to the superstition and "folklore" that constitute the greater part of any particular common sense. By putting our practically confirmed good sense to work against the prevailing common sense, we may begin to achieve greater coherence, systematic unity, and consensus.

Gramsci wrote "The Study of Philosophy" around 1932,[8] while he was one of thousands of political prisoners in Benito Mussolini's Italy. This accounts for the scarcity of citations in the text and for his occasionally odd manner of expression, which was intended to evade the prison censors. All of the footnotes to the Gramsci text below are those of the editors of the *Selections from the Prison Notebooks*, except where indicated.

It is essential to destroy the widespread prejudice that philosophy is a strange and difficult thing just because it is the specific intellectual activity of a particular category of specialists or of professional and systematic philosophers. It must first be shown that all men are "philosophers," by defining the limits and characteristics of the "spontaneous philosophy" which is proper to everybody. This philosophy is contained in (1) language itself, which is a totality of determined notions and concepts and not just of words grammatically devoid of content; (2) "common sense" and "good sense";[9]

---

[8]According to Giuseppe Cospito, Professor of the History of Philosophy at the University of Pavia, Gramsci composed the notes for "the Study of Philosophy" in 1932. ("Verso l'edizione critica e integrale dei «Quaderni del carcere»," *Studi Storici* 52, no. 4 (2011): 881–904.) I wish to thank an anonymous reviewer for Bloomsbury Academic for kindly bringing this important fact to my attention, and for providing the source citation, too.

[9]The meaning that Gramsci gives to these two terms is explained in the paragraphs that follow. Broadly speaking, "common sense" designates the incoherent set of generally held assumptions and beliefs common to a society, while "good sense" means practical empirical common sense, in the English sense of the term. —M. M.

and (3) popular religion and, therefore, also the entire system of beliefs, superstitions, opinions, ways of seeing things and of acting, which are collectively bundled together under the name of "folklore."

Having first shown that everyone is a philosopher, though in his own way and unconsciously, since even in the slightest manifestation of any intellectual activity whatever, in "language," there is contained a specific conception of the world, one then moves on to the second level, which is that of awareness and criticism. That is to say, one proceeds to the question: is it better to "think," without having a critical awareness, in a disjointed and episodic way? In other words, is it better to take part in a conception of the world mechanically imposed by the external environment, i.e. by one of the many social groups in which everyone is automatically involved from the moment of his entry into the conscious world (and this can be one's village or province; it can have its origins in the parish and the "intellectual activity" of the local priest or aging patriarch whose wisdom is law, or in the little old woman who has inherited the lore of the witches, or the minor intellectual soured by his own stupidity and inability to act)? Or, on the other hand, is it better to work out consciously and critically one's own conception of the world and thus, in connection with the labors of one's own brain, choose one's sphere of activity, take an active part in the creation of the history of the world, be one's own guide, refusing to accept passively and supinely from outside the molding of one's personality?

> *Note I.* In acquiring one's conception of the world one always belongs to a particular grouping which is that of all the social elements which share the same mode of thinking and acting. We are all conformists of some conformism or other, always man-in-the-mass or collective man. The question is this: of what historical type is the conformism, the mass humanity to which one belongs? When one's conception of the world is not critical and coherent but disjointed and episodic, one belongs simultaneously to a multiplicity of mass human groups. The personality is strangely composite: it contains Stone Age elements and principles of a more advanced science, prejudices from all past phases of history at the local level and intuitions of a future philosophy which will be that of a human race united the world over. To criticize one's own conception of the world means therefore to make it a coherent unity and to raise it to the level reached by the most advanced thought in the world. It therefore also means criticism of all previous philosophy, in so far as this has left stratified deposits in popular philosophy. The starting point of critical elaboration is the consciousness of what one really is, and is "knowing thyself"[10]

---

[10]"Know thyself," the inscription on the forecourt of the temple at Delphi in Greece, became a principle of Socratic philosophy.—M. M.

as a product of the historical process to date which has deposited in you an infinity of traces, without leaving an inventory.

Note II. Philosophy cannot be separated from the history of philosophy, nor can culture from the history of culture. In the most immediate and relevant sense, one cannot be a philosopher, by which I mean have a critical and coherent conception of the world, without having a consciousness of its historicity, of the phase of development that it represents and of the fact that it contradicts other conceptions or elements of other conceptions. One's conception of the world is a response to certain specific problems posed by reality, which are quite specific and "original" in their immediate relevance. How is it possible to consider the present, and quite specific present, with a mode of thought elaborated for a past that is often remote and superseded? When someone does this, it means that he is a walking anachronism, a fossil, and not living in the modern world, or at the least that he is strangely composite. And it is in fact the case that social groups that in some ways express the most developed modernity, lag behind in other respects, given their social position, and are therefore incapable of complete historical autonomy.

Note III. If it is true that every language contains the elements of a conception of the world and of a culture, it could also be true that from anyone's language one can assess the greater or lesser complexity of his conception of the world. Someone who only speaks dialect, or understands the standard language incompletely, necessarily has an intuition of the world which is more or less limited and provincial, which is fossilized and anachronistic in relation to the major currents of thought that dominate world history. His interests will be limited, more or less corporate or economistic,[11] not universal. While it is not always possible to learn a number of foreign languages in order to put oneself in contact with other cultural lives, it is at least necessary to learn the national language properly. A great culture can be translated into the language of another great culture, that is to say a great national language with historic richness and complexity, and it can translate any other great culture and can be a worldwide means of expression. But a dialect cannot do this.

Note IV. Creating a new culture does not only mean one's own individual "original" discoveries. It also, and most particularly, means the diffusion in a critical form of truths

---

[11]Workers as a class can be merely "economistic" when they come together solely to defend their economic position (wages, hours, and conditions of work, health benefits, pensions, and so forth), without aspiring to a position of political and social leadership (Gramsci, xiv).—M. M.

already discovered, their "socialization" as it were, and even making them the basis of vital action,[12] an element of co-ordination and intellectual and moral order. For a mass of people to be led to think coherently and in the same coherent fashion about the real present world, is a "philosophical" event far more important and "original" than the discovery by some philosophical "genius" of a truth that remains the property of small groups of intellectuals.

Connection between "Common Sense," Religion, and Philosophy

Philosophy is intellectual order, which neither religion nor common sense can be. It is to be observed that religion and common sense do not coincide either, but that religion is an element of fragmented common sense. Moreover common sense is a collective noun, like religion: there is not just one common sense, for that too is a product of history and a part of the historical process.[13] Philosophy is criticism and the superseding of religion and "common sense." In this sense it coincides with "good" as opposed to "common" sense.

Relation between Science, Religion, and Common Sense

Religion and common sense cannot constitute an intellectual order, because they cannot be reduced to unity and coherence even within an individual consciousness, let alone collective consciousness. Or rather they cannot be so reduced "freely"—for this may be done by "authoritarian" means, and indeed within limits this has been done in the past.

---

[12]"Vital action." The concept here would appear to derive from French philosopher Henri Bergson, some of whose ideas were filtered to Gramsci through radical thinker Georges Sorel, and in a sense provided him with a psychological antidote to the fatalism of Austro-Marxism. There is no question, however, of Bergson having had a systematic influence on Gramsci's Marxism as such.

[13]"Part of the historical process." In the original, "*undivenire storico*"—historical becoming. For this aspect of common sense see Int., p. 144 [not included in this selection—M. M.]: "Every social stratum has its own 'common sense' and its own 'good sense,' which are basically the most widespread conception of life and of man. Every philosophical current leaves behind a sedimentation of 'common sense': this is the document of its historical effectiveness. Common sense is not something rigid and immobile, but is continually transforming itself, enriching itself with scientific ideas and with philosophical opinions that have entered ordinary life. 'Common sense' is the folklore of philosophy, and is always halfway between folklore properly speaking and the philosophy, science, and economics of the specialists. Common sense creates the folklore of the future, that is as a relatively rigid phase of popular knowledge at a given place and time."

Note the problem of religion taken not in the confessional sense but in the secular sense of a unity of faith between a conception of the world and a corresponding norm of conduct. But why call this unity of faith "religion" and not "ideology," or even frankly "politics"?[14]

Philosophy in general does not in fact exist. Various philosophies or conceptions of the world exist, and one always makes a choice between them. How is this choice made? Is it merely an intellectual event, or is it something more complex? And is it not frequently the case that there is a contradiction between one's intellectual choice and one's mode of conduct? Which therefore would be the real conception of the world: that logically affirmed as an intellectual choice? or that which emerges from the real activity of each man, which is implicit in his mode of action? And since all action is political, can one not say that the real philosophy of each man is contained in its entirety in his political action?

This contrast between thought and action, i.e., the coexistence of two conceptions of the world, one affirmed in words and the other displayed in effective action, is not simply a product of self-deception [*malafede*]. Self-deception can be an adequate explanation for a few individuals taken separately, or even for groups of a certain size, but it is not adequate when the contrast occurs in the life of great masses. In these cases the contrast between thought and action cannot but be the expression of profounder contrasts of a social historical order. It signifies that the social group in question may indeed have its own conception of the world, even if only embryonic; a conception which manifests itself in action, but occasionally and in flashes—when, that is, the group is acting as an organic totality. But this same group has, for reasons of submission and intellectual subordination, adopted a conception which is not its own but is borrowed from another group, and it affirms this conception verbally and believes itself to be following it, because this is the conception which it follows in "normal times"[15]—that is when its conduct is not independent and autonomous, but submissive and subordinate. Hence the reason why philosophy cannot be divorced from politics. And one can show furthermore that the choice and the criticism of a conception of the world is also a political matter.

What must next be explained is how it happens that in all periods there coexist many systems and currents of philosophical thought, how these currents are born, how they are diffused, and why in the process of diffusion they fracture

---

[14]For Gramsci's uses of "ideology" in its various senses see Gramsci, 375–7 [not included here; however, Gramsci will have more to say about ideology below.—M. M.]. By "politics" Gramsci means conscious action (praxis) in pursuit of a common social goal.

[15]"Normal times": as opposed to the exceptional (and hence potentially revolutionary) moments in history in which a class or group discovers its objective and subjective unity in action.

along certain lines and in certain directions. The fact of this process goes to show how necessary it is to order in a systematic, coherent and critical fashion one's own intuitions of life and the world, and to determine exactly what is to be understood by the word "systematic," so that it is not taken in the pedantic and academic sense. But this elaboration must be, and can only be, performed in the context of the history of philosophy, for it is this history which shows how thought has been elaborated over the centuries and what a collective effort has gone into the creation of our present method of thought which has subsumed and absorbed all this past history, including all its follies and mistakes. Nor should these mistakes themselves be neglected, for, although made in the past and since corrected, one cannot be sure that they will not be reproduced in the present and once again require correcting.

What is the popular image of philosophy? It can be reconstructed by looking at expressions in common usage. One of the most usual is "being philosophical about it," which, if you consider it, is not to be entirely rejected as a phrase. It is true that it contains an implicit invitation to resignation and patience, but it seems to me that the most important point is rather the invitation to people to reflect and to realize fully that whatever happens is basically rational[16] and must be confronted as such, and that one should apply one's power of rational concentration and not let oneself be carried away by instinctive and violent impulses. These popular turns of phrase could be compared with similar expressions used by writers of a popular stamp—examples being drawn from a large dictionary—which contain the terms "philosophy" or "philosophically." One can see from these examples that the terms have a quite precise meaning: that of overcoming bestial and elemental passions through a conception of necessity that gives a conscious direction to one's activity. This is the healthy nucleus that exists in "common sense," the part of it that can be called "good sense" and that deserves to be made more unitary and coherent. So it appears that here again it is not possible to separate what is known as "scientific" philosophy from the common and popular philosophy that is only a fragmentary collection of ideas and opinions.

But at this point we reach the fundamental problem facing any conception of the world, any philosophy that has become a cultural movement, a "religion," a "faith," any that has produced a form of practical activity or will in which the philosophy is contained as an implicit theoretical "premise." One might say "ideology" here, but on condition that the word is used in its highest sense of a conception of the world that

---

[16]*Rational* in G. W. F. Hegel's special sense of the word, as in his dictum, "the rational alone is real." Gramsci's point here is that, in the study of history, one can always describe *causes* of events, even when (as is typically the case) *reasons* are lacking.—M. M.

is implicitly manifest in art, in law, in economic activity and in all manifestations of individual and collective life. This problem is that of preserving the ideological unity of the entire social bloc[17] that that ideology serves to cement and to unify. The strength of religions, and of the Catholic Church in particular, has lain, and still lies, in the fact that they feel very strongly the need for the doctrinal unity of the whole mass of the faithful and strive to ensure that the higher intellectual stratum does not get separated from the lower. The Roman church has always been the most vigorous in the struggle to prevent the "official" formation of two religions, one for the "intellectuals" and the other for the "simple souls." This struggle has not been without serious disadvantages for the Church itself, but these disadvantages are connected with the historical process that is transforming the whole of civil society, and which contains overall a corrosive critique of all religion, and they only serve to emphasize the organizational capacity of the clergy in the cultural sphere and the abstractly rational and just relationship that the Church has been able to establish in its own sphere between the intellectuals and the "simple."

[...]

The question posed here was the one we have already referred to, namely this: is a philosophical movement properly so called when it is devoted to creating a specialized culture among restricted intellectual groups, or rather when, and only when, in the process of elaborating a form of thought superior to "common sense" and coherent on a scientific plane, it never forgets to remain in contact with the "simple" and indeed finds in this contact the source of the problems it sets out to study and to resolve? Only by this contact does a philosophy become "historical," purify itself of intellectualistic elements of an individual character, and become "life."[18]

---

[17]A *social bloc* forms within a particular society at a particular time, from an alliance of social classes or fractions of classes (whether politically dominant or "subaltern"), and their "organic intellectuals." *Organic intellectuals* are thinkers and agents that represent the social bloc by articulating and advancing its interests. (Kate Crehan, *Gramsci's Common Sense*, 38, cited in the Further Readings section below; Gramsci, 60–1; 334; 418.)—M. M.

[18]Perhaps it is useful to make a "practical" distinction between philosophy and common sense in order to indicate more clearly the passage from one moment to the other. In philosophy the features of individual elaboration of thought are the most salient: in common sense on the other hand it is the diffuse, uncoordinated features of a generic form of thought common to a particular period and a particular popular environment. But every philosophy has a tendency to become the common sense of a fairly limited environment (that of all the intellectuals). It is a matter therefore of starting with a philosophy which already enjoys, or could enjoy, a certain diffusion, because it is connected to and implicit in practical life, and elaborating it so that it becomes a renewed common sense possessing the coherence and the sinew of individual philosophies. But this can only happen if the demands of cultural contact with the "simple" are continually felt. [Gramsci's note.].

A philosophy of praxis[19] cannot but present itself at the outset in a polemical and critical guise, as superseding the existing mode of thinking and existing concrete thought (the existing cultural world). First of all, therefore, it must be a criticism of "common sense," basing itself initially, however, on common sense in order to demonstrate that "everyone" is a philosopher and that it is not a question of introducing from scratch a scientific form of thought into everyone's individual life, but of renovating and making "critical" an already existing activity. It must then be a criticism of the philosophy of the intellectuals out of which the history of philosophy developed and which, in so far as it is a phenomenon of individuals (in fact it develops essentially in the activity of single particularly gifted individuals) can be considered as marking the "high points" of the progress made by common sense, or at least the common sense of the more educated strata of society but through them also of the people. Thus an introduction to the study of philosophy must expound in synthetic form the problems that have grown up in the process of the development of culture as a whole and which are only partially reflected in the history of philosophy. (Nevertheless it is the history of philosophy which, in the absence of a history of common sense, impossible to reconstruct for lack of documentary material, must remain the main source of reference.) The purpose of the synthesis must be to criticize the problems, to demonstrate their real value, if any, and the significance they have had as superseded links of an intellectual chain, and to determine what the new contemporary problems are and how the old problems should now be analyzed.

The relation between common sense and the upper level of philosophy is assured by "politics," just as it is politics that assures the relationship between the Catholicism of the intellectuals and that of the simple. There are, however, fundamental differences between the two cases. That the Church has to face up to a problem of the "simple" means precisely that there has been a split in the community of the faithful. This split cannot be healed by raising the simple to the level of the intellectuals (the Church does not even envisage such a task, which is both ideologically and economically beyond its present capacities), but only by imposing an iron discipline on the intellectuals so that they do not exceed certain limits of differentiation and so render the split catastrophic and irreparable. In the past such divisions in the community of the faithful were healed by strong mass movements, which led to, or were absorbed

---

[19]To evade the prison censors, Gramsci used "philosophy of praxis" as a code term for Marxism.—M. M.

in, the creation of new religious orders centered on strong personalities (St. Dominic, St. Francis).[20]

[...]

The position of the philosophy of praxis is the antithesis of the Catholic. The philosophy of praxis does not tend to leave the "simple" in their primitive philosophy of common sense, but rather to lead them to a higher conception of life. If it affirms the need for contact between intellectuals and "simple," it is not in order to restrict scientific activity and preserve unity at the low level of the masses, but precisely in order to construct an intellectual–moral bloc which can make politically possible the intellectual progress of the mass and not only of small intellectual groups.

The active man-in-the-mass has a practical activity, but has no clear theoretical consciousness of his practical activity, which nonetheless involves understanding the world in so far as it transforms it.[21] His theoretical consciousness can indeed be historically in opposition to his activity. One might almost say that he has two theoretical consciousnesses (or one contradictory consciousness): one which is implicit in his activity and which in reality unites him with all his fellow workers in the practical transformation of the real world, and one, superficially explicit or verbal, which he has inherited from the past and uncritically absorbed. But this verbal conception is not without consequences. It holds together a specific social group, it influences moral conduct and the direction of will, with varying efficacy but often powerfully enough to produce a situation in which the contradictory state of consciousness does not permit of any action, any decision, or any choice, and produces a condition of moral and political passivity. Critical understanding of self takes place therefore through a struggle of political "hegemonies" and of opposing directions, first in the ethical field and then in that of politics proper, in order to arrive at the working out at a higher level of one's own conception of reality. Consciousness of being part of a particular hegemonic force (that is to say, political consciousness) is the first stage toward a further progressive selfconsciousness in which theory and practice will finally be one.

---

[20]The heretical movements of the Middle Ages were a simultaneous reaction against the politicking of the Church and against the scholastic philosophy which expressed this. They were based on social conflicts determined by the birth of the Communes, and represented a split between masses and intellectuals within the Church. This split was "stitched over" by the birth of popular religious movements subsequently reabsorbed by the Church through the formation of the mendicant orders and a new religious unity. [Gramsci's note.].

[21]A reference to the 11th of Marx's *Theses on Feuerbach,* which Gramsci interprets as meaning that philosophy (and, in particular, the philosophy of praxis) is a socio-practical activity, in which thought and action are reciprocally determined.

Thus the unity of theory and practice is not just a matter of mechanical fact, but a part of the historical process, whose elementary and primitive phase is to be found in the sense of being "different" and "apart," in an instinctive feeling of independence, and which progresses to the level of real possession of a single and coherent conception of the world. This is why it must be stressed that the political development of the concept of hegemony represents a great philosophical advance as well as a politico-practical one.[22] For it necessarily supposes an intellectual unity and an ethic in conformity with a conception of reality that has gone beyond common sense and has become, if only within narrow limits, a critical conception.

[...]

When you don't have the initiative in the struggle, and the struggle itself comes eventually to be identified with a series of defeats, mechanical determinism becomes a tremendous force of moral resistance, of cohesion and of patient and obstinate perseverance. "I have been defeated for the moment, but the tide of history is working for me in the long term." Real will takes on the garments of an act of faith in a certain rationality of history and in a primitive and empirical form of impassioned finalism[23] which appears in the role of a substitute for the Predestination or Providence of confessional religions. It should be emphasized, though, that a strong activity of the will is present even here, directly intervening in the "force of circumstance," but only implicitly, and in a veiled and, as it were, shamefaced manner. Consciousness here, therefore, is contradictory and lacking critical unity, etc. But when the "subaltern"[24] becomes directive and responsible for the economic activity of the masses, mechanism at a certain point becomes an imminent danger and a revision must take place in modes of thinking because a change has taken place in the social mode of existence.[25] The boundaries and the dominion of the "force of circumstance"

---

[22]The reference here is not only to Marx's argument about "ideas becoming a material force," but also to Lenin and the achievement of proletarian hegemony through the Soviet revolution.

[23]"Finalism": the notion that history is always working toward a determined end. The idea that Gramsci is attacking is that of historical inevitability, and in particular of the "inevitable" spontaneous collapse of capitalism and its replacement by the socialist order.

[24]As Gramsci used the term, a *subaltern group* is a social group that is subordinate to some other group, or that occupies a subordinate location within an overarching institution such as the state (refer to Crehan, 185). In his prison writings, Gramsci describes the modern proletariat as a subaltern group, as well as slaves, peasants, various religious and racial groups, and women.—M. M.

[25]This is an echo of Marx's statement (in his Preface to *A Contribution to the Critique of Political Economy*) that it is not consciousness that determines being, but man's social being that determines his consciousness. This conception is very important to Gramsci and constantly recurs in his prison writings, as do other ideas from the same Preface.

become restricted. But why? Because, basically, if yesterday the subaltern element was a thing, today it is no longer a thing but an historical person, a protagonist; if yesterday it was not responsible, because it was "resisting" a will external to itself, now it feels itself to be responsible because it is no longer resisting but an agent, necessarily active and taking the initiative.

But even yesterday, was it ever mere "resistance," a mere "thing," mere "non-responsibility"? Certainly not. Indeed one should emphasize how fatalism is nothing other than the clothing worn by real and active will when in a weak position. This is why it is essential at all times to demonstrate the futility of mechanical determinism: for, although it is explicable as a naive philosophy of the mass and as such, but only as such, can be an intrinsic element of strength, nevertheless when it is adopted as a thought-out and coherent philosophy on the part of the intellectuals, it becomes a cause of passivity, of idiotic self-sufficiency. This happens when they don't even expect that the subaltern will become directive and responsible. In fact, however, some part of even a subaltern mass is always directive and responsible, and the philosophy of the part always precedes the philosophy of the whole, not only as its theoretical anticipation but also as a necessity of real life.

That the mechanicist conception has been a religion of the subaltern is shown by an analysis of the development of the Christian religion. Over a certain period of history in certain specific historical conditions religion has been and continues to be a "necessity," a necessary form taken by the will of the popular masses and a specific way of rationalizing the world and real life, which provided the general framework for real practical activity. This quotation from an article in *La Civiltá Cattolica* (*Individualismo pagano e individualismo cristiano*, March 5, 1932) seems to me to express very well this function of Christianity:

> Faith in a secure future, in the immortality of the soul destined to beatitude, in the certainty of arriving at eternal joy, was the force behind the labor for intense interior perfection and spiritual elevation. True Christian individualism found here the impulse that led it to victory. All the strength of the Christian was gathered around this noble end. Free from the flux of speculation which weakens the soul with doubt, and illuminated by immortal principles, man felt his hopes reborn; sure that a superior force was supporting him in the struggle against Evil, he did violence to himself and conquered the world.

But here again it is naive Christianity that is being referred to: not Jesuitized Christianity, which has become a pure narcotic for the popular masses.

The position of Calvinism, however, with its iron conception of predestination and grace, which produces a vast expansion of the spirit of initiative (or becomes the form of this movement) is even more revealing and significant.[26]

What are the influential factors in the process of diffusion (which is also one of a substitution of the old conception, and, very often, of combining old and new), how do they act, and to what extent? Is it the rational form in which the new conception is expounded and presented? Or is it the authority (in so far as this is recognized and appreciated, if only generically) of the expositor and the thinkers and experts whom the expositor calls in in his support? Or the fact of belonging to the same organization as the man who upholds the new conception (assuming, that is, that one has entered the organization for other reasons than that of already sharing the new conception)?

In reality these elements will vary according to social groups and the cultural level of the groups in question. But the enquiry has a particular interest in relation to the popular masses, who are slower to change their conceptions, or who never change them in the sense of accepting them in their "pure" form, but always and only as a more or less heterogeneous and bizarre combination. The rational and logically coherent form, the exhaustive reasoning which neglects no argument, positive or negative, of any significance, has a certain importance, but is far from being decisive. It can be decisive, but in a secondary way, when the person in question is already in a state of intellectual crisis, wavering between the old and the new, when he has lost his faith in the old and has not yet come down in favor of the new, etc.

One could say this about the authority of thinkers and experts: it is very important among the people, but the fact remains that every conception has its thinkers and experts to put forward, and authority does not belong to one side; furthermore, with every thinker it is possible to make distinctions, to cast doubt on whether he really said such and such a thing, etc.

One can conclude that the process of diffusion of new conceptions takes place for political (that is, in the last analysis, social) reasons, but that the formal element, that of logical coherence, the element of authority and the organizational element have a very important function in this process immediately after the general orientation has been reached, whether by single individuals or groups of a certain size. From

---

[26]On this question see: Max Weber, *L'etica protestante e lo spirito del capitalismo*; published in *Nuovi Studi*, volume for 1931, *et seq.* (*The Protestant Ethic and the Spirit of Capitalism*, trans. Talcott Parsons [London: Allen and Unwin, 1930].) And see Groethuysen's book on the religious origins of the bourgeoisie in France. (*Origines de l'esprit bourgeois en France* vol. I. *L'Eglise et la bourgeoisie* [Paris: Gallimard, 1927].) [Gramsci's note.]

this we must conclude, however, that in the masses *as such,* philosophy can only be experienced as a faith.

Imagine the intellectual position of the man of the people: he has formed his own opinions, convictions, criteria of discrimination, and standards of conduct. Anyone with a superior intellectual formation with a point of view opposed to his can put forward arguments better than he does and really tear him to pieces logically, and so on. But should the man of the people change his opinions just because of this? Just because he cannot impose himself in a bout of argument? In that case he might find himself having to change every day, or every time he meets an ideological adversary who is his intellectual superior. On what elements, therefore, can his philosophy be founded? And in particular his philosophy in the form which has the greatest importance for his standards of conduct?

The most important element is undoubtedly one whose character is determined not by reason but by faith. But faith in whom, or in what? In particular in the social group to which he belongs, in so far as in a diffuse way it thinks as he does. The man of the people thinks that so many like-thinking people can't be wrong, not so radically, as the man he is arguing against would like him to believe; he thinks that, while he himself, admittedly, is not able to uphold and develop his arguments as well as the opponent, in his group there is someone who could do this and could certainly argue better than the particular man he has against him, and he remembers, indeed, hearing expounded, discursively, coherently, in a way that left him convinced, the reasons behind his faith. He has no concrete memory of the reasons and could not repeat them, but he knows that reasons exist, because he has heard them expounded, and was convinced by them. The fact of having once suddenly seen the light and been convinced is the permanent reason for his reasons persisting, even if the arguments in its favor cannot be readily produced.

These considerations lead, however, to the conclusion that new conceptions have an extremely unstable position among the popular masses; particularly when they are in contrast with orthodox convictions (which can themselves be new) conforming socially to the general interests of the ruling classes. This can be seen if one considers the fortunes of religions and churches. Religion, or a particular church, maintains its community of faithful (within the limits imposed by the necessities of general historical development) in so far as it nourishes its faith permanently and in an organized fashion, indefatigably repeating its apologetics, struggling at all times and always with the same kind of arguments, and maintaining a hierarchy of intellectuals who give to the faith, in appearance at least, the dignity of thought. Whenever the continuity of relations between the Church and the faithful has been violently interrupted, for political reasons, as happened during the French Revolution, the losses suffered by the Church have been incalculable. If the conditions had persisted for a long time in which it was difficult to carry on practicing one's own religion, it is quite possible that these losses would have been definitive, and a new religion would have emerged, as indeed one did emerge in France in combination with the old Catholicism. Specific necessities can be deduced from this for any cultural movement which aimed to replace common sense and old conceptions of the world in general:

1. Never to tire of repeating its own arguments (though offering literary variation of form): repetition is the best didactic means for working on the popular mentality.

2. To work incessantly to raise the intellectual level of ever growing strata of the populace, in other words, to give a personality to the amorphous mass element. This means working to produce *élites*[27] of intellectuals of a new type that arise directly out of the masses, but remain in contact with them to become, as it were, the whalebone in the corset.[28]

This second necessity, if satisfied, is what really modifies the "ideological panorama" of the age. But these *élites* cannot be formed or developed without a hierarchy of authority and intellectual competence growing up within them. The culmination of this process can be a great individual philosopher. But he must be capable of re-living concretely the demands of the massive ideological community and of understanding that this cannot have the flexibility of movement proper to an individual brain, and must succeed in giving formal elaboration to the collective doctrine in the most relevant fashion, and the one most suited to the modes of thought of a collective thinker.

It is evident that this kind of mass creation cannot just happen "arbitrarily," around any ideology, simply because of the formally constructive will of a personality or a group that puts it forward solely on the basis of its own fanatical philosophical or religious convictions. Mass adhesion or nonadhesion to an ideology is the real critical test of the rationality and historicity of modes of thinking. Any arbitrary constructions are pretty rapidly eliminated by historical competition, even if sometimes, through a combination of immediately favorable circumstances, they manage to enjoy popularity

---

[27]"*Élite*." Gramsci uses this word (in French in the original) in a sense very different from that of the reactionary post-Pareto theorists of "political *élites*." The *élite* in Gramsci is the revolutionary vanguard of a social class in constant contact with its political and intellectual base.

[28]For Gramsci's theory of the "organic" intellectual see the essay "The Formation of the Intellectuals," in Gramsci, 5–14. [Not included here, but refer to the note on the term *social bloc*, above.—M. M.]

of a kind; whereas constructions which respond to the demands of a complex organic period of history always impose themselves and prevail in the end, even though they may pass through several intermediary phases during which they manage to affirm themselves only in more or less bizarre and heterogeneous combinations.

These developments pose many problems, the most important of which can be subsumed in the form and the quality of the relations between the various intellectually qualified strata; that is, the importance and the function that the creative contribution of superior groups must and can have in connection with the organic capacity of the intellectually subordinate strata to discuss and develop new critical concepts. It is a question, in other words, of fixing the limits of freedom of discussion and propaganda, a freedom which should not be conceived of in the administrative and police sense, but in the sense of a self-limitation which the leaders impose on their own activity, or, more strictly, in the sense of fixing the direction of cultural policy. In other words—who is to fix the "rights of knowledge" and the limits of the pursuit of knowledge? And can these rights and limits indeed be fixed? It seems necessary to leave the task of researching after new truths and better, more coherent, clearer formulations of the truths themselves to the free initiative of individual specialists, even though they may continually question the very principles that seem most essential. And it will in any case not be difficult to expose the fact whenever such proposals for discussion arise because of interested and not scientific motives. Nor is it inconceivable that individual initiatives should be disciplined and subject to an ordered procedure, so that they have to pass through the sieve of academies or cultural institutes of various kinds and only become public after undergoing a process of selection.

It would be interesting to study concretely the forms of cultural organization that keep the ideological world in movement within a given country, and to examine how they function in practice. A study of the numerical relationship between the section of the population professionally engaged in active cultural work in the country in question and the population as a whole, would also be useful, together with an approximate calculation of the unattached forces. The school, at all levels, and the Church, are the biggest cultural organizations in every country, in terms of the number of people they employ. Then there are newspapers, magazines and the book trade and private educational institutions, either those that are complementary to the state system, or cultural institutions like the Popular Universities. Other professions include among their specialized activities a fair proportion of cultural activity. For example, doctors, army officers, the legal profession. But it should be noted that in all countries, though in differing degrees, there is a great gap between the popular masses and the intellectual groups, even the largest ones, and those nearest to the peripheries of national life, like priests and school teachers. The reason for this is that, however much the ruling class may affirm to the contrary, the State, as such, does not have a unitary, coherent and homogeneous conception, with the result that intellectual groups are scattered between one stratum and the next, or even within a single stratum. The Universities, except in a few countries, do not exercise any unifying influence: often an independent thinker has more influence than the whole of university institutions, etc.

With regard to the historical role played by the fatalistic conception of the philosophy of praxis one might perhaps prepare its funeral oration, emphasizing its usefulness for a certain period of history, but precisely for this reason underlining the need to bury it with all due honors. Its role could really be compared with that of the theory of predestination and grace for the beginnings of the modern world, a theory which found its culmination in classical German philosophy and in its conception of freedom as the consciousness of necessity.[29] It has been a replacement in the popular consciousness for the cry of "'tis God's will," although even on this primitive, elementary plane it was the beginnings of a more modern and fertile conception than that contained in the expression "'tis God's will" or in the theory of grace. Is it possible that a "formally" new conception can present itself in a guise other than the crude, unsophisticated version of the populace? And yet the historian, with the benefit of all necessary perspective, manages to establish and to understand the fact that the beginnings of a new world, rough and jagged though they always are, are better than the passing away of the world in its death throes and the swan song that it produces.

---

[29]"The consciousness of necessity." This notion, which originated with Spinoza, plays a particularly important role in Hegelian philosophy.

Chapter 19

The Intramural Warfare between Thought and Common Sense

Hannah Arendt

In his novel *1984*, George Orwell wrote that, for Big Brother, "The heresy of heresies was common sense," which led its subjects to deny "not merely the validity of experience, but the very existence of external realty."[1] This was the baneful effect of "totalitarianism," according to Orwell's self-identified successors. Common sense, which comprises the shared judgments of the diverse individuals who make up a community, makes public discourse possible, and without public discourse, there is also no democracy, in one or another honorific use of that word. So claimed Hannah Arendt and other public intellectuals in the camp that would eventually win the Cold War.

Following Aristotle, Arendt viewed the *sensus communis* as a "sixth sense" that "fits our five senses into a common world," a shared community. When people, each from their necessarily unique perspective, judge in keeping with their shared common experience, they move beyond their merely subjective experiences and make space for a "common world." Because common sense gives us a way of talking together about the passing scene, it is both "the ground on which true democracy forms and the product that true democracy creates."[2] For this reason, Arendt described common sense as "the political sense par excellence."[3]

Philosophers, Arendt writes, must have been the first to note the conflict between common sense and thinking, because they were the first to turn away

---

[1] George Orwell, 1984 (New York: Harcourt Brace Jovanovich, 1949), 69.

[2] Rosenfeld, 252. Arendt looked to ancient Athens for a picture of civic engagement. More accurately, she looked to an idealized Athens, one that managed to mask off slave production in that city-state, as well as the exclusion of women from the public sphere and the many violent upheavals that pitted the haves against the have-nots.

[3] From Arendt's essay, "Understanding and Politics," quoted in Rosenfeld, 252.

from the world of appearances. Common sense is at odds with reason, which demands that the philosopher, "one who spends his whole life in thought," regard the body as the cage of the soul. Philosophers, epitomized by Plato and the Stoics, have turned away from life toward death, as liberation from the illusions of the bodily senses. They have turned common sense upside down, proclaiming hostility toward the body and also toward politics, "the petty affairs of men."

But even the philosopher—who, after all, is a human like any other—shares with others the common-sense suspicion that a life spent in solitary thought disrupts the proper functioning of the body. Turning it around, though, the philosopher contends that the body obstructs reason. And yet reason never quite has the last word: the conflict between the philosopher and the unthinking "many" plays out within the mind of the philosopher herself.

Reviewers assure us that Hannah Arendt (1906–1975) was one of the leading social theorists of the last century. Like Mortimer Adler, she might be described as a modern follower of Aristotle, the ancient thinker who famously held that humans are a "political animal." Above all, she was a highly original public intellectual and advocate of civic republicanism and "participatory democracy," the view that a citizenry can and should engage maximally in the policy decisions that affect it.

"Take on the color of the dead"[4]—so indeed the philosopher's absentmindedness and the style of life of the *professional*[5] who devotes his entire life to thinking, thus monopolizing and raising to an absolute what is but one of the many human faculties, must appear to the common sense of common men, since we normally move in a world where the most radical experience of disappearing is death, and withdrawal from appearance is dying. The very fact that there have always—at least since Parmenides[6]—been men who chose this way of life deliberately without being candidates for suicide shows that this sense of an affinity with death does not come from the thinking activity and the experiences of the thinking ego itself. It is, rather, the philosopher's own common sense—his being "a man like you and me"—that makes him aware of being "out of order" while engaged in thinking. He is

[4]This was the puzzling advice that the oracle at Delphi gave to the stoic philosopher Zeno, when the latter asked what he should do to lead the best life.—M. M.
[5]Arendt is alluding here to a formulation of the German philosopher Immanuel Kant (1724–1804), who once described philosophers as "professional thinkers."—M. M.
[6]The fifth-century Greek thinker who declared that, according to "the way of truth" (as opposed to the way of mere opinion), reality is "one" and unchanging.—M. M.

not immune from common opinion, because he shares, after all, in the "common-ness" of all men, and it is his own sense of realness that makes him suspect the thinking activity. And since thinking itself is helpless against the arguments of common-sense reasoning and the insistence on the "meaninglessness" of its quest for meaning, the philosopher is prone to answer in common-sense terms, which he simply turns upside down for the purpose. If common sense and common opinion hold that "death is the greatest of all evils," the philosopher (of Plato's time, when death was understood as the separation of soul from body) is tempted to say: on the contrary, "death is a deity, a benefactor to the philosopher, precisely because it dissolves the union of soul and body"[7] and thus seems to liberate the mind from bodily pain and pleasure, both of which prevent our mental organs from pursuing their activity, just as consciousness prevents our bodily organs from functioning properly.[8] The whole history of philosophy, which tells us so much about the objects of thought and so little about the process of thinking and the experiences of the thinking ego, is shot through with an *intramural warfare* between man's common sense, this sixth sense that fits our five senses into a common world, and man's faculty of thought and need of reason, which determine him to remove himself for considerable periods from it.

The philosophers have interpreted that intramural warfare as the natural hostility of the many and their opinions toward the few and their truth, but the historical facts to support this interpretation are rather scanty. There is, to be sure, the trial of Socrates, which probably inspired Plato to declare at the end of the Cave parable (when the philosopher returns from his solitary flight into the sky of the ideas to the darkness of the cave and the company of his fellow men)[9] that the many, if they only could, would lay hands on the few and kill them. This interpretation of Socrates's trial echoes through the history of philosophy up to and including Hegel.[10] Yet, leaving aside some very justified doubts about Plato's version of the event,[11] the fact is, there are hardly any

---

[7]*Hagigah*, chapter II, 1. Quoted from Hans Blumenberg, *Paradigmen zu einer Metaphorologie* (Bonn: Bouvier, 1960), 26 note 38.

   [Note: The *Tractate Hagigah* is a collection of writings, forming part of the Jewish Talmud, that details the laws of the thrice-yearly pilgrimage to the Holy Temple. As this citation shows, it appears that not all of the original footnotes in this reading correspond to the requirements of the published text. This might be due to the fact that *The Life of the Mind* was published posthumously, from an unfinished manuscript. In any case, in the present text the original footnotes remain unchanged, mostly without comment.—M. M.]

[8]Book XI, Chapters xii and xxx. [It is not clear what work is cited here.—M. M.]

[9]Plato's famous Allegory of the Cave appears in his *Republic*, Book VII.—M. M.

[10]Hegel ascribed a pivotal role to Socrates in the history of philosophy. Socrates' accusers viewed him as a threat to a fragile democracy. By Hegel's lights, though, he personified a new relationship between the "individual consciousness" and the "universal law of the state," and between morality and the individual.—M. M.

[11]See Niccolo Machiavelli, *Discourses on Livy* (c. 1517), Book II, Chapter xix.

instances on record of the many on their own initiative declaring war on philosophers. As far as the few and the many are concerned, it has been rather the other way round. It was the philosopher who of his own accord quitted the City of men and then told those he had left behind that, at best, they were deceived by the trust they put in their senses, by their willingness to believe the poets and be taught by the populace, when they should have been using their minds, and that, at worst, they were content to live only for sensual pleasure and to be glutted like cattle.[12] It seems rather obvious that the multitude can never resemble a philosopher, but this does not mean, as Plato stated, that those who do philosophy are "necessarily blamed" and persecuted by the many "like a man fallen among wild beasts."[13]

The philosopher's way of life is solitary, but this solitude is freely chosen, and Plato himself, when he enumerates the natural conditions favorable to the development in "the noblest natures" of the philosophical gift, does not mention the hostility of the many. He speaks, rather, of exiles, of a "great mind born in a petty state whose affairs are beneath ... notice," and of other circumstances such as ill health that cut such natures off from the public affairs of the many.[14] But this turning-of-the tables, to make the warfare between thought and common sense the result of the few turning against the many, though perhaps a shade more plausible and better documented—to wit, on the philosopher's claim to rule—than the traditional persecution mania of the philosopher, is probably no nearer the truth. The most plausible explanation of the quarrel between common sense and "professional" thinking still is the point already mentioned (that we are dealing here with an intramural warfare) since surely the first to be aware of all the objections common sense could raise against philosophy must have been the philosophers themselves. And Plato—in a different context, where he is not concerned with a polity "worthy of the philosophical nature"—dismisses with laughter a question raised as to whether a man who is concerned with divine things is also good at things human.[15]

Laughter rather than hostility is the natural reaction of the many to the philosopher's preoccupation and the apparent uselessness of his concerns. This laughter is innocent and quite different from the ridicule frequently turned on an

---

[12]Heraclitus, in John Burnet, ed., *Early Greek Philosophy* (London: Adam and Charles Black, 1908), 154, fragment 111, 23.

[13]The phrase "like a man fallen among wild beasts" is to be found in Plato's *Republic*, Book VI. —M. M.

[14]*Discourses*, Book II, Chapter 16.

[15]All the works we have, including the *Discourses*, are "apparently almost a stenographic record of his lectures and informal discussions taken down and compiled by one of his pupils, Arrian." See Whitney J. Oates, *The Stoic and Epicurean Philosophers* (New York: Modern Library, 1940), whose translation I often follow.

opponent in serious disputes, where it can indeed become a fearful weapon. But Plato, who argued in the *Laws* for the strict prohibition of any writing that would ridicule any of the citizens,[16] feared the ridicule in all laughter. What is decisive here are not the passages in the political dialogues, the *Laws* or the *Republic*, against poetry and especially comedians, but the entirely serious way in which he tells the story of the Thracian peasant girl who bursts out laughing when she saw Thales fall into a well while he was watching the motions of the heavenly bodies above him, "[the Thracian girl] declaring that he was eager to know the things in the sky, but what was ... just at his feet escaped him." And Plato adds: "Anyone who gives his life to philosophy is open to such mockery. ... The whole rabble will join the peasant girl in laughing at him ... [as] in his helplessness he looks like a fool."[17] It is strange that in the long history of philosophy it occurred only to Kant— who was so singularly free of all the specifically philosophical vices—that the gift for speculative thought could be like the gift "with which Juno honored Tiresias, whom she blinded so that she might give him the gift of prophecy." He suspected that intimate acquaintance with another world could be "attained here only by forfeiting some of the sense one needs for the present world." Kant, at any rate, seems to have been unique among the philosophers in being sovereign enough to join in the laughter of the common man. Probably quite unaware of Plato's story of the Thracian girl, he tells in perfectly good humor a virtually identical tale about Tycho de Brahe and his coachman: the astronomer had proposed that they take their bearings from the stars to find the shortest way during a night journey, and the coachman had replied: "My dear sir, you may know a lot about the heavenly bodies; but here on earth you are a fool."[18]

On the assumption that the philosopher does not need the "rabble" to inform him of his "foolishness"—the common sense he shares with all men must be alert enough for him to anticipate their laughter—on the assumption, in short, that what we are dealing with is an intramural warfare between common-sense reasoning and speculative thinking going on in the mind of the philosopher himself; let us examine more closely the affinity between death and philosophy. If we take our perspective from the world of appearances, the common world in which we appeared by birth and from which we shall disappear by death, then the wish to know our common habitat and amass all kinds of knowledge about it is natural. Because of thinking's need to transcend it, we have turned away; in a metaphorical sense, we have *dis*appeared from

---

[16]*Discourses*, Book I, Chapter xv.

[17]Ibid., Book II, Chapter xviii.

[18]Ibid., Book I, Chapter xxvii.

this world, and this can be understood—from the perspective of the natural and of our common-sense reasoning—as the anticipation of our final departure, that is, our death.

That is how Plato described it in the *Phaedo*: Seen from the perspective of the multitude, the philosophers do nothing but pursue death, from which the many, if they cared at all, might conclude that philosophers had better die.[19] And Plato is not so sure that the many are not right, except that they do not know in what sense that is to be construed. The "true philosopher," one who spends his whole life in thought, has two desires: first, that he may be free from all kinds of business and especially be rid of his body, which always demands to be taken care of, "falls in our way at every step … and causes confusion and trouble and panic,"[20] and second, that he may come to live in a hereafter where those things with which thinking is concerned, such as truth, justice, and beauty, will be no less accessible and real than what now can be perceived with the bodily senses.[21] Even Aristotle, in one of his popular writings, reminds his readers of those "islands of the blessed" that are blessed because there "men would not need anything and none of the other things could be of any use to them so that only thinking and contemplating (*theōrein*) would be left, that is, what even now we call a free life."[22] In short, the turning-about inherent in thinking is by no means a harmless enterprise. In the *Phaedo,* it reverses all relationships: men, who naturally shun death as the greatest of evils, are now turning to it as the greatest good.

All of this is of course spoken with tongue in cheek—or, more academically, it is put into metaphorical language; philosophers are not famous for their suicides, not even when they hold with Aristotle (in a surprisingly personal remark in the *Protreptikos*)[23] that those who want to enjoy themselves should either philosophize or depart from life: all else seems to be foolish talk and nonsense. But the metaphor of death, or rather, the metaphorical reversal of life and death—what we usually call life is death, what we usually call death is life—is not arbitrary, although one can see it a bit less dramatically: If thinking establishes its own conditions, blinding itself against the sensorily given by removing all that is close at hand, it is in order to make room for the distant to become manifest. To put it quite simply, in the proverbial

---

[19]Ibid., Book II, Chapter i.
[20]Ibid., Book II, Chapter xvi.
[21]*The Manual*, 23 and 33.
[22]*Discourses*, Book II, Chapter xvi.
[23]Ibid., Book I, Chapter i.

absentmindedness of the philosopher, everything present is absent because something actually absent is present to his mind, and among the things absent is the philosopher's own body. Both the philosopher's hostility toward politics, "the petty affairs of men,"[24] and his hostility toward the body have little to do with individual convictions and beliefs; they are inherent in the experience itself. While you are thinking, you are unaware of your own corporality—and it is this experience that made Plato ascribe immortality to the soul once it has departed from the body and made Descartes conclude "that the soul can think without the body except that so long as the soul is attached to the body it may be bothered in its operations by the bad disposition of the body's organs."[25]

Mnemosyne, memory, is the mother of the Muses, and remembrance, the most frequent and also the most basic thinking experience, has to do with things that are absent, that have disappeared from my senses. Yet the absent that is summoned up and made present to my mind—a person, an event, a monument—cannot appear in the way it appeared to my senses, as though remembrance were a kind of witchcraft. In order to appear to my mind only, it must first be desensed, and the capacity to transform sense objects into images is called "imagination." Without this faculty, which makes present what is absent in a desensed form, no thought processes and no trains of thought would be possible at all. Hence, thinking is "out of order" not merely because it stops all the other activities so necessary for the business of living and staying alive, but because it inverts all ordinary relationships: what is near and appears directly to our senses is now far away and what is distant is actually present. While thinking I am not where I actually am; I am surrounded not by sense objects but by images that are invisible to everybody else. It is as though I had withdrawn into some never-never land, the land of invisibles, of which I would know nothing had I not this faculty of remembering and imagining. Thinking annihilates temporal as well as spatial distances. I can anticipate the future, think of it as though it were already present, and can remember the past as though it had not disappeared.

Since time and space in ordinary experience cannot even be thought of without a continuum that stretches from the nearby into the distant, from the *now* into past or future, from *here* to any point in the compass, left and right, forward and backward, and above and below, I could with some justification say that not only distances but also time and space themselves are abolished in the thinking process. As far as space is concerned, I know of no philosophical or metaphysical concept that could plausibly

---

[24]Ibid.
[25]Ibid., Book I, Chapter xvii.

be related to this experience, but I am rather certain that the *nunc stans*, the "standing now," became the symbol of eternity—the *nunc aeternitatis* (Duns Scotus)—for medieval philosophy because it was a plausible description of experiences that took place in meditation as well as in contemplation, the two modes of thought known to Christianity.

Just now, I chose to speak first of desensed sense objects, that is, of invisibles belonging to the world of appearances that have temporarily disappeared from or have not yet reached our field of perception and are drawn into our presence by remembering or anticipation. What actually occurs in these instances is told for all time in the story of Orpheus and Eurydice. Orpheus went down to Hades to recover his dead wife and was told he could have her back on condition that he would not turn to look at her as she followed him. But when they approached the world of the living, Orpheus did look back and Eurydice immediately vanished. More precisely than could any terminological language, the old myth tells what happens the moment the thinking process comes to an end in the world of ordinary living: all the invisibles vanish again. It is fitting, too, that the myth should relate to remembrance and not to anticipation. The faculty of anticipating the future in thought derives from the faculty of remembering the past, which in turn derives from the even more elementary ability to desense and have present *before* (and not just *in*) your mind what is physically absent. The ability to create fictive entities *in* your mind, such as the unicorn and the centaur, or the fictitious characters of a story, an ability usually called *productive* imagination, is actually entirely dependent upon the so-called reproductive imagination; in "productive" imagination, elements from the visible world are rearranged, and this is possible because the elements, now so freely handled, have already gone through the desensing process of thinking.

Not sense perception, in which we experience things directly and close at hand, but imagination, coming after it, prepares the objects of our thought. Before we raise such questions as What is happiness? What is justice? What is knowledge? and so on, we must have seen happy and unhappy people, witnessed just and unjust deeds, experienced the desire to know and its fulfillment or frustration. Furthermore, we must repeat the direct experience in our minds *after* leaving the scene where it took place. To say it again, every thought is an afterthought. By repeating in imagination, we *desense* whatever had been given to our senses. And only in this immaterial form can our thinking faculty now begin to concern itself with these data. This operation precedes all thought processes, cognitive thought as well as thought about meaning, and only sheer logical reasoning—where the mind in strict consistency with its own laws produces a deductive chain from a given premise—has definitely cut all strings to living experience, and it can do so only because the premise, either fact or hypothesis, is supposed to be self-evident, and therefore not subject to examination by thought. Even the simple *telling* of what has happened, whether the story then tells it as it was or fails to do so, is *preceded* by the desensing operation. The Greek language has this time element in its very vocabulary: the word "to know," as I pointed out earlier, is a derivative of the word "to see." To see is *idein,* to know is *eidenai,* that is, to *have* seen. First you see, then you know.

To vary this for our purposes: All thought arises out of experience, but no experience yields any meaning or even coherence without undergoing the operations of imagining and thinking. Seen from the perspective of thinking, life in its sheer thereness is meaningless; seen from the perspective of the immediacy of life and the world given to the senses, thinking is, as Plato indicated, a living death. The philosopher who lives in the "land of thought" (Kant) will naturally be inclined to look upon these things from the viewpoint of the thinking ego, for which a life without meaning *is* a kind of living death. The thinking ego, because it is not identical with the real self, is unaware of its own withdrawal from the common world of appearances; from its perspective, it is rather as though the invisible had come forward, as though the innumerable entities making up the world of appearances, which through their very presence distract the mind and prevent its activity, had been positively concealing an always invisible Being that reveals itself only to the mind. In other words, what for common sense is the obvious withdrawal of the mind from the world appears in the mind's own perspective as a "withdrawal of Being" or "oblivion of Being"—*Seinsentzug* and *Seinsvergessenheit* (Heidegger). And it is true, everyday life, the life of the "They," is spent in a world from which all that is "visible" to the mind is totally absent.

And not only is the quest for meaning absent from and good for nothing in the ordinary course of human affairs, its results also remain uncertain and unverifiable; even thinking is somehow self-destructive. In the privacy of his posthumously published notes, Kant wrote: "I do not approve of the rule that if the use of pure reason has proved something, the result should no longer be subject to doubt, as though it were a solid axiom"; and "I do not share the opinion … that one should not doubt once one has convinced oneself of something. In pure philosophy this is impossible. Our *mind has a natural aversion to it*" (italics added).[26] From which it follows that the business of thinking is like Penelope's web; it undoes every morning what it has finished the night before.[27] For the need to think can never be stilled by allegedly definite insights of "wise men"; it can be satisfied only through thinking, and the thoughts I had yesterday will satisfy this need today only to the extent that I want and am able to think them anew.

We have been looking at the outstanding characteristics of the thinking activity: its withdrawal from the common-sense world of appearances, its self-destructive tendency

---

[26]*Discourses*, Book I, Chapter xviii.
[27]Ibid., Book II, Chapter xi.

with regard to its own results, its reflexivity, and the awareness of sheer activity that accompanies it, plus the weird fact that I know of my mind's faculties only so long as the activity lasts, which means that thinking itself can never be solidly established as one and even the highest property of the human species—man can be defined as the "speaking animal" in the Aristotelian sense of *logon echōn,* in possession of speech, but not as the thinking animal, the *animal rationale.* None of these characteristics has escaped the attention of the philosophers. The curious thing is, however, that the more "professional" the thinkers were and the greater they loom in our tradition of philosophy, the more they were inclined to find ways and means of reinterpreting these inherent traits so as to be armed against common-sense reasoning's objections to the uselessness and unreality of the whole enterprise. The lengths to which philosophers went in these reinterpretations as well as the quality of their arguments would be inexplicable if they had been directed at the famous multitude—which has never cared anyway and remained happily ignorant of philosophical argumentation—rather than prompted primarily by their own common sense and by the self-doubt which inevitably accompanies its suspension. The same Kant who confided his true thinking experiences to the privacy of his notebooks announced publicly that he had laid the foundations of all future metaphysical systems, and Hegel, the last and most ingenious among the system builders, transformed thinking's undoing of its own results into the mighty power of the negative without which no movement and no development would ever come to pass. For him, the same inexorable chain of developmental consequences which rules organic nature from germ to fruit, in which one phase always "negates" and cancels out the earlier one, rules the undoing of the mind's thinking process, except that the latter, since it is "mediated through consciousness and will," through mental activities, can be seen as "making itself": "Mind is only that which it makes itself, and it makes itself actually into that which it is itself (potentially)." This, incidentally, leaves unanswered the question of who made the potentiality of the mind to begin with.

[…]

Chapter 20

Inherit the Whirlwind

Thomas Frank

Our next reading consists of a chapter from the bestselling book *What's the Matter with Kansas?* The author, historian and journalist Thomas Frank, describes the hazy but strongly felt "common sense" assumptions, attitudes, and resentments of "mainstream conservatives" in Middle America. He covers a lot of ground, touching on such populist phenomena as anti-intellectualism, suspicion of experts, opposition to real or imaginary elites, and the politics of "backlash"—and like Gramsci, he directs much of his attention to education and schooling. Frank notes that less than a century ago, these "anti-elitist" themes and attitudes had been the currency of left-wing populists, in the state of Kansas as much as anywhere else, just as much as they are today the obsessions of self-described conservatives. These days, however, the "big government" that the most vocal populists rail against "is, by and large, their government."

Thomas Carr Frank is an American historian and journalist born in Kansas City, Missouri. His other books include *The Wrecking Crew* (2008), *Pity the Billionaire* (2011), *Listen, Liberal* (2016), and *Rendezvous with Oblivion* (2018).

[…]

The Republicans today are the party of anti-intellectualism, of rough frontier contempt for sophisticated ideas and pantywaist book learning. *Harvard Hates America,* screamed an early backlash classic, and today's GOP hates Harvard right back. Today's Republicans are doing what the Whigs did in the 1840s: putting on backwoods accents, telling the world about their log-cabin upbringings, and raging against the overeducated elites. (Even George W. Bush, Yale '68, has complained about how Easterners regard his Texas cronies "with just the utmost disdain.") The symbols of aristocracy have to be trashed so that the real lives of the aristocracy might be made ever more comfortable.

Much has been invested in this war against intellectuals: in addition to all the familiar bestselling denunciations of life on campus, conservatives have built counterinstitutions and alternative professional associations from which they denounce the claims of traditional academia; they have set up think tanks that support writers strictly for partisan reasons; and they publish pseudoscholarly magazines that openly do away with the tradition of peer review.

All this has not come without a certain amount of pain for old-fashioned Republicans who, like so many of our Kansas Mods [Moderate Republicans], are often highly educated suburban professionals and no strangers to intellectual achievement. Expertise is something such people deplore only when it is wielded by government bureaucrats or interfering liberals. But having spent decades unleashing the ferocious language of anti-intellectualism on federal commissions that, say, want to study the effects of their businesses on the groundwater, these Republicans are now chagrined to find the same language turned on them for, say, believing in the theory of evolution. Here, too, the old-fashioned Republicans are reaping the whirlwind, trapped by the success of their own strategies.

Hence the situation in Kansas, where the most prominent conservatives, themselves an assortment of millionaires and lawyers and Harvard grads, lead a proletarian uprising against the millionaires, lawyers, and Harvard grads—and also against the doctors, architects, newspaper owners, suburban developers, and the corporate types who make up the moderate faction.

As it happens, there is considerable precedent for a pseudopopulist war against the professions in Kansas. In the twenties and thirties, the state was home to a quack of national celebrity, Dr. John Brinkley of Milford, who claimed to cure impotence by surgically transplanting bits of goat testicle to humans. Brinkley was also a pioneer in radio, obtaining a license in 1923 for a clearchannel station on which he broadcast word of his miraculous cure across the entire country. (The station was voted the most popular in America in 1929.) His hospital in Milford had long waiting lists, and Brinkley himself prospered spectacularly from his practice, sporting large diamond rings on both hands and driving a magnificent Cadillac that bore his monogram in gold in thirteen places.

Brinkley's goat operation was a fraud, though, and his medical credentials were questionable,[1] and since he was the most prominent quack in the country, the American

---

[1] Brinkley's medical degree was from an "eclectic" institution, one of the philosophies of medicine, such as osteopathy and homeopathy, that stood apart from "regular" AMA practice, or "allopathy." At that time, Kansas was one of the few remaining states where "irregular" medical degrees were officially considered to be on an equal footing with mainstream degrees. Stamping out the legitimacy of these irregular disciplines was, in addition to exposing quackery, one of the cardinal objectives of the AMA.

Medical Association (AMA) was determined to make an example of him. In this effort they were joined by the Federal Radio Commission, which revoked his broadcasting license, and the *Kansas City Star,* the owner of a rival radio station, which ran a series of articles exposing Brinkley's medical failures. Instead of destroying Brinkley, however, this awesome combination of the professions, the government, and the media only served to make him a martyr.[2]

So in the Depression years of 1930 and 1932, Brinkley ran for governor, always seeking to identify his victimization with the victimization of ordinary Kansans at the hands of the bankers and the big landowners. Brinkley fever swept the state as the doctor barnstormed with a country music band and a series of local preachers, often arriving at campaign events in his private plane. Old-timers compared the feeling in the state to the mood during the Populist days of the 1890s. The doctor was only beaten through prodigious underhanded efforts on the part of the state's traditional rulers—the responsible fathers of today's responsible Moderate Republicans.

Political Brinkleyism was just as strange as Brinkley himself. The doctor was a fervent fundamentalist and an enemy of Darwinian evolution, and yet the politics he espoused were standard-issue thirties' radicalism. *Leftist* radicalism, that is to say: pro-labor, anticorporate, and in favor of state-subsidized health care and old-age retirement schemes. (Brinkley also had a plan for increasing rainfall in Kansas.)

Brinkley was a charlatan and an opportunist, but in those days when an opportunist wanted to take up the politics of antiprofessionalism, he turned naturally to the left. This made sense in the larger context as well; the AMA, remember, was for decades the power that blocked any effort to set up a national health program. It was no friend of the working class. Today, however, the obvious political home for a man with Brinkley's beef against the professions would be the backlash right. We fight the impositions of the AMA and the Bar Association and all the rest of the bulwarks of middle-class power by railing against evolution, by decrying liberal bias in the news, and above all, by protesting abortion.

Its power as an anti-intellectual rallying point is one of the things that make the anti-abortion crusade so central to contemporary conservatism. Free-market libertarians of a purist bent often express exasperation at the larger Republican embrace of the

---

[2]For my description of Brinkley's doings, I am relying on R. Alton Lee, *The Bizarre Careers of John R. Brinkley* (Lexington: University Press of Kentucky, 2002; the quote can be found on p. 115), W.G. Clugston, *Rascals in Democracy* (New York: R. R. Smith), 1941; and Francis W. Schruben, *Kansas in Turmoil: 1930–1936* (Columbia: University of Missouri Press, 1969).

right-to-life crowd, seeing in the crusade to ban abortion a clear violation of the principles of privacy and limited government. There's nothing more private, they figure, than individual choices concerning our own bodies.

But it is important when trying to understand the pro-life movement to keep in mind that, whatever else the 1973 *Roe v. Wade* decision might have been, it was also a monument to the power of the professions. In fact, according to the sociologist Kristin Luker, almost the entire history of abortion law can be understood in the context of medical professionalization. Just as the nineteenth-century laws banning the procedure were passed at the behest of physicians just then establishing their own expertise, so the wave of reforms that unbanned the procedure in the sixties and seventies reflected the profession's changing views of itself. Abortion law remained tangled with medical professionalism right to the end: the list of groups that submitted amicus briefs to the Supreme Court in favor of abortion rights in 1973 reads like a veritable Who's Who of the nation's medical hierarchy. Furthermore, the justice who wrote the *Roe* decision, Harry Blackmun, had spent his legal career as the attorney for the Mayo Clinic, and, according to two journalists who have studied the controversy, it was the "rights of the physician" to treat his patient "according to his best professional judgment" that was foremost in Blackmun's mind in *Roe,* not the rights of the pregnant woman.[3]

Roe v. Wade also demonstrated in no uncertain manner the power of the legal profession to override everyone from the church to the state legislature. The decision superseded laws in nearly every state.[4] It unilaterally quashed the then-nascent debate over abortion, settling the issue by fiat and from the top down. And it cemented forever a stereotype of liberalism as a doctrine of a tiny clique of experts, an unholy combination of doctors and lawyers, of bureaucrats and professionals, securing their "reforms" by judicial command rather than by democratic consensus.

---

[3]Luker: See Chapters 2 and 4 of Kristin Luker, *Abortion and the Politics of Motherhood* (Berkeley: University of California Press, 1985). On the list of groups submitting amicus briefs, see Luker, 142. Luker argues that abortion reform and *Roe v. Wade* effectively removed medical expertise from the abortion debate, making the issue a political competition between different nonelite constituencies, but the pro-life movement, as well we shall see, insists on magnifying the role of the various professions in the controversy. Two journalists who have studied: Jim Risen and Judy Thomas, *Wrath of Angels* (NY: Basic Books), 2003, 34.

[4]Four states had legalized abortion altogether before *Roe v. Wade,* while thirteen others, including Kansas, had passed legislation recommended by the American Law Institute and the AMA in which a number of doctors had to agree on the procedure and then could only authorize it in order to protect the life or health of the woman, because of a fetal deformity, or in cases of rape or incest (Risen and Thomas, 11, 14). Under *Roe v. Wade* these medical limitations were largely swept away; abortion became available for almost any reason in the early stages of pregnancy. However, since the early nineties, state legislatures have passed numerous nonmedical restrictions on abortion, including parental notification for minors, counseling and waiting periods, and bans on state funding, all three of which are in effect in Kansas today.

When Antonin Scalia accused his Supreme Court colleagues in 2003 of striking down state sodomy laws more out of deference to "the law profession's anti-anti-homosexual culture" than respect for any particular provision of constitutional law, he was invoking this stereotype. As was Ann Coulter when she drew a similar line between judges and the media, arguing only semifacetiously that liberals were interpreting the constitution willy-nilly "so as to better reflect the storylines in this week's episode of *Ally McBeal*."[5] And as were conservatives generally when the rumor went around in the summer of 2003 that certain Supreme Court justices were now skipping the Constitution altogether and looking to the legal traditions of other, more sophisticated countries when striking down the laws of heartland communities like Kansas and Missouri.

Making *Roe v. Wade's* legal, medical, and governmental impositions seem even more monstrous was the field in which the liberal elite was apparently interfering: the very definition of human life. With jurisdiction over such a fundamental philosophical matter claimed by doctors and lawyers, the anti abortion movement found it easy to convince itself that further degradation lurked around the corner. Movement literature now abounds in lurid tales of the medical profession gone mad, of doctors giving the thumbs-up to infanticide and euthanasia, of abortionists trafficking in fetal body parts, and of deranged scientists manufacturing embryos from which stem cells can then be harvested. The Nazi eugenics programs, they will even tell you, were sanctioned by the German medical community, the flower of European professional rectitude. "Where the destruction will end depends only on what a small scientific elite and a generally apathetic public will advocate and tolerate," wrote Dr. Everett Koop and the theologian

---

[5] "Today's opinion is the product of a Court, which is the product of a law-profession culture that has largely signed on to the so-called homosexual agenda," Scalia wrote in his famous dissent in *Lawrence v. Texas*, "by which I mean the agenda promoted by some homosexual activists directed at eliminating the moral opprobrium that has traditionally attached to homosexual conduct. I noted in an earlier opinion the fact that the American Association of Law Schools (to which any reputable law school *must* seek to belong) excludes from membership any school that refuses to ban from its job-interview facilities a law firm (no matter how small) that does not wish to hire as a prospective partner a person who openly engages in homosexual conduct."

Coulter: This was in Coulter's column for December 3, 2003, putatively a response to the Massachusetts Supreme Court's decision legalizing gay marriage. In it she insists that liberals have essentially abandoned the rule of law, and she flat-out rejects the legal authority of the courts, writing that the Massachusetts chief justice "has as much right to proclaim a right to gay marriage from the Massachusetts Supreme Court as I do to proclaim it from my column." Coulter's columns are available at http://www.anncoulter.com/columns.html.

[*Ally McBeal* was a television show about a single professional woman.—M. M.]

Francis Schaeffer back in 1983. "Any hope of a comprehensive standard for human rights has already been lost."[6]

Each aspect of the backlash nightmare seems to follow a similar path. Overweening professionals, disdainful of the unwashed and uneducated masses, force their expert (i.e., liberal) opinions on a world that is not permitted to respond. Thus we read about church hierarchs decreeing that God has changed His mind about this sin or that and then using their episcopal authority to shut down or excommunicate congregations that don't agree. Thus we process endless complaints about scurrilous professors, answerable only to one another, rewriting history to suit their liberal preferences and pounding their thoughts into the heads of impressionable college students. And thus do we hear, over and over and over again, about the news media, staffed exclusively these days by graduates of journalism schools, ignoring critics and screening out stories that don't reflect their universally shared liberal views of the world.[7] Maybe what George Bernard Shaw once wrote is true: "All professions are conspiracies against the laity."

---

[6]Everett Koop and Francis Schaeffer, *Whatever Happened to the Human Race?* revised edn. (Westchester, IL: Crossway Books, 1983), 42. *Whatever Happened to the Human Race?* was one of the most influential anti-abortion tracts of the eighties. Its coauthor, Everett Koop, went on to become President Reagan's Surgeon General. Among other things, the book is a meditation on the rightful role of the medical profession, which the authors believe has overstepped its field of expertise.

[7]Indeed, the most convincing elements of Jack Cashill's study of TWA 800 are his attacks on the hypocrisies of journalistic professionalism. When Cashill's coauthor, independent investigator James Sanders, discovered what he believed to be evidence that a missile had struck the airplane, he was rebuffed by the mainstream media and, eventually, charged by the Justice Department with conspiracy to steal part of the wreckage. Although journalists are customarily highly protective of their First Amendment rights, on this occasion the profession did not rally around the accused. The obvious message is that those who are not part of the great news organizations are not worthy of even elementary levels of professional courtesy or respect. Another incident described in the book makes the point more chillingly. At an FBI press conference, a man described as "an unkempt figure among the reporters" asked a critical question, to which the FBI agent in charge responded by ordering flunkies to haul the man out of the room. "There was something very disquieting about the goonish tactics," writes a reporter who was there, but there is no mention of protest from the man's journalistic brethren. Jack Cashill and James Sanders, *First Strike* (Nashville: WND Books), 2003, 205, 212, 137, 140, 89.

Ironically, the rise of professionalism among journalists is also one of the cultural factors that have made possible the right's erasure of the economic. As the media scholar Robert McChesney has pointed out, professionalism's emphasis on legitimacy and expertise has caused mainstream journalism to define news almost exclusively as the doings of the state, government officials, and rival politicians; the corporate world is not considered a legitimate subject for critical inquiry or the attention of the general public. As McChesney points out, this lack of true journalistic scrutiny is what made possible such costly debacles as the Enron and WorldCom bankruptcies. Robert W. McChesney, *The Problem of the Media* (NY: Monthly Review Press, 2004), Chapter 2.

If so, it is only natural that education should become a major battleground in political wars like the one we see in Kansas. In Kansas as in many states, education is the largest discretionary item of the budget, the inevitable victim of the Cons' [conservatives'] many rounds of tax cutting. As it happens, education is also what defines and unifies the Cons' enemies.

For the Johnson County Mods, many of them members in good standing of the professional middle class, education is largely a positive thing. They may be willing to mouth the standard denunciations of interfering experts that one hears in the business world, but education is also the basis of their own status, the source of all the JDs and MDs and MBAs and PhDs that make them elite to begin with. Education is one of the things that distinguish them from lesser mortals: It gives them expertise and credibility, it determines an individual's merit, and it links them to the larger world of the national elite.

The Mods respect public education; they support it virtually without reservation. The public schools that they have built in Johnson County are first-class, routinely ranking among the best in the nation. Indeed, public-school excellence is one of Johnson County's most basic *raisons d'etre*. The schools keep up real estate values. They encourage families and companies to move to Overland Park instead of Kansas City, Missouri. They give suburban life meaning and purpose. Supplying the public schools with whatever they require is a fundamental article of moderate Republican faith.

Admission to a selective college, the ultimate goal of these fine public schools, is the object of a sort of cult in the affluent Johnson County suburbs. I suppose the same is true to some degree in any upscale American suburb, but out here the awesomeness of the Ivy League is magnified by Kansas's remoteness and by its great fear of the hick stigma. I knew a person in high school who was able to recite the address of the Harvard admissions office from memory. To this day I can recall precisely which of my classmates got into which snob colleges, how they immediately accreted the various sweatshirts, notebooks, and other paraphernalia needed to tell the world about their feat, and how they developed an irritating, instant intimacy with the lore of the beloved institution. Meanwhile, the students' parents, the Mods (back then known simply as Republicans), would contentedly add another sticker to the rear window of the Buick. They would throw parties celebrating the glorious occasion. They would fly university flags.

College admission is an achievement that lasts a lifetime in the Mod world, often overshadowing what one does later in life. So important is it that within a few minutes of meeting a Mod you will invariably have been asked where you went to school or, conversely, have discovered that he is himself a Harvard man, but that he also got degrees from Yale and Oxford.

The Cons generally don't give a damn. Their rank and file—and also certain of their leaders, including their candidate for governor in 2002—typically have no college degrees at all. For many of them, higher education is part of the problem, the institution that generates all these damnable know-it-alls in the first place. Leftists like to explain the disaffection of working-class people with public education as a natural reaction to the patriotism, conformity, and civility pushed by what they call the "ideological state apparatus." The object of education, according to this view, is to police class boundaries by transforming most kids into unquestioning drones while selecting a small number of others for management positions. Kids from blue-collar homes are supposed to know intuitively that this is the case, and they respond accordingly, cutting class and getting high and listening to *The Wall* over and over again. A more nuanced version of this critique, the 1995 book *Lies My Teacher Told Me*, points out that high school American history textbooks give "a Disney version of history": heroic, egalitarian, jam-packed with progress, and almost entirely free of class conflict. Teaching such an "Officer Friendly" account of reality, the author concludes, is merely to "make school irrelevant to the major issues of the day."[8] The kids know bullshit when they see it.

The disaffection of the Kansas conservatives with public education is almost precisely the opposite. They do not have a problem with the idea that schools should be designed to churn out low-wage workers; indeed, Kay O'Connor told me that was a worthy goal. The Cons are pissed off because they think the schools don't provide *enough* Disney, *enough* Officer Friendly.

For the fancy colleges so venerated in Mission Hills and Leawood, the Cons have only contempt. Universities, in today's conservative mythology, are not so much founts of useful knowledge as they are playgrounds of political correctness, dens of sedition where tenured radicals revile our nation and brainwashed students march and chant. The treason of the intellectuals is such a hardy backlash perennial that there are entire websites dedicated to the plen-T-plaint[9] on campus, to documenting each unpatriotic utterance by a professor or outrageous incident of offense-taking by a thin-skinned minority group. A hundred years ago, Harvard students earned the enmity of the working class by scabbing the jobs of strikers just for fun. Today, the right tells us, students at that same bastion of privilege thumb their noses at workers

---

[8] James W. Loewen, *Lies My Teacher Told Me: Everything Your American History Textbook Got Wrong* (New York: New Press, 1995), 25, 288.
[9] The petty gripe.—M. M.

by cheering for the very scum that guns down the sons of blue-collar Boston when they fight for freedom on foreign shores.

Education at the K-12 level, meanwhile, is the main place where average Kansans routinely encounter government, and for the Cons that encounter is often frustrating and offensive. School is where big government makes its most insidious moves into their private lives, teaching their kids that homosexuality is OK or showing them their way around a condom. Cons find their beliefs under attack by another tiny, insular group of arrogant professionals—the National Education Association—that stands above democratic control, and they look for relief in vouchers, homeschooling, or private religious schools.

Ask Con leaders publicly how they feel about the state's public schools, and they will insist that they love education as much as the next guy, that they are proud of Johnson County's high test scores and the state's fine basketball teams. They have nothing against public schools. God forbid! And how dare the Mods imply that they are anything less than 100 percent on this matter.

But read the screeds they circulate privately to one another, and their loathing of public education comes out in the open. When a high-profile court case ended in June 2003 with the removal of the Ten Commandments from an Ohio public school, the Kansas Conservative Listserv exploded in outrage. Public schools were "snakepits," declared a former county GOP chairman, and the authorities that caused the Commandments to be removed were "totalitarian liberal judges," "crypto-Nazis" who longed to "ghettoize" Christians. Another participant objected to the very term *public schools,* calling them "government schools" and later upgrading that to "government indoctrination centers." A third helpfully pointed out that "Christian children in public schools are deliberately subjected nearly daily to the leftist pro homosexual pro-evolution pro-abortion propaganda of the leftist socialist NEA." The consensus eventually reached was that conservatives should have no dealings with public schools at all, although one participant gamely suggested that the kids ought to go as "warriors" against the satanic regime.

An even more powerful condemnation of public education, by virtue of its lurid (but imagined) specifics, comes up in Jack Cashill's account of the nightmarish year 2006. It is only five years into the Al Gore administration, but education has already become a baroque exercise in p.c. horror. Cashill's hero attends a high school graduation ceremony at which two "diversity trainers" in bizarre indigenous-person costumes mount the stage and lecture the audience contemptuously about "the nation's original sin," that is, slavery. The diplomas they hand out are said to represent the students' "new understanding of 'our shameful history and our hereditary responsibility for it.

Each of our graduates has submitted to rigid self-criticism and is purer for it."[10] *Hey, teacher, leave those kids alone!*

Of the many barking idiocies to which Kansas proudly affixed its good name over the last decade and a half, the most memorable by far was the 1999 decision by the State Board of Education to delete references to macroevolution and the age of the earth from the state's science standards.[11] So perfectly did the move fit the larger cultural set piece of Rubes versus Reality that the national media could not resist. They descended on the state in multitudes and commenced immediately to file stories alternately deploring and scolding. The cynical mocked Kansas on the late-night talk shows. The moralistic reprimanded Kansas on the editorial pages. The contemplative found in Kansas a timeless illustration of fundamentalism's tragic inability to accept or understand our advanced secular world.

As every high schooler knows, fundamentalism had taken this route before. The nation had laughed Nebraska Democrat William Jennings Bryan into the grave for it after the Tennessee "Monkey Trial" in 1925. Embracing biblical creationism has been synonymous with backwoods cluelessness ever since. "It is not often that a single state can make a whole continent ridiculous," wrote George Bernard Shaw after the trial, "or a single man set Europe asking whether America has ever really been civilized. But Tennessee and Mr. Bryan have brought off this double event."

To ask for a rematch on this battlefield was to embrace a legacy of folly, ignorance, and humiliation. For let's say the opposing team granted the Cons' request, allowed the rematch, agreed to let their doctrine—"young-earth creationism," "Intelligent Design," whatever it was—take the field against the massed critical scrutiny of professional science. All the Cons had to look forward to in such a case was certain, humiliating defeat.[12]

That prospect did not deter the Cons. For them the importance of the evolution issue arose not so much from the possibilities it offered to change the way Americans

---

[10]Jack Cashill, *2006: The Chautauqua Rising* (Dunkirk, NY: Olin Frederick, 2000), 84.

[11]As in other places, the State Board of Education in Kansas sets broad "standards" for what is supposed to be taught and learned in its public schools. These standards are not mandatory directives, dictating precisely what goes on in the classroom, but they do determine the content of the state's assessment tests, by which it judges the progress being made by students at different grade levels. And since teachers inevitably focus on what is on the tests, the standards gradually make their influence felt.

[12]This is even the case for Intelligent Design, the doctrine widely believed by the Kansas Cons to be a valid, legitimate, academically accepted critique of evolution. Separated from the religious and political cant that always accompanies it, Intelligent Design falls apart when subjected to searching criticism. See, for example, paleontologist Kevin Padian's review of the anthology *Intelligent Design Creationism and Its Critics* in *Science* magazine, March 29, 2002.

thought as from the allegorical resonance of the gesture. And like the abortion controversy or the jihad against gangsta rap, the battle over evolution seems almost to have been designed to keep Kansas polarized, keep its outrage levels high and its Con pot boiling, while changing the way things are actually done not a bit. The combat was purely symbolic; the board only changed high school standards, the general guidelines for teaching science. At no point did the board outlaw evolution or mandate the teaching of creationism.

It was symbolic combat, however, of the most momentous kind. To read through the conservatives' materials on the subject, you'd think the assault on evolution was the greatest and noblest culture cause of them all. Evolution, one of them claims, is nothing less than a part of a sinister "war against God." Another maintains that evolution is a "pagan religion" masquerading as science that exists to legitimate materialism and teach "that there is no meaning to life, no inherent value in humans and no absolute source of moral authority."

> If it feels good ... Do it! If it is inconvenient to have a baby ... kill it ... we get rid of spare cats, why not spare kids? If it's inconvenient to have a wife, get rid of her ... neither marriage vows, nor their participants have any intrinsic value.

Getting down to hideous specifics is the creationist text that blames "naturalistic evolutionary teaching in our schools" for "teen drug use, the rampant spread of sexually transmitted diseases, despair and suicide in teens as well as youth violence."[13] That is why a concentrated attack on evolution is the thing that will put God back in charge, pull the rug out from under socialism, abortion, divorce, et cetera, and solve all the teen troubles listed above. With this one silver bullet we will fix it all.[14]

The Cons know, even as they make these claims, that this is one silver bullet they will never be allowed to fire. The real object of their anti-evolution gambit, I believe, was not getting Kansans right with God but getting themselves reelected.

---

[13]"War against God": this line is found in a pamphlet distributed at the Intelligent Design Symposium in Kansas City that is described later in this chapter. John D. Morris, "The Dayton Deception," in *Scopes: Creation on Trial* (Green Forest, AR: Master Books, 1999), 31. The teachings of the "pagan religion" are from the flyer *Is Evolution Science?* that was written by Tom Willis, president of the Creation Science Association for Mid-America (dated October 10, 1995), a Missouri group that was instrumental in writing the Kansas science standards of 1999. Ellipses in original. See also the infamous "wedge" document, discussed in the introduction, note 4 [not included in this excerpt]. "More and more commentators": Paul Ackerman and Bob Williams, *Kansas Tornado: The 1999 Science Curriculum Standards Battle* (El Cajon, CA: Institute for Creation Research, 1999), 6.

[14]Ironically, William Jennings Bryan hoped to accomplish exactly the opposite by defeating evolution. In his mind evolution led irresistibly to social Darwinism and the savagery of nineteenth-century capitalism; undermining it would make the country *less* capitalist, not *more*.

As we have seen, conservatives grandstand eloquently on cultural issues but almost never achieve real-world results. What they're after is cultural turmoil, which serves mainly to solidify their base. By deliberately courting the wrath of the educated world with the evolution issue, the Cons aimed, it seems, to reinforce and to sharpen their followers' peculiar understanding of social class. In a word, it was an exercise in anti-intellectualism.

Anti-evolution strategists are no doubt aware that if you put aside all the scientific squabbles surrounding evolution (as 99 percent of observers surely do), the issue can be easily transformed into a moral battle between the democratic impulses of the common people and the hardest core of the liberal elite—the intellectuals. Polls show that vast majorities of Americans support the teaching of "both theories" (evolution and creationism), but conservatives know that any effort to put such a scheme into practice will automatically trigger a forceful smackdown from the science establishment. And here is the key: this science establishment may be the most turf-conscious, credential-flaunting, undiplomatic bunch of pedagogues in all of academia. Provoke them, and they inevitably pull rank on you. Get them to do their high-hat, critic-squashing routine against some nice, unassuming Kansans—just as they did against old Doc Brinkley in the thirties—and you've set up a war-pitting humble, God-fearing, blue-collar folk against an arrogant intellectual elite, a populist melodrama where the victims can't lose. On the right, the class-based interpretation of the evolution controversy is a common one. David Brooks, for example, understands the popularity of those little "Darwin" fishes that people put on their cars as nothing but upper-crust boastfulness, just a way for elitist smarty-pants "to show how intellectually superior to fundamentalist Christians they are."[15] Turning specifically to the Kansas events, Jack Cashill once attacked a moderate, pro-evolution school board candidate by informing readers of the *Weekly Standard* that she was popular in Mission Hills, where she gave comfort to "the rich and the scared." The incumbent conservative, who had led the

[15]David Brooks, "One Nation, Slightly Divisible," *The Atlantic* (December 2001), 53–65. Brooks seems to base this pronouncement on his personal observation of Darwin-fish people. When they are actually asked why they put the Darwin-fish on their cars, though, they say they are doing it for precisely the opposite reason. A University of Georgia professor who has actually conducted a study of people who put Darwin-fishes on their cars finds that many of them see the fish as "a kind of defense, a way for persecuted atheists to fight back against the onslaught of religion." The newspaper story describing the Darwin-fish study does not mention anyone using the fish as a symbol of upper-class caste or as a put-down of intellectual inferiors. Carol Kaesuk Yoon, "Unexpected Evolution of a Fish Out of Water," *The New York Times*, February 11, 2003.

board in its famous stand against evolution, was said to be a hero to residents of "more modest quarters."[16]

According to *Kansas Tornado,* a right-wing narrative of the evolution controversy, the whole thing started with a humble "Prairie Village homemaker,"[17] who decided to get involved in formulating the science standards by which the progress of the state's public school students is evaluated. However, the committee charged with writing the standards, she found, was taking its cues from distant, elitist professional associations like the National Academy of Sciences. It wasn't interested in hearing the opinions of regular people, and so our unpretentious homemaker called a meeting of the alienated at the home of a prominent local creationist and set up what they called the Citizen's Writing Committee. This group produced much of the language that the state school board later adopted, to the scandalized horror of the entire world. But the housewife and her citizen's crusade are just there to lend drama to our populist parable. The real subject of conservative anti-evolution literature is the "experts" on the other side of the battlefield and, more important, their expertise. "Should we 'leave it to the experts?'" asks *Kansas Tornado.* Obviously we should not. The scientists who showed up for the Kansas board hearings, the pamphlet goes on to assert, were petulant and selfish, demanding "special treatment" during the board's hearings as though they were a notch above the average run of citizens. Their strategy for dealing with the board was not democratic; it was "to engage in name-calling" and "to invoke the authority of the scientific establishment." They showed "disrespect for the board and contempt for any who would oppose them." The scientists' version of the standards, if adopted, would have made believers into "second-class citizens" who were not to be educated so much as indoctrinated.[18]

It is fortunate for historians that the fulminating John D. Altevogt was writing his short-lived column for the *Kansas City Star* at the time the evolution decision was handed down. In Altevogt's seething prose we can make out the inverted populist mentality at the very end of its tether, perpetually offended, raging against this or that elitist slight and storming at "liberal science and liberal reporting," those partners in deception. After the school board had taken its stand against evolution and the laughter of the nation had duly commenced, Altevogt raised his voice to condemn "the arrogant authoritarianism that just drips from many of those who oppose the board's new standards."

---

[16]Cashill, "The Natural Selection Election," *Weekly Standard*, July 31, 2000.

[17]Despite its name, Prairie Village is one of the more comfortable Johnson County suburbs and, coincidentally, the town where my high school was located.

[18]Ackerman and Williams, 27, 15, 19, 15, 23.

If they can't have their way through an elected body, they'll get rid of the board and appoint one. Better yet, they'll sue the board. They don't know for what, but hey, get a liberal judge and this is not a problem either.

In Altevogt's view, class arrogance was the *real* problem, the unmoved mover behind this charade. The liberals and evolutionists simply believe that they were born to rule everyone else, and they just will not allow things to be any other way. Their claims of expertise are merely a means to this aristocratic end. Two months after the controversy hit the front pages, Altevogt had a run-in with one of the offenders, an evolution-believing science teacher from one of the prized Johnson County schools, and he proceeded to inform readers of the *Star* that although this teacher was unable to answer science questions dreamed up by Altevogt himself, he persisted in believing that "the science curriculum should be determined by his group, not by elected officials." Such arrogance! But Altevogt had news for this nabob: "Our country is governed by elected representatives, not groups of self-proclaimed 'experts.'"[19]

By sidestepping the scientific issues involved and keeping strictly to this narrative of intellectual snobs lording it over the common people, the Cons were then able to go down the list of fundamentalism's supposed offenses against democracy and turn each one back against their opponents. For example, Kansas's anti-evolution crusaders insist that it is the science community—not the fundamentalists—that is trying to impose its religious views on everyone else; that it is the science community—not the fundamentalists—that engages in "censorship of contrary evidence"; that it is the science experts who are "dogmatic" and "narrow-minded"; that it is these same experts who are irrational and emotional, unable to face reality; and that the reason no articles refuting evolution are ever published in professional, peer-reviewed journals is that those journals are biased.[20] (This last, incidentally, was a line once used to defend Dr. Brinkley from the professional inquisitors of the AMA.) What's more, these arbiters of professional rectitude wanted no backtalk. "Once you weren't supposed to question God," wrote Gregg Easterbrook of *The New Republic*, clearly caught up in the Kansas

---

[19]*Kansas City Star*, columns by John Altevogt for August 25, 1999, and October 21, 1999.

[20]Three of these allegations appear in *Kansas Tornado* (see pp. 11, 6, 7). *Dogmatic* and *narrow-minded* are terms used by Linda Holloway, the chairman of the State Board of Education when it made its historic decision. The item about the bias of peer-reviewed journals is a frequent plaint of the Intelligent Design movement, which sees itself as an academically respectable version of creationism. See Jonathan Wells, "Design Theorist Charges Academic Prejudice Is a 'Catch-23,'" *Research News & Opportunities in Science and Theology*, July–August 2002. See also the related article by Wells in the *American Spectator*, December 2000–January 2001.

spirit. "Now you're not supposed to question the head of the biology department."[21] Sometimes the Cons were even moved to declare that it was the damnable scientists, in their megalomaniac desire to impose their obscene views on the rest of the world, who started the Kansas fight in the first place.[22]

Having provoked the inevitable reaction, the Cons promptly began to scream "religious persecution," recasting themselves as the victims of a secular world's determination to stamp out the godly. Just as the small-minded hillbillies in *Inherit the Wind* persecute the high school science teacher for his views,[23] so the Cons carefully totted up each bit of criticism that was leveled at the Kansas board by the national media and imagined themselves nailed to the cross. All the ridicule, they believe, is merely the followers of "naturalism" expressing their irrational hatred for "people of faith." The Cons are thus, in their own minds, victims of bigotry as surely as any of the usual populations of the discriminated-against—the "people of color."

Altevogt, for one, saw the Inquisition coming only weeks after the decision, warning in the *Kansas City Star* of a "Christian-bashing chorus of lies and distortions" that would bring the Holocaust itself to mind. Later he claimed that the reason so many news stories didn't get the precise wording of the Kansas School Board's decision exactly right (for example, the board didn't strike Darwin from textbooks although early reports claimed it did) is that "the truth would have failed to generate the hatred for conservative Christians and public outrage sought by our liberal media

---

[21]Easterbrook apparently believes that the science community is trying to suppress doubts about itself because it is being genuinely challenged by Intelligent Design. "The New Fundamentalism," *Wall Street journal*, August 8, 2000.

[22]The reasoning goes like this: the science standards the state was considering before the Cons got into the act represented "an attempt ... to establish the worldview of philosophical naturalism as the official, state-sanctioned belief for science education in Kansas," and that the good parents of Kansas simply said no to this outrageous imposition (Ackerman and Williams, 21; see also 44). Others argue that liberals generally are responsible. John Altevogt, for example, said at a public forum discussing the school board's deed that "this has been one of the biggest nonoutrages that the left has ever tried to put together" (*Kansas City Star*, September 16, 1999).

   Although widely held among the Kansas Cons, the view that the whole evolution imbroglio was started by uppity scientists is contradicted by the fact that the Cons themselves had already declared their support for presenting "the scientific facts supporting creationism presented on an equal basis with evolution" in the 1996 Kansas Republican platform and had reaffirmed that stance in their 1998 platform. The school board's decision was not made until August 1999.

[23]Contemporary anti-evolution literature returns again and again to the 1960 movie *Inherit the Wind* (a dramatization of the Monkey Trial starring Spencer Tracy) and the need to reverse the "paradigm" that this movie supposedly established.

establishment."[24] An even weirder expression of conservative persecution mania surfaced during the 2000 election campaign, when many of the board members who had made the now-infamous decision came up for reelection. It is a flyer showing Linda Holloway, a member of the State Board of Education from the Johnson County suburb of Shawnee, seated and smiling pleasantly, and surrounded by a halo of epithets in boldface type. This is a flyer *promoting* Holloway's reelection, mind you, and it is doing so by reminding you that she has been called "Pond scum," "Pinhead," "Fanatic," and "Neanderthal."[25] All that, just for standing up to the "liberal academic establishment" and its drive to "silence any voices that challenge their atheistic orthodoxy." Ah, it's so unfair.[26]

Let us pause for a moment to assess the delusions of martyrdom that all this requires the Cons to embrace. What they mean by *persecution* is not imprisonment or excommunication or disenfranchisement, but *criticism,* news reports that disagree with them: TV anchormen shaking their heads over Kansas, editorials ridiculing creationism, Topeka columnists using the term *wing nut.* This comes from the faction given to taunting their opponents as "pro-aborts," "totalitarians," and "Nazis." The disproportion between dish-it-out and take-it is positively staggering.

The flip side of the Cons' persecution mania is a gleeful sense of subversiveness. Even while they cry about rude words from Kansas University science professors and moan over a world that is coming apart, Con leaders like Jack Cashill are capable of backing the evolution decision because it causes headaches for what he calls "the country club cognoscenti."[27] Cons also provide a lively market for T-shirts proclaiming

---

[24]*Kansas City Star*, Altevogt columns for August 25, 1999, and September 8, 1999.

[25]The Moderates, for their part, fell back on precisely the opposite theme. For them the denunciation of the outside world had summoned the dread specter of embarrassment—what Jack Cashill calls "the big E"—and they exhorted voters to oust the Cons from whatever positions they held on the grounds of status anxiety alone. *Don't let them think Kansas is a hick state!* So great was the perceived crisis in status that this theme spilled over from school board elections into all manner of other contests. A moderate Republican running for Congress from Johnson County even aired radio commercials that quoted from the East Coast editorials mocking Kansas and erected a billboard reading, simply, "Embarrassed?"

[26]Holloway lost. The flyer I describe was accompanied by a letter noting that "there has been an overwhelming display of bigotry and intolerance by those who claim to be 'Moderate.' Why is the Sacred Cow of Evolution guarded so closely by the Liberal Educational and political establishments? Truth to tell is that Evolution has more to do with the Political correctness of Revolution, Socialism, and World government than it does Science!" Sic sic sic sic sic. Both flyer and letter from the archives of the Mainstream Coalition.

[27]Ironically, Cashill made this point to an audience of executives in *Ingram's*, the Kansas City business magazine, July 2000.

that students who pray are "a Real Menace to Society," and even for T-shirts screaming "Subvert the Dominant Paradigm" under a picture of Charles Darwin.

I saw the latter for sale at the second annual Darwin, Design, and Democracy Symposium, a get-together at Rockhurst College in Kansas City. Modeled after an academic conference, the keynote speeches and panel discussions all aimed to publicize the much-ballyhooed theory of Intelligent Design. The inevitable Jack Cashill kicked things off with a denunciation of Hollywood for accepting a God-free vision of the universe. He kept things lively by showing clips from sinful films supposedly influenced by the doctrines of Darwin, such as *Hud* and *High Plains Drifter*. Cashill was followed, however, by an Intelligent Design theorist who lectured monotonously on the faked evidence supposedly used by evolutionists, and heads began to nod. To everyone's relief, the speaker finally yielded the stage to the Mutations, "three fine Christian ladies" in pink dresses who strutted and whirled like an early-sixties girl group and proceed to sing "Overwhelming Evidence," a ditty set to the pulsing beat of "Ain't No Mountain High Enough." Comically assuming the voice of the arrogant science establishment, the women pretend-derided the audience, singing that "the truth is what we say" and that, as professional scientists, "we don't have to listen to you!" The audience had plainly been bored by the preceding recitation of science's errors, but this lighthearted bit of persecuto-tainment hit exactly the right note, and sent everyone home with a smile on his or her face.[28]

---

[28]The full lyrics of "Overwhelming Evidence," as well as the description of the Mutations as "three fine Christian ladies," can be found on the website of Phillip Johnson, one of the leaders of the Intelligent Design movement: http://www.am.org/docs/pjweel<ly/pj_weel<ly_O10702.htm.

Chapter 21

Common-Sense Neoliberalism

Stuart Hall and Alan O'Shea

Stuart Hall and Alan O'Shea examine the movement that was personified in its early years by British Prime Minister Margaret Thatcher,[1] a movement that they describe as a project to "reshape common sense." Appropriately, the original subtitle of their article was "The Battle over Common Sense Is a Central Part of Our Political Life." "Common sense," the authors write, "is key to how we negotiate politics collectively." Since the article is an intervention in recent political debates in the UK, some of the references might not be familiar to readers; however, the editor's annotations should provide some context.

The term *neoliberalism* might be unfamiliar or vague to some readers. Commentators have suggested that, despite the fact that neoliberalism is pervasive—or perhaps *because* of that fact—it has not been widely understood, as an economic policy model and as what Gramsci has called an *ideology*.[2] Proponents of neoliberalism advocate shifting control of economic factors from the state and the public sector to the private sector: the state, they say, must cut taxes, tariffs, and subsidies; reduce the influence of unions; privatize public resources and services; deregulate banks, financial markets, and industries; abolish fixed-rate exchanges; and reduce deficit spending.[3]

---

[1] Thatcher (1925–2013) was the Conservative Party Prime Minister of the UK from 1979 to 1990.

[2] The British environmentalist and author George Monbiot wrote: "So pervasive has neoliberalism become that we seldom even recognise it as an ideology." ("Neoliberalism: The Ideology at the Root of All Our Problems," *The Guardian*, April 15, 2016, accessed May 3, 2019, https://www.theguardian.com/books/2016/apr/15/neoliberalism-ideology-problem-george-monbiot.) Since the onset of the Great Recession (2007 to the early 2010s), however, the words *neoliberalism* and *neoliberal* have gained greater currency.

[3] Neoliberals profess to embrace "limited government"; however, state institutions and public funding have played a large and indispensable role in the pursuit of their goals. State agencies advance neoliberal goals through monetary and fiscal policy, the privatization of public services and resources, and the police, courts, electronic surveillance, and prison systems. The state also provides direct and

Paradoxically, proponents of neoliberal policies, whether of the Conservative Party in the UK or of the Labor Party, often frame their case for neoliberal policies in terms of "fairness." As Hall and O'Shea observe, large sections of a public that stands to lose benefits as a result of neoliberal policies embrace neoliberal claims of fairness. The upshot of Hall and O'Shea's review is that laypeople who hold strong opinions on matters of public policy are considerably less decided about issues than published opinion polls suggest.

The late Stuart Hall (1932–2014), one of the founding luminaries of the field of Cultural Studies, was an influential Jamaican-born cultural theorist, political activist, and sociologist who lived and worked in the UK from 1951. Alan O'Shea is Emeritus Professor of Cultural Studies at the University of East London.

And let this be our message—common sense for the common good.

—David Cameron, April 24, 2011[4]

When politicians try to win consent or mobilize support for their policies, they frequently assert that these are endorsed by "hard-working families up and down the country." Their policies cannot be impractical, unreasonable, or extreme, they imply, because they are solidly in the groove of popular thinking—"what everybody knows," takes for granted, and agrees with—the folk wisdom of the age. This claim by the politicians, if correct, confers on their policies popular legitimacy.

In fact, what they are really doing is not just invoking popular opinion but shaping and influencing it so they can harness it in their favor. By asserting that popular opinion already agrees, they hope to produce agreement as an effect. This is the circular strategy of the self-fulfilling prophecy.

But what exactly is common sense? It is a form of "everyday thinking" which offers us frameworks of meaning with which to make sense of the world. It is a form of popular, easily available knowledge which contains no complicated ideas, requires no sophisticated argument and does not depend on deep thought or wide reading. It works intuitively, without forethought or reflection. It is pragmatic and empirical,

---

indirect public subsidies for private enterprise, including public funding of infrastructure; publicly funded research and development; hundred-billion-dollar bailouts of banks and corporations, and state expenditures to offset "externalities," notably environmental degradation and anthropogenic global warming.

[4]Cameron (b. 1966) was the leader of the Conservative Party of Great Britain and Prime Minister from 2010 to 2016.—M. M.

giving the illusion of arising directly from experience, reflecting only the realities of daily life and answering the needs of "the common people" for practical guidance and advice.

It is not the property of the rich, the well-educated or the powerful, but is shared to some extent by everybody, regardless of class, status, creed, income, or wealth. Typically, it expresses itself in the vernacular, the familiar language of the street, the home, the pub, the workplace, and the terraces. The popularity and influence of the tabloid press—one of its main repositories—depend on how well it imitates, or better, *ventriloquizes* the language and gnomic speech patterns of "ordinary folk." In the now-famous example, it must say not "British Navy Sinks Argentinean Cruiser" but, simply, "Gotcha."

According to Antonio Gramsci, the Italian political philosopher who has written perceptively on this subject, common sense "is not critical and coherent but disjointed and episodic."[5] However, it does have a "logic" and a history. It is always, Gramsci argues, "a response to certain problems posed by reality which are quite specific and 'original' in their relevance." It draws on past ideas and traditions, but it also keeps evolving to give meaning to new developments, solve new problems, and unravel new dilemmas. "Common sense," as Gramsci argued, "is not something rigid and immobile, but is continually transforming itself."

It also has a content. It is a compendium of well-tried knowledge, customary beliefs, wise sayings, popular nostrums, and prejudices, some of which—like "a little of what you fancy does you good"—seem eminently sensible, others wildly inaccurate. Its virtue is that it is obvious. Its watchword is *Of course!* It seems to be outside time. Indeed it may be persuasive precisely because we think of it as a product of Nature rather than of history. Common sense tends to be socially conservative, leaning toward tradition (even if, as Eric Hobsbawm argued,[6] much tradition was only "invented" yesterday!). Its pace of change seems glacial. In fact, it is constantly being reconstructed and refashioned by external pressures and influences.

Common sense feels coherent. But Gramsci argues that, like the personality, it is "strangely composite": "It contains Stone Age elements and principles of a more advanced science, prejudices from all past phases of history ... and intuitions of a future philosophy." For these and other reasons, it is fundamentally contradictory. It tells not one narrative, but several conflicting "stories" stitched together—while failing to resolve the differences between them. Bits and pieces of ideas from many

---

[5] All quotations from Gramsci are from *Selections from the Prison Notebooks* (see the item in the Readings That Appear in This Book section below).
[6] Hobsbawm (1917–2012) was one of the foremost British historians of the twentieth century.—M. M.

sources—what Gramsci calls "stratified deposits"—have slowly settled or sedimented, in truncated and simplified forms, into "popular philosophy," without leaving behind an inventory of their sources. Many common-sense moral judgments—for example about sexuality—have a Judeo-Christian lineage, though we do not know where in the Bible they are to be found.

Many people intuitively favor an "eye for an eye, a tooth for a tooth" conception of justice—while at the same time believing that Muslim Sharia Law is a barbarous form of law. Some who depend on benefits to survive believe all the other claimants are "scroungers." Some who hold that unbridled competition driven by self-interest is the only way to succeed also believe "we should love our neighbours as ourselves." Margaret Thatcher, the mistress of common-sense language, and of squaring circles, supported both the "free market" (i.e., one without much state regulation) and a "strong state."

However, as well as being conservative in outlook, common sense also contains critical or utopian elements, which Gramsci calls "the healthy nucleus ... which deserves to be made more unitary and coherent." He is referring to the apparently obvious taken-for-granted understandings that express a sense of unfairness and injustice about "how the world works": landlords tend to exploit tenants, and banks responsible for the "credit crunch" expect to be bailed out by taxpayers rather than take the crunch themselves. CEOs receive immense bonuses even when their companies perform badly; profitable businesses will avoid paying tax if they can; and companies profiting from a fall in commodity prices will not pass the gains on to consumers.

Gramsci called these apparently "natural" insights into the wicked ways of the world *good sense*. Common sense and good sense coexist. Our ability to live with this incoherent structure may be due to the fact that the "stratified deposits" of common sense represent the outlook and interests of very different social groups: "Every philosophical current leaves behind a sedimentation of 'common sense': this is the document of its historical effectiveness." It is this that allows us to hold contradictory opinions simultaneously, and to take up contradictory subject positions.

As citizens, we expect public services in return for paying taxes. But as taxpayers we are invited to think that we should pay as few taxes as possible, whatever the social consequences. Margaret Thatcher exploited such contradictions, arguing that, as workers, we have sectional interests, "but we are all consumers and as consumers we want a choice. We want the best value for money." Hence: "the same trade unionists, as consumers, want an open market." The difficulty is that most of us are simultaneously citizens, taxpayers, and workers. So discourses which try to win us over must privilege one way of positioning ourselves over others. Common sense thus becomes a contested arena. As Doreen Massey argued in "Vocabularies of the Economy," we know that doctor/patient, teacher/student, citizen/state, client/provider, shopper/supermarket relationships all have specific, and very different, social contents.[7] However, if we can be persuaded to see ourselves simply as "customers," then all the other relationships are reduced to one common denominator: the fact that we are consuming a product (sic) in a market (sic) which only has value because we pay for it (sic). Everything becomes a commodity, and this aspect of our activities overrides everything. In this way, a whole new way of seeing society (as a market) is coming into play. If developed, it could provide the cornerstone for a new kind of (neoliberal) common sense.

Slowly but surely, neoliberal ideas have permeated society and are transforming what passes as common sense. The broadly egalitarian and collectivist attitudes that underpinned the welfare state era are giving way to a more competitive, individualistic market-driven, entrepreneurial, and profit-oriented outlook. There is no proof as to how far this process has gone: the evidence is hard to read, and the trend is certainly not one-way. However, after forty years of a concerted neoliberal ideological assault, this new version of common sense is fast becoming the dominant one.

One common-sense assertion that has become widely acceptable is: "You can't solve a problem just by throwing money at it"—often aimed at Labour's "tax and spend" policies. True, perhaps. But there are very few problems which would not be considerably alleviated by being better funded rather than having their budgets savagely cut. The right's use of this slogan is of course highly selective: they have no qualms about money being "thrown" at the banks or at the economy via quantitative easing.

Taxpayers, it is said, want "value for money" and "greater efficiency." Citizens certainly have a right to see their money well spent. But are the fire service, the police, ambulance crews, youth and community workers, mental health staff, or childminders necessarily more efficient because there are fewer of them? Can their benefit to society be measured exclusively in terms of their exchange value? If policing is more efficient when information-led, how come the "backroom" staff who provide the information are seen as dispensable, on the grounds that they are "not front-line staff"? More and more, these common-sense "truths" serve as a cover-up for savaging the public sector in line with the dominant neoliberal, anti-state ideology.

These days, we are told, we all want greater freedom and personal choice. Indeed, not only are we given "freedom to choose," we are required to choose: which hospital to

---

[7] Doreen Massey, "Vocabularies of the Economy," *Soundings* 54 (Summer, 2013), 9–21. www.lwbooks. co.uk/journals/soundings/manifesto.html.

be ill in, which lifestyle to adopt, which identity to fashion, which celebrity role model to imitate. Certainly, there is no reason why only the well off should exercise choice. However, there is also strong evidence that the responsibility which comes with so much choice can create unfulfillable expectations, anxiety and a sense of the precariousness of life.[8] This sense of insecurity is then further exacerbated by the increasing introduction in the workplace of personal targets, appraisals, and performance-related pay, to keep staff up to the mark. Michael Gove now plans to introduce the latter into the teaching profession. But "it's all down to us"—apart from being untrue—is a hard "truth" to live with. What if we make the wrong choice?

The structural consequences of neoliberalism—the individualization of everyone, the privatization of public troubles and the requirement to make competitive choices at every turn—has been paralleled by an upsurge in feelings of insecurity, anxiety, stress and depression. These are now responsible for one in every three days sick leave from work.[9] We need to acknowledge these affective dimensions that are in play, and which underpin common sense.

How then does common sense make sense of these changes in lived experience? Have most people accepted that it is inevitable and natural to understand most of our life as consumers and market competitors?

There are in fact many signs of resistance to be found. These include older forms of political protest, such as the trade unions, and newer, emerging, forms such as Occupy, UK Uncut, or 38 Degrees. However, these do not in any way constitute a single social force, as happened to some extent with the Greater London Council in the 1980s,[10] when, although the traditional left and the new social movements did not always agree—and certainly were not unified—they did occupy the same space, and struggle over the same budget, and together offered a broader and more effective political force than we have seen since then.

There is also much individualized disaffection. To fall ill with anxiety is itself a symptom that some people are finding it difficult to live with neoliberal culture. Another is a marked retreat, in popular culture, to an isolated self-sufficiency. There is unfocused anger, a grudging, grumbling resentment at one's lot, and a troubled uncertainty about what to do next. There is a sense of being abandoned by the political class and widespread cynicism, disaffiliation, and de-politicization. Many groups, of course, do have cultural resources to resist these trends; these include historic

[8]Renata Salecl, *The Tyranny of Choice* (London: Profile Books), 2010.
[9]The Young Foundation, *Sinking and Swimming*, online report, 2011.
[10]The Greater London Council was a municipal administrative body for the larger London area. Founded in 1965, Margaret Thatcher's Conservatives abolished it in 1986.—M. M.

working-class solidarities, defensive organizations, strong local loyalties, and a culture of mutual support. Others have insight into new processes, such as digital technologies and communication, which are changing the shape of society. But these have not resulted in any coming together in a vigorous, effective response.

Fairness

The resistance which lies in the "good sense" components of common sense is more elusive, but still possible to illustrate. To attempt this, and to demonstrate why this understanding of common sense is valuable for fighting the spread of neoliberal discourse, we will now focus on one pivotal element—the idea of *fairness* and its role in popular discourse during the winter of 2012/2013. We have selected "fairness" as our instance because no one is against it. It is a term that groups along the whole political spectrum struggle to inflect to their own projects.

[…]

What counts as fair has been pivotal to our political history. The welfare state was set up in the 1940s as a collective contract between all members of the society to guarantee a fairer distribution of wealth, and a chance for everyone to flourish and make a useful contribution. These aspirations were supported by a broad consensus across the population.

The neoliberal right has been working hard to undermine and trans-code this inclusive meaning of "fairness" since the 1970s. Margaret Thatcher made it her project to break up the consensus and substitute a market approach. But she also validated this by a common sense appeal to "what we all already think":

> A great number of people in Britain are becoming increasingly alarmed about a society which depends on the state's help—on entitlement. What has happened is that so many of the people who have done everything right and saved for their old age and put a bit by, seem to have had a raw deal. Some of those who have done only too little and have not done it very well have been on the beneficial end of what has been going … You can't have welfare before someone else has created national wealth.
>
> —Speech to party workers, Berwick, August 30, 1978

Decades later, David Cameron echoed the same sentiment:

> For too long we've lived in an upside down world where people who do the right thing, the responsible thing, are taxed and punished, whereas those who do the wrong thing are rewarded … And for that person intent on ripping off the system,

we are saying—we will not let you live off the hard work of others. Tough sanctions. Tougher limits. In short we're building a system that matches effort with reward … instead of a system that rewards those who make no effort.

—Speech, May 23, 2011[11]

Here "fairness" is a quasi-market relation, a reward for personal effort—a long way from the collectivism of the 1940s.

Recent attitude surveys (from the Joseph Rowntree and Resolution Foundations) suggest that the decades of playing off "hard-working families" against those who for one reason or another are unable to find work have achieved the intended result. The surveys found a decline in sympathy for the poor and those on benefits. The concept of fairness was generally disconnected from any notion of rights ("No-one is owed a living"), and seen simply in terms of fair rewards for effort.

The 2012–2013 fairness debate focused on George Osborne's decision to cap benefit payments below the rate of inflation, and Iain Duncan Smith's welfare reforms, which were accompanied by the launch of a large-scale "moral panic" demonizing claimants, which was amplified enthusiastically by the press, and not strongly resisted by broadcasters (including the BBC).[12]

In his now notorious contribution, Osborne asked:

Where is the fairness, we ask, for the shift-worker, leaving home in the dark hours of the early morning, who looks up at the closed blinds of their next door neighbour sleeping off a life on benefits? When we say we're all in this together, we speak for that worker. We speak for all those who want to work hard and get on.

—Conservative Party Conference, October 8, 2012

This vivid image has been amplified by personal stories, and profiles of specific out-of-work families on benefits greater than the average wage (with no reference to the fact that a very large chunk of this is housing benefit paid directly to profiteering landlords). A YouGov poll found that people on average thought that 41 percent of the welfare budget went on benefits to the unemployed, while the true figure is 3 percent; and that 27 percent of the welfare budget was claimed fraudulently, while the

[11]Available at www.conservatives.com/News/Speeches/2011/05/David_Cameron_Building_a_bigger_stronger_society.aspx.

[12]Osborne (b. 1971) was a British Conservative Party politician, former Chancellor of the Exchequer, and Member of Parliament. George I. D. Smith was a Conservative Party politician and Secretary of State for Work and Pensions from 2010 to 2016. Both of these men strongly supported neoliberal policies.—M. M.

government's own figure is 0.7 percent.[13] This suggests that the folk-devil figure of the scrounger/skiver/shirker/fraudster living a life of idle luxury has resonated with many people's concerns, resentments and insecurities.

This is the ideological climate in which both polling and online responses have to be understood. The debate has been conducted within a neoliberal framing of the agenda across most of the political spectrum and media output. This frame takes for granted that the market relation is central (you can only have what you pay for), the deficit is the problem, and cutting public expenditure is the only solution, and, within this, cutting welfare benefits is the priority—and it's all a result of "Labour's mess." (The Labour Party itself hasn't strongly challenged this!) In the context of this closing down of the debate, along with the onslaught of propaganda and misinformation, it is not surprising that polls show that support for capping benefits below the rate of inflation can be rallied.

But we have to beware taking poll findings as the unquestionable truth, or as reflecting deeply held political positions. The YouGov poll also showed that when respondents were given the correct figures, their views changed and they became more sympathetic toward benefit claimants. This demonstrates that the earlier responses were a result of an effective misinformation campaign by the government and the press, and not of some "uncontaminated" opinion of those polled. As David Stuckler has recently pointed out:

> People's support for welfare depends greatly on how the question is framed. When the question links taxes to specific programmes and recipients, the young tend to express stronger support. For example, only 20 per cent of British youth agree with the very broad idea of giving more money to the poor, but when asked about support for specific vulnerable groups, such as the disabled or working parents, more than 90 per cent would like to increase or maintain existing levels of support.[14]

Opinion polls are taken—especially by the media—as objective fixities, as an indisputable tide against which politicians turn at their peril—rather than as yes/no answers to questions framed from within the dominant agenda of the moment. They are a tool in the struggle over common sense, rather than an objective reflection of it.

People are less decided about issues than polls suggest. To get a better sense of the way discourse works, and of how people are engaging with neoliberal frames and agendas and reworking their common sense in response, we need to do more than work with simple answers to questions commissioned by vested interests. We have

---

[13]www.tuc.org.uk/social/tuc-21796-f0.cfm.

[14]David Stuckler and Aaron Reeves, "We Are Told Generation Y Is Hard-Hearted but It's a Lie," *Guardian*, July 30, 2013.

to capture discourse which is volunteered, which arises from the writer's own set of concerns, and is as spontaneous and unfettered by what others may think as possible. Online comments are rather like this, especially as everyone contributes under a pseudonym.

[…]

The left and the Labour Party must take the struggle over common sense seriously. Politics, as Gramsci insisted, is always "educative." We must acknowledge the insecurities which underlie common sense's confusions and contradictions, and harness the intensity and anger which comes through in many of the readers' comments. Labour must use every policy issue as an opportunity, not only to examine the pragmatics, but also to highlight the underlying principle, slowly building an alternative consensus or "popular philosophy." It must harness to this the already strongly existing sense of unfairness and injustice. In other words, it must engage in a two-way learning process, leading to what Gramsci called "an organic cohesion in which feeling-passion becomes understanding." This may be complicated in the context of a popular cynicism toward the political class in general, but there is no alterative. […]

FOR DISCUSSION OR ESSAYS

- What is the relationship between what Gramsci calls *philosophy*, properly speaking, and a "conception of the world"?

- Does Gramsci provide insights into the "unsurprising" phenomenon that Scott O. Lilienfeld described in our reading from Part II? In considering this question, you might focus on (i) Gramsci's conception of *hegemony*, or (ii) his observations about the fragmented, incoherent character of common sense, or (iii) his distinction between *good sense* and the "folkloric" part of common sense.

- In our reading above, Arendt writes that "thinking itself is helpless against the arguments of common-sense reasoning." What did she mean by "thinking," and how does it contrast to common-sense reasoning?

- A related prompt: Arendt describes the "intramural warfare" between common sense and "man's faculty of thought and need of reason." Compare and contrast this view to Reid's view of common sense.

- Echoing passages we have encountered in our readings, American philosopher Marcus G. Singer wrote that "It seems likely, indeed, that Common Sense holds nothing precisely."[15] How might Arendt respond to Singer's claim?

- Like Gramsci, Arendt, too, viewed common sense as unavoidably political. What Gramsci meant by "politics," however, was very different from what Arendt meant. In the book *Gramsci's Common Sense*, anthropologist Kate Crehan compares Gramsci to Arendt, when it comes to what they had to say about common sense:

  > Unlike Hannah Arendt and that strain of philosophical thinking that sees common sense as a reliable touchstone to which intellectual speculation must always return, Gramsci insists on its unreliability. [...] The importance of common sense is not that it represents some "common inherited wisdom" [...] but rather that it provides subalterns with the maps they use to navigate the worlds they inhabit.[16]

---

[15]Singer (refer to the entry in the Further Readings section for Part IV, above), 221.

[16]Crehan (refer to the entry in the Further Readings for Part VI section, 333), 186.

With this in mind, compare, contrast, and evaluate the conflicting views of Gramsci and Arendt when it comes to common sense and politics.

- How might Gramsci describe "what's the matter with Kansas"?

- Stuart Hall and Alan O'Shea describe common sense as "a form of 'everyday thinking' which offers us frameworks of meaning with which to make sense of the world." And yet they also acknowledge, with Gramsci, that it is "fundamentally contradictory." How are we to square these two seemingly inconsistent views?

FURTHER READINGS FOR PART VI

Burke, Barry. "Antonio Gramsci, Schooling and Education." In *The Encyclopedia of Informal Education*, 1999, 2005. http://www.infed.org/thinkers/et-gram. htm, accessed March 18, 2019. This short, readable article begins with a sketch of Gramsci's life, followed by a clearly written introduction to his ideas of *ideological hegemony*, "civil society," and *organic intellectuals*. Burke also explores Gramsci's observations on elementary and secondary education.

Crehan, Kate. *Gramsci's Common Sense: Inequality and Its Narratives*. Durham and London: Duke University Press, 2016. The first four chapters provide a nice introduction to Gramsci on common sense, and Chapter 6 complements Thomas Frank's discussion in *What's the Matter with Kansas?*

Linker, Damon. "Against Common Sense." In *The New Republic*, November 30, 2009. http://www.newrepublic.com/blog/damon-linker/against-common-sense, accessed September 12, 2014. This is "advocacy journalism" in the manner of Thomas Frank, with commentary, from a liberal perspective, bewailing the largely successful attempt by "right-wing rabble-rousers" in the first decade of twenty-first-century America to capture common sense for their exclusive use.

Locke, John. *Two Treatises of Government*. Cambridge: Cambridge University Press, 1988. First published in 1690. According to Locke, all humans are created equal and free, but subject to "the law of nature," which "teaches all mankind who will but consult it that, being all equal and independent, no one ought to harm another in his life, health, liberty, or possessions." In Chapter II of the *Second Treatise of Civil Government*, titled "Of the State of Nature," he examines the "natural rights" that correspond to these nature-imposed obligations.

Paine, Thomas. *Common Sense*. Bedford, MA: Applewood Books, 2002. The celebrated pamphlet first appeared in early 1776. A few months later that year, James Chalmers penned and published a point-by-point rebuttal of Paine, in his similarly titled pamphlet, *Plain Sense*.

Rawls, John. *A Theory of Justice*. Cambridge, MA: Harvard University Press, 1971. A watershed work of political philosophy, *A Theory of Justice* shifted the attention of political philosophers in the United States to an almost exclusive emphasis on normative questions, rather than explanatory descriptions. Combining social contract theory with a Kantian approach to the problem of a just distribution of goods in society, Rawls appeals to what he believes is the intuitively reasonable principle that a just system of distribution would guarantee the greatest freedom to each member of society, as long as that freedom does not infringe upon the freedom of others.

Rush, Benjamin. "Thoughts on Common Sense." In *Essays Literary, Moral, and Philosophical*, edited by Michael Meranze, 146–150 (Schenectady New York: Union College Press, 1988). First published in 1791. These several pages might serve as a brief critical companion to our Reid reading from Part I, and perhaps to Paine's *Common Sense*, too. Rush, the physician and Founding Father, defines common sense not as a faculty of the mind, but simply as *"Opinions and feelings in unison with the opinions and feelings of the bulk of mankind."* He then delivers verdicts on several topics of the day, including the relation of common sense to republican governance. At one point he quips that, after all that has been said in favor of common sense, "I cannot help thinking that it is the characteristic only of common minds."

Readings That Appear in This Book

Reid, Thomas. "Of Judgment." In *The Works of Thomas Reid*, 650–653. Charlestown, MA: *Samuel Etheridge Jr.*, 1813–1825. Our selection consists of Chapter Two from Reid's essay "Of Judgment," included in his *Essays on the Intellectual Powers of Man* (first published in 1785).

Moore, G. E. "A Defence of Common Sense." In *Contemporary British Philosophy*. 2nd edn. Series editor J. H. Muirhead, 193–223. London: Allen & Unwin, 1925. Reprinted in G. E. Moore, *Philosophical Papers*. London: George Allen & Unwin Publishers, 1959, 32–45. Our extract consists of Moore's introductory paragraph, as well as Sections I–III of the five sections of the original paper.

Ludwig Wittgenstein. *On Certainty*. New York: Harper Torchbooks, 1969, 1972. Our selection consist of forty-four of the total 676 notes. Republished with permission of Blackwell Publishing; permission conveyed through Copyright Clearance Center, Inc.

Kingwell, Mark. "The Plain Truth about Common Sense: Skepticism, Metaphysics, and Irony." In *Journal of Speculative Philosophy* IX, no. 3 (1995), 169–188. Our selection includes all of Sections 1, 2 and 3, as well as the first paragraph of Section 4 (181) and the last paragraph (184–185). It omits most of the final section of the original paper, which includes a difficult discussion of common sense and irony. Republished with permission of *The Journal of Speculative Philosophy*; permission conveyed through RightsLink.

Quine, W. V. O. "The Scope and Language of Science." In *The Ways of Paradox and Other Essays*, 215–232. New York: Random House, 1966. The paper was first published in 1954. The selection consists of only the first three sections, I–III, of the chapter.

Popper, Karl R. "Two Faces of Common Sense: An Argument for Common-Sense Realism and against the Common-Sense Theory of Knowledge." In *Objective Knowledge: An Evolutionary Approach*, 32–105. Oxford: Oxford University Press, 1973. The excerpt comprises Sections 2–5 (pp. 33–44), and Sections 12–16 (pp. 60–70). Reprinted with permission of Oxford University Press. All rights reserved.

Lilienfeld, Scott O. "Why Scientists Shouldn't Be Surprised by the Popularity of Intelligent Design." In *Skeptical Inquirer* 30, no. 3 (May–June 2006), 46–49. Used by permission of *The Skeptical Inquirer* (www.csicop.org).

Clarke, Samuel. "A Cosmological Argument for the Existence of God." In *A Demonstration of the Being and Attributes of God*, 9–15. London: W. Eatham, for James Knapton, 1719. First published in 1705, the essay has appeared in various editions since then.

William Paley. "An Analogical Argument from Design." In *Natural Theology: Or, Evidences of the Existence and Attributes of the Deity*. American 1st edn. Published in 1802. https://archive.org/details/naturaltheologyo1802pale, accessed September 1, 2018. Our selection is from Chapters I and II, pp. 1–13.

Baron d'Holbach. *Good Sense without God: Or Free Thoughts Opposed to Supernatural Ideas*. 1st French edn. 1772. Translator unknown. London: W. Stewart & Co. Our selection consists of twenty-seven of the original 206 sections of the work.

Plantinga, Alvin. "The Reformed Objection to Natural Theology." In *Christian Scholar's Review* 11, no. 3 (1982), 187–198. Republished with permission of *Christian Scholar's Review*; permission conveyed through Copyright Clearance Center, Inc.

Darwin, Charles. *The Descent of Man and Selection in Relation to Sex*. Revised edn., 112–142. New York: Lovell, Coryell & Company, 1871. Our selection is from Chapter IV, "Comparison of the Mental Powers of Man and the Lower Animals—Continued."

Rosen, Stanley. "Common Sense." In *The Journal of General Education* 18, no. 2 (July1966), 112–136. Republished with permission of *The Journal of General Education*; permission conveyed through RightsLink.

Adler, Mortimer J. "The Common-Sense View Philosophically Developed: A Teleological Ethics." In *The Time of Our Lives: The Ethics of Common Sense*, 157–169. New York: Holt, Rinehart and Winston, 1970. Section 1 has been omitted. Republished with permission of Fordham University Press; permission conveyed through Copyright Clearance Center, Inc.

Mankiw, N. Gregory. "Ten Principles of Economics." In *Principles of Macroeconomics*, 3rd edn., 4–14. Mason, OH: Thomson, 2004. Republished with permission of South-Western College Publishing; permission conveyed through Copyright Clearance Center, Inc.

Becker, Gary and Posner, Richard A. "'Income Inequality' and 'Corporate Social Responsibility.'" In *Uncommon Sense: Economic Insights, from Marriage to Terrorism*, 185–196. Chicago: University of Chicago Press, 2009. Reprinted with permission of University of Chicago Press. All rights reserved.

Swanson, Jacinda. "Economic Common Sense and the Depoliticization of the Economic." In *Political Research Quarterly* 61, no. 1 (March 2008), 56–67. Our selection consists of most of the introductory material, plus the first section, most of the second section, and the fourth and final section of Swanson's original paper. Reprinted by permission of SAGE Publications, Inc.

Gramsci, Antonio. "The Study of Philosophy." In *Selections from the Prison Notebooks*, edited and translated by Quintin Hoare and Geoffrey Nowell Smith, 323–343. New York: International Publishers, 1971. Republished with permission of International Publishers Company; permission conveyed through Copyright Clearance Center, Inc.

Arendt, Hannah. "The Intramural Warfare between Thought and Common Sense." In *The Life of the Mind*, 80–89. New York and London: Harcourt Brace Jovanovich, 1971, 1978. Reprinted by permission of Houghton Mifflin Harcourt Publishing Company. All rights reserved.

Frank, Thomas. "Inherit the Whirlwind." In *What's the Matter with Kansas? How Conservatives Won the Heart of America*, 191–214. New York: Picador/Henry Holt & Co., 2004. The selection, starting at p. 195, comprises most of the chapter. Reprinted by permission of Henry Holt and Company. All rights reserved.

Hall, Stuart and O'Shea, Alan. "Common-Sense Neoliberalism." In *Soundings* (2013), 1–18. www.lwbooks.co.uk/journals/soundings/pdfs/Manifesto_commonsense_ neoliberalism.pdf, accessed May 2016. Our selection consists of slightly more than the first half of the original paper, plus a paragraph towards the end. Most of the material from the original paper that has been omitted from our excerpt consists of a critical review of reader responses to newspaper articles that appeared in recent years in the online version of the large-circulation British tabloid, *The Sun*. Our selection is reproduced with permission of the Licensor through PLSclear.

Index

Note: Locators with letter 'n' refer to notes.

Aberdeen Philosophical Society (The "Wise Club") 20
abortion law 306
Active Powers of Man (Reid) 219
Adler, Mortimer 172, 205–18, 294
afterlife 128
Allegory of the Cave (Plato) 295
Ally McBeal (TV series) 307
alternative medicine 117
Altevogt, John D. 315–16, 317
Althusser, Louis 259
American Ethos, The (McClosky and Zaller) 254–5
American Medical Association (AMA) 304–5
analytic philosophy 15, 28
anatman (no-mind) 2
antirealism 65
appearance *vs.* reality 16–17, 55, 64, 96, 97 n.7, 273 n.4
Aquinas, Thomas 156, 162, 163, 206, 211 n.4
Arendt, Hannah 271, 273, 293–302, 331
Aristotle 6 n.12, 58 n.8, 128 n.1, 159, 172, 205, 212 n.4, 273, 293–4, 298
astrology 117, 164
astronomy 1–2, 3, 101, 125, 153, 297
atheism 127, 128, 129, 140, 144, 153, 158, 166–7, 318
Augustine of Hippo 211 n.4

Bach, Johann 99
Bacon, Francis 121, 178 n.7
Bagehot, W. 182 n.11, 183 n.14
Bain 175
Baldwin, J. M. 108
basic knowledge *vs.* common sense 58
Becker, Gary 226–7, 241–50, 267
being certain, concept of 49, 79 n.4
Bentham, Jeremy 185 n.21

Bergson, Henri 280 n.12
Berkeley, George 13–15, 19 nn.1–2, 28, 44, 55, 62–3, 65, 91, 106
Blackmun, Harry 306
Bradley, F. H. 60, 64 n.16
Brinkley, John 304–5, 314, 316
Broad, C. D. 64 n.16
Brooks, David 314 n.15
Bryan, William Jennings 312, 313 n.14
Buchanan, Patrick J. 115–6
bucket view (theory of knowledge) 79, 91–107 *See also* common-sense theory of knowledge; epistemology; Popper, Karl R.
Buddhism 2
bundle theory 2, 14–15
Bush, George W. 229, 303
Butler, Joseph 220
Butler, Judith 258 n.17
Buttigieg, Joseph A. 253 n.4, 256 n.12, 258 n.18

Calvin, John 155, 156–9, 163–4, 165
Calvinism 156–9, 288
Cameron, David 322, 327
Campbell, Donald T. 108
capitalism 226–7, 241, 253, 254–64, 286 n.23, 313 n.14
Carlile, Richard 141
Carnap, Rudolf 81
Cashill, Jack 308 n.7, 311–2, 314–19
Categorical Imperative 221
category mistakes 57
Catholicism 156, 282–92
cause and effect 6, 125, 127–8, 145, 148, 166
caution, idea of 194, 198
Cavell, Stanley 69
Chalmers, James (pseud. "Candidus") 272

China, economic development 241–3, 251
Christianity 125 n.2, 287, 300
    beliefs 155–65
Churchill, Winston 100–1, 105
Cicero, Marcus Tullius 25
Clarke, Samuel 125, 127–31, 145 n.2, 166
Clarke, Thompson 58, 67–70
classical theism 125
common sense
    definitions 3–8, 13, 20, 58, 171, 191, 227,
        255, 271, 273–4
    as insecure starting point 92–3
    limitations 195–7
    philosophical 16–7, 55, 58–9, 60, 273 n.4.
        See also plain common sense
    pragmatic value 59, 308, 322
Common Sense (Paine) 271–2
Common Sense: A Political History (Rosenfeld)
    3–4
common-sense theory of knowledge 91–111
    and criticism 92–4
    criticism of 104–7
    pre-Darwinian character of 107–8
"communism" 235–6
Communist Manifesto (Engels and Marx) 241
Compaq (personal computer) 235
Conjectures and Refutations (Popper) 92, 107
    n.16, 111 n.21
consciousness 19, 21, 157, 175, 185, 202, 295,
    302
    ideology as false 257
    of necessity (Spinoza, Hegel) 292
    theoretical (Gramsci) 285–6
conservatism 305
conservatism as a virtue of a theory 81, 120
Conservative Party (UK) 321 n.1, 322, 326
    n.10, 328
contemplation 216, 300
copy theory, of language 86
corporate social responsibility 247–50
Coulter, Ann 307
Crehan, Kate 283 n.17, 286 n.24, 331
"Critical Notes on an Attempt at Popular
    Sociology" (Gramsci) 275
criticism 17, 79, 91–4, 104–6, 107, 111, 273,
    277, 278, 281
    of common sense 284
    philosophy as 280
Cromer, Alan 117

Dalton, John 120
Darwin, Charles 108, 133, 171, 173–89, 219,
    317, 319
Dawkins, Richard 115, 118
deductive logic 89, 300
"Defence of Common Sense, A" (Moore) 15,
    27–45, 245
democracy 254–5, 256, 259–60, 271, 293,
    316
depoliticization of economics 227, 251–65
    conceptual vs. practical features 252, 257,
        267
    examples 261–5
    politicizing process 257–61
    problems with 252–7
Depression 305
Descartes, Rene 6 n.12, 27, 55, 61–2, 65, 68,
    79, 93, 94–5, 97, 109, 162–3, 299
    dreamer 68
Descent of Man, and Selection in Relation to
    Sex, The (Darwin) 171, 173, 174
Dewey, John 6 n.11, 104
d'Holbach, Baron 126, 141–53
DNA 114
Dobzhansky, Theodosius 113, 174
duty 142, 172, 181, 196–7, 205, 219–20
    sense of 173, 180
    to shareholders 250

Easterbrook, Gregg 316–17
Eastern Europe 235
econometrics 225
economic common sense 225–65, 266–7
    corporate social responsibility 247–50
    principles of 229–40
economic determinism/economism 252, 253,
    256, 258, 261–2, 286–7
economics of scarcity 197, 264
Economics (Samuelson) 225
efficiency vs. equity 231, 237–8, 266
Einstein, Albert 77, 78, 96 n.5, 100, 106
élites 273, 290, 303
empiricism 92, 104
Encyclopédie 141
Engels, Friedrich 78, 241 n.1, 259
Engles, Eric 264
Enron 255, 308 n.7
envy 178 n.7, 245. See also jealousy
Epicurus 149

epistemic rights (Plantinga) 155, 157–8,
      159–60, 163
epistemology 28, 62, 66, 67, 100, 120
      evolutionary 91–2, 108–11
      Reformed (Plantinga) 163–4, 165, 166
      subjectivist 101
equilibrium theory 227, 261
Essay Concerning Human Understanding, An
      (Hume) 148 n.3
Essays on the Intellectual Powers of Man (Reid)
      21
ethical skepticism 21 n.4
ethics (of common-sense) 28, 172, 191,
      205–18, 219
      philosophical development 208–14
      teleological and deontological approaches
      205–8
      vs. metaethics 171
Euclid 2
Evolution and Modification of Behaviour
      (Lorenz) 110 n.20
evolutionary biology (or theory) 78, 110,
      113–8, 119, 125, 171
evolutionary epistemology 91–2, 108–11, 120
exploitation (economic) 257, 258, 276
extrasensory perception 117

Failure of Capitalism, A (Posner) 241
fairness, idea of 327–30
fallibilism 79, 91–4
false consciousness 257
feminism 253
Fénelon, François 13, 25
finalism 286
Fingarette, Herbert 58
Ford (automobile company) 235
Ford, Gerald 239
form of life 47–8
fortitude (as a moral virtue) 184,
      211 n.4
Foucault, Michel 257 n.15
foundationalism 159–64, 166
      rejection of 163–4 *See also* fallibilism;
      pragmatism
Frank, Thomas 272, 303–19
freedom 172, 211–3, 215, 256–7, 291, 292, 325
      fear of (Sartre) 262
French Revolution 290
Freud, Sigmund 96 n.5
Frontiers of Legal Theory 245

fundamentalist Christianity 115, 305, 312,
      314, 316
Funder, David 115

Gadamer, Hans-Georg 58 n.8
Gallup poll 113, 114, 255 n.8
Galton, Francis 188
game theory 225
Geertz, Clifford 171
general good 173, 186
geology 125
George III, King 272
globalization 243
God's existence 125–6
      argument from design 133–40
      cosmological argument 125–6, 127–31
      Plantinga (the Reformed position)
      155–65
Golden Rule 178 n.7, 219
Goodman, Nelson 88
Goods (objects of desire) 205–18
good sense 8, 13, 22, 23, 78, 126, 197, 277, 280
      n.13, 282, 324, 327, 331
      d'Holbach on 141–53
Gore, Al 311
Gramsci, Antonio 7, 8, 197 n.3, 253, 254–5,
      257, 259–63, 272–3, 274, 275–92,
      323–5, 330, 331–2
Greater London Council 326
"greatest happiness principle" 173, 176 n.5,
      185–6. *See also* happiness
Great Pumpkin objection 164–5, 166. *See also*
      God's existence; Plantinga, Alvin
Great Recession 241, 255 n.8, 321 n.2
Groethuysen, Bernard 288 n.26
Groundwork (or *Foundations*) *of the
      Metaphysics of Morals* (Kant) 221
guns-or-butter trade-off 230, 266

habit 85, 87, 117, 153, 175, 177–82, 185 n.22,
      187–9, 211 n.4
      common sense as a belief-habit 7
Hall, Stuart 274, 321–30, 332
happiness 148–50, 157, 172–3, 207–8,
      209–14, 216, 220, 300 *See also* "greatest
      happiness principle"
      pursuit of 192, 210
Heckman, James 244
Hegel, Georg W. F. 28, 282 n.16, 292 n.29,
      295, 302

hegemony 254, 260, 275, 276–7, 286, 331
  cultural 260, 273, 276–7
hell-torments 149
Heraclitus 97
Hereditary Genius (Galton) 188 n.25
Hesiod 5
hierarchy of needs 192
Hobbes, Thomas 1
Hobhouse, L. T. 59
Hobsbawm, Eric 323
Holloway, Linda 318
Horgan, John 115
Howe, Leo 265
human capital 244, 266–7. *See also* job
  readiness
human nature (and common sense) 17, 115,
    191–203, 213 n.5, 219, 226, 253 n.3
  qualities of 194–5
  variability of 195
Hume, David 2, 13–5, 18, 69, 70, 79, 95, 148
    n.3, 175 n.3
  "bundle theory" of the self 2, 14–5
Hutcheson, Francis 19 n.1, 21–2

idealism (philosophical) 13, 28, 95, 97, 105–6,
    109 n.19, 219
  Berkeley's 62–3, 91
  Popper's arguments against 98–101
ideas 19–20, 22, 28, 109, 202, 219
  a priori 81 n.2
  Berkeley vs. Hume 13–5, 28, 109
  d'Holbach on 142, 147
  as "impressions" 2
  Moore on 44
  Popper on 103–4, 109
  Reid on 5, 21–2, 109
ideology 282–3, 290, 291, 321
immanent criticism 93
immigration reform 271
incentives 225, 233–5
income inequality 242–6
India, economic development 242, 251
indicator words 82, 88–9
infanticide 307
  female 182
infinity 2–4, 142
  actual 128–30, 166
  potential 128 n.1
  succession 128–30

inflation 239–40
Inherit the Wind (movie) 317 n.23
initial public offering (IPO) 249
*Inquiry into the Nature and Causes of the
    Wealth of Nations, An* (Smith) 236
intelligent design (ID) 113–8, 126, 312,
    316 n.20, 317 n.21, 319
intersubjectivity 85, 87–8
irony 56, 70
Islam 125 n.2

James, William 4, 59
jealousy 184. *See also* envy
Jennings, H. S. 108
job readiness (or "human capital") 267
Jones, John 114
Judaism 125 n.2
justice 193, 211 n.4, 298, 300, 324
  divine 150–1
  economic 254, 256–7

Kansas City Star 305, 315, 317
Kansas Tornado 315
Kant, Immanuel 79, 93, 97, 109 n.19, 156, 158,
    173, 175, 205, 208 n.3, 294 n.5, 297,
    301, 302
Katha Upanishad 3 n.2
Kingwell, Mark 16–8, 55–70, 71, 119, 120,
    272–3
knowing, concept of (G. E. Moore) 49, 79 n.4
knowledge 13, 19–20, 25, 37, 47, 58, 62, 68,
    83–4, 126, 155, 191–203, 206, 215,
    216, 300
  common-sense/bucket theory 79, 91–111,
    120
  direct 6, 92, 103, 105
  and doubt 15–16, 21 n.4, 52, 65, 68
  external world, of the 28
  of human nature 193–5
  innate 81 n.2
  intuitive 105
  as moral wisdom 209–10
  objective 70, 107
  positivist notion of scientific 264
  practical 205–6
  "rights of knowledge" 291
  subjectivist theory 105–6, 107–8, 121
  theory of 65, 79, 94, 119–20 *See also*
    fallibilism, foundationalism

"know thyself" 278–9
Koop, Everett 307–8
Krauss, Lawrence 3
Krueger, Joaquim 115 n.6

Labour Party (UK) 329, 330
labor unions 238, 258, 266, 321, 324, 326
language game 48–50, 71
language learning (or acquisition) 82, 85–6,
        87–8, 107
Laozi (Lao Tzu) 3 n.2
Law of Honor 186
Laws (Plato) 297
Le Bon Sens (d'Holbach) 126, 141
Leibniz, Gottfried Wilhelm 163
Lenin, V.I. 286 n.22
Lilienfeld, Scott O. 77, 79, 113–18, 119–20,
        125, 126, 331
Liptak, Adam 242
Listen, Liberal (Frank) 303
Lloyd Morgan, C. 108
Locke, John 19, 21, 22, 79, 93, 95, 97, 104,
        109, 163
logic, laws, method, basic principles 2, 3, 50,
        89–90, 300
Lorenz, Konrad 110 n.20
Luker, Kristin 306

Mach, Ernst 98
macroeconomic policy 227, 266
Mankiw, Gregory 226, 229–40, 266
marginal changes 232–3, 234
market failure 237
market power 237
Marx, Karl 241 n.1, 258–9, 262, 285 n.21, 286
        n.22
Marxism 252, 259, 260 n.23, 280 n.12
Massey, Doreen 325
materialism 201, 219
material morality 176 n.5
Mates, Benson 55
McChesney, Robert 308 n.7
McClosky, Herbert 254–5
McInerny, Ralph 156
memory 6 n.12, 19, 21, 116, 299
mental facts 28, 39–45
metaethics 171
metaphysics 3, 16, 28, 60-6, 66–70, 71, 98, 139,
        153, 176 n.5, 302 *See also* realism

Metaphysics (Aristotle) 128 n.1
Mill, John Stuart 1, 185 nn.21–2, 208 n.3
Miller, Richard W. 8, 77
Milton, John 61
Mnemosyne 299
Monbiot, George 321 n.2
Montaigne, Michel de 61
Moore, George Edward 6, 15–7, 27–45, 47–8,
        49–52, 66–69, 71, 95, 120, 219 *See also*
        knowing, concept of
morality (and common sense) 25, 171–89,
        191–203, 205–21, 276, 285
    Darwin's account 173–89, 219
    duty 151–2, 159, 173, 205, 208
    intuitive theory 185 n.22
    material and formal morality, distinction
        between 176 n.5
    virtue 182–5, 191–2, 194–5, 205, 209–14
moral philosophy 9, 25, 171–2, 191, 193,
        205–6, 208
moral sense 21, 22, 173, 176, 182, 184
Mussolini, Benito 277
Myers, Jason 262

Nader, Ralph 233
Nagel, Thomas 67 n.22
National Education Association (NEA) 311
national health insurance 271
naturalism (ontological) 122, 141, 173
natural kind 85
natural selection 114, 115, 173, 174
necessity, consciousness of 292
neoliberalism 321–30
Newman, John Henry 49
New Republic, The 316–17
Newton, Isaac 120
    Newton's theory 96 n.5, 101
New York Times 114, 242
noetic structure (index of degree of belief)
        159–62, 163
nothing from nothing 1, 3, 8, 127

Occupy 326
O'Hair, Madalyn Murray 164–5
On Certainty (Wittgenstein) 47–53
ontology 78, 119–20
opportunity cost 229, 231–2, 266
Origin of Species by Means of Natural Selection
        (Darwin) 133, 173

Orpheus and Eurydice 300
Orwell, George 293
Osborne, George 328
O'Shea, Alan 274, 321–30, 332

Paine, Thomas 60, 271–2
Paley, William 126, 133–40, 166
Pappas, George 62
Parfit, Derek 2 n.1
Park, Mungo 183
Parmenides 3 n.2, 127, 294
Peltzman, Sam 234
Pena, Pablo 243–4
Phaedo (Plato) 298
phenomenalism 97 n.6, 100
phenomenology 97 n.6, 100
Philosophical Investigations (Wittgenstein) 48
phronesis 58 n.8
physical facts 28, 40–5
Physics (Aristotle) 128 n.1
Pierce, C. S. 7
Pity the Billionaire (Frank) 303
plain common sense 16–17, 55, 56–60. *See*
    also common sense, philosophical
    common sense
  essential features 59
  and science 61
Plain Truth (Chalmers/pseud. "Candidus") 272
Planned Parenthood 249
Plantinga, Alvin 126, 155–65, 166
Plato 294, 295–301
political liberty 212–13, 215
politicization, of economics 257–61
politics (and common sense) 271–319, 321–32
  and philosophy 275–92
polygamy 184
Pope, Alexander 23
Popper, Karl R. 78–9, 91–111, 119–20
positivism 81–2, 92, 95 n.4, 97 n.6, 100, 104, 264
Posner, Richard A. 227, 241–50, 251
poststructuralism 253, 254
poverty 196, 197, 200, 242, 246, 251, 255–6
power, wealth and 9, 205, 227, 238, 251–2,
    261–2, 264
pragmatism 81–2
praxis, philosophy of 260, 284-5, 292
predestination 286, 288, 292
Priestley, Joseph 22, 25
Principles of Economics (Mankiw) 229

probability calculus 98
productivity 238–9, 244, 247
profit maximization 249–50
propositions 15–16, 27, 89–90, 141, 142–53,
    159–60, 162–3, 163–4, 166–7
  Kingwell's 55, 59–60
  Moore's 16, 27–45, 66–8, 71
  Wittgenstein's 47–8, 48–53
Protestantism 156, 288
Protreptikos (Aristotle) 298
Proverbs, Book of 7
Providence 17, 286
prudence 23, 171, 172, 183–4, 193–6, 198, 209,
    210–11, 212
  common sense, and 193–4
pseudoscience 57, 91, 117, 120
public education 114, 264, 271, 309–19

quantum theory 3, 78, 98
Quine, Willard Van Orman 5, 77, 78–9,
    81–90, 119, 120, 272, 275

Reagan, Ronald 242
realism ("common-sense," naive, scientific) 16,
    62, 78–9, 91–2, 94–101, 105–7, 118
reality, independent of language 78, 82, 86,
    87, 88
reality, mind-independent 14–15, 27–8, 34,
    71, 91, 95
Rée, Jonathan 61–2
Reformation 156
Reid, Thomas 4, 5, 6, 14–5, 19–26, 63, 71, 95,
    128 n.2, 155, 219, 271, 275 n.1, 331
reification 86
religion (and common sense) 9, 25, 125–6,
    133–40, 141, 142–53, 155–65, 166–7,
    280–92. *See also* God's existence
Rembrandt van Rijn 99
remorse 179–80
Rendezvous with Oblivion (Frank) 303
repentance 179–80
Republic (Plato) 297
Ricardo, David 227
Roe v. Wade 306–7
Rosen, Stanley 5, 171, 191–203, 219
Rosenfeld, Sophia 3–7, 271, 272, 273
Routledge, Hugh 94
Rush, Benjamin 334
Russell, Bertrand 4 n.5, 28, 95, 100, 105–6, 164

same-sex marriage 271
Samuelson, Paul 225
Sanders, James 308 n.7
"savage society" 174 n.1
Scalia, Antonin 307
Schaeffer, Francis 308
school vouchers 271, 311
science (and common sense) 55, 61, 63, 77–9,
     81–111, 113–8, 119–121, 141, 192,
     195–9, 275, 278, 280–5
   and language 81–90
   vs. pseudoscience 57, 91
   and religion 125, 280–92, 313
   teaching in schools 264, 312–3, 315–18
science *vs.* pseudoscience 91, 117, 120, 314
scientific community 314, 316
scientific realism 98–9, 109
Scottish Enlightenment 21 n.5, 63
Scottish School of Common Sense 20–1
Selections from the Prison Notebooks
     (Gramsci) 275
self-command 175, 181–4
self-preservation 176–8, 191, 198, 205
self-realization 191
self-regarding virtues 183–4, 185 n.22, 187
semantic theory of truth 99 n.11
sense perception 79, 300–1
senses, external *vs.* internal 6 n.12, 19, 21–2
Sensus Communis 24–5, 58 n.8, 293
Shaftesbury, Lord 24, 25
shame 179, 180, 186–9
Shaw, George Bernard 308, 312
simplicity 51, 87
Singer, Marcus 58, 64, 331
skepticism 9, 13–45, 47–53, 55–70, 71, 94–5
   Benson Mates on 55–6
   epistemological 21 n.4, 91–2
   ethical 21 n.4
   metaphysical claims 60–6, 77–9, 81–2
Smith, Adam 236
socialism 255 n.8, 286 n.23
social media 252
Socrates 295
solipsism 99
"something exists" 127
Soviet Union, collapse of 235–6
Sowell, Thomas 227 n.5, 229 n.1
Spinoza, Baruch 93, 292
Sprigge, Timothy 57, 63
standard of living 230, 238–9, 267

Staunton, George 184
Stiglitz, Joseph 227, 266
Strawson, P. F. 4 n.5
Stroud, Barry 65 n.19, 68–9
Stuckler, David 329
"Study of Philosophy, The" (Gramsci) 272,
     275–7, 277–92
subjectist theory of knowledge 95 n.4, 97 n.6,
     100–2, 105–6
   subjective idealism 13–14
suicide 116, 182–3, 294, 298, 313
superstition 8 n.18, 57, 60, 164, 180, 277,
     278
Swanson, Jacinda 227, 251–65, 267
sympathy 173–5, 177–81, 184–9, 219, 328
Systeme de la Nature (d'Holbach) 141

Tarksi, Alfred 99
taxation 60, 231, 233, 237–8, 240, 244, 245,
     249–50, 263, 266, 329
teleology 115
teleological ethics 172, 205–8, 219–20
temperance 211 n.4
Thatcher, Margaret 321, 324, 327
theism, classical 125
Theses on Feuerbach (Marx) 285 n.21
38 Degrees 326
*Time of Our Lives: The Ethics of Common
     Sense, The* (Adler) 206
Toshiba (personal computer) 235
totalitarianism 293
Toyota 235
Tractatus Logico-Philosophicus (Wittgenstein)
     48, 81
Treatise of Human Nature, The (Hume) 2, 14
truisms 1–6, 8, 27–45, 55, 78, 110, 273
truth 22, 50, 60, 62–3, 70, 79, 89–90, 95 n.4,
     103, 108–10, 183
   all is relative 198, 219
   certain and evident 129, 207
   faculty of 5–6
   love of 183, 187
   moral and philosophical 25–6
   necessary 161
   objective 51
   philosophical truth about common
     sense (Kingwell) 60–63
   plain truth about common sense
     (Kingwell) 56–60, 70 See also plain
     common sense

semantic theory of (Tarski) 99 n.11
   standards of 105, 106
Truth and Method (Gadamer) 58 n.8
Twain, Mark 117
Tycho de Brahe 297

UK Uncut 326
Uncommon Sense: Economic Insights, from Marriage to Terrorism (Becker and Posner) 241
Universe from Nothing, A (Lawrence Krauss) 3
Unsafe at Any Speed (Nader) 233
utilitarian/utilitarianism 126, 173, 185 nn.21–2, 197, 205, 208
utopia/utopian 264, 274, 324

verificationism 57
vital action 280 n.12
von Eschenbach, Marie Ebner 97 n.7

Wallace, Alfred R. 187 n.23
Walrus, Léon 227

watchmaker analogy 133–4
Watson, James D. 114, 115
Weekly Standard 314
What's the Matter with Kansas? (Frank) 273, 303–19
Wigner, Eugene P. 98
Wise Club 20–1
Wittgenstein, Ludwig J. J. 15–16, 17, 47–53, 71, 79 n.4, 81, 272
Wolff, Richard 256 n.13, 257 n.16, 259, 261 n.28, 263 n.32, 263 n.35
Wolpert, Lewis 77–8, 117
Woozley, A. D. 21
World Bank 242
WorldCom 255, 308 n.7
Wrecking Crew, The (Th. Frank) 303
Wright, Frank Lloyd 16

YouGov poll 328–9

Zaller, John 254–5
Zande people 72